INTERNATIONAL WATERCOURSES LAW FOR THE 21ST CENTURY

International Watercourses Law for the 21st Century

The Case of the River Ganges Basin

Edited by
SURYA P. SUBEDI, OBE
Leeds University, UK

ASHGATE

Published by
Ashgate Publishing Limited
Gower House
Croft Road
Aldershot
Hampshire GU11 3HR
England

Ashgate Publishing Company
Suite 420
101 Cherry Street
Burlington, VT 05401-4405
USA

Ashgate website: http://www.ashgate.com

British Library Cataloguing in Publication Data
International watercourses law for the 21st century : the case of the River Ganges Basin
1. Water resources development - Law and legislation - Ganges River Valley (India and Bangladesh) - Congresses 2. Water resources development - Law and legislation - Congresses 3. Water resources development - Ganges River Valley (India and Bangladesh) - International cooperation - Congresses 4. Water resources development - International cooperation - Congresses 5. Water rights (International law) - Congresses 6. International rivers - Congresses
I. Suvedi, Suryaprasada, 1957-
341.4'4'09541

Library of Congress Cataloging-in-Publication Data
International watercourses law for the 21st century : the case of the river ganges basin / edited by Surya P. Subedi.
p. cm.
Includes bibliographical references and index.
ISBN 0-7546-4527-4
1. Water resources development--Ganges River (India and Bangladesh) 2. Ganges River (India and Bangladesh)--Law and legislation. 3. Water resources development--Law and legislation--India. 4. Water resources development--Law and legislation--Bangladesh. I. Suvedi, Suryaprasada, 1957-
KNC660.G36I58 2005
346.54'104691--dc22

2005011871

ISBN 0 7546 4527 4

Printed and bound by Athenaeum Press, Ltd.
Gateshead, Tyne & Wear.

Contents

List of Contributors

Professor Graham P. Chapman
He is Professor of Human Geography at the University of Lancaster, UK.

Professor B.S. Chimni
He is Professor of International Law at Jawaharlal Nehru University, New Delhi.

Mr Anjan Datta
He is Programme Officer at the United Nations Environment Programme, GPA Coordination Office, The Hague, The Netherlands.

Professor Malgosia Fitzmaurice
She is Professor of International Law at Queen Mary University of London.

Mr Ramaswamy R. Iyer
He is Senior Adviser at Winrock International India and Honorary Research Professor at the Centre for Policy Research, India. Formerly he was Secretary to the Government of India.

Mr Mohammad Humayun Kabir
He is Research Director at the Bangladesh Institute of International and Strategic Studies (BIISS), Dhaka, Bangladesh.

Professor Gerhard Loibl
He is Professor of International Law at the Vienna Diplomatic Academy, Vienna.

Professor André Nollkaemper
He is Professor of Public International Law and Director of the Amsterdam Center for International Law, University of Amsterdam, the Netherlands.

Dr. Bantita Pichyakorn
She is a Diplomat/Researcher at the Ministry of Foreign Affairs, Thailand.

Professor Surya P. Subedi, OBE
He is Professor of International Law at the University of Leeds, UK.

Mr Surya Nath Upadhaya
He is Chief Commissioner for the Commission of Investigation of Abuse of Authority, Nepal. He was formerly Secretary to the Ministry of Water Resources, Government of Nepal.

Dr. Trilochan Upreti
He is a Joint-Secretary to the Government of Nepal and is at present working for the Nepal Law Commission.

Introduction

International Watercourses Law for the 21st Century and the Case of the River Ganges Basin

Surya P. Subedi

The River Ganges, with a length of 2,510 km, is one of the major international rivers of the world. The river and its tributaries pass through several densely populated areas of India, Bangladesh and Nepal. Millions of people in these countries are dependent upon this river for drinking water, irrigation, navigation and the provision of hydroelectric power. However, the Ganges has become one of the most polluted rivers in the world and the quality of life of its people has fallen to an alarming scale within the past few decades. Many small tributaries of the Ganges have either dried up or the volume of water in these rivers has decreased alarmingly during the dry season owing to deforestation across northern India and Nepal Himalayan region and other climatic changes.

Consequently, the tributaries of the Ganges are finding it increasingly difficult to meet the growing demand for clean water by the people of northern India, Nepal and Bangladesh. Tensions have erupted not only among the upper and lower riparian states of the river, but also among the communities within the same state regarding the sharing of the water of these rivers or their use. As a result, not only environmentalists but also development oriented agencies and organisations have called for a regional approach to this regional problem.

A major breakthrough was achieved in 1996 when not only India and Nepal, but also India and Bangladesh were able to conclude two long-term treaties of far reaching implications regarding the sharing and utilisation of the water resources of the River Mahakali between Nepal and India and of the River Ganges between India and Bangladesh. Nevertheless, unlike regional co-operation schemes regarding international rivers of other regions, there is as yet no single international instrument for the management of the resources of the Ganges and its tributaries. What is more, even after the conclusion of these treaties the riparian states have encountered a number of major problems in the implementation of the provisions of these bilateral treaties. In spite of these changes, little has been written about them. Whatever writing is there in this area is mainly about politico-economic issues of a long-standing problem of water sharing and utilisation between the co-basin states of this major river of South Asia. Accordingly, a two-day international conference on the problems and prospects for co-operation between the riparian states of the River Ganges basin was organised in June 2001 at Middlesex University, London.

The objective of the conference was to examine all the major legal issues involved in the use, development, management and sharing of the waters of the river Ganges basin in the light of the extant and evolving law on international watercourses. What are the major problems of water sharing and utilisation between these states? To what extent do the existing treaties address the problem of pollution and environmental degradation of the River Ganges basin? Do they provide for sustainable utilisation of the water resources of the river basin? What are the principles of international law applicable to these problems and have such rules been applied in the context of the River Ganges and its tributaries? How well developed or clear are the rules of international watercourses law themselves in resolving problems such as those encountered by the riparian states of the River Ganges? Is the existing legal regime satisfactory for the management of the present and future problems concerning the sustainable use and sharing of the water resources of the River Ganges and its tributaries? These are the questions that the various papers presented at the conference sought to examine.

The conference analysed the extent of the problem, the rights and duties of the lower and upper riparian states of the River Ganges in international law. It discussed the application of the principles of international watercourses law (concerning joint management and sharing of the resources of the River Ganges and its tributaries) to the problems of the region. Various speakers invited from India, Nepal and Bangladesh as well as other international experts examined the major problems of water sharing and utilisation between these states. Some of the speakers also looked at the problem of pollution and environmental degradation of the River Ganges basin and analysed to what extent the existing legal framework had provided for sustainable utilisation of the water resources of the river basin.

It was attended by leading international lawyers and practitioners in the field and the representatives of all three riparian states of the River Ganges. It brought together leading people from the academia, civil society and policy-making sector to discuss the problem of the River Ganges basin. Consequently, a decision was taken to publish the rich content of the deliberations of the conference in a book form so that a wider community of academics, researchers and policy makers can benefit from it. All of the contributors were invited to submit their papers for publication as chapters in a book.

Accordingly, what is included in this volume is an up-dated, revised and substantially expanded version of the papers presented and presents a comprehensive and comparative picture of the law of international watercourses with special reference to the issues facing the River Ganges Basin. In my own introductory chapter I have made an attempt to outline the state of the law today and the direction for future development in this area. Next, the chapter jointly authored by Professors Fitzmaurice and Loibl analyses the development of international watercourses law by the International Law Association and outlines the essentials of the 1997 UN Convention on Non-Navigational Uses of International Watercourses. Professors Chapman and Chimni, Mr Iyer and Mr Datta focus in their chapters on the nature of relations between the three riparian states of the River Ganges and examine the potential for co-operation among these states. The next two chapters provide a comparative picture of interesting developments taking place in the Rhine and the Mekong River basins. Professor Nollkaemper's chapter presents a comparative perspective of the legal regime that exists for the River Rhine. Similarly, Dr Pichyakorn's chapter outlines the developments taking place in the River Mekong basin and compares the Mekong experience with that of South Asia.

The chapters by Mr Upadhyay and Mr Kabir outline the domestic legal regime of Nepal and Bangladesh respectively. In doing so, they also assess the political dimension of the issues concerning the sharing of the waters of the river Ganges basin. Last, but not least important is the chapter by Dr Upreti presenting the Nepalese perspective on the whole gamut of Indo-Nepal water relations. Two of the delegates expected to attend the conference from Nepal were unable to travel to the UK due to the most unfortunate royal massacre in Nepal which took place two days prior to the conference. Consequently, a chapter outlining Nepalese points of view was commissioned in order to present a comprehensive picture looking at the issues involved from different perspectives.

I am grateful to the Indo-Dutch Programme on Alternatives in Development (IDPAD), The Hague, and the Middlesex University Business School, London, for their financial support towards the organisation of the conference. The conference was organised as part of a research project on the 'Development of a Legal Framework for Co-operation between India, Bangladesh and Nepal on the Management of the Water Resources of the River Ganges Basin' supported by the IDPAD, Institute of Social Studies, The Hague, and Jawaharlal Nehru University, New Delhi. I wish to record my sincere thanks to Professor B.S. Chimni of Jawaharlal Nehru University for kindly agreeing to work with me as a Co-Director of the project from India. Thanks are also due to Dr Bantita Pichyakorn (formerly of Middlesex University and now with the Ministry of Foreign Affairs of Thailand) for lending her invaluable support in making the conference a success and to Ms Christabel Silva, Mr Veramani Tuthirapathy of Middlesex University and my son Pranay Subedi for their assistance in putting this volume together.

PART I:

INTERNATIONAL PERSPECTIVE

Chapter 1

Regulation of Shared Water Resources in International Law: The Challenge of Balancing Competing Demands

Surya P. Subedi

1.1 Introduction

Water is essential for the survival of not only human beings but also all forms of life on our planet. Owing to a number of dramatic man-made and natural changes taking place in our planet water-related issues have come to occupy a place high on international agenda in recent years. A report published by the World Bank at the end of the last century, the twentieth century, stated that 'many of the wars of this century were about oil, but wars of the next century [i.e., the present one] will be over water'.[1] This was echoed in a report published by the UN on the state of the freshwater resources of the world.[2] There was a worldwide attempt to highlight the water problem in the run-up to a global ministerial conference on water held in The Hague in March 2000 and in the subsequent World Water Forums. A quick scan of certain leading newspapers reflects the anxiety about the looming water crisis of the world. 'World is running out of water', proclaimed *The Independent* on its front page not long ago,[3] 'the water bomb' was the headline of a report published in *The Guardian*,[4] and 'UN appeals for action to avert wars over water' was the headline of a report in *The Times*.[5] The problem of fresh-water is becoming more acute in various parts of the world[6] and is likely to pose a threat to international peace and security in certain areas of the world such as the Middle East, South Asia and Northern Africa. Rivers are the main source of freshwater and there are some 260 rivers in the world that are shared by two or more countries. If there is going to be

---

[1] As cited in Environmental Policy and Law 1995 s25(6).

[2] United Nations, 'Comprehensive Assessment of Freshwater Resources of the World' (1997).

[3] See *The Independent* (London) 25 January 1997 [1].

[4] See 'No Water World' *The Guardian* (London) (Part 2) 8 August 1995 [2].

[5] See 'UN appeals for action to avert wars over water' *The Times* (London) 23 June 1997 [13].

[6] For a comprehensive picture, see Peter H. Gleick, 'Water in Crisis: A Guide to the World's Fresh Water Resources' (Pacific Institute for Studies in Development, Environment and Security, Stockholm Environmental Institute) (OUP Oxford 1993).

a conflict about freshwater it is likely to be about the sharing of the waters of international rivers.

Many of the rivers around the globe have become unusable as sources and some others could become liabilities rather than lifesavers if no action is taken. According to the World Water Commission, 'more than one-half of the world's major rivers are being seriously depleted and polluted, degrading and poisoning the surrounding eco-systems, thus threatening the health and livelihood of people who depend upon them for irrigation, drinking and industrial water'. The Commission adds, 'Many of the rivers are being depleted because global demand for water is rising sharply. The problem will be further aggravated by having to meet the needs for food, drinking water, and water for economic development of the additional two billion people on Earth by 2025'.[7] In the opinion of the Commission, global water shortages will become so catastrophic over the next 25 years that two in three people on the planet will face regular depletion of water supplies.[8] In this context this chapter[9] aims to examine the attempts made through international law to address this problem since the primary function of international law is to manage conflicts and above all, to prevent conflicts.

1.2 Development of International Watercourses Law

International law-making in the area of sharing, utilising, managing and developing the waters of international watercourses between riparian States reached a new height in 1997 with the adoption by the UN General Assembly of a Convention on the Law of the Non-Navigational Uses of International Watercourses.[10] There was little international law on international watercourses until the 1950s. There were a few declarations specific to a geographical region or resolutions of non-

[7] Press Release of the World Water Commission *World Water Vision* 29 November 1999.

[8] This prediction was made by the World Water Commission in a report released to mark the World Water Day on 22 March 2000. See 'Global thirst will turn millions into water refugees' *The Independent* (London) 23 March 2001.

[9] An earlier version of this Chapter was published as an article by the present author in *Nepal Law Review* (Faculty of Law, Tribhuvan University) Vol. 15 (1 & 2) July 2002 [1]-[14].

[10] The Convention was adopted on 21 May 1997 by Resolution 51/229 of the General Assembly. It was adopted by a vote of 103 in favour to 3 against (Burundi, China, Turkey), with 27 abstentions (Andorra, Argentina, Azerbaijan, Belgium, Bolivia, Bulgaria, Colombia, Cuba, Ecuador, Egypt, Ethiopia, France, Ghana, Guatemala, India, Israel, Mali, Monaco, Mongolia, Pakistan, Panama, Paraguay, Peru, Rwanda, Spain, Tanzania and Uzbekistan). For text of the Convention, see 36 ILM 700, 1997; UN Doc A/51/869 of 11 April 1997. For the reasons given by some of the States for voting against or abstentions, see UN Doc A/51/PV99 of 21 May 1997. The Convention has not yet entered into force. It was opened to signature on 21 May 1997 and remained open to signature until 20 May 2000.

governmental organisations, but they did not achieve international application.[11] States used to invoke different principles of international law to justify their claims over the waters of international rivers. It was in 1895 that the U.S. Attorney General, Harmon, relied on the doctrine of absolute sovereignty in support of the U.S. position in relation to a water dispute with Mexico.[12] However, if an upper riparian State invokes the doctrine of absolute sovereignty to justify the use or diversion of more than its fair share of the waters of an international river to the detriment of a lower riparian State, the latter can also invoke the doctrine of territorial integrity to demand the supply of a fair share of the water of the river to meet its existing and potential use.[13]

The conflict between these two doctrines gave rise to the application of the principle of equitable utilisation in apportioning the water resources of an international river between the riparian States. It is this principle that constitutes the cornerstone of the current law on international watercourses.[14] As can be seen from various international water law cases decided by various national and international courts and tribunals prior to the 1950s, judicial opinion favoured the application of this principle to either the principle of absolute and exclusive sovereignty or the principle of territorial integrity in disputes between States.[15] The

---

[11] For a summary of such declarations and resolutions, see United Nations General Assembly 'Legal Problems Relating to the Utilisation and Use of International Rivers' UN Doc A/5409 of 15 April 1963, Part IV and Annex I.

[12] 21 Ops Attorney General (1895) [274], [283]; 1 Moore, Digest of International Law, 654 (1906), cited in Jerome Lipper, 'Equitable Utilisation', in A.H. Garreston et al. (eds.), *The Law of International Drainage Basins* (Dobbs Ferry, New York: Oceana, 1967; published for the Institute of International Law, New York University School of Law) [15]-[88]. Harmon issued the opinion in connection with a complaint by Mexico alleging the U.S. of interference with the flow of the Rio Grande on the U.S. side of the border, in violation of international law. His opinion:

'The case presented is a novel one. Whether the circumstances make it possible or proper to take any action from considerations of comity is a question which does not pertain to this Department [ie the U.S. Dept of Justice]; but that question would be decided as one of policy only, because, in my opinion, the rules, principles, and precedents of international law impose no liability or obligation upon the United States'.

[13] See F.J. Berber *Rivers in International Law* (Stevens & Sons London 1959) [19]-[25].

[14] Both the Helsinki Rules of 1966 of the ILA and the 1997 UN Convention on International Watercourses Law treat this principle as central to the whole legal regime on international watercourses.

[15] Examples of such cases are: The Case Concerning the River Meuse (*Belgium v the Netherlands*), *P.C.I.J.* Series A/B, No.70 1937; the Arbitral Awards of 19 August 1872 and 10 April 1905 in the *Helmand River Delta Case* between Afghanistan and Persia, Report of the Helmand River Delta Commission, Afghanistan and Iran, February 1951; Award of 22 March 1888 by Grover Cleveland, the President of the United States of America, as Arbitrator, in the *San Juan River Case* between Costa Rica and Nicaragua, Moore, International Arbitrations Vol. 2 [1964]; U.S. Foreign Relations 1888 [456]; Award in the *Faber Case* by a German-Venezuelan Mixed Claims Commission constituted under the Protocol of 13 January 1903, United Nations, Reports of International Arbitral Awards, Vol. X [466]; Awards of 16 April

development of international law in other areas of the environment has had a profound effect on this area of law and hence we now also have the principle of sustainable development and utilisation of the waters of international watercourses.[16] Added to this are the principles concerning the prevention of the pollution of water, and intergenerational equity, etc.[17] These latest developments become clear if one looks at the recent judgement of the ICJ on the *Gabcikovo/Nagymaros Case* between Slovakia and Hungary and various individual opinions of the judges appended to it.[18]

The attempts at codification and progressive development of international watercourses law began as early as 1910[19] within the International Law Institute (ILI) and resulted in the adoption of a declaration in 1911.[20] When the ILI returned

1938 and 11 March 1941 by an Arbitral Tribunal in the *Trail Smelter Case*, United Nations, Reports of International Arbitral Awards, Vol. III, [1905]-[1982]. Although the last of these arbitral awards deals mainly with the question of air pollution, the pronouncements of the awards have direct relevance to the question of the pollution of waters of an international river. The main cases concerning the disputes relating to the waters of an international water course after the establishment of the UN are the Arbitral Award of 16 November 1957 by an Arbitral Tribunal in the *Lake Lanoux Case* between Spain and France, Revue Generale de Droit International Public, Vol. LXII 1958, [79] and the case concerning the Gabcikovo-Nagymaros Project (*Hungary v Slovakia*, 37 ILM 162 (1998)).

16 See, generally, Edward H.P. Brans et al. (ed.) *The Scarcity of Water: Emerging Legal and Policy Responses* (Kluwer Law International The Hague 1997); R. Zacklin and L. Caflisch (eds.) *The Legal Regime of International Rivers and Lakes* (Martinus Nijhoff The Hague 1981); P. Sands *Principles of International Environmental Law, Vol. I: Frameworks, Standards and Implementation* (Manchester University Press Manchester 1995) Ch 9; P.W. Birnie and A.E. Boyle *International Law and the Environment* (Clarendon Press Oxford 1992) Ch 6; J. Lammers *Pollution of International Watercourses* (Martinus Nijhoff The Hague 1984); A. Noellkaemper *The Legal Regime for Transboundary Water Pollution: Between Discretion and Constraint* (Kluwer, Dordrecht 1993).

17 For instance, see Edith B. Weiss 'Intergenerational Fairness for Fresh Water Resources' 25 (4/5) *Environmental Policy and Law* (1995) [231]-[236].

18 The case concerning the Gabcikovo-Nagymaros Project (*Hungary v. Slovakia* 37 ILM 162 (1998). See generally on this judgement, Charles B. Bourne 'The Case Concerning the Gabcikovo-Nagymaros Project: An Important Milestone in International Water Law' 8 Yearbook of International Environmental Law (1997) [6]-[12]; A.E. Boyle 'The Gabcikovo-Nagymaros Case: New Law in Old Bottles' Law' 8 *Yearbook of International Environmental Law* (1997) [12]-[20]; Paulo C de Castro 'The Judgement in the Case Concerning the Gabcikovo-Nagymaros Project: Positive Signs for the Evolution of International Water Law' Law' 8 *Yearbook of International Environmental Law* (1997 [21]-[31].

19 At its session held in Paris in 1910, the ILI decided to study the question of 'Determining the rules of international law relating to international rivers from the point of view of the utilization of their energy'. See the report of the rapporteur of the ILI in: *Annuaire de l'Institut de Droit International*, Vol.24, Madrid Session, April 1911, Paris, 1911. The report was also published in the *Revue Generale de Droit International Public*, 1910 [281]-[288].

20 See the resolution of 1911 on 'International regulations regarding the use of international watercourses' in: *Annuaire de l'Institut de Droit International*, Vol. 24, Madrid Session, April 1911, Paris, 1911 [365]-[367]. It has been reproduced in UN General Assembly, 'Legal

to the subject in 1956, its work resulted in the adoption of a resolution of historic importance – the Salzburg Declaration in 1961.[21] The work of the ILI was further enhanced by the International Law Association (ILA), which resulted in the adoption of the famous Helsinki Rules in 1966.[22] The work of these two professional bodies of international lawyers was advanced by the UN General Assembly in 1970 when it recommended that the International Law Commission (ILC) take up the study of the law on the non-navigational uses of international watercourses.[23] Accordingly, the ILC began its work on this subject in 1974.

After numerous rounds of deliberations and the production of several reports by the Special Rapporteurs,[24] the ILC completed its work on the subject in 1994 when it adopted the Draft Articles on the law.[25] When the report of the ILC containing the Draft Articles was presented to the UN General Assembly, it decided upon the recommendation of its Sixth (Legal) Committee, to convene a Working Group of the Whole to elaborate a framework Convention on the subject matter on the basis of the ILC draft articles.[26] Ultimately, upon the recommendation of the Working Group the General Assembly adopted the UN Convention on 21 May 1997.

Thus, the 1997 UN Convention has been viewed, as the result of international efforts of the last four decades, as both the codification and progressive development of the law. Since we now have an international treaty designed to govern the activities of States concerning the utilisation of international

---

Problems Relating to the Utilization and Use of International Rivers' UN Doc A/5409 of 15 April 1963.

[21] ILI Resolution on the 'Use of International Non-Maritime Waters' Salzbourg 11 September 1961. In: *Annuaire de l'Institut de Droit International*, Vol. 49-II Salzbourg Session September 1961 (Basle 1961) [381]-[384].

[22] The ILA Helsinki Rules on the 'Uses of the Waters of International Rivers' Helsinki 20 August 1966. In: *The International Law Association, Report of the Fifty-Second Conference Helsinki 14-20 August 1966* (London 1967) [484]-[532].

[23] GA Resolution 2669(XXV) of 8 December 1970. See for a succinct summary of developments leading to the adoption of the Draft Articles on the subject by the ILC in 1994 in: Stephen C. McCaffrey 'The International Law Commission adopts Draft Articles on International Watercourses' 89 *AJIL* (1995) [395]-[404].

[24] There were several reports on the subject produced by various rapporteurs of the ILC. Richard D. Kearney was Special Rapporteur between 1974 and 1977, Stephen M. Schwebel between 1977 and 1981, Jens Evensen between 1982 and 1985, Stephen C. McCaffrey between 1985 and 1992 and finally Robert Rosenstock between 1992 and 1994. See for an account of the work of these rapporteurs and of the ILC: [1976] 2 *Y.B.Int'l L.Comm'n*, pt.1 [147]; [1980] 2 *Y.B.Int'l L.Comm'n*, pt.2 [110]-[136]; [1982] 2 *Y.B.Int'l L.Comm'n*, pt.1 [65]; [1983] 2 *Y.B.Int'l L.Comm'n*, pt.1 [155]; [1984] 2 *Y.B.Int'l L.Comm'n*, pt.1 [101]; [1987] 2 *Y.B.Int'l L.Comm'n*, pt.2 [25]-[38]; [1991] 2 *Y.B.Int'l L.Comm'n*, 66; UN Doc A/CN 4/451 (1993) and A/CN 4/462 (1994).

[25] See Report of the International Law Commission on the Work of Its Forty-Sixth Session, 2 May –22 July 1994; Supplement No.10 UN Doc A/49/10 of 1994.

[26] GA Resolution 49/52 of 9 December 1994, adopted by a vote of 143 in favour, 0 against, with 8 abstentions.

watercourses, it is proposed to examine how influential and effective the principles embodied in the UN Convention have been, or are likely to be, in shaping and resolving the existing and potential problems and issues surrounding the sharing, managing, utilising and development of water resources of major international river basins around the world.

1.3 Regulation of Competing Demands for Water Under the 1997 UN Convention

Although the 1997 UN Convention is designed as a framework convention to prescribe basic principles governing the utilisation of international watercourses between the watercourses States, it also contains significant provisions designed to protect the watercourse from pollution and other harmful activities, the preservation of water and the protection of the marine and other aquatic life of the watercourse. The Convention provides in Article 5 for equitable and reasonable utilisation of the waters of an international watercourse between the watercourse States. It also requires the watercourse States to develop the watercourse in order to attain optimal and sustainable utilisation thereof and therefrom. In doing so, they are required to ensure that there is adequate protection of the watercourse.

When agreeing on the utilisation of the watercourses the watercourse States should take into account the non-exhaustive factors outlined in Article 6 of the Convention. There is also an obligation on the part of a watercourse State not to cause significant harm to other watercourse States in utilising an international watercourse in its territory. The Convention imposes an obligation on a watercourse State to co-operate with other watercourse States on the basis of sovereign equality, territorial integrity, mutual benefit and good faith in order to attain optimal utilisation and adequate protection of an international watercourse. It also imposes a duty on watercourse States to protect and preserve the ecosystems and marine environment of the international watercourse, and to prevent, reduce and control pollution of the watercourse.

However, the 1997 Convention states, at the outset, that, provisions of the Convention will 'not affect the rights or obligations of a watercourse State arising from agreements in force for it'. Thus, whatever progress we have made with regard to the development of international norms for the utilisation of international watercourses, the law applicable to most major international watercourses is the law based on bilateral or multilateral agreements between the watercourse States concerned. This state of affairs has a number of consequences. For instance, even when the provisions of a bilateral or multilateral agreement are not consistent with the principle of equitable and reasonable utilisation enunciated in the 1997 Convention, that situation would continue and an aggrieved State would continue to suffer.

States make use of the waters of any given river for a variety of purposes. The main types of uses are: (i) uses for domestic and sanitary purposes; (ii) uses for navigation; (iii) uses for power generation; and (iv) uses for irrigation purposes. Indeed, Article VI of the 1966 Helsinki Rules on the Uses of the Waters of

International Rivers states that 'A use or category of uses is not entitled to any inherent preference over any other use or category of uses'.[27] A similar provision can be found in Article 10(1) of the 1997 UN Convention on the Law of the Non-Navigational Uses of International Watercourses:

1. In the absence of agreement or custom to the contrary, no use of an international watercourse enjoys inherent priority over other uses.
2. In the event of a conflict between uses of an international watercourse, it shall be resolved with reference to Articles 5 to 7, with special regard being given to the requirements of vital human needs.[28]

The reference to Articles 5 to 7 is to the principle of equitable and reasonable utilisation (Article 5), the factors relevant to equitable and reasonable utilisation (Article 6) and the obligation not to cause significant harm (Article 7). In the Statement of Understanding Pertaining to Certain Articles of the Convention issued by the Chairman of Working Group of the Whole some clarification was offered to the term 'vital human needs': 'In determining "vital human needs", special attention is to be paid to providing sufficient water to sustain human life, including both drinking water and water required for production of food in order to prevent starvation.'[29] Having said that international watercourses law provides for no clear hierarchy between different uses of water of an international watercourse, the watercourse States will have to abide by the provisions of existing agreements with regard to the terms and modalities of sharing the waters of shared international watercourses.

However, there are a number of areas around the world where the existing bilateral or multilateral agreements have not been able to provide satisfactory solutions to the problems faced by the watercourse States of the region. Those States, which feel aggrieved, have challenged the validity of many of such existing bilateral and multilateral treaties. The whole idea behind the making of new laws is to change the existing situation. However, the new law on international watercourses adopted in 1997 is not likely to change the existing situation to any great extent. Although, as demonstrated in the *Gabcikovo/Nagymaros Case,* international courts and tribunals would be inclined to give effect to the principles of the UN Convention by virtue of their customary law character, the impact of the Convention on non-parties and on those agreements concluded before the entry into force of the Convention is likely to be limited.

Consequently, the need is to look at the international legal picture as a whole, rather than just the 1997 UN Convention, as a way forward. A network of treaties and international instruments include provisions relevant to the problems of water and water sharing between States. A State in question may not be a party to the

---

[27] *The International Law Association, Report of the Fifty-Second Conference*, Helsinki 14-20 August 1966 (London 1967) [484]-[532].

[28] 36 ILM 700 (1997) [707].

[29] 36 ILM 719 (1997).

1997 Convention but may have given its consent to the principles embodied in other international instruments. If the obligations of States are considered in their totality rather than in isolation, there are other provisions in international law, which require a State to submit itself to the principles of the 1997 Convention.

1.4 Looking Beyond the UN Convention

The principle of sustainable development and the right to a clean and healthy environment can be invoked in arguing that a watercourse State is under an obligation to adhere to the principle of equity and fairness in utilising the waters of an international watercourse. In relation to a shared international watercourse, the principle of sustainable development requires a watercourse State to do its utmost to develop the water resources of the watercourse, to protect and preserve the ecosystems and marine environment of the international watercourse, and to prevent, reduce and control pollution of the watercourse. The term 'sustainable development' entered the lexicon of international law and international relations as late as in the 1980s.[30] However, by the early 1990s it had become a major policy goal of the international community. Within a matter of a decade it had become a significant 'soft law' principle of international environmental law[31] thanks mainly to its incorporation into the 1992 Rio Declaration[32] and a number of other international environmental law treaties. In fact, it has become a bridging principle that combines the developmental aspects of international economic law with the environmental considerations of development. In doing so, this principle seeks to reconcile the developmental aspirations of States with the need for environmental protection while carrying out their development projects.[33]

Both Principles 2 and 4 of the 1992 Rio Declaration[34] try to introduce

---

[30] The 1980 World Conservation Strategy of the IUCN (the World Conservation Union) seems to be the first international instrument to put the words 'sustainable' and 'development' together. See M.C.W. Pinto 'The Legal Context: Concepts, Principles, Standards and Institutions' in Weiss et al., op.cit note 1 [13]-[30] at (n 17).

[31] See, generally, A. Boyle and D. Freestone (ed.), *International Law and Sustainable Development* (OUP Oxford 1999).

[32] It is mainly Principle 4 of the Rio Declaration that establishes the link between economic development and environmental protection: 'In order to achieve sustainable development, environmental protection shall constitute an integral part of the development process and cannot be considered in isolation of it.'

[33] See for the views of the present author on the concept of sustainable development, S.P. Subedi 'Sustainable Development Perspectives in International Economic Law' in A.H. Qureshi (ed.) *Perspectives in International Economic Law* (KluwerLaw International Law The Hague 2002) [261]-[276].

[34] Principle 2 reads as follows: 'States have, in accordance with the Charter of the United Nations and the principles of international law, the sovereign right to exploit their own resources pursuant to their own environmental and developmental policies, and the

environmental considerations and the element of sustainable development into the agenda of economic development, an area of activity traditionally governed by international economic law. These two Principles of Rio accommodate the interests and concerns of both the developed and developing countries; no wonder the Rio Declaration has been described as 'a text of uneasy compromises, delicately balanced interests, and dimly discernible contradictions, held together by the interpretative vagueness of classic UN-ese'.[35] Thus, the delicate balance that the international community has tried to achieve between economic development and environmental protection through the introduction of the principle of sustainable development is relevant to the issues relating to the utilisation of international watercourses. Similarly, the right to a clean and healthy environment embodied in the Stockholm and Rio Principles would also include a right to clean water. In fact, the right to life, the most fundamental human right, would also encompass the right to clean water since life cannot be sustained without water.

If people have a right to clean water this right is valid *erga omnes*. Thus, not only the State of their nationality but also all other States would be under an obligation not to violate this right. As with other human rights, the responsibility to ensure that a right to clean water is respected rests with the State. Thus, to ensure that people have access to clean water, the first and foremost responsibility of any civilised State would be to develop the water resources of the watercourses within its territory, to protect and preserve the ecosystems and marine environment of the international watercourse, and to prevent, reduce and control pollution of the watercourse.

Similarly, if the right to clean water is a right valid *erga omnes* a watercourse State would not be in a position to commit any action that would deny this right to the people residing in other watercourse States. This obligation invokes the principle of equitable and reasonable utilisation even if the State in question is not a party to the 1997 UN Convention. This combined obligation on the part of both of these States gives rise to the duty jointly to develop the water resources of the basin of a watercourse by the watercourse States, to co-operate to protect and preserve the ecosystems and marine environment of the international watercourse, and to prevent, reduce and control pollution of the watercourse.

The next question to be examined is whether the right to water is an individual right or a collective or community right. Alternatively, is this a right of States? If communities have a right to clean water, what happens when there is not enough clean water to meet the competing demands? Similarly, if the right to water is a right of the State, how can the State have its right enforced and against whom? These are the problems faced by communities and States in the developing world. Since the 1997 New York Convention is limited in scope, these and other ancillary issues have not been properly considered by any international law instrument.

---

responsibility to ensure that activities within their jurisdiction or control do not cause damage to the environment of other States or of areas beyond the limits of national jurisdiction.'

[35] I. Porras 'The Rio Declaration: A New Basis for International Co-operation' in P. Sands (ed.) *Greening International Law* (Earthscan London 1993) [20].

1.5 From Demand Management to Resource Management

The focus of the law on international watercourses has thus far been on devising the rules for the sharing and utilising the available water on an equitable and reasonable manner between the riparian States concerned. There are not many direct obligations imposed on States to work towards ensuring that the amount of water needed for the communities and States is maintained at the optimum level. The 1997 UN Convention should have included the concept of sustainable utilisation along with the principle of equitable and reasonable utilisation. The element of sustainability is also missing from many bilateral treaties. The Ganges Treaty of 1996 concluded between India and Bangladesh in an example. Owing, *inter alia*, to deforestation in the hills of Nepal and northern India the capacity of the topsoil to preserve water has diminished. Consequently, whatever water rains drains quickly into the Ganges and ultimately into the Bay of Bengal during the monsoon season, creating floods and havoc in the plains of Nepal, India and Bangladesh.[36]

However, when the dry season approaches there is too little water in the Ganges to meet the needs of both India and Bangladesh. For this reason, these two countries have, since the conclusion of the 1977 Agreement, been talking about augmenting the flows of the Ganges during the dry season and the same empty rhetoric has been repeated in Article VIII of the new Treaty.[37] In the past 30 years or so, these States have not taken any serious strategic measures to address their long-term problem. This is a part of the world where population as well as industrial growth has been phenomenal in the past several decades and the trend is likely to continue. The Ganges and its tributaries have to meet the needs of the people and industry upstream before the waters reach Farakka and beyond.

What is disappointing is the absence of any long-term conservation plans to augment the flows of the Ganges or to improve the quality of water in this region of the world. Whatever plans have been proposed relate to the exploitation and

---

[36] For a detail analysis of the water treaties concluded between India and Nepal as well as between India and Bangladesh, see S.P. Subedi 'The Legal Regime Concerning the Utilization of the Water Resources of the River Ganges Basin' 46 *German Yearbook of International Law* (2003) [452]-[493].

[37] 36 ILM 525 (1997). This article reads as follows:

'The two Governments recognise the need to co-operate with each other in finding a solution to the long-term problem of augmenting the flows of the Ganga/Ganges during the dry season.'

However, unlike the 1977 agreement, in this article there was no mention of any schemes that could be implemented through Nepal's participation for the augmentation of the flows of the Ganges. With the conclusion of the Mahakali Treaty, India seems to have believed that the waters of the rivers between Nepal and India had effectively become bilateral issues, not to be brought on to any agenda of sub-regional or tripartite negotiations. As stated by Dixit, the Pancheswar storage scheme covered by the bilateral Mahakali Treaty 'was, after all, one of the seven dams in Nepal proposed by Dhaka for flood control and augmentation'. See Ajaya Dixit 'Regionalism Washed Away' *HIMAL* South Asia, January/February 1997 [60]-[62].

optimal utilisation of the rivers of the region without having paid serious attention to the concept of sustainable utilisation of the waters of the rivers of the region. Whether it be a treaty between Nepal and India or between India and Bangladesh, all are about exploitation and the optimal use of the existing resources without having in place any plans to sustain the resources, to improve the quality of water and to address the broader and bigger environmental issues of the region affecting the water resources in the longer term. These two treaties are examples of demand management rather than resource management. The factor required is resource management rather than merely demand management.

1.6 Conclusion

The 1997 UN Convention is basically designed for demand management rather than resource management. The law on the management of water as a resource is weak. That is where the problems lie. The emphasis of the law is on the utilisation or exploitation of water and prevention of conflicts in use of international watercourses rather than on the conservation of their invaluable ecosystems. The management of water could best be addressed by adopting an integrated policy of resource management and demand management. Article 20 of the UN Convention requires the basin States of an international watercourse to act, individually and, where appropriate, jointly, to protect and preserve the ecosystems of international watercourses. Similar provisions are to be found in Articles 21-26 with regard to the prevention, reduction and control of pollution and management and regulation of international watercourses.[38]

However, these provisions are couched in a vague and hortatory language rather than as legal requirements. Consequently, many of the watersheds lack co-ordinated management schemes for the development of the water resources of the area. The idea of a basin-wide sub-regional co-operation has not yet been materialised with regard to the rivers in very many developing regions. For instance, both the Ganges Treaty between India and Bangladesh and the Mahakali Treaty between India and Nepal concluded in 1996 are conducive neither to sub-regional or basin-wide management of the entire Ganges basin nor to the concept of sustainable use and management of the water resources of the region. They represent a piecemeal or fragmented bilateral approach to what is basically a sub-regional or trilateral problem.[39]

---

[38] Nicholas A. Robinson (ed.) *Agenda 21 & The UNCED Proceedings Vol. IV* (Oceana New York 1993) [358]. Agenda 21 adopted by the Rio Conference on Environment and Development states in Chapter 18 that 'Transboundary water resources and their use are of great importance to riparian States. In this connection, co-operation among those States may be desirable in conformity with existing agreements and/or other relevant arrangements, taking into account the interests of all riparian States concerned' (Para 19.4).

[39] See S.P. Subedi 'Hydro-diplomacy in South Asia: The Conclusion of the Ganges and the Mahakali River Treaties' 93(4) *American Journal of International Law* (October 1999) [631]-[640].

To conclude, international law has a role not only in managing and preventing conflicts between States relating to water but also in managing water for use in a sustainable manner. Until now, international law has sought to prevent conflicts relating to water by providing rules for water sharing between the riparian States. It is resource management rather than demand management that can address the competing demands for water between States and balance water rights with environmental needs for the long-term welfare of the people residing in the watersheds. As seen in the preceding paragraphs, international law on shared water resources is rather weak. In its present form it is unlikely to be able to address fully the situations facing the world today. The 1997 UN Convention embodies the basic principles of international law concerning the utilisation of international watercourses. However, these provisions need to be fleshed out to provide a comprehensive legal regime not only for the utilisation of water but also for the management of water as a valuable resource and the treatment of water as a social good rather than an economic good. While the 1997 New York Convention has not yet entered into force and is unlikely to do in the foreseeable future, the world has moved on and the problems surrounding water have become more acute. The time has come for the international community to adopt a more comprehensive international instrument designed to deal with all major aspects of water, including sustainable use of water, right to water, control of pollution of water, conservation of water as well as equitable and reasonable use of water to be found everywhere rather than just in international watercourses.

Indeed, the Water Resources Committee of the ILA has come up with a comprehensive set of rules on all major aspects of the utilisation, management and conservation of water resources, which was adopted by the Berlin Conference of the ILA in the summer of 2004. These ILA rules have been reproduced in Appendix VIII of this volume. This latest work of the ILA has added yet another significant chapter to the evolution of the law of international watercourses. As stated by Fitzmaurice and Loibl in Chapter II of this volume, it can be hoped the rules recommended by the ILA Water Resources Committee will facilitate future law-making in this area and guide States in concluding bilateral or regional agreements relating to the utilisation or management of the watercourses shared by them. It can also be expected that international and regional organisations will take on board the 2004 Berlin Rules of the ILA in formulating their own policies concerning the management, conservation, and development of the waters of international watercourses around the globe.

Chapter 2

Current State of Development in the Law of International Watercourses

Malgosia Fitzmaurice and Gerhard Loibl

2.1 The Main Issues

This chapter will be presented in two main parts: part one will deal with main theories pertaining to the law of international watercourses and will describe the fundamental issues concerning the 1997 United Nations Convention on the Law of the Non-Navigational Uses of International Watercourses. Part two will focus on the main provisions of the 1966 International Law Association (the ILA) Helsinki Rules and the work of the ILA Water Resources Committee leading to the revision of these Rules.

2.2 Part One: Historical Overview and the Current Developments

2.2.1 The Problem of Scarcity of Water

The problem of scarcity of water is one of major problems of the contemporary world. This was noted by Agenda 21 that refers to 'the widespread scarcity, gradual destruction and increased pollution of fresh water reserves in many parts of the world.' It also mentions 'fresh water as a finite and vulnerable natural resource, on which all social and economic activities are highly dependent' (Agenda 21 paragraph 3). It may be said that there are four major problems concerning fresh water:

> (a) shortage of renewable supplies; (b) unequal distribution of supplies; (c) problems of water quality and health; and (d) disastrous effects of unrestricted construction of dams and reservoirs.[1]

---

[1] H.L.F. Saeijs and M.J. van Berkel 'The Global Water Crisis: The Major Issue of the Twenty-first Century, A Growing and Explosive Problem', in E.H.P. Brans, E.J. de Haan, A. Nollkaemper and J. Rizma (eds.) *The Scarcity of Water, Emerging Legal and Policy Responses* (KluwerLaw International, Hague 1997) [3]-[20].

While '[t]he majority of the countries with limited renewable water supplies are in the Middle East, North Africa, Central Asia and Sub-Saharan Africa',[2] there are other countries which have 'shortage of water ... in [some] parts only, such as in the north of China'.[3] Agenda 21 noted this problem and also noted that 'one in three people in developing countries does not have access to drinking water in sufficient quantities and quality to cover basic needs'. It noted further that 'in all parts of the world, the availability of fresh water per head of population from its own resources is declining alarmingly fast' (Agenda 21 paragraph 18.46).

The problems of scarcity of water will escalate due to the growth of population (it has been estimated that the earth can only supply 4.5 to 9 billion people with fresh water on a sustainable basis). Millions of people will flee their homes as a result of floods, drought and erosion problems. These people constitute a new group of refugees called 'eco-refugees'. It was estimated that in 1994 there were '25 million people who ... had to leave their own countries because of drought, erosion, desertification and floods'.[4] Yet another problem with fresh water supplies is the lack of concern in big cities for maintaining adequate supplies of fresh water or adequate purification systems. In order to provide for sustainable management of fresh water, certain general principles must be followed:

> [(a)] the problem of fresh water resources must be dealt with in an integrated way at the level of the river basin;
> (b) this integrated approach must include both surface and groundwater, both quantity and quality;
> (c) integrated management of water resources should be based on the awareness that water is an inseparable part of the ecosystem and a social and economic resource;
> (d) priority needs to be given to the fulfilment of basic human needs as well as the protection of ecosystems;
> (e) users of water should be charged a reasonable amount, to encourage people to save water;
> (f) local communities in the countryside should participate in all stages of water management – it is especially important for women to be involved, in view of their decisive practical role in supplying, managing and using water on a daily basis; and

---

[2] Saeijs and Berkel (n 1) [7].

[3] ibid. See also R. Hirji and D. Grey 'Managing International Waters in Africa: Process and Progress', in S.M.A. Salman and L.B. de Chazournes, (eds.) *International Watercourses, Enhancing Co-operation and Managing Conflict, proceedings of A World Bank Seminar* (1998) [77]-[99]. They say as follows:
'[g]rowing water scarcity is afflicting many African countries. The primary causes are: increasing demand due to population growth and urbanisation; and decreasing water resources availability, due to deteriorating water quality because of pollution, to flashier river flows caused by river degradation, and possibly to effects of climate change.'

[4] Saeijs and Berkel (n 1) [13].

(g) the management of water reserves needs to be developed within a comprehensive package of policy measures covering the following aspects:

(i) public health,
(ii) the production, protection and distribution of food,
(iii) disaster contingency plans,
(iv) environmental protection, and
(v) conservation of natural resources.[5]

In order to establish a sustainable system of water management, an adequate legal framework is necessary: '[r]ules of international law cannot by themselves alleviate the scarcity of water, but they can both prevent one state from causing another to suffer needlessly from it, and promote co-operative efforts by states in managing their shared water resources so as to avoid conditions of water scarcity to the extent permitted by natural conditions.'[6]

2.3 Water Management in General International Law: Legal Issues

2.3.1 Theories Relating to the Utilisation of International Watercourses

The various theories, which have existed relating to the utilisation of international watercourses, derived their legal background from general international law, and in particular from the doctrine of territorial sovereignty. Depending on the interpretation, four main theories may be identified as relating to the utilisation of international watercourses: the theory of absolute territorial sovereignty, the theory of absolute territorial integrity, the theory of community of interests, the theory of limited territorial sovereignty, which at present is commonly referred to as the doctrine of 'equitable utilisation', and finally the common management theory which in fact is a variation of the doctrine of equitable utilisation.[7]

2.3.2 The Absolute Sovereignty Theory (the 'Harmon Doctrine')

The cornerstone of this theory is that the state exercises full and unlimited sovereignty over its national territory. It was originally formulated by the United States Attorney-General Harmon, in 1895, and concerned the diversion of the Rio Grande. Harmon asserted the unilateral and unequivocal right of the United States

---

[5] Saejis and Berkel (n 1) [15].

[6] S. McCaffrey 'Water Scarcity: Institutional and Legal Responses', in E.H.P. Brans, E.J. de Haan, A. Nollkaemper and J. Rizma (eds.) *The Scarcity of Water, Emerging Legal and Policy Responses* (Kluwer Law International Hague 1997) [56].

[7] See generally, P. Birnie and A. Boyle *International Law and the Environment* (2ed. OUP Oxford 2002) [298]-[346].

to divert the river, based on the grounds that the jurisdiction of the United States over the territory was absolute and exclusive.[8] According to this theory, '... State has an absolute right to do as it pleases with the water in its territory'.[9] The Harmon Doctrine today is obsolete and only of historical importance. In the contemporary world and under modern international law, there has been no support, either in practice or in theory, for the doctrine of absolute territorial sovereignty due to its egoistic, unjust character, which favoured the rights of upper riparian states, thereby making it subject to much criticism.[10]

2.3.3 The Theory of Absolute Territorial Integrity

'[T]his theory, which is an obverse theory to the Harmon Doctrine, is based on the principle which stipulates that since water is part of state territory, the lower riparian states have an absolute right to the continuation of the flow of water from an upstream state, which must, therefore, refrain from obstructing the flow of water to lower riparian states.'[11] Similar to the Harmon Doctrine, this theory has no bearing on the modern management of watercourses, and was widely criticised.[12]

2.3.4 The 'Community of Interest Theory'

The third of the theories approaches international watercourse management as an integrated whole. '[T]he basic premise of this theory is that administration can only be achieved by means of joint management'.[13] Joint management would include, for example, joint planning or joint construction. This approach also envisaged by the 1997 UN Convention on the Non-Navigational Uses of International Watercourses (*infra*), provides for the creation of a joint management body; an International River Commission. The principle of community of interests was adopted by the Permanent Court of International Justice (the PCIJ) in the *River Oder Case*.[14]

---

[8] Official Opinions of Attorney General of the United States 1895 [274].

[9] D. Caponera 'Shared Waters in International Law' in G. Blake et al. (eds) *Peaceful Management of Transboundary Resources* (Graham Trotman/Martinus Nijhoff 1995) [121]-[126].

[10] See for example as stated in J. Lammers *Pollution of International Watercourses* (Martinus Nijhoff Publishers 1984).

[11] J. Lipper 'Equitable Utilisation', in Garrestson, Hayton, Olmstead (eds.) *The Law of International Drainage Basins* (Oceana Publications New York 1967) [18].

[12] B.B. Chauhan *Settlement of International Disputes in International Drainage Basins* (Erich Schmidt Verlag Berlin 1981) [18]-[110]; Lammers (n 10) [562]-[563].

[13] See S. Schwebel II *Y'Book of the International Law Commission* (1982) pt. 1 [76]-[81]. See also para. 70.

[14] Territorial Limits of the Jurisdiction of the International Commission of the River Oder (1929) *PCIJ* Series A No 23.

Although the dispute concerned navigational rights, its fundamental statement that 'the community of interest in a navigable river becomes the basis of a common legal right, the essential features of which are the perfect equality of all riparian states, in the user of the whole course of the river and the exclusion of any preferential privilege of any riparian state in relation to the others'.[15]

The importance of this principle was further reaffirmed by the International Court of Justice in the 1997 *Gabcikovo-Nagymaros Project Case* (Hungary/Slovakia) in which the Court pronounced as follows: 'modern development of international law has strengthened this principle for non-navigational uses of international watercourses as well as evidenced by the adoption of the Convention of 21 May 1997 on the law of the Non-Navigational Uses of International Watercourses by the United Nations General Assembly.' [16]

2.3.5 Equitable Utilisation

The doctrine of equitable utilisation (or limited territorial sovereignty) 'has gained the overwhelming support of the international community'.[17] It is the underlying principle for the 1997 Watercourse Convention (*supra*).[18]

---

[15] Territorial Limits of the Jurisdiction of the International Commission of the River Oder (1929) *PCIJ* Series A No 23 [27].

[16] Judgment 25 September 1997 37 ILM 162 (1998) para 85 from http://www.icj-cij/org/idocket/his/ihsjudgment/ihsjudcontent.html7.

[17] H.L. Dickstein 'International Lake and River Pollution: Question of Method' 12 *Columb. J. of Transnnat'l Law* (1973). The same views were expressed by the International Law Commission during its work on the law of non-navigational uses of international watercourses. The *ILC Rapporteur* said as follows: '... all available evidence of general practice of states, accepted as law, in respect of non-navigational uses of international watercourses – evidence including treaty provisions, positions taken by states in specific disputes, decisions of international bodies, the views of learned commentators, and decisions of municipal courts in cognate cases-demonstrate that there is overwhelming support for the doctrine of equitable utilisation as general guiding principle of law for the determination of the rights of states in respect of the non-navigational uses of international watercourses.' S. McCaffrey, Second Report on the Law of Non-navigational Uses of International Watercourses, *Y'book of the ILC*, (1986) vol. II part I [130]. See also, Separate Opinion of Judge P. Kooijmans in Kasikili/Sedudu Island (Botswana /Namibia), Judgment of 13 Dec 1999 para 29 at http://www.icj.cij.org/icjwww/idocket/ibono/ibono/ibonoframe.htm.

[18] Convention on the Non-Navigational Uses of International Watercourses, 36 *ILM* 713-720 (1997). Numerous publications gave the overview of this Convention, e.g. M. Fitzmaurice 'Convention on the Law of Non-Navigational Uses of International Watercourses' *Leiden Journal of International Law* (LJIL) vol. 10 (1997) [501]-[508]; S. McCaffrey, 'The UN Convention on the Law of the Non-Navigational Uses of International Watercourses: Prospects and Pitfalls' in S.M.A. Salman and L.B. de Chazournes (eds.) 'International Watercourses: Enhancing Co-operation and Managing Conflict, Proceedings of a World Bank Seminar' World Bank Technical Paper No. 414 (1998) [17]-[28]; L. Caflish 'Regulation of the Uses of International Watercourses' in S.M.A. Salman and L.B. de Chazournes (eds.) 'International

In attempting to solve practical and theoretical problems relating to non-navigational uses of international watercourses, two main principles were formulated: the principle of equitable utilisation and the principle of non-significant harm. The uneasy relationship between these two principles and the attempts to reconcile them were very much in evidence in the drafts of the ILC leading to the 1997 Convention.[19] These two principles constitute the core of the Convention in the part II General Principles: Articles 5-7.[20]

Watercourses: Enhancing Co-operation and Managing Conflict, Proceedings of a World Bank Seminar' World Bank Technical Paper No. 414 (1998) [3]-[16].

[19] M. Fitzmaurice 'The Law of Non-Navigational Uses of International Watercourses-The International Law Commission Completes its Draft' *LJIL* vol. 8 (1995) [361]-[375].

[20] Article 5: 'Equitable and reasonable utilisation and participation. 1. Watercourse States shall in their respective territories utilise an international watercourse in an equitable and reasonable manner. In particular, an international watercourse shall be used and developed by watercourse States with a view to attaining optimal and sustainable utilisation thereof and benefits there from, taking into account the interests of the watercourse States concerned, consistent with adequate protection of the watercourse. 2. Watercourse States shall participate in the use, development and protection of an international watercourse in an equitable and reasonable manner. Such participation includes both the right to utilise the watercourse and the duty to co-operate in the protection and development thereof, as provided in the present Convention.'

Article 6 'Factors relevant to equitable and reasonable utilisation: 1. Utilisation of an international watercourse in an equitable and reasonable manner within the meaning of Article 5 requires taking into account all relevant factors and circumstances, including:

(a) Geographic, hydrographic, hydrological, climactic, ecological and other factors of a natural character; (b) The social and economic needs of the watercourse States concerned; (c) The population dependent on the watercourse in each watercourse State; (d) The effects of the use or uses of the watercourse in each watercourse State on other watercourse States; (e) Existing and potential uses of the watercourse; (f) Conservation, protection, development and economy of use of the water resources of the watercourse and the costs of measures taken to that effect; (g) The availability of alternatives, of comparable value, to a particular planned or existing use.

2. In the application of article 5 or paragraph 1 of this article, watercourse States concerned shall, when need arises enter into consultations in a spirit of co-operation. 3. The weight to be given to each factor is to be determined by its importance in comparison with that or other factors. In determining what is a reasonable and equitable use, all relevant factors are to be considered together and conclusion reached on the basis of the whole.

Article 7: 'Obligation not to cause significant harm: 1. Watercourse States shall, in utilising an international watercourse in their territories, take all appropriate measures to prevent the causing of significant harm to other watercourse States. 2. Where significant harm nevertheless is caused to another watercourse State, the States whose use causes such harm shall, in the absence of agreement to such use, take all appropriate measures, having due regard for the provisions of articles 5 and 6, in consultation with the affected State, to eliminate or mitigate such harm and, where appropriate, to discuss the question of compensation'.

On the negotiating history of the Convention see: T. Nussbaum 'Report of the Working Group to Elaborate a Convention on International Watercourse' 6 *Review of European Community & International Environmental Law* (RECIEL) (1996) [47]-[53]; A. Tanzi 'Codifying the Minimum Standards of the Law of International Watercourses: Remarks on part One and Half' 21(2) *Natural Resources Forum* (1997) [109]-[117]; Caflish (n 18).

The question of the mutual relationship between these two principles, i.e., which principle has the priority in the case of conflict, or in other words, the order of subordination, was the subject of most of the discussion within the ILC during the drafting process which lasted twenty years. The first Special Rapporteur, S. Schwebel, took the view that the no-harm principle should be subordinate to the principle of equitable and reasonable utilisation. It meant that this principle was taken into account only if a planned new or expanded use was likely to exceed what is equitable or reasonable. The harm caused by such use was one of the elements to be taken into consideration to ascertain whether such a use was equitable. The next two Special Rapporteurs, J. Evens and S. McCaffrey, took a different view and accorded the role of a leading principle to the no-harm rule. It became 'the fundamental rule' of the draft. Furthermore, this rule was no longer used as one of the elements to be taken into consideration while assessing what is equitable and reasonable. This reversal of priorities was criticised by some states. This prompted the next Special Rapporteur, R. Rosenstock, to re-draft Article 7 in an attempt to reconcile the conflicting views.[21] The reception given to the new draft Article 7 was not very encouraging. Conceptually, Article 7 was subject to two main objections: first, for 'its lack of clarity';[22] and secondly, 'that responsibility and liability under the no-harm rule were maintained except, that where they were not attributable to a lack of due diligence, their consequences were reduced to consult over the equitableness of the measures of abatement or indemnization'.[23]

The discussion ensued within the Working Group of the Sixth Committee of the General Assembly. There were three distinct groups of views. The '... upper riparian [states] ... favoured strengthening the principle of equitable and reasonable utilization, and ... suggested the deletion of article 7'.[24] A second group, '... of varied riparian status ... supported the ILC text of the articles ...'[25] On the other hand, the 'downstream [states] and environment-minded States ... favoured amending the text of articles 5 and 7 to strengthen the "no-harm" principle, and insert language reflective of developments in the field of environmental law'.[26]

---

[21] This draft Article 7 reads as follows: '[w]atercourse States shall exercise due diligence to utilise an international watercourse in such a way as not to cause significant harm to other watercourse States; 2. Where despite the exercise of due diligence, significant harm is caused to another watercourse State, the State whose use causes the harm shall in the absence of an agreement to such a use, consult with the State suffering harm over: (a) the extent to which such a use is equitable and reasonable taking into account the factors listed in Article 6; (b) the question of ad hoc adjustments to its utilisation, designed to eliminate or mitigate any such harm caused and, where appropriate, then question of compensation.'

[22] Caflish (n 18) [14].

[23] Ibid.

[24] Nussbaum (n 20) [49].

[25] Ibid.

[26] Ibid.

These states were in favour of inclusion of the principle of sustainable development and the precautionary principle. They achieved at least partial success by the new formulation of Article 5.

The non-significant harm principle as formulated in the ILC's draft also generated many adverse comments from states. They can be divided into three main groups. The first group consisting of upstream states felt that Article 7, 'despite the modification … [created] an unacceptable restriction on the principle of equitable and reasonable utilization, supported the deletion of the article, or the insertion of [a safeguard clause] wording … such as "without prejudice to the principle of equitable and reasonable utilization"'.[27] The second group favoured the ILC draft Articles as they stood. The third group criticised the ILC's draft Articles as '… [weakening] the no-harm principle in general'.[28] As a result of the discussion within the Working Group, the final texts of Articles 5-7 differ greatly from the draft ones and constitute a 'package deal'. The Convention was accepted by 103 votes with 3 votes against (Burundi, China, and Turkey), and 27 abstentions, 'a rate of approval, which raises doubts over the viability of the new Convention'.[29]

The standard of due diligence has been abandoned and rather, reference is made to 'all appropriate measures'. This standard is equally vague and in fact, they mean almost exactly the same.[30] It has to be observed, however, that this standard is in line with another important Convention, which is in force, namely, the 1992 Convention on the Protection and Use of Transboundary Watercourse and Lakes ('The Helsinki Convention'), which is based on this standard rather than that of due diligence.[31]

The careful analysis of Articles 5-7 convinced McCaffrey that '… paragraph 2 of Article 7 of the Convention gives precedence to equitable utilisation over no-harm doctrine'. The very existence of a second paragraph implicitly acknowledging that harm may be caused without engaging the harming state's responsibility supports this conclusion. Also indicating a recognition that significant harm may have to be tolerated by a watercourse state are the numerous mitigating clauses in paragraph 2, especially the phrase 'having due regard for the provisions of articles 5 and 6' – the two equitable utilisation Articles. Finally, the proposition that 'non-significant-harm' rule does not enjoy inherent pre eminence is supported by Article 10 of the Convention, which provides that any conflict between uses of an international watercourse is to be resolved 'with reference to articles 5 to 7', '…the conflict is not be resolved solely by applying the 'no-harm' rule of Article 7, but rather through reference to the 'package' of articles setting

[27] Nussbaum (n 20) [50].

[28] Ibid.

[29] Caflisch (n 18) [18].

[30] See McCaffrey (n 18) [21], '[i]n my view, the deletion of "due diligence" from paragraph 1 and its replacement with 'all appropriate measures' is merely saying the same thing in different words'.

[31] Text in: 31 ILM (1992).

forth principles of both equitable utilisation and 'no-harm'.[32] The threshold of harm that is permissible has been set at 'significant' level. The threshold of harm caused some heated discussions within the ILC. In the earlier drafts (including the 1991 draft) the Commission used the term 'substantial harm'. In the view of the ILC, however, the term 'substantial' might have had a variety of meanings and this ambiguity caused it ultimately to be considered undesirable for use in the ILC's drafts. Therefore the term 'substantial' was changed into 'appreciable'. The ILC explained that 'appreciable' harm means harm that is 'significant' not trivial, or inconsequential but less than 'substantial'. In other words, 'appreciable' harm was to be that which is not significant or barely detectable, but, was nonetheless, not necessarily 'serious'. The 1994 draft has replaced 'appreciable' with 'significant' in order to bring the terminology of the watercourse draft in line with that of the ILC draft on Liability for Injurious Consequences Arising out of Acts Not Prohibited by International Law ('State Liability Draft'). The Commentary to the 1997 Convention contains an interpretation of the meaning of 'significant'. It is different from 'substantial'. 'As used in the Convention, significant adverse effect must be capable of being established by objective evidence and not be trivial by nature.'[33] In fact, this discussion appears to be slightly futile, since it shows that there is not much difference, if any, between 'appreciable' and 'significant'.[34]

It is indisputable that the cornerstone of the Convention is its Article 5. It imposes an obligation on states to use an international watercourse in its relation with other states in an equitable and reasonable manner. Of great importance is Article 5, which provides that in order to be equitable and reasonable, the use must be consistent with adequate protection of the watercourse from pollution and other forms of degradation.

The same Article has introduced the new concept of equitable participation. The underlying idea behind this concept is that in order to complete a regime of equitable and reasonable utilisation, riparian states must co-operate with each other by taking affirmative steps, individually or jointly, with regard to watercourse. ' a regime of equitable utilisation of an international watercourse system, together with the protection and preservation of its ecosystems, cannot be achieved solely through individual action by each riparian state acting in isolation; again, affirmative cooperation will often be necessary.'[35]

Other watercourses conventions also use the principle of equitable and reasonable participation as the basis of their co-operation. For example, the above-mentioned 1992 Helsinki Convention, postulates that '[t]he riparian Parties shall on the basis of equality and reciprocity enter into bilateral or multilateral agreements or other arrangements, where these do not yet exist, or adapt existing

[32] McCaffrey (n 18) [22].

[33] Commentary on the 1997 UN Convention, UN Doc/A/61.869 (1997).

[34] McCaffrey (n 18) [21], rightly points out that '… is also changed [the Convention as opposed to the Draft)] 'appreciable' to 'significant'. I don't regard this in any way as a terribly 'significant' change, however'.

[35] McCaffrey (n 18) [20].

ones, where necessary to eliminate the contradictions with the basic principles of this Convention, in order to define their mutual relations and conduct regarding the prevention, control and reduction of transboundary impact. The Riparian Parties shall specify the catchment area, or part(s) thereof, subject to cooperation. These agreements or arrangements shall embrace relevant issues covered by this Convention, as well as any other issues on which the Riparian Parties may deem it necessary to cooperate' (Article 9(1)).

This principle was fully endorsed by the Court in *Gabcikovo-Nagymaros Case* (*supra*), which held that: '[r]e-establishment of a joint regime will also affect in an optimal way the concept of common utilisation of shared water resources for the achievement of several objectives mentioned in a Treaty, in concordance with Article 5, paragraph 2, of the Convention on the Law of Non-Navigational Uses of International Watercourses …' (paragraph 147 of the Judgment). The Court further held that '[r]eparation must "as far as possible", wipe out all consequences of the illegal act. In this case, the consequences of the wrongful acts of both parties will be wiped out "as far as possible" if they resume their co-operation in the utilisation of the shared water resources of the Danube, and if the multi-purpose programme, in the form of a co-ordinated single unit, for that use, development and protection of the watercourse is implemented in an equitable and reasonable manner. What is possible for the parties to do is to re-establish co-operative administration of what remains of the project. To that end, it is open to them to agree to maintain the works at Cunovo, with changes in the mode of operation in respect of the allocation of water and electricity, and not to build works at Nagymaros' (paragraph 150 of the Judgment).[36]

2.3.6 Common Management

Common management is a variation of the equitable utilisation theory. It derives from the premise that an international watercourse is better managed as an integrated whole, and that it is most efficiently administered through efficient institutional machinery established in order to secure equitable utilisation and development. It is also an expression of the community of interest approach (as enunciated in the *River Oder* case), which, apart from adhering to the equitable utilisation principle, goes beyond it and suggests the integrated development and international regulation of the watercourse environment. Thus, the comprehensive approach is different from the basin or hydrologic approach to watercourse

[36] See also: J. Lammers 'The *Gabcikovo-Nagymaros* Case Seen in Particular From the Perspective of the Law of International Watercourses and the Protection of the Environment' 11 *LJIL* (1998) [287]-[320]; see also: P. Sands 'Watercourses, Environment and the International Court of Justice: The *Gabcikovo-Nagymros* Case' in S.M.A. Salman and L.B. de Chazournes (n 3) 'International Watercourses, Enhancing Co-operation and Managing Conflict, Proceedings of a World Bank Seminar' World Bank Technical Paper No. 414 (1998) [103]-[127].

management. This approach presupposes an establishment of international institutions in which all riparian states participate in order to formulate policies applicable to a watercourse. Although there are many river commissions, there are only a few bodies that would assume an integrated approach, including environmental protection of a watercourse.[37]

2.4 Other Fundamental Provisions of the 1997 UN Convention

The 1997 Convention contains several other provisions other than the general provisions in Articles 2, 3, 8 and 10 already discussed above.

The Convention adopts a broad definition of an international watercourse. It does not only refer to an international river but takes into account groundwaters, which constitutes 'by virtue of their physical relationship, a unitary whole and normally flowing into a common terminus'.

Article 3 of the Convention was the subject of a heated discussion within the Sixth Committee. The problem as regards Article 3 originated generally from the lack of certainty and understanding by states of the relationship between already existing bilateral and multilateral watercourse agreements and the new framework Convention. The views of states in connection with this relationship may be divided into two groups: one group of states of the same region that are not party to existing watercourse agreements and that opposed the insertion of the exclusion clause to Article 3 paragraph 1; and a second group of states that are already bound by existing watercourse treaty obligations. The first group of states voiced their concern that the provisions of existing agreements might exclude or contravene principles of the framework Convention that would benefit them. In order to satisfy to some extent the wishes of these states, Article 3 paragraph 2 envisages the possibility for states to harmonise such agreements with the provisions of the framework Convention. The second group felt threatened by the new Convention as constituting a potential danger to existing agreements.[38] The Convention in Article 3 paragraph 3 seems to provide for the possibility of adjusting the framework Convention by states entering into new watercourse agreements by taking into consideration characteristics of a particular watercourse. In general, it may be said that the wording of the Convention indicates that agreements may depart from the provisions of the Convention. This confirms the view that the

---

[37] See also the dissenting opinion of Weeramantry J. in Kasikili/Sedudu Island *(Botswana/Namibia)* Judgment of 13 December 1999 at http://www.icj.cij.org/icjwww/idocket/ibono/ibono/ibonoframe.htm. He said as follows: Joint management regimes have been established for integrated development of resources in river basins with States splitting costs and responsibilities and sacrificing sovereignty as needed to facilitate the management process (paragraph 109).

[38] See Nussbaum (n 20) [48]-[49]. He notes the example of the upper riparian states of the Nile. He states that 'This position seemed to stem from their concern over an existing agreement between Egypt and Sudan that apportions almost all of the waters of the Nile to themselves'.

Convention does not contain norms of the character of *jus cogens*; and that its provisions serve mainly as guidelines for those states, which are ready to negotiate new watercourse agreements. Thus, '... [t]he conventional freedom of States is fully maintained'.[39]

Furthermore, the Convention adheres to the principle of law of treaties; *pacta tertii nec nosunt nec prosunt*. This is evidenced by Article 3 paragraph 6, which expressly excludes the legal effect of the Convention in relation to third parties.

Article 4 paragraph 1 did not present any difficulties during the negotiation process. The problem was Article 4 paragraph 2, which applies to partial agreements. These agreements are concluded only by some states of a watercourse agreement *inter se*, and limited to their respective segments, but with a potential of affecting other states of the same watercourse. A compromise was reached by allowing the third states to participate in consultations on such an agreement and, when appropriate, in the negotiations thereof in good faith with a view to becoming a party thereto, to the extent that its use is thereby affected. Caflisch observes that '[f]rom the viewpoint of legal orthodoxy, this solution is questionable. It was found acceptable, however, because of the inclusion of the words "where appropriate", which give considerable leverage to the original parties to the agreement, and also because the participation of the third State in the agreement will be limited "to the extent that its use is thereby affected"'.[40]

Article 8 of the Convention imposes the general obligation to co-operate.[41] An interesting provision is contained in Article 8 paragraph 2 which gives states an opportunity to consider the establishment of a joint mechanism or a commission. A solution already adopted in many regions of the world. Finally, mention must be made of Article 10 that deals with relationship between different kinds of uses. Firstly, as a general principle, no use of an international watercourse enjoys priority over other uses; and in the event of conflict between uses it will be resolved with special reference to Articles 5 to 7 but with special regard given to the requirements of vital human needs.[42]

As regards other provisions of the Convention of fundamental importance, mention must be made of Article 32, which deals with the procedure for dispute

---

[39] Caflisch (n 18) [11].

[40] ibid [12].

[41] Article 8 reads as follows: 'General obligation to cooperate: 1. Watercourse States shall cooperate on the basis of sovereign equality, territorial integrity, mutual benefit and good faith in order to obtain optimal utilisation and adequate protection of an international watercourse. 2. In determining the manner of such cooperation, watercourse States may consider the establishment of joint mechanisms or commissions, as deemed necessary by them, to facilitate cooperation on relevant measures and procedures in the light of experience gained through co-operation in existing joint mechanisms and commissions in various regions.'

[42] Article 10 reads as follows: 'Relationship between different kinds of uses: 1. In the absence of agreement or custom to the contrary, no use of any watercourse enjoys inherent priority over other uses; 2. In the event of a conflict between uses of an international watercourse, it shall be resolved with reference to Articles 5 to 7, with special regard being given to the requirement of vital human needs.'

settlement. This provision has also proved to be controversial due to the introduction of compulsory fact-finding at the request of any party. This Article provides that states have to declare, upon becoming parties to the Convention, that they accept as compulsory the submission of disputes to the International Court of Justice or to arbitration in accordance with procedures established in the Annex to the Convention.

2.4.1 The Protection of the Watercourse Environment

The new part, which traditionally did not belong to the law of international watercourses, is Part IV on protection, preservation and management of the riparian environment (Articles 20-26). The fundamental provision for the whole Part is contained in Article 20, 'Protection and preservation of ecosystems'. It provides that: '[w]atercourse states shall, individually and where, appropriate, jointly, protect and preserve the ecosystems of international watercourse'. This provision was modelled on Article 192 of the 1982 Law of the Sea Convention. This is undoubtedly, a due diligence obligation.[43] Article 21 which deals with the pollution of international watercourses was also modelled on the provisions of the Law of the Sea Convention, in that riparian states must 'prevent, reduce and control pollution' of international watercourses. This Article is only operative, however, if the pollution 'may cause significant harm to other watercourse states or to their environment ...'.

Article 24 deals with the issue of management. The Article is couched in very careful terms, again to reconcile the interests of states. The main focus of this Article is to enter into consultations between watercourse states in matters concerning the management of an international watercourse. One of the possibilities may be the establishment of a joint management mechanism. The Article explains what is meant by the expression 'management': planning of sustainable development of an international watercourse and providing for implementation of any plans adopted; and other wise promoting the rational and optimal utilisation, protection and control of the watercourse.

2.4.2 The Procedural Obligations

A number of special provisions are devoted to procedural obligations of riparian states. They are contained in Part III of the Convention, 'Planned Measures' (Articles 11-19). They are quite elaborate and we may safely presume that they do

[43] Although, in a 'statement of understanding', the Working Group in which the Convention was negotiated indicated that Articles 21-23 are based on the due diligence standard (not, however, general Article 20), it is assumed in the theory and practice of international environmental law that the obligation to protect the environment is a due diligence obligation.

not reflect international customary law. The main Article 11 advocates the full exchange of information on planned measures.[44]

2.4.3 International Watercourse as a 'Shared Resource'

A problem in which there is still insufficient clarity and which is a source of differing opinions is whether international watercourses belong to the group of 'shared resources'.[45] The ILC, having initially included the notion of shared resources in its Draft Articles, subsequently abandoned it.[46] In 1980, the ILC explicitly recognised the minimal value of the use of the concept of shared resources in relation to international watercourses. 'The reasons for the abandoning of this concept were its novelty and the lack of certainty as to its legal consequences.'[47]

The concept was, though in a way that stresses its limited utility, cited as underlying the principle of prevention of transboundary pollution. The essence of this concept was said to be that '... it links the factual and legal interdependence of states'.[48] Factual interdependence results simply from the fact that the activities of each state affect a watercourse that is shared by other states. According to Nollkaemper, however, the usefulness of the theory in this context is very limited due to the existence of multiple elements affecting this factual interdependence between states, which renders the establishment of direct links almost impossible. Another crucial problem is to define the link between factual inter-relationships and the rights and duties of states. 'The doctrine of shared resources is of no help in establishing the character of the content of these rights and duties.'[49]

However, The Court, in the *Gabcikovo-Nagymaros* case, returned to this concept and interestingly linked it with the equitable and reasonable utilisation. It said as follows: 'Modern development of international law has strengthened this principle for non-navigational uses of international watercourses as well, as evidenced by the adoption of the Convention of 21 May 1997 on the Law of Non-Navigational Uses of International Watercourses by the United Nations General

---

[44] Article 11 reads as follows: 'Information concerning planned measures: Watercourse States shall exchange information and consult each other and, if necessary, negotiate on the possible effects of planned measures on the condition of an international watercourse.'

[45] See e.g. UNEP Principles on Conservation and Harmonious Utilisation of Natural Resources Shared by Two or More States, 19 May 1978, P.W. Birnie and A. Boyle *International Law and Environment* (OUP Oxford 2002) Ch 3 [139]-[141].

[46] This concept was present in Draft Article 5 (proposed by Schwebel) II *Y'book ILC*, vol. II (Part One) [69].

[47] P. Buirrete 'Genese D'un Droit Fluvial International General (Utilisation a des fines autres que navigations)' *RGDIP* (1992) [32]-[33]; A. Nollkaemper *The Legal Regime for Transboundary Water Pollution: Between Discretion and Constraint* (Kluwer Law International Hague 1993) [26].

[48] ibid. Also see E.H.P. Brans, E.J. de Haan, A. Nollkaemper and J. Rizma (eds.) *The Scarcity of Water, Emerging Legal and Policy Responses* (Kluwer Law International Hague 1997) [26].

[49] Nollkaemper (n 48) [26]-[28].

Assembly. The Court considers that Czechoslovakia, by unilaterally assuming control of a shared resource, and thereby depriving Hungary of its right to an equitable and reasonable share of the natural resources of the Danube with the continuing effect of the diversion of these waters on the ecology of the riparian area of the Szigetkoz, failed to respect the proportionality which is required by international law' (paragraph 85 of the Judgment).

'[I]t has to be observed, however, that many authors refer to international watercourses as a shared resource.'[50]

2.4.4 Conclusions

The survey of the legal approaches to modern management of international watercourses indicates that the principle of equitable utilisation is of fundamental importance. Although, widely used in practice by states, it has been fully elaborated by the 1997 UN Convention. It is noteworthy, however, that some unresolved problems still persist. The most important of them is the relationship between this principle and the non-significant harm rule. As pointed out above, this relationship was the subject of a heated argument between upper and lower riparian states during negotiations of the Convention. The International Court of Justice also endorsed the principle of equitable utilisation. It is clear that this principle is an elaboration of the development of the community of interest theory as enunciated by the Permanent Court of International Justice in the *River Oder* case and which presupposes the equality of all riparian states and the integrated common management (see *supra*).[51]

Finally, one more feature of the modern management of international watercourses must be mentioned: the protection of the environment. This element indicates that in contemporary water law, the integral approach to the problems of the administration of an international watercourse has been introduced. This approach requires a legal framework of watercourse administration that is farther-reaching and more comprehensive than the one applied in the past. Therefore, states are encouraged to enter into watercourse agreements that establish a body or a commission to manage jointly the common watercourse.

The complexity of problems covered calls for some institutional structure to carry out all the varied functions that relate to water management, taking into consideration the interests of all riparian states equally.

It has to be mentioned that several international watercourse agreements include provisions setting up such a structure. The most developed, however, is the Finnish-Swedish Frontier River Commission (the 'FSFRC') which is a body

---

[50] See e.g. N. Schrijver *Sovereignty over Natural Resources, Balancing Rights and Duties* (Cambridge University Press, Cambridge 1997) [129]-[130].

[51] See also the Kasikili/Sedudu Island (Botswana /Namibia) Judgment of 13 December 1999, also Dissenting Opinion of Judge C. Weeramantry and Separate Opinion of Judge P. Kooijmans at http://www.icj.cij.org/icjwww/idocket/ibono/ibono/ibonoframe.htm.

established under the Boundary Rivers Agreement of 16 September 1971.[52] The Commission's functions are much broader than those of any other similar body. In the area under its jurisdiction (which comprises of the vast northern territories of Finland and Sweden), its functions include virtually all matters both judicial and administrative, which may affect the use and the development of the watercourses, including matters relating to construction, regulation of water flow, fishing and protection of the watercourses from pollution. As to its judicial functions, the Commission, acting as the Court of first instance performs the functions, which are accorded to Water Courts in the judicial systems of Finland and Sweden. The matters, which belong to the Commission's judicial functions, cover examination of the legality of constructions affecting the watercourse; compensation; protection against water pollution; water regulation. Administrative functions are very broad and they include granting of fishing rights. Other types of functions are the so-called supervisory functions over water use, water conditions and fishing. These functions clearly indicate the enormous extent of the Commission's powers. In implementation of these functions, it may impose a penalty of fine or even a year imprisonment for a person who acts without the FSFRC permission, by setting unauthorised fish traps. Such vast powers and extensive functions, accorded to a river commission are only possible under judicial systems which are so integrated as these of the Nordic states and among states having very close, common policy.

2.5 Part Two: Main Provisions of the 1966 ILA Helsinki Rules and the Ongoing Work of the ILA Water Resources Committee

The International Law Association ('ILA') has since 1966 worked to elaborate general rules on international water resources. Its work has served as a basis for the codification of international water law of the International Law Commission and the UN Convention on International Watercourses 1997.

This contribution intends to give an overview of the main provisions of the 1966 Helsinki Rules, the evolution of additional rules and its work on elaborating 'new rules' as well as revising the existing rules in the light of the evolution of international water resources law in recent years.

2.5.1 The 1966 ILA Helsinki Rules[53]

In 1966, the ILA Conference, which was held in Helsinki, adopted the final report of the 'Committee on the Uses of Waters of International Rivers' the 'old Rivers Committee', which had been established in 1954. It had been the task of this committee to elaborate general rules applicable to international rivers drawing on

---

[52] Text in; 825 UNTS [191].

[53] *Yearbook of the International Law Commission* II (1974), Part Two [357]-[359]; *Yearbook of the International Law Commission* II (1980), Part One [194].

the bilateral and regional practice and experience of states. Thus, for the first time, 'international water law' had been codified. The so-called 'Helsinki Rules on the Uses of International Rivers' contained chapters on general rules, equitable utilisation of the waters of an international drainage basin, pollution, navigation, and procedures for the prevention and settlement of disputes.

2.5.2 The Main Provisions of the Helsinki Rules

2.5.2.1 Application of the Helsinki Rules – international drainage basin

In dealing with international water resources, the question of geographical definition arises. The ILA adopted the concept of an 'international drainage basin'. Article II of the Helsinki rules defines 'an international drainage basin as a geographical area extending over two or more states determined by the watershed limits of the system of waters, including surface and underground waters, flowing into a common terminus'. Thus, the International Law Association has opted for a broad definition for the application of its rules. This approach – although it has been followed in a number of treaties, such as the 1972 Senegal River Basin Treaty, the 1987 Zambesi River Treaty,[54] the 1978 Treaty on Amazonian Co-operation, the 1994 Convention on Co-operation for the Protection and Sustainable Use of the Danube River and the 1995 Agreement on the Co-operation for the Sustainable Development of the Mekong River Basin[55] – it has been criticised as putting too heavy a burden on upstream states, in particular with regard to environmental protection.

The International Law Commission, therefore, did not follow the concept of 'international drainage basin' but referred in its draft articles to 'international watercourses'.[56] One of the arguments which had been put forward in the discussion in the ILC and the Sixth Committee of the General Assembly was that the ''basin'' concept put too much emphasis on the land areas within the watershed, indicating that the physical land area of a basin might be governed by the rules of international water resources law'.[57]

It has been argued in international academic writings that the practical difference between the two concepts on the geographical scope of international water resources law, as also the more limited definition obliges states to control pollution in the wider drainage basin in order to produce the desired results for the

[54] ILM 27 (1988) 1109 ff.

[55] ILM 34 (1995) 864 ff.

[56] Art. 2 define 'watercourse' as 'a system of surface waters and ground waters constituting by virtue of their physical relationship a unitary whole and normally flowing in a common terminus'.

[57] cf Evensen *Yearbook of the International Law Commission II* (1983), Part One [167]-[168] para 71.

waters of the international water course.[58] Although it should be noted that in the case of the bilateral relations between Canada and the United States the two concepts which have been used to deal with transboundary water issues concerning the two countries have led to different results.[59]

In light of the above-mentioned treaty practice the ILA has not changed its approach. Also, in the current on-going work of the ILA, the concept of 'international drainage basin' has been followed.

2.5.2.2 Equitable and reasonable use

The central question that has been discussed in international water law is the question of allocation of transboundary water resources. The International Law Association has discussed this question intensively. The 1966 Helsinki Rules devote a whole chapter to the question of equitable utilisation of transboundary water resources.

Article IV of the Helsinki Rules is to be seen as the key principle. It reads as follows: 'Each basin state is entitled, within its territory, to a reasonable and equitable share in the beneficial uses of the waters of an international drainage basin.' Although the term 'reasonable and equitable' is not capable of a precise determination in general,[60] the issues turn on a balancing of relevant factors and must be responsive to the circumstances of individual cases. Article V paragraph 2 lists some of the factors to be considered in an individual case, such as the geography of the basin, including in particular the extent of the drainage area in the territory of each basin state; the hydrology of the basin, including in particular the contribution of water by each basin state; the climate affecting the basin; the past utilisation of the waters of the basin, including in particular existing utilisation; the population dependent on the waters of the basin in each basin state; and the avoidance of unnecessary waste in the utilisation of waters of the basin.

According to Article V paragraph 3, 'the weight to be given to each factor is to be determined by its importance in comparison with that of other relevant factors. In determining what is a reasonable and equitable share, all relevant factors are to be considered together and a conclusion reached on the basis of the whole'. Furthermore, the 1966 Helsinki Rules deal with the relationship between certain uses: Article VI states that 'a use or category of uses is not entitled to any inherent preference over any other use or category of uses'. According to Article VII, 'a basin state may not be denied the present reasonable use of the waters of an international drainage basin to reserve for a co-basin state a future use of such waters'. Moreover, Article VIII paragraph 1 determines that 'an existing reasonable use may continue in

---

[58] cf Lammers *Pollution* [110]–[113].

[59] See Birnie & Boyle *International Law and the Environment* (2002) [326]-[328].

[60] Art. V para 1 of the Helsinki Rules reads as follows: 'What is a reasonable and equitable share within the meaning of Article IV is to be determined in the light of all the relevant factors in each particular case.'

operation unless the factors justifying its continuance are outweighed by other factors leading to the conclusion that it be modified or terminated so as to accommodate a competing incompatible use'. According to Article VIII paragraph 3, 'a use will not be deemed an existing use if at the time of becoming operational it is incompatible with an already existing reasonable use'.

The Helsinki Rules did not mention the 'no-harm' principle as a specific rule of its own. Article V paragraph 2 lists as one of the factors determining equitable and reasonable utilisation 'the degree to which the needs of a basin state may be satisfied, without causing substantial injury to a co-basin State'. Thus, 'the harm a given use may inflict on a watercourse state is an element, but not the decisive element, for measuring equitable and reasonable utilisation. This is so because otherwise, in the case of a fully exploited watercourse, any new activity would be prohibited since it would, necessarily, harm present uses and users'.[61]

Similar provisions as contained in Articles IV and V of the 1966 Helsinki Rules have been elaborated by the International Law Commission in its draft articles on the 'non-navigational uses of international watercourses' and are contained in the 1997 UN-Convention on the law of the non-navigational uses of international watercourses.[62] However, it should be noted that the question on the relationship between uses, the line taken by the ILA has not been followed in the UN-Convention as a whole. Although the UN Convention states that in the absence of an agreement or custom to the contrary, no use of an international watercourse enjoys inherent priority over other uses, it underlines that special regard is to be given to the requirements of vital human needs.

2.5.2.3 Pollution

Article X of the Helsinki Rules states that consistent with the principle of equitable utilisation of the waters of an international drainage basin, a state must prevent substantial injury in the territory of a co-basin state, and should take all reasonable measures to abate existing water pollution to such an extent that no substantial damage is caused in the territory of a co-basin state.

2.5.2.4 Further elaboration of the 1966 Helsinki Rules between 1966 and 1999

Already in 1966, when the Conference adopted the final report it established a new Committee to deal with the numerous theoretical and practical problems still awaiting international legal codification. The Helsinki Conference instructed the Committee on International Water Resource Law:

---

[61] L. Caflisch 'Regulation of the Uses of International Watercourses'in Salman/Boission de Chazournes (eds.) 'International Watercourses – Enhancing Co-operation and Managing Conflict, Proceedings of a World Bank Seminar' (1998) 3ff, 8f and 13.

[62] cf Articles 5 and 6 of the UN-Convention (ILM 36 (1997) 700ff).

> to carry on a programme of codification and study certain selected aspects of water resources law, of which the following topics are illustrative: underground waters, the relationship of water to other natural resources, domestic uses of water, hydraulic uses of water including the generation of power and irrigation, flood control and siltation, regulation of water flow, detailed rules on the navigation of rivers, and further consideration of the subject of pollution of coastal areas and enclosed seas.[63]

Since 1966, the Committee elaborated rules on a number of issues:

> flood control; marine pollution of continental origin; maintenance and improvement of naturally navigable waterways separating or traversing several states; protection of water resources and water installations in times of armed conflict; administration of international water resources; regulation of the flow of international watercourses; relationship of international water resources and environmental elements; water pollution in an international drainage basin; law of international groundwater resources; complementary rules applicable to international water resources; private law remedies for transboundary damage in international watercourses; cross-media pollution resulting from the use of the waters of an international drainage basin;[64] and adequate stream flows.[65]

In particular, the rules on administration of international water resources are to be seen in the context of the key principle of 'equitable utilisation' of international water resources. It lays down rules on the establishment of institutional or other arrangements by agreement among two or more basin states, which shall be a forum to determine in a particular case, the 'equitable utilisation' by the riparian states.

Furthermore, the rules adopted on groundwater resources extended the scope of the Helsinki Rules to groundwater resources in general.

Thus, the ILA elaborated a set of rules concerning international water resources over the last decades. However, it must be borne in mind that the sectoral approach followed by the Water Resources Committee has led to a large number of rules which both cover new areas of international water resources law – such as the regulation of the flow of water of international watercourses – or have elaborated

---

[63] Al Utton (ed.) *The Work of the International Law Association on the Law of International Water Resources* (1996).

[64] The rules which have been adopted by the International Law Association are reproduced in Al Utton (ed.) *The Work of the International Law Association on the Law of International Water Resources* (1996).

[65] An article on Adequate Stream Flows had been adopted by the Water Resources Committee at its Rotterdam meeting in 1998. At its London Conference 2000, the ILA took note 'of the draft Article on Adequate Stream Flows as a provision deserving further consideration by the Committee' (Resolution No. 18/2000).

the Helsinki Rules further – e.g. on water pollution in an international drainage basin.

2.6 The Campione Consolidation of the ILA Rules on International Water Resources (1966-1999)

Taking into account the intensive work of the ILA in the last decades on various issues concerning transboundary water resources, the ILA Committee decided that a consolidation of the rules so far elaborated should be undertaken. The Committee under the Chairmanship of Prof. Charles Bourne undertook a consolidation of the rules it had adopted in the past. The Campione Consolidation did not consider whether the rules approved by the ILA over the past 34 years needed to be revised to correspond to the present state of the law.[66] It restated the existing rules in a comprehensive manner, but did not consider developments in international water law that have occurred since the original rules were adopted. The main aim of this undertaking was to provide a comprehensive document on the work of the ILA.

At its London Conference 2000, the ILA '[took] note of The Campione Consolidation of the ILA Rules on International Water Resources' and 'request[ed] the Committee on Water Resources to continue to consider possible new rules on water resources'.[67]

2.7 The Work of the ILA Water Resources Committee

In light of the developments concerning bilateral and regional watercourses as well as recent developments in international law, such as the adoption on the 1997 UN-Convention on the Law of the Non-Navigational Uses of International Watercourses, as well as the evolution of other areas of international law, e.g. environmental law, the ILA started to review the bulk of international rules it had elaborated in the last decades.

The question of whether and how to proceed with a possible revision of the work of the Association regarding the waters of international drainage basins were discussed extensively at meetings of the Committee between June 1997 and February 2000. The Committee finally adopted by consensus the following motion:

> The future work of the Committee will be the consideration of possible new rules on water resources, working on the basis of the Rapporteur's draft of January 2000.

As this motion indicates, the Committee was considering 'new rules'. The new rules considered to some extent revised and updated the international rules on

[66] cf Report of the Water Resources Committee (Report of the 69th Conference 2000, 858f).

[67] cf Resolution No. 18/2000 (Report of the 69th Conference 2000, 40).

water resources already approved by the ILA, and to some extent addressed new matters not previously addressed by the Association.

2.8 Issues Discussed in the New Work of ILA

The discussion within the Water Resources Committee has shown that a number of new issues had emerged in the last years, other issues had become less important in international water law. Although, as has been pointed out above, the rules were to be seen as general rules or guidelines as more detailed rules had to be elaborated, taking into account the specific circumstances of each international drainage basin. The revised rules intended to take into account recent developments in state practice.

The discussions at the London Conference on the Campione Consolidation pointed out that the general principles dealing with 'equitable and reasonable utilisation' (Articles 3 to 12) needed to be discussed in the light of recent treaty practice and the ongoing work in other international fora. Furthermore, Article 10 – which had not been adopted by the ILA at earlier Conferences, needed to be further elaborated. Article 10 provides as follows: 'Consistent with the principle of reasonable and equitable utilisation, states shall, individually and, where appropriate, in co-operation with other basin states, take all reasonable measures to ensure stream flows adequate to protect the biological, chemical, and physical integrity of international watercourses, including their estuarine zones.'

This provision – which was based on the conclusion of a study undertaken by Professor Utton – tried to provide a general rule dealing with the issue of 'adequate minimum stream flows' which had been addressed in a number of international fora in recent years. As the commentary to Article 10 noted, there 'is an early and extensive treaty practice which provides for the regulation of flows of international watercourses for a variety of purposes such as hydro-power, commercial fisheries, log-floating and flood control, but does not deal with modern environmental protection as such.' But recent treaties, such as the Mekong River Basin Treaty[68] explicitly requires minimum stream flows, and the UN-Convention recognises the range of environmental issues and obliges states to take measures to protect the environment. It is suggested in the commentary that although the maintenance of minimum stream flows is not addressed explicitly, the environmental protection obligation might often require the maintenance of adequate flow levels in international watercourses. The commentary further noted that the suggested Article 10 would not impose a mandatory obligation to maintain adequate stream flows as it is subject to the principle of equitable utilisation.[69]

The London Conference felt that the adoption of such a provision might be premature in view of the work undertaken to revise the Helsinki Rules. Thus, the issue of 'adequate stream flows' was going to be one of the issues to be considered further in the future work.

---

[68] Article 6 (ILM 34 (1995) 864ff.

[69] cf Report of the 69th Conference 2000, 834ff.

Furthermore, the Water Resources Committee ('WRC') had already undertaken work on a number of issues, such as environmental harm and the no-harm rule, which are closely connected to issues raised by the proposed Article 10.

Moreover, a number of issues had emerged in recent years, which needed to be addressed in the work of the WRC. Among them were 'the management of an international watercourse'; 'environmental issues' such as sustainable development, minimisation of environmental harm and environmental impact assessment; the protection of rights of existing communities; and water quality objectives and criteria.

The 'management of an international watercourse' had been already addressed in the earlier work of the ILA by stating that 'basin states shall co-operate in a spirit of good faith and good neighbourliness in matters relating to the waters of the basin'. Taking into account recent treaty practice, the WRC discussed three general provisions on 'management': they deal with co-operative management, conjunctive management and integrated management.

The provision on co-operative management stated that: 'Basin states shall co-operate in the development, use, protection and control of fresh waters and related resources.' 'Conjunctive management' means: 'In dealing with fresh waters and related resources, basin states shall use their best efforts to manage the surface waters, the groundwater, and other pertinent water resources of the basin together in a comprehensive managerial system.' The general principle on 'integrated management' reads: 'Basin states shall use their best efforts to integrate appropriately the management of the water resources of a drainage basin with the management of other natural resources of the basin.'

These three provisions ascertain the important principle that 'management' of international water resources have not only to be seen one-dimensionally, but states have to take into account more dimensions in the management of an international watercourse.

The principle of 'sustainable development', which has emerged as the objective to be achieved by developmental and environmental policies, has also to be integrated in international water law. It is to be seen as one of the general principles to be applied to the uses of an international watercourse. The relevant provision reads as follows: 'States, acting individually or jointly, shall exercise due diligence to achieve the sustainable use of the fresh waters and related resources subject to their jurisdiction.'

Recent developments in the area of international environmental law, such as environmental impact assessment, had to be considered. Environmental impact assessment has not only been included in the 1992 Rio Declaration on Environment and Development,[70] but has also been included in international treaties[71] as an obligation to be undertaken by states before activities are implemented. Thus, a revision of the Helsinki Rules had to discuss this issue and

[70] Principle 17.
[71] e.g. 1991 Espoo Convention.

determine the relationship between environmental impact assessment and rules on notification and consultations with other states.

Another issue which, has emerged in recent years in regard to international water resources, is the question of the rights of pre-existing communities, i.e. rights of indigenous and local communities. This issue has been addressed in international fora, e.g., in the context of the 1992 Convention on Biological Diversity: the rights of indigenous and local communities had been addressed in a broader context.[72]

Furthermore, the Committee discussed whether new rules had evolved in recent years concerning flood control, rules applicable during armed conflict as well as prevention and settlement of disputes. As regards the latter, recent treaty practice in the area of international water law as well as new emerging trends in other areas of international law were taken into consideration.

Other rules, such as those on timber floating or navigation were reviewed in regard to recent treaty practice as the work of international bodies to elaborate general rules on international watercourses have concentrated on the non-navigational uses of international watercourses. Navigation has not been at the centre of the discussions. This may be partly due to the fact that practice of states concerning the freedom of navigation on a specific watercourse varies to a large extent between continents.

The provision of timber floating which has been an important use in certain parts of the world seems to have lost importance in recent years.

2.9 Concluding Remarks

After several rounds of meetings and lengthy deliberations, the Water Resources Committee prepared its final report in April 2004, which was discussed and adopted by ILA Conference in August 2004. The rules have been elaborated taking into account developments on the national, regional and international level. They address all the issues which have been stated earlier in this Chapter as issues to be discussed in the Committee's work, e.g., the concept of sustainability has been incorporated into the rules, the principle of cooperation has been strengthened and the principles of conjunctive and integrated management have been further elaborated. Furthermore, the participation of affected persons in the management of the water resources has been strengthened. Moreover, recent developments in the protection of the aquatic environment as well as the general practice of impact assessment have been incorporated.

Thus, the work of the International Law Association has contributed significantly to the evolution of international law concerning international water resources. The work of the Committee was to review comprehensively and to revise to the extent necessary to assure that the ILA Rules correctly stated the law

---

[72] cf Article 8(j) and the work undertaken within the framework of the Convention's bodies.

and to indicate emerging developments resulting from practice in recent years.[73] As has been stated earlier, water issues were also discussed by the ILA Committee within the framework of the Rio process. The summit held in Johannesburg in September 2002 ('Rio+10') discussed, among other issues, the question of water supply and water distribution.

To conclude, it can be hoped that the recommendations of the Water Resources Committee of the ILA as adopted by the Berlin Conference in August 2004 will have an important influence on the further evolution of international law regarding water resources and will shape the practice states as well as of international organisations and institutions, such as the World Bank, FAO and UNDP.

---

[73] The final rules of the Committee have been published on the ILA Water Resources Committee's webpage and are reproduced in Annex VIII of this volume.

PART II:

THE ISSUES IN THE GANGES RIVER BASIN

Chapter 3

A Maverick View

Ramaswamy R. Iyer

3.1 Part I

The title of the Conference is an interesting one. It is not a simple indication of a theme or topic but virtually a synoptic statement of a thesis. Consider its various components. The term basin brings in the idea of 'basin planning', with the word 'integrated' not mentioned but implicitly present; similarly, the word 'sustainable' is not used but it is there in the climate of opinion and is bound to be encountered. Ganges is a river that flows through several countries, and issues of inter-country relationships (riparian and other) are involved, and the notion of 'regional cooperation' will inevitably come up in this context. These implications are made explicit by the word *international*. The word *law* brings in the themes water-sharing principles, riparian rights and obligations, the old Helsinki Rules and the recent UN convention, conflicts and their resolution, a legal and institutional framework for inter-country cooperation, and so on. Finally, the reference to *the 21st century* brings in the themes of future needs (with particular reference to aspirations for 'development'), projected scarcities and possible conflicts, their security implications, the 'water wars' theory, and so on. All this can be woven together into some kind of a composite thesis arguing for large supply-side solutions, regional cooperation, and so on. Some such thesis is implicit in the title of this Conference. Some reservations in this regard will be put forward later, but first it is necessary to understand the mainstream view more fully.

In recent years there has been a growing perception of a looming water scarcity. There is a currently fashionable thesis that future wars will be fought over water, not oil. That is a debatable proposition, but the prognosis of acute water scarcity in the not too distant future cannot easily be disputed. The water available to us on earth today is no different in quantity from what was available thousands of years ago. That finite quantity has to be juxtaposed against increasing demands from a growing population. The population of the world, currently around 6 billion, is expected to exceed 8 billion by the year 2050. Apart from sheer numbers, the processes of urbanisation and 'development' are also expected to result in a vast increase in the demand for fresh water. It is this projection that leads to predictions of water scarcity, which could be severe in some parts of the world. (Incidentally, global figures are not of much practical significance: water is not an internationally traded commodity to an extent comparable to oil, and the availability of water in a distant part of the world is not of much significance to a water-short country or region. A new concept of 'virtual water trade' has made its appearance in this context, but we need not go into it here).

A common trend in most of the discussions on the subject is to proceed *from* projections of enormous future needs (basic and 'developmental') of a growing (and urbanising) population and the severe pressure that this will exert on finite supplies, *to* the need for large supply-side solutions, the massive investments and the kind of integrated planning that these will require, the imperative of regional cooperation in that context, and at the same time, given the limitations on the managerial capacities of states and their resource constraints, the need for private sector participation and investments (and related to this, the fostering of water markets), and the legal and institutional underpinning that all this will call for.

Turning to India, the National Commission on Integrated Water Resources Development Plan (NC) in its Report (September 1999) has made various assumptions in regard to the growth of population and the processes of urbanization and 'development' (high, medium and low rates of change), and come to the conclusion that by the year 2050 the total water requirement of the country will be 973 to 1180 km^3 under 'low' and 'high' demand projections, as against its estimate of 1086 km^3 as the 'usable' water resources of the country, which means that supply will barely match demand by that date. It is the NC's view that there will be a difficult situation but no crisis, *provided* that a number of measures on both the demand side and the supply side are taken in time. However, there are wide variations, both temporal and spatial, in the availability of water in the country. The standard engineering response to these temporal and spatial variations is to propose (a) the storing of river waters in reservoirs behind large dams to transfer water from the season of abundance to that of scarcity (as also from good years to bad), and (b) long-distance water transfers from 'surplus' areas to water-short areas. Both large 'storages' (i.e., reservoirs) and the 'linking of rivers' (i.e., 'inter-basin transfers') have played an important part in the thinking of Indian water resource planners, and both involve major engineering interventions in the form of large 'water resource development' (WRD) projects.

Thus, both at the regional/international level and at the national (Indian) level there seems to be widespread agreement that to the projected water needs of the future an important (if not the major) part of the answer lies in WRD projects. As most of these projects (whether in the private sector or in the public sector) will have to be undertaken on large rivers that run through more than one country, inter-country understandings (or, in their absence, conflicts) become matters of considerable importance.

3.2 Part II

For more than nine years (May 1990 – September 1999) the present writer was involved in a study of the possibilities of cooperation by India, Bangladesh and Nepal on the utilisation of the water resources of the Himalayan river systems for the benefit of all three countries. That study (funded by the Ford Foundation) was a joint project of three non-governmental institutions in the three countries, namely, the Centre for Policy Research, New Delhi, Bangladesh Unnayan Parishad, Dhaka, and Institute for Integrated Development Studies, Kathmandu. Behind that ten-year study laid the firm belief that inter-country cooperation was essential for the beneficial utilisation of these water resources. That belief has some relevance to the theme of this Conference. However, before proceeding further it is necessary to refer to an important definitional issue.

The title refers to the 'Ganges Basin', but is it a basin or a sub-basin? The term 'Eastern Himalayan Rivers' that has gained considerable currency in recent years is a slightly imprecise expression, but it is generally known that it refers to the rivers Ganga, Brahmaputra and Barak or Meghna. Nepal has several rivers, all of which are a part of the Ganga system; that country has nothing to do with the Brahmaputra or the Barak. Bhutan, on the other hand, is entirely within the Brahmaputra system. Both India and Bangladesh are concerned with all three rivers. In India, the Ganga, the Brahmaputra and the Barak are far apart whereas in Bangladesh they all join and flow together into the sea; and yet Bangladesh argues that they are three separate basins and India holds the view that they constitute one basin because of the common terminus. On the surface, this seems a definitional or conceptual difference, but in fact it is primarily a political difference arising from certain concerns and objectives that the two countries have: each country tends to adopt the position that best suits the purposes it has in view. We need not go into that controversy here. In any case, despite this difference between the Indian and Bangladeshi (official) positions, the non-governmental Three Country Study did in fact treat the Ganga-Brahmaputra-Meghna system(s) as constituting a unity of some kind. 'Region' was the preferred word, and the abbreviation GBM has come into vogue. Though the title of the present Conference refers only to the Ganges basin, we must keep in mind the fact that it is part of a larger system or basin or region or whatever else we wish to call it.

3.3 Part III

For a brief account of the Ganges or Ganga basin, we cannot do better than refer to the book 'Cooperation on the Eastern Himalayan Rivers' which was the final outcome of the Three-Country Study mentioned above. An extract is reproduced in the Annexe to this chapter. Against that background, what are the various benefits that the riparian countries can expect and plan cooperatively for?

Reverting to the larger 'system' or 'region', the countries concerned (leaving China aside for the present) can be classified (in relation to these water-resources) as follows:

1. Nepal/Bhutan: upper riparians, mountainous countries;
2. India: middle riparian (lower riparian to Nepal/Bhutan, upper to Bangladesh), largely plains (though there is also the Himalayan part);
3. Bangladesh: lowest riparian, deltaic country.

To Nepal and Bhutan, given their relatively limited cultivable land areas, their water endowment largely represents a source of hydro-electric power, whether for use within the two countries or for earning revenues through export; to Nepal, the rivers also hold promise of an escape from its land-locked condition through a navigable outlet to the sea. To India, the water resources represent possibilities of hydroelectric power, navigation and irrigation, but also the danger of floods. To Bangladesh, criss-crossed as it is by a vast network of rivers and streams, they represent a formidable source of recurrent and often devastating floods, but they also act as conveyors of commerce, sustain fisheries, offer possibilities of irrigation, and play a role in the control of salinity.

3.4 Part IV

Against the background outlined above, inter-country cooperation is obviously necessary, and it is equally evident that conflicts might occur. Assuming that there is no deliberate intention on the part of any party to cause harm to others, how do conflicts in relation to water or over WRD projects arise, whether between countries or between constituent units within a country? They could arise from one or more of the following causes:

1. wrong principles (Harmon Doctrine, prior appropriation, prescriptive rights, etc., asserted in an absolute manner);
2. limited vision (myopic nationalism, blind assertion of local perceptions);
3. lack of sensitivity on the part of the stronger party, excessive touchiness on the part of the weaker;
4. inadequate understanding of implications and consequences; failure to study these fully;
5. ignorance; lack of data/ information;
6. unwillingness to share information; failure to consult all concerned; failure of imagination about others' needs, rights or concerns; and
7. politicisation, i.e., the tendency for differences over water or environmental concerns to become elements in domestic electoral politics.

How can conflicts relating to river waters (and in particular large projects) be avoided or minimised? In this context we often come across two kinds of 'ideal' recommendations. From a hydrological point of view, the recommendation is that national or political boundaries should be ignored, that a hydrological unit such as a basin or sub-basin should be taken as a whole, and that there should be integrated water-resource planning for such a unit. From a political/economic perspective, the recommendation is that regional planning is superior to national planning. There is much force in these propositions, but there are also some difficulties that must be taken note of. These will be referred to later.

In relation to principles, neither the Harmon Doctrine (that of territorial sovereignty) nor that of prescriptive rights or prior appropriation has found general approval. What commands a fair degree of international acceptance is the principle of equitable apportionment for beneficial uses. That was the language of the old Helsinki Rules. The present UN Convention on the Non-Navigational Uses of International Water Courses (passed by the General Assembly in 1997, but still awaiting ratification by the stipulated number of countries) requires the watercourse states to 'utilize an international watercourse in an equitable and reasonable manner' (Article 5, cl.1). (It will be noticed that the idea of 'apportionment' has disappeared.) Again, the next clause requires the watercourse states to 'participate in the use, development and protection of an international watercourse in an equitable and reasonable manner'. (The word 'protection' brings in the idea of 'sustainable development'.) What is 'equitable' has of course to be determined with reference to many criteria, and there is enormous scope for differences here, but there is some merit in a general subscription to the principles of equity and reasonableness.

The short point is that if countries falling within a river basin or sub-basin wish to avoid conflict while planning a project, there are enough principles and guidelines to go by. As regards institutional mechanisms, there are many models to choose from: bilateral or multilateral commissions; purely governmental bodies or bodies with a large non-official component; advisory or empowered bodies; private sector projects; and so on. What are feasible in a given case will be a function of the felt needs and the facts of geography on the one hand, and the state of political relations between the countries concerned on the other. It is important that institutional mechanisms appropriate to a given case should be established very early, before differences of perception grow sharp and attitudes harden.

That brings us to the political dimension. Regarded simply as disputes relating to water sharing, conflicts are not particularly difficult to resolve: a reasonable agreement can always be worked out. Why then do these disputes become so difficult and loom so large in the minds of ordinary people? The answer in one word is 'politics'. There is a complex interaction between water issues and political relations. It is not always a case of conflicts over water resources leading to a worsening of political relations, though that may happen on occasion; it is more often a case of a difficult political relationship rendering the water issue more intractable. This is particularly so when other issues become prominent from time to time: for instance, Nepal's grievances as a land-locked country and its concerns over trade and transit issues; or India's security concerns and its apprehensions about Nepal's relations with China; or in the Indo-Bangladesh context, the question of illegal immigrants, Chakma refugees, insurgency operations, border demarcation issues, trade balance, etc. Water issues in turn can become the most dominant factor at certain times, and can have an impact on the general political relationship.

More than anything else, one factor tends to influence Indo-Nepal and Indo-Bangladesh relations, namely, India's size. India's relations with the smaller neighbours have doubtless improved significantly in recent years, but the old distrust of the 'Big Brother' has not wholly disappeared either in Nepal or in Bangladesh. The twin dangers of big-country insensitivity or arrogance and small-country touchiness, diffidence and proneness to suspicion, are the Scylla and Charybdis that can wreck even a good relationship.

In the light of the foregoing, do we need new principles, laws or institutions in the new century (to which the title of this Conference refers)? To this writer the answer seems to be 'No', though this is a tentative and not a dogmatic statement. The real problem in most cases is, as mentioned earlier, politics.

3.5 Part V

At this stage, it may be useful to look at some of the issues that have actually come up between these countries in inter-governmental talks and/or in non-official academic exchanges of the kind referred to above. Out of the many under discussion, only those of a general nature having a bearing on the theme of this Conference will be referred to.

First, in relation to the basic question of the relative rights of upper and lower riparians, there is an asymmetry that must be taken note of. India's position as the middle riparian (between Nepal and Bangladesh), together with its desire to avoid accusations of big-country dominance, places it in a somewhat difficult situation. For instance, vis a vis Nepal, India as the lower riparian has conceded to the upper riparian the right to use whatever waters the latter needs, including the right to make inter-basin transfers. Thus, primacy has been given to Nepal, and the lower riparian's rights have been subordinated to those of the upper riparian. On the other hand, vis a vis Bangladesh, it is the primacy of the lower riparian that has been implicitly (partly) granted. The whole complaint of Bangladesh for years was that the flows coming down had been reduced by the upper riparian; and it continues to express apprehensions about upstream uses in UP and Bihar. To meet the concerns of Bangladesh, India as the upper riparian has undertaken to protect the flows reaching Farakka, which means that it has undertaken the responsibility of regulating upstream uses. This is a politically difficult undertaking, given the quasi-federal structure of India. In particular, there is a sense of grievance in the state of Bihar that its interests were not kept in mind by the Central Government when it negotiated the Ganges Treaty with Bangladesh. Be that as it may, India has undertaken an obligation under the Treaty and will have to fulfil it. It may be added that Bangladesh sometimes tends to argue that it is a 'stakeholder' in the entire Ganga system and should be consulted or kept informed about any intervention, major or minor, at any point in the system from the Gangotri downwards. This will need extended discussion, which is not feasible here; the point is mentioned in passing only as an indication of an extreme lower riparian position.

Secondly, in both the Mahakali (India-Nepal) and Ganga (India-Bangladesh) Treaties the principle of 'no harm to either side' has been incorporated. That seems very reasonable, but it could present some difficulties on a future date. It is fair enough to say that the upper riparian, in planning its own water uses, should keep the interests of the lower riparian in mind and refrain from causing undue injury or distress to it; but the absolute assertion of 'no harm' could put the upper riparian in some difficulty, as any use by it of the waters of the river in question may conceivably reduce downstream flows, and therefore cause some harm, however minor, to the lower riparian. The Helsinki Rules wanted the upper riparian to avoid causing substantial harm, and the present UN Convention uses the expression 'significant' adverse effects. In the Treaties mentioned above there is no such qualification. In practical terms, this may not cause any difficulty in the near future, but the potential for a difference in perceptions at some stage does exist. This will need to be avoided by wisdom and goodwill on both sides.

Thirdly, we need to take note of the issue of 'bilateralism' versus 'regionalism'. The Government of India has in the past preferred to deal with Nepal and Bangladesh separately and bilaterally, and though there was some rethinking on this at one stage, the official policy still remains one of bilateralism. The considerations behind this position seem to include (a) the feeling that negotiations are difficult and protracted enough between two countries, and that they will become vastly more complicated and intractable when three or more countries are involved; and (b) the fear that the smaller countries may join hands and make common cause against the bigger country. These are somewhat exaggerated fears but they cannot be dismissed as totally unfounded and absurd. On the other hand, a view that has gained considerable currency not only in Nepal and Bangladesh but even among many in India is that 'regional cooperation' has better solutions to offer to most problems than purely national or bilateral approaches. This is a complex subject that will require a separate chapter. All that can be said here is that on this, as on many other subjects, we have to be guided by practical considerations. Some problems and issues are best dealt with on a national or local basis; some call for cooperation between two countries or units; and others demand a regional approach. The circumstances vary from case to case, and in each case the most appropriate route needs to be followed. On the one hand, a rigid bilateralism such as that adopted by the Government of India is unwise and unduly self-limiting; on the other, a dogmatic advocacy of regionalism as inherently superior to a national or bilateral approach would unnecessarily complicate simple issues and render them more difficult to resolve. What is called for is pragmatism rather than doctrine.

Fourthly, the ratification of the Mahakali Treaty by the Nepal Parliament was accompanied by a set of resolutions that are generally referred to in that country as 'strictures'. If the Nepal Parliament had been deeply troubled by certain questions, it could have refused to ratify the Treaty. To say that it has ratified the Treaty but has at the same time passed a series of 'strictures' seems inconsistent. The Government of Nepal must of course take note of their Parliament's concerns, and if necessary, go back to the Government of India for a fresh round of negotiations; but in that event, the Treaty must be treated as dormant (if not as non-existent) until the re-negotiation is completed and a fresh document is agreed upon. And of course the negotiations may fail, or may yield results somewhat different from what the Nepalese Parliament might have had in mind. It would appear that there can only be 'ratification' or 'non-ratification' of a Treaty, and not a conditional ratification; and that a conditional ratification is the same as non-ratification. It could be seriously argued that the Mahakali Treaty does not stand ratified and therefore is not operative. However, the general view is that the Treaty has been ratified, and the two countries have exchanged instruments of ratification. Thus a somewhat confused situation prevails.

Fifthly, from the fact that the Mahakali is described in the Treaty as 'a boundary river on major stretches' the Nepalese draw the inference that it belongs equally to the two countries, and therefore that half of the waters of the river belong to Nepal. Speaking subject to correction, these doctrines ('boundary river', ownership of half the waters, etc) seem to be Nepalese innovations. The Indian view (if one has understood it correctly) is that the river can be used by the two countries but does not 'belong' to either; that in particular, any doctrine of ownership of flowing water and the implied right of the upper riparian to 'sell' the water so owned to the lower riparian (who would in any case receive that water naturally by gravity flow) seems non-maintainable in international law; that 'equal sharing' really applies to the incremental benefits to be created by the Pancheswar Project; and that the relative benefits gained by the two countries would determine their respective shares of the capital costs of the project. There is a clear divergence of views here. In so far as this is the result of inadequate negotiation or poor wording, both sides must share the blame for leaving this nebulousness in the Treaty. Nothing will be gained by taking a dogmatic position on this issue; this is a matter for discussion between the two countries with a view to arriving at an agreed position.

Certain other issues such as the territorial Kalapani question, the issue of protection of existing consumptive uses, the question of basing the power tariff on the 'avoided cost' principle, etc, will not be discussed here, as these, while being important, have no significant bearing on the theme of this conference. In the India-Bangladesh context, a point on which the two Governments are agreed is that the Ganga is water-short and cannot meet the combined requirements of the two countries and that there is a need for the 'augmentation' of the lean-season flows of the river. This again will not be discussed here as being too narrow and specific to be put into a chapter that seeks to cover a larger canvas. The present writer's reservations on this 'augmentation' proposition are set forth in an article in the Economic and Political Weekly of Mumbai in the issue dated 14 August 1999.

3.6 Part VI

Returning to the main theme of the Conference, what can one envision for the Ganges Basin in the 21st century? There is no doubt that the population of the basin – in all three countries – will increase; that there will be greater pressure on the available natural resources, particularly water (both for drinking – including all domestic use under that rubric – and for food production, not to mention industrial use); that energy needs will also increase; that the protection of the river (and of course all surface water and groundwater) from pollution and contamination will become major concerns; that the minimisation of damage from floods will also be a major objective; that the utilisation of the river system for commerce (inland navigation) may increase; and that the three countries will need to reach understandings on a whole range of matters relating to the management, utilisation, protection and conservation of the water resources of the basin (or sub-basin, if that is what one wishes to call it).

What in fact are the three Governments' plans? The first point to note is that there are a few unresolved questions arising out of the Mahakali and Ganges Treaties on which agreements need to be arrived at quickly. As for the future, India and Nepal have been talking about (but making little progress on) a series of large projects in the Himalayan region: Karnali, Pancheswar, Sapta Kosi, etc, with varying combinations of hydro-electric power, irrigation, flood-moderation, and navigation components. The twin interests of Nepal, as mentioned earlier, will be in revenues from the sale of power and a navigational outlet to the sea. Bangladesh is also interested in some if not all these projects, partly for the augmentation of the lean season flows of the Ganga at Farakka, partly for the purchase of electric power, and partly for such flood moderation as may be achievable with some of these projects. Bangladesh is also planning a big barrage across the Ganges for the better utilisation of the waters that it receives under the 1996 Treaty.

Apart from 'projects', there has also been some talk of cooperation in the 'real-time' sharing of information on floods and in 'disaster-preparedness and management', but these ideas have not become effective and operational as yet.

In the past, water quality had not been a major theme in inter-governmental talks, but it is likely to become as important as, if not more important than, water-sharing as a subject for discussion and a source of friction in the future. Already the problem of arsenic contamination of groundwater is a particularly severe one in Bangladesh and serious enough in West Bengal in India. Arsenic, of course, is a naturally occurring contaminant and not an inter-country problem; if anything, it could lead to inter-country cooperation in identifying causes and solutions. However, the quality of flowing surface waters as they cross boundaries and the need for protocols on the subject could become major subjects for inter-country negotiations in the future.

3.7 Part VII

At the beginning of this chapter, some reservations on the thesis implicit in the title were hinted at. That indication has now to be elaborated. As planners and policy-formulators think of the future, they tend to present rosy pictures of regional cooperation or gloomy predictions of conflicts and water wars. Underlying those two divergent visions there are some commonalities: they are both based on huge projections of future demand derived from a certain view of 'development', and they both presume a similar supply-side response of large, technology-driven projects and the kind of Promethean, adversarial relationship to nature that these imply. We need not spend much time on the implausible water wars theory based on a highly misleading analogy with oil. Those who are interested might look up this writer's article 'Scarce Natural Resources and the Language of Security' in the Economic and Political Weekly issue of 16 May 1998. Turning to the more 'positive' picture, one still has reservations on many elements in it, and indeed on the entire approach.

The trouble starts with projections of future 'demand'. These are generally based (a) on current patterns of water-use with some adjustments for improvements in efficiency and resource-conservation, and (b) on prevailing notions of 'development'. If we assume ('realistically', as some may say) that no more than moderate improvements in efficiency and economy in water-use are likely to happen, and if we assume further (even more 'realistically') that there will be no change in our ideas of 'development' (i.e., the pursuit of higher and higher 'standards of living', with all countries aspiring to the condition of America), then there will indeed be a horrendous water scarcity necessitating massive supply-side projects. We must then also 'realistically' acknowledge that sustainable development is an impossibility, and that planet earth (and along with it humanity) is doomed. Instead of such apocalyptic forecasts, it will surely be *more realistic* to recognise that given the precious nature of this life-sustaining element and its finite supply on this planet, a tremendous effort needs to be made at efficiency, economy and conservation, so that the benefit derived from a unit of water is maximised. With that kind of reversal of approach, which implies changes in ways of living, the 'demand' projections will undergo drastic reductions. (The reference here is to water for irrigation, industry, etc., and not to water for drinking, cooking and washing, though even here there is much scope for economy in the case of the middle and rich classes.)

Further, we must shake ourselves free of the usual engineering conventions of defining 'available water resources' in terms of river-flows and 'usable water resources' in terms of what is stored behind a dam. What is available in nature is rainfall, not just flows in rivers; and while storing river waters behind a dam doubtless converts 'available' water into 'usable' water, so does *in situ* rainwater harvesting (i.e., 'catching the raindrop as it falls') and local watershed development. These are also part of the supply-side answers to the demand.

If we combine those two propositions, namely, if we learn to reduce our draft on this finite and precious resource, and if we learn to augment supplies locally through watershed development and water-harvesting in every locality and area where this is feasible, then we may find that the available water will go a long way indeed, and that a crisis can be averted with very little (if any) recourse to big WRD projects and huge investments. The predilection for large, technology-driven, supply-side projects, the tendency towards centralisation and the implicit belief that the state must be the principal actor in WRD, are inter-linked. It is that combination that we need to turn away from.

How is this approach to be reconciled with the generally accepted idea of 'basin planning'? There is no contradiction here, but this needs a bit of explanation. The term 'basin planning' derives from hydrology and is essentially an engineer's language. How did this idea originate? It arose from recognition of the limitations and dangers of isolated project planning. Engineers built a dam here, a barrage there, a run-of-the-river scheme in a third place, flood-control embankments in a fourth, and so on. By experience they learnt that this was not the best thing to do, and that in planning any such intervention in a river they needed to take into account the river as a whole. That logic cannot be faulted. Discrete project planning is certainly inferior to project planning within a larger framework. However, this is still a very limited vision for two reasons. The first is that while widening our vision from a point on the river to the river as a whole we are still thinking only of the river, and not of the ecological system of which it is a part – by which it is sustained and which it in turn sustains. A basin is primarily a hydrological concept, not an ecological one. In fact, even from a hydrological point of view, a river-basin approach suffers from the limitation that the boundaries of the basin may not coincide with those of groundwater aquifers. Secondly, we are thinking of the river in terms of 'planning'; and if we ask 'What are we planning?' the answer is clear: 'projects'. We want to 'harness' the water resources of a river for human use through the application of science and technology ('S&T'), and it is in that context that the idea of basin planning emerges: the engineer wants to build better and larger projects. This is essentially a centralising tendency. Thus, the idea of 'basin planning and management', which *prima facie* seems eminently sound, contains within itself the seeds of centralisation and gigantism. We need to be aware of and on our guard against such tendencies.

It is often argued that in our water resource planning we must take note of the immense possibilities offered by regional cooperation, particularly cooperation with Nepal and Bangladesh, on the utilisation of the water resources of the Ganga, Brahmaputra and Meghna. As mentioned earlier, this was the subject of a collaborative three-country study project undertaken by the Centre for Policy Research, New Delhi, the Bangladesh Unnayan Parishad, Dhaka, and the Institute for Integrated Development Studies, Kathmandu. Though the present writer was closely associated with that study throughout its nine-year period, he developed some doubts over the years. The basic thesis underlying the entire project was the following:

> The GBM region is a resource-rich area, but it is home to a large concentration of the world's most poor; the water resources of the immense rivers that flow through the region hold promise of an escape from this paradox; water is in fact the magic key to future prosperity in this region; and the countries of the region must learn quickly to cooperate to bring about that prosperity or remain forever locked in grinding poverty.

That is not a quotation but an encapsulation by this writer. Leaving aside some reservations that one has on that seemingly compelling statement, and wholly endorsing the plea for cooperation, one still needs to ask: in concrete terms, what does 'cooperation' mean here? It means essentially cooperation in 'harnessing' the water resources of the GBM system(s) by means of a number of major projects such as Karnali, Pancheswar and Sapt Kosi (on major tributaries of the Ganga) in Nepal; Manas and Sankosh in Bhutan and Dihang and Subansiri in India (on the Brahmaputra); Tipaimukh in India (on the Barak); the Ganges Barrage in Bangladesh; and so on. It is by now widely recognised that while providing certain benefits such projects also have serious adverse consequences not all of which can be foreseen or remedied. Further, even if these projects do create wealth, they will not eliminate poverty: the wealth and the poverty will be in different hands.

The alleviation of poverty, the ensuring of equity and social justice, the removal of the disabilities of women, children and disadvantaged groups and the 'empowerment' of the community, are hard tasks to be tackled with patience, imagination and determination *within* each of the countries of this region. A preoccupation with big, multi-country projects and the naive belief that they hold the magic key to prosperity will produce complacency and distract us from what needs to be done.

If water is the key to prosperity, how can one explain the distress that repeatedly strikes Kalahandi in Orissa State, which has water enough to produce rice? The waters of the Ganga, Brahmaputra and Meghna rivers are not a new discovery. They have been known to, and are being used by, the people living in the areas concerned for generations. The new element that is expected to transform the economies of the three countries is essentially hydroelectric power. However, this needs giant dams and reservoirs in a fragile and seismically active ecosystem. Considering the opposition to such projects, and the enormous investments that they call for, the question whether, and if so when, any or all of these projects will in fact come up is one that cannot be answered with any confidence. Meanwhile, the pursuit of such chimeras may lead to a loss of valuable time and a failure to pursue more modest but also more effective alternatives.

This is not to argue that there is no need for inter-country cooperation. Inter-country treaties or agreements over river systems that run along or straddle boundaries will of course be necessary. Conflicts may arise in the absence of such understandings, or even in relation to the interpretation of clauses or the actual operation of such agreements; and mechanisms will be needed to resolve such conflicts. The point that is being made here is merely that such cooperation should not be identified with a clutch of big projects or confined to the sphere of governments. There are many other possibilities and compulsions of cooperation. The protection of water sources (rivers, lakes, mountains, forests, aquifers) from pollution, degradation or denudation; the preservation and regeneration of deteriorating wetlands (e.g., the Sunderbans); improving and maintaining water quality; dealing with common problems such as drainage in the Indus basin in both India and Pakistan, or the occurrence of arsenic in aquifers in both India and Bangladesh; coping with floods and minimising damage; sharing experiences in local water-harvesting and watershed development and in the related social mobilization and transformation: these are among the areas in which inter-country cooperation will be very fruitful, and in some instances very necessary. Such cooperation can be at the level of governments, NGOs, academic institutions or 'think tanks', or 'people-to-people'.

If engineers and administrators tend to argue for supply-side projects, 'liberal' economists and officials of the multilateral financial institutions tend to argue for water markets. To them water is a commodity like any other, governed by the laws of supply and demand: if the state steps out of the sphere and leaves it to the private sector and to the operation of market forces, then supply will meet demand, prices will be right, economy and conservation will be ensured, and conflicts will be automatically resolved by the market. The slogan is: 'water is an economic and social good'. Water is indeed an 'economic good' when it is used for industry or agriculture, and perhaps a 'social good' when used for sanitation or in hospitals or for fire-fighting; but is even the term 'social good' an adequate description of water as a basic human and animal need (and as the sustainers of the environment of which it is a part)? Can water in that basic aspect, be reduced to a commodity like cement or steel or fertilisers or soap? Is it not more akin to the air? One is not ruling out water markets; they may have a role to play; but there are important issues of equity, social justice and sustainability that cannot be left to market forces. The glib answer to that will be that these can be taken care of through 'regulation', but regulation is far from easy.

The doctrinaire call for 'privatisation' includes allowing the corporate private sector to build and operate dams across rivers for hydroelectric power and/or for irrigation. Assuming that the private sector is interested in investing in such capital-intensive, long-gestation, modest-return projects, how are the environmental and social impacts (which have presented serious difficulties to the state in past projects) going to be handled by the private entrepreneur and manager? Supply may match demand but resource conservation may receive scant consideration; resettlement and rehabilitation aspects are likely to be given grudging attention only to the extent that resistance by those affected and public opinion compel such attention; and it is naïve to imagine that market forces will obviate conflicts or provide a magical route to their resolution. Whatever the position in relation to industry, water cannot be left to market forces. One is not arguing for a dominant role for the state, but the alternative is civil society, not the corporate sector.

Those reservations are not intended to deprecate the recommendations of inter-country or regional cooperation, or to question the recognition that the private sector has a role to play, or even to rule out all large projects. They merely constitute a plea to look at these matters with reference to a larger framework of a re-examination of our notions of 'development' and 'sustainability'.

If by 'sustainability' we mean the long-term maintenance of an ecological balance and thus the survival of planet earth and with it humanity; if we approach this in a positive spirit of fostering a harmonious relationship with nature rather than merely limiting the harm that we do; if we think of rivers as deities to be worshipped and not as horses to be harnessed and ridden; if we think of them not as separate entities but as integral parts of larger ecological systems; then our planning might take different forms. On the one hand we might look at a larger framework than a river basin, and on the other, we might focus on smaller land-and-water complexes such as micro-watersheds as well as the enormous possibilities of local rainwater-harvesting. We would also learn to think not merely of human need but also of the needs of other species and forms of life – birds, animals, aquatic life, vegetation, indeed the river itself. We could still plan 'projects' but with reference to a much wider and more complex framework; there could still be room and need for basin commissions or authorities but they will cooperate and live with the river, not 'manage' or 'harness' it.

As regards 'development', it seems appropriate to recall some words of Mahatma Gandhi. An epigrammatic remark of his that is often quoted runs as follows: 'The world has enough for everyone's need but not enough for anyone's greed'. By 'greed' he meant the desire for higher levels of consumption than needed, his definition of 'need' being quite austere. In reply to a speculative question of what would happen if India were to attain the standards of consumption reached in the West, he is said to have remarked: 'My God! We shall soon strip the earth bare, like locusts'. Those were prescient words and early adumbrations of the environmental movement that was to emerge much later. Conflicts, whether within or between countries, often arise from the 'greed' (in Gandhi's sense) that underlies the prevailing notions of 'development' and makes unsustainable demands on nature; we cannot learn to live in harmony with our neighbours until we have learnt to live in harmony with nature.

ANNEXE

Extract from 'Cooperation on the Eastern Himalayan Rivers'

The Ganga/Ganges

The Bhagirathi, the traditional source of the river, rises from the Gangotri glacier in the Himalaya, India at an elevation of about 7,010m. It is joined by the Alakananda at Deva Prayag and thereafter the river is known as the Ganga. From Hardwar to Allahabad, a distance of about 720km, it flows in a generally south/southeastern direction. Starting from the Uttarkashi district of Uttar Pradesh the river practically covers the whole of northern India between the Himalayas and the Vindhyas except Punjab and Jammu and Kashmir. The Ganga is joined by a number of tributaries on the right and left banks in Uttar Pradesh and Bihar. The Ram Ganga, the Gomati, the Ghagra, the Gandak, the Bagmati and the Kosi are the important Left bank tributaries, and the Yamuna and the Sone are the important Right Bank tributaries. The Ghagra (Karnali in Nepal), the Gandak and the Kosi, which flow from Nepal, contribute a significant part of the flows in the Ganga particularly in the dry season.

After its confluence with the Kosi, the Ganga continues its eastward flow in Bihar for another 40km and as it enters West Bengal it swings round the Rajmahal hill range. The Delta of the river can be said to start soon thereafter, below Farakka. From about 16km below Farakka, it forms the common boundary between India and Bangladesh for about 140km. Downstream of Farakka the river divides into two arms, one flows eastward into Bangladesh as the Padma (Ganges) and the other flows southwest and becomes the Hooghly. The river then flows eastwards inside Bangladesh and joins the Brahmaputra at Goalunda. Bhagitrathi/ Hooghly takes off in India about 40km below Farakka while the Gorai, the Arial Khan, the Kumar, the Mathabhanga are other important distributors in Bangladesh. The combined flow of the Ganges and the Brahmaputra continues under the name of Padma till it joins the Megna near Chandpur.

The drainage area of the Ganga/Ganges system is 1,080,000km^2 of which 861,000km^2 lie in India, 140,000km^2 in Nepal and 46,000km^2 in Bangladesh with the balance lying in Tibet. The length of the river from the source to the sea along the Bhagirathi-Hooghly route in India is about 2,525km. The average annual flow in the river as recorded at Farakka in India (1948-1973) is around 380 BCM and as recorded at Hardinge Bridge in Bangladesh around 383 BCM.

The cultural area in the Ganga/Ganges basin is estimated to be about 65.8 million ha, of which 60.2 million ha is in India. The basin is also densely populated particularly in the lower reaches, and it is estimated that the present population (1996) is about 427 million.

Chapter 4

A Tale of Two Treaties: The Ganga and Mahakali Agreements and the Watercourses Convention*

B.S. Chimni

4.1 Introduction

Water scarcity consciousness has today come to pervade the international community of States, particularly in the Third World, as either the present or projected quantity of water available to a large number of States falls short of expected needs.[1] The sharing of river water resources has therefore become a potential area of conflict. Yet, there are no enforceable international legal rules, which regulate the allocation and use of international waters. The principal reason being that States perceive rigid and detailed rules as inhibiting rather than encouraging international cooperation. On 21 May 1997, the United Nations General Assembly adopted a framework Convention on the Non-Navigable Uses

---

* This chapter forms an integral part of a report written for an Indo-Dutch Project on Alternative Development (IDPAD) on 'Development of a Legal Framework for Cooperation between India, Nepal and Bangladesh on the Management of the Water Resources of the River Ganga Basin'. I wish to thank Professor Surya P. Subedi for inviting me to be a Co-Director of the project and the IDPAD cell in the Indian Council for Social Science Research for all the support received.

[1] P. Wallensteen and A. Swain *Comprehensive Assessment of the Freshwater Resources of the World* (Stockholm Environment Institute Stockholm 1997) [2], [7]:

> 'Almost all the developing countries are in the arid and semi-arid, tropical and subtropical regions and many of them are facing severe water shortages. The volume of the rivers, which is the major source of the fresh water, is also unequally distributed among the countries within these regions … . In 88 developing countries, with nearly 40 per cent of the world's population, water shortages are already a serious constraint of development.'

See also A.K. Biswas 'Management of international rivers: Opportunities and constraints' [1]-[7] in A.K. Biswas and J.I. Uitto (eds.) *Sustainable Development of the Ganges-Brahmaputra-Meghna Basins* (United Nations University Press Tokyo 2001) [1]-[17]; and R.R. Iyer 'Water; Charting a Course for the Future' *Economic and Political Weekly*, 31 March–6 April 2000 [1115]-[1123].

of International Watercourses (hereafter the 'Watercourses Convention').[2] But even this framework agreement is yet to enter into force. Meanwhile, there are few rules that may be deemed to be part of customary international law. And even if certain core rules are characterised as such (for example, the principle of reasonable and equitable utilisation) it is of no great help for these are marked by a high degree of interpretive ambiguity. In short, within certain broad legal parameters, the problem of sharing and use of international waters is left to the riparian states to resolve through bilateral or multilateral agreements.

Among the hotspots of international water disputes is the Ganga basin in South Asia. River Ganga is nearly 2,525km in length. About 80 per cent of the Ganga Basin is in India, around 18 per cent in Bangladesh, and approximately 2 per cent is in Nepal and China.[3] The Ganga basin is one of the most densely populated basins in the world, with a total population of more than 300 million, of whom about 10 million are in Nepal, 40 million in Bangladesh and the rest in India. Within India the river is an inter-state river shared by the states of Uttar Pradesh (UP), Himachal Pradesh, Rajasthan, Haryana, Madhya Pradesh, Bihar, West Bengal, and the National Capital Territory of Delhi. Of the total of 2,525km 1450km lie in UP, 110km along the UP-Bihar border, 445km in Bihar and 520km in West Bengal. It is also among the most polluted rivers in the world.

The disputes between the riparian states Bangladesh, India and Nepal are a multifaceted one. There are complex scientific, technical, legal, constitutional, policy and political issues involved. The problem, which has received most attention where Bangladesh and India are concerned, is the sharing of Ganga waters in the dry season (albeit there are related issues concerning augmentation

---

[2] The Convention was adopted by 104 votes in favour, 3 against and 26 abstentions. India and Pakistan abstained while Burundi, China and Turkey voted against the adoption of the Convention. For the text of the Convention see *International Legal Materials* Vol. 36 (1997) [300].

[3] S.A. Salman 'Co-Management of Resources: The Case of the Ganges River' October 1998 at www.http//gurukul.ucc.american.edu/maksoud/water 98/present/.htm:

> 'Although it is known internationally by the name "the Ganges", it carries this name neither in India, nor in Bangladesh. In India it is called the Ganga, and in Bangladesh the Padma. The Ganges originates in the Indian state of Uttar Pradesh where it is known as the Bhagirathi, and is joined by a number of tributaries originating inside India such as the Yamuna, the Tons and the Gomti. It is also joined by other tributaries originating in Nepal such as the Kamala and Mahakali, and the Nepal China borders in Tibet such as the Kosi and the Gandak. After reaching Farakka in the Indian state of West Bengal, the river splits into two: one branch flowing eastward into Bangladesh, and the other southward into West Bengal. The latter which is known as the Bhagirathi is joined by the Jalangi River, and the combined river is known as the Hooghly River. Calcutta city, the capital of West Bengal and one of India's most important ports, is situated on the Hooghly River. South of Calcutta, the Hooghly River is joined by the Damodar River and flows into the Bay of Bengal. In Bangladesh, the Ganges, which is known as the Padma, is joined by both the Brahmaputra River, which is known in Bangladesh as the Jamuna River, and also by the Meghna River. The combination of the three rivers, which continues to be called the Padma, splits downstream into a number of channels, all flowing into the Bay of Bengal.'

and the changes introduced in the aquatic environment).[4] This is in keeping with the past trend of 'the narrow focus of most [freshwater] agreements'.[5] Where India and Nepal are concerned the issues extend to both developments of, and through, water resources. Nepal in particular places an excessive reliance on utilising water resources to achieve rapid economic development.[6] Bilateral agreements relating to the sharing of waters or water resource development have not been easy to arrive at given the general climate of suspicion and mutual distrust prevailing in the South Asia region. Each interpretation of the different elements of the dispute offered by one State is eagerly contested by the other. The lack of transparency where data and official papers are concerned has only added to the problems.

This Chapter seeks to, first, analyse the two agreements arrived at in 1996 between India and Nepal on the one hand, and India and Bangladesh on the other. It especially looks at some of the controversial issues, which have arisen in connection with the implementation of the two historic agreements. Second, in this background, it considers the evolving law of international watercourses. It looks in particular at the Watercourses Convention and contends that its provisions do not offer any ready-made formula to resolve the existing disputes between the three riparian States.

---

[4] S. Postel 'Changing the course of transboundary water management' *Natural Resources Forum* Vol. 21 no 2 (1997) [85]-[90]:

> 'The mighty Ganges in South Asia is one of the several major rivers that no longer reach the sea for all or part of the year. India's heavy diversions upstream during the dry season have left almost no water in the river for Bangladesh, much less to reach the river's natural outlet in the Bay of Bengal. The lack of fresh water flowing out to sea has caused the rapid advance of a saline front across the western portion of the river delta, which is damaging valuable mangroves and fish habitats, important resources for local inhabitants. Unless more water is allowed to flow into the delta during the dry season, damage to vegetation and fisheries will continue, spreading disruption to the local economy.'

[5] See J. Brunnee and S.J. Toope 'Environmental Security and freshwater Resources: Ecosystem Regime Building' *American Journal of International Law* Vol. 91 (1997) [26]-[59]. By way of criticism it is pointed out that 'an exclusively sectoral approach, particularly when combined with rigid allocation arrangements, cannot promote environmental security. New issues that an agreement does not address or even anticipate inevitably arise. Because a sectoral agreement's specific concern is embedded in and affected by a larger ecosystem, the agreement may not even prove successful in achieving its narrow goals. Moreover, its effectiveness may ultimately be reduced by the spill over of conflicts relating to issues not covered by the agreement.'

[6] See also G.D. Shreshtha 'Perspectives on Regional Cooperation' in B.B. Thapa and B.B. Pradhan (eds.) *Water Resource Development: Nepalese Perspectives* (Konarak Publishers Delhi 1995). [Almost any Nepalese writing you read on water resources states the same sentiment]:

> '… the only resource that Nepal can rely on to propel the country towards rapid economic development, is water. The Nepalese people, for decades, have pinned their hopes on the utilisation of this resource … this resource, more than anything else, holds the key to Nepal's progress.'

4.2 The Mahakali Treaty

4.2.1 An Overview of Treaty and Ratification Process

4.2.1.1 Objectives and principal features

In February 1996 a Treaty Between His Majesty's Government of Nepal and the Government of India 'Concerning the Integrated development of the Mahakali River including Sarada Barrage, Tanakpur Barrage and Pancheswar Project' (hereafter is known as the 'Mahakali Treaty') was signed. The Preamble to the treaty records that it is entered into 'on the basis of equal partnership to define their obligations and corresponding rights and duties thereto in regard to the waters of the Mahakali River and its utilisation'.[7] The Mahakali Treaty is to remain in force for a period of seventy-five years and is to be 'reviewed by both the Parties at ten years interval or earlier as required by either party and make amendments thereto, if necessary'.[8]

The principal features of the Mahakali Treaty are the following: First, it lays down the entitlement of Nepal to waters from the Sarada barrage (Article 1). Second, subject to 'the continued sovereignty and control of Nepal' (Article 2), it gives its consent to the use of 2.9 hectares of Nepalese territory for the construction of the eastern afflux bund of the Tanakpur Barrage. In return Nepal is entitled to (a) an agreed supply of 300 ft3/s of water in the dry season (i.e. from 16th October to 14th May); (b) 'a supply of 70 millions kilowatt – hour (unit) of energy on a continuous basis annually, free of cost …'; (c) the construction by India of a new electricity transmission line, and (d) additional water and electricity in the event that the flow of the Mahakali river is subsequently augmented by new works (Article 2(2) and 2(3)). Third, it provides the framework rules for the construction of the integrated Pancheswar Multipurpose Project on the 'boundary' Mahakali River. The total energy generated is to be shared equally and the cost of the project is to be borne in proportion to the benefits accruing to each party (Article 3). A portion of Nepal's share is to be sold to India on the basis of price that is to be agreed upon later. Fourth, it commits India to supplying irrigation water to Nepal

---

[7] S.A. Salman and K. Uprety 'Hydro-Politics in South Asia: A Comparative Analysis of the Mahakali and the Ganges Treaties' *Natural Resources Journal* Vol. 39 (1999) [295]-[343].

'The Mahakali River begins where two rivers, the Kali river beginning in the Taklakot area in the east, and the Kuthi-Yankti River originating in the Zanskar range of the Himalayas, meet at the Kawa Malla in the Drachula District in Nepal. The merging of the Kali and Kuthi-Yankti Rivers is known as the Mahakali River. … The Mahakali River serves as a western boundary for long distances between Nepal and India along the border of the Indian State of Uttar Pradesh. It is called the Sarada River in India, and after it is joined by the Ghaghra River in the State of Uttar Pradesh, it is called the Ghaghra River. The Ghaghra River continues to flow eastward, and joins the Ganges River immediately after crossing the State of Uttar Pradesh in the State of Bihar.'

[8] See Article 12(2) and (3) respectively. For the text of the agreement see *International Legal Materials* Vol. 36 (1997) [531].

(Article 4). Fifth, it lays down the basis of all future projects on the boundary Mahakali River: 'Any project, other than those mentioned herein, to be developed in the Mahakali River, where it is a boundary river, shall be designed and implemented by an agreement between the Parties on the principles established by this Treaty' (Article 6).

4.2.1.2 The Mahakali River Commission

The Treaty establishes a Mahakali River Commission, which is to be guided by 'the principles of equality, mutual benefit and no harm to either Party' (Article 9). It is to be composed of equal number of representatives from either side and is to have the following functions:

1. To seek information on and, if necessary, inspect all structures included in the Treaty and make recommendations to both the Parties to take steps which shall be necessary to implement the provisions of the Treaty;
2. To make recommendations to both the Parties for the conservation and utilisation of the Mahakali River as envisaged and provided in the Treaty;
3. To provide expert evaluation of projects and recommendations thereto;
4. To co-ordinate and monitor plans of actions arising out of the implementation of the Treaty; and
5. To examine any differences arising between the parties concerning the interpretation and application of the Treaty.

The Mahakali Commission is yet to be established. However, at least on paper it represents 'a breakthrough' for 'rarely are such projects [i.e. the Pancheswar Multipurpose Project] between countries financed, implemented, and operated jointly by a binational authority'.[9] One may also note that the function of the Commission includes making recommendations to both parties with regard to 'conservation' of the Mahakali River and that in this respect it is empowered to 'seek information'.

4.2.1.3 Dispute settlement: provision for arbitration

In the event the Commission fails to resolve any differences between the two parties within a period of three months, or either party disagrees with the recommendations made by the Commission, 'a dispute shall be deemed to have arisen which shall then be submitted to arbitration for decision' (Article 11). The arbitral tribunal is to be composed of three arbitrators: one nominated by Nepal, one by India and the third jointly. If the two sides are unable to agree upon the third arbitrator within 90 days either party may decide to request the Secretary-

---

[9] Salman and Uprety (n 7) [319].

General of the Permanent Court of Arbitration at the Hague to appoint the arbitrator who must not be a national of either country. The procedure of arbitration is left to be determined by the tribunal. Both the parties have agreed to accept the decision of the arbitral tribunal as 'final, definitive and binding'.

4.2.1.4 Ratification of the treaty and strictures of Nepali parliament: status in international law

The Mahakali Treaty was approved, as is required by Article 126 of the Constitution of Nepal, by a two-thirds majority of the joint upper and lower houses of the Parliament. However, the Parliament also passed a stricture on the Treaty ('*sankalpa prastav*'), which is said to be 'binding on the Nepal government'.[10] The four elements of the stricture, perceived as redefining water rights between the two parties, are:

1. Nepal's electricity to be bought by India will be sold as per the 'avoided cost principle';
2. When the Mahakali Commission is constituted, it will be done only upon agreement with the main opposition party in parliament as well as parties recognised as national parties;
3. 'Equal entitlement in the utilisation of the waters of the Mahakali River without prejudice to their respective existing consumptive uses of the Mahakali River' means equal rights to all the waters of the Mahakali; and
4. Saying that 'Mahakali is a boundary river on major stretches between the two countries' is the same as saying it is 'basically a border river'.[11]

But Nepal exchanged the instrument of ratification with India on June 4, 1997 without any formal reference to the *sankalpa prastav*. However, notwithstanding this absence of reference to the *sankalpa prastav* in the ratification process, Gyawali and Dixit consider it as amounting to 'conditional ratification'. Indeed, they go so far as to contend that 'a Treaty ratified with strictures is no ratification, especially since the Indian side has not accepted those strictures and the Nepali side cannot move away from those strictures'.[12]

On the other hand, in terms of international law the stricture would appear to have no consequences for it did not form any part of the official ratification process. In the circumstances it would be incorrect to designate the act of ratification as 'conditional ratification'. The stricture is, to put it differently, not a 'reservation' within the meaning assigned to it in international law. Article 2(d) of the Vienna Convention on the Law of Treaties, 1969 defines the term 'reservation' as follows:

---

[10] D. Gyawali and A. Dixit 'Mahakali Impasse and Indo-Nepal Water Conflict' *Economic and Political Weekly*, 27 February 1998 [553]-[564].
[11] ibid [559].
[12] ibid [559], [562].

'reservation' means a unilateral statement, however phrased or named, made by a State, when signing, ratifying, accepting, approving, or acceding to a treaty, whereby it purports to exclude or to modify the legal effect of certain provisions of the treaty in their application to that State.

No such statement accompanied the ratification of the treaty by Nepal. On the mode of making a reservation, Article 23 of the Vienna Convention clearly states (in the context of a multilateral treaty):

1. A reservation, an express acceptance of a reservation and an objection to a reservation must be formulated in writing and communicated to the contracting States and other States entitled to become parties to the treaty.
2. If formulated when signing the treaty subject to ratification, acceptance or approval, a reservation must be formally confirmed by the reserving State when expressing its consent to be bound by the treaty. In such a case the reservation shall be considered as having been made on the date of its confirmation.

Clearly the Nepalese Parliament did not instruct the executive to ratify subject to certain reservations. In any case, to claim that the strictures are 'reservations' in the context of a bilateral treaty is in reality a call for its renegotiation. In the words of Shaw:

> The problem [of reservations] does not really arise in the case of bilateral treaties, since a reservation by one party to a proposed term of the agreement would necessitate a renegotiation. An agreement between two parties cannot exist where one party refuses to accept some of the provisions of the treaty.[13]

However, while the stricture has no validity in international law, it does point to the unstable nature of the regime that has been established. In fact, it cannot be ruled out that a future government in Kathmandu may refuse altogether to cooperate with India on its implementation. At least the strong sentiments that Nepali scholar have expressed on the treaty, points in that direction. According to Gyawali and Dixit:

> Agreements through political pressure, diplomatic manoeuvring and legal point scoring from a strong and large neighbour may bring forth agreements in the short term but, as Mahakali has shown, nothing will move forward in the long term. Even if it did, the social and political costs may make the victory too expensive.[14]

---

[13] M.N. Shaw *International Law* (Cambridge University Press Cambridge 1997) [642].
[14] Gyawali and Dixit (n 10) [563].

But was there really political pressure? What do Gyawali and Dixit understand by 'diplomatic manoeuvring'? Are the problems relating to the implementation of the agreement (on which more presently) a case of legal point scoring or simply that Nepal seeks to evade voluntarily undertaken obligations? Be that as it may, Gyawali and Dixit concede that the possibility of India modifying the terms of the Treaty is difficult to envisage:

> Given the continuing preoccupation of the Indian water establishment with new constructions and a failure to conduct a credible review of past mistakes, there is little hope that South Asia's largest water bureaucracy can provide the required statesmanship. This job is made all the more difficult because of the colossal vested interests built into the political economy of embankment and canal construction industry in India.[15]

This understanding significantly points towards the links between international agreements with domestic water management policies, a problem that cannot be discussed within the scope of this chapter. Instead, I will turn to examining certain controversial aspects of the Mahakali Treaty.

4.2.2 Controversial Issues

According to Salman and Uprety, disputes relating to the Mahakali Treaty have arisen because the provisions contained in it, as in earlier treaties, lack specificity: 'This has left room for ambiguity and controversy in the interpretation and enforcement of the provisions…'[16] I would however like to pre-empt a detailed analysis of this theme to offer a brief excursus into the history of Indo-Nepal cooperation on water resource development. For, in my view, this history is the matrix in which differences have arisen and cast a shadow on the implementation of the Mahakali Treaty.

4.2.2.1 Conspectus on history of Indo-Nepal cooperation on water resources development

While the history of cooperation in water resource development between India and Nepal is traced back to 1920, the critical dates are 1954 and 1959 when the Kosi and the Gandak treaties respectively were signed between the two countries. Most Nepalese, according to Salman and Uprety, 'are convinced that they have not been equitably treated by the treaties'.[17] They believe that 'India is draining Nepal's watershed for its own benefit'.[18] Learned papers endorse this popular view: 'In the

---

[15] ibid.
[16] Salman and Uprety (n 7) [299]-[300].
[17] Salman and Uprety (n 7) [300].
[18] ibid.

case of Kosi and Gandak projects there is a general feeling that Nepal was deprived of her due share of benefits.'[19] In other words, what it received were only 'negligible' or 'marginal' benefits.[20] It is contended that while Nepal contributed land and material to the projects its agricultural needs were not met even as there was substantial submergence of scarce agricultural land, little benefit from flood protection, and the problem of displaced persons who had to be rehabilitated. It was further felt that Nepal was not sufficiently consulted in the course of the implementation of the two agreements.[21]

On the other hand, India has drawn attention to the fact that it planned, implemented and financed both the Kosi and Gandak projects, that it alone possessed the technology and skills to implement them and that Nepal received considerable benefits pertaining to irrigation, flood protection, hydropower and even infrastructure (the bridge across river Kosi). The Indian view is supported by the fact that Nepal's political leadership has itself stated from time to time that these projects have been made the target of criticism by vested interests.[22] Perhaps the truth lies somewhere in between. But meanwhile the environment of mistrust and suspicion of the charges created in relation to cooperation on water projects left its indelible mark. All subsequent projects were confronted with the same criticism. These included the Karnali and the Tankapur. Projects[23] leading to the inclusion of a provision in the Constitution of Nepal requiring approval of any future agreement by a two-thirds majority of members present in a joint session of its Parliament. In brief, the four and half decades of water cooperation has been marked in Nepal by a strong sense of being used by a powerful neighbour. The result is that what may be described as water grievance has acquired an existence of its own, and the expression of water resentment takes priority over finding solutions to differences, including those which have arisen over the terms of the Mahakali Treaty.

4.2.2.2 The equal sharing principle: meaning of 'consumptive use'

The first grievance relates to Article 3 of the Mahakali Treaty which *inter alia* states that 'both the parties agree that they have *equal entitlement* in the utilisation of the Mahakali River…'. The inclusion of the equal entitlement principle was seen by Nepal as a concession, which was extracted from India as it represents a *voluntary* departure from the equitable and reasonable utilisation principle

---

[19] See B.B. Thapa and B.B. Pradhan (eds.) *Water Resources Development: Nepalese Perspectives* (Konark Publishers Delhi 1995) [250].
[20] ibid [212]-[213].
[21] ibid [215].
[22] See generally B.C. Upreti *Politics of Himalayan River Waters* (Nirala Publications Jaipur 1993) [92]-[123].
[23] B.G. Verghese and R.R. Iyer (eds.) *Harnessing the Eastern Himalayan Rivers: Regional Cooperation in South Asia* (Konark Publishers New Delhi 1993) [203]-[208].

incorporated in the Watercourses Convention.[24] However, it is claimed by the Government of Nepal and Nepali scholars that this equal entitlement principle has been negated by the interpretation that India has given to the words 'without prejudice to their respective existing consumptive uses of the waters of the Mahakali River' which follow immediately afterwards.

Nepal has questioned the protection of 'existing consumptive use' on the grounds that 'this use had not been mentioned earlier; that the treaty covers the Mahakali river as a border river, and not the river after it crosses the border and becomes an Indian river; and that the farmers at the lower Sarada are really drawing upon the Karnali, and make only occasional use of the Sarada waters'.[25] According to Gyawali and Dixit, Article 3 has compromised Nepal's rights to 50 per cent share of the waters of the border river.[26] They claim that it is at a meeting of a joint group of experts in September 1997 that India first came up with proposals, which 'stunned' the Nepali technicians.

Their proposal was that the sharing of Mahakali waters should be done only after ensuring that the flow of water to the lower Sarada project situated about 160km downstream from the Sarada barrage at the Nepal-India border is assured as prior use. In fact, India made prior rights claims based on the size of its canals (built without Nepal's cooperation or permission), which amounts to more water than there is in the river itself. India thus used Article 3 of the Mahakali Treaty to its advantage as suspected by many when the Treaty was initialled.[27]

Salman and Uprety support the Nepali standpoint on Article 3 and wrote:

> The term 'existing consumptive use' is a key phrase … Its full and meaningful implementation requires that the countries first identify the 'existing consumptive use' of both India and Nepal. Only then can the phrase 'without prejudice to their respective existing consumptive uses' be objectively applied. Unfortunately, the Mahakali Treaty defines Nepal's existing consumptive use, but does not do so for India and therefore, leaves open an opportunity for India to unilaterally define the scope of its consumptive use.[28]

It is difficult to appreciate in terms of international law the objections of Nepal and those who support its standpoint. First, the phrase 'existing consumptive use' is nowhere defined in the treaty. It would therefore have to be given its ordinary meaning viz., that each party is entitled to continue to use the quantity of waters that were being availed immediately prior to the treaty being signed. This is strictly an empirical issue. Thus, whether a particular consumptive use was mentioned at the time of negotiations is not relevant.

---

[24] R.R. Iyer 'Conflict Resolution: Three River Treaties' *Economic and Political Weekly* 12 June 1999 [1509]-[1519].

[25] ibid [1511]-[1512].

[26] Gyawali and Dixit (n 10) [557].

[27] ibid [560].

[28] Salman and Uprety (n 7) [322].

The question is whether there was an 'existing consumptive use' at the time the treaty was ratified. Second, the protection of 'existing consumptive use' is along with the principle of equal entitlement a part of a package deal. It also explains why India agreed to Article 5 paragraph (1), which states that, the 'water requirements of Nepal shall be given prime consideration in the utilisation of the waters of the Mahakali River'. Consequently, individual elements cannot be redefined without unravelling the entire package. Third, Nepal as the upper riparian State has the option; vide Article 5(1), of drawing waters beyond its 'existing consumptive use', albeit subject to India's right to its 'existing consumptive use'. It is therefore not meaningful to say that Nepal's existing consumptive use has been permanently fixed by the treaty. Fourth, the Preamble to the Treaty clearly states that 'the Mahakali River is a boundary river on *major stretches* between the two countries'. It is therefore *not* a boundary river. In any case, there is no basis in international law of exercising ownership rights over flowing water but merely to participate in its equitable utilisation, and in this case, by the terms of the treaty, equal utilisation. Fifth, if the question raised relates to the justice of the agreement then it should be resolved at the level of diplomacy.

It is true that 'ordinarily, conflicts over consumptive uses are more difficult to resolve than conflicts over non-consumptive uses where all one need is to assure that all interested parties have access to the river ...'[29] But as Iyer has pointed out, in this instance the issue 'can easily be resolved' if answers can be found to the following questions:

> Is there an existing consumptive use of Mahakali waters in the Lower Sarada area? If so, what is the quantum? How old is the use? Is it regular or occasional? Is it a fact that the farmers depend essentially on the Karnali and draw upon the Sarada only infrequently, when for certain reasons they are unable to use Karnali waters, and if so, how important is that occasional use? (ii) What would be the consequences of not recognising this as 'existing use'? Is it merely a question of reckoning this against India's share of the benefits arising from the Pancheswar project, and thus requiring India to pay more (perhaps a few hundred crore) towards the capital cost of the project? Or is there a danger of an actual denial of Mahakali waters to the farmer in question... (iii) In the event of the farmers being denied Mahakali waters do they have any alternative source, or will they be subjected to distress?[30]

Therefore, Nepal should instead of assuming a rigid position on the question of 'existing consumptive use' collect appropriate data and facts and present it to India.

---

[29] T. Natt and R.C. Matson (eds.) *Water in the Middle East: Conflict or Cooperation?* (Westview Replica Edu Boulder 1989) [163].

[30] R.R. Iyer (n 24) [1512].

4.2.2.3 Financial gains

A second grievance relates to the prospective financial gains that are likely to accrue to Nepal. It is argued that it is unlikely that Nepal will reap financial gains from the operation of the treaty. According to Gyawali, the 'cost plus approach' of India, as opposed to 'avoided cost' approach, has meant that given 'the near anarchy of the adjacent power and irrigation markets in UP and Bihar ... Nepali hopes of any returns on investments is an extremely risky proposition'.[31] Likewise, Thapa points out that the financial benefits from the planned mega projects are unlikely to be large.[32]

First, unlike oil, water is not an internationally tradable commodity with an identifiable market price. Second, since India is to be the sole buyer it can resist higher prices. Third, electricity distribution in India is carried out by State Electricity Boards, which are insolvent due to the subsidised price of electricity and their inability to efficiently collect charges from their customers. And, 'if this distribution structure in India is to remain unchanged, the excess in the price of power paid to Nepal from the price the State Boards receives from its customers will in effect be a direct subsidy incurred by the Indian Central Government. The Indian government has lots of other competing interests in allocating such subsidy expenditure'.[33] In summary, according to Thapa:

> Far from being a panacea for Nepal's economic ills, projects such as the Karnali-Chisapani or Pancheswar high dams are ill-advised. At best, if everything comes out as planned (including cheap concessional credit), they will have a minimal impact on Nepal's development path.[34]

Now, it is true that the side letter to the Mahakali Treaty written by the Prime Minister of Nepal to his Indian counterpart states that in assessing the benefits from the Pancheswar Multipurpose Project, 'net power benefit shall be assessed on the basis of, *inter alia*, saving in costs to the beneficiaries as compared with relevant alternatives available'. In this respect the natural question arises as to what are these 'alternatives available'? Second, should the tariff be the same as the 'avoided cost'? Iyer responds to these questions in the following way:

> In regard to the first question, there are many possibilities (other hydro-electric projects, thermal projects, gas-based projects, etc) and thermal generation need not be assumed to be the only alternative available; and in regard to the second question, if in fact the generation cost at Pancheswar is

[31] D. Gyawali 'Water Beyond the State: Resolving Conflicts with Institutional Pluralism' paper read at the International Conference in South Asia: Resolution of Inter-State Conflicts held at Jawaharlal Nehru University, New Delhi, 29-30 March 1999 [3].

[32] P.J. Thapa 'Water-Led Development in Nepal: Myths, Limitations and Rational Calculations' *Water Nepal* Vol. 5 No. 1 (Jan-July 1997) [35]-[57].

[33] ibid [45].

[34] ibid [44].

> lower, the gain surely would have to be shared between the two countries: if the 'alternative cost' is to be fully paid by India to Nepal, what is India's gain, and what has it 'avoided'.[35]

Given the dispute between the two countries the Detailed Project Report (DPR) on the Pancheswar Multipurpose Project, which was to be finalised within a period of six months, has yet to see the light of the day. *Albeit*, there are indications that the DPR may be completed in the near future.

Meanwhile, on 17 February 1996, the Nepal-India Agreement 'Concerning the Electric Power Trade' (hereafter the 'Power Trade Agreement') was signed. According to Crow, the Power Trade Agreement transferred negotiations 'from the diplomatic to the economic sphere':[36]

> The principal parties in the exchange are no longer the diplomatic arms of the government, but various private, semi-government and non-governmental agencies. These parties, subject to the laws of both states, set the terms and conditions of the exchange. The raising of finance, organisation of construction and the day-to-day operation of any hydroelectric facilities agreed upon may be in the hands of a private corporation or government agency.[37]

Under the Power Trade Agreement:

> Any governmental, semi-governmental and private enterprise in Nepal or India can enter into an agreement for power trade between the two countries. Parties entering into such power trade arrangements may determine the terms and conditions, including the quantum and parameters of supply, points of delivery and the price of electricity.

It is in the aftermath of the Mahakali Treaty and the Power Agreement that transnational corporations started showing interest in the hydel projects in Nepal. Through adopting a framework agreement that governed all future hydel projects, it created the necessary conditions of political stability.[38] But was the advent of

---

[35] R.R. Iyer (n 24) [1512].

[36] B. Crow 'New Actors and New Space for Environmental Agreement' *Water Nepal* Vol. 6 No. 1 (1998) [25]-[41].

[37] ibid.

[38] S.A. Aiyar 'Multinational oil on troubled Indo-Nepalese Waters' *Times of India* (on file with author). Aiyar writes:

> 'Statkraft and ABB of Norway are building a 60MW project at Khimit. Panda International and Harza, two US companies, are setting up a 36MW project on the Upper Bhote Kosi. These are small projects for local Nepalese consumption ... but giant projects based on sales to India are on the anvil too. Snowy Mountain Engineering Corporation of Australia has been awarded a 750MW project on the West Seti river, which could cost over $6 billion. Nepal now plans competitive negotiations for hydel projects, and so Karnali and the 210 MW Arun-3 project have been opened up for bidding.'

TNCs unavoidable and will they bring much benefit to the peoples of the two countries are questions awaiting an answer.

4.2.3 Evaluation

Despite the interpretative disputes which have delayed the implementation of the Mahakali Treaty moderate critics concede that it represents a way forward:

> In spite of its shortcomings, the Mahakali Treaty has made attempts to reconcile the conflicting interests between the two countries as much as possible. When compared with the two previous agreements relating to the Mahakali River, that is the Sarada Treaty and the Tanakpur Agreement, the Mahakali Treaty has made significant noticeable progress both in terms of broadening the scope of water resource development as well as defining the rights and obligations of the two countries.[39]

It may also be said along with Salman and Uprety that 'each country may need to temper its nationalist ego' and approach the problem in the spirit of compromise.[40] If necessary the treaty provision for arbitration can be invoked to resolve a dispute. Its presence should assure Nepal that its interests will be protected.

4.3 The Ganga Treaty

The treaty between the Government of the Republic of India and the Government of the People's Republic of Bangladesh on Sharing of the Ganga/Ganges Waters at Farakka (hereafter the 'Ganga Treaty') was signed on 12th December 1996. Before turning to its key features and areas of controversy a synoptic review of the dispute is in order so as to stress the contexts in which the treaty should be evaluated.

4.3.1 Synoptic History of Dispute 1971-1996

The story of the dispute between India and Bangladesh on sharing the waters in river Ganga can be told in six phases:

---

[39] Salman and Uprety (n 7) [341].

[40] ibid [339]. On the notion of 'compromise' see *infra.*

Phase	Period	Issue Focus
Phase I	1951-1971	Discussion over the Farakka Bridge
Phase II	1971-1977	Division of Dry Season Flow (leading to Ganga Water Treaty)
Phase III	1977-1982	Augmentation of the Flow
Phase IV	1983-1987	Independent national river development
Phase V	1988-1996	Arriving at 1996 Ganga Water Sharing Treaty
Phase VI	1996-	Implementation of the Ganga Treaty

The first phase (1951-1971) of the dispute revolved around India's decision to construct the Farakka barrage about ten miles from India's border with Bangladesh (then an integral part of Pakistan). In order to resolve the differences, five meetings of water resource experts were held between June 1960 and May 1968 followed by Secretary level meetings between December 1968 and July 1970. But the talks between India and Pakistan got nowhere.[41] In 1971, Bangladesh became independent. In March 1972, the Indo-Bangladesh Treaty of Friendship and Co-operation and Peace was signed. India and Bangladesh agreed, among other things, to 'make joint studies and take joint action in the fields of flood control, river basin development, and the development of hydro-electric power and irrigation'. Pursuant to it a decision was taken to establish the Joint Rivers Commission (JRC) and in November 1972 its Statute was adopted. In the years 1975-1976 the relations between the countries soured and little progress was made over the dispute on sharing and augmentation of Ganga waters. The dispute had by then become an integral part of the domestic politics of Bangladesh, making it difficult to resolve; opposition parties inevitably positioned themselves to brand any future agreement as being pro-India and a sell-out.[42]

In 1976, Bangladesh unsuccessfully attempted to internationalise the dispute by taking it to the Special Political Committee (SPC) of the United Nations General Assembly. Lammers has pointed out that 'during the debate before the GA Special Political Committee, the differences of view between India and Bangladesh appeared [...] to be less than claimed by Bangladesh. India no longer denied the international character of the Ganges as it had previously done in respect of Pakistan. Nor did it claim a right to dispose of the Ganges waters at Farakka as it pleased'.[43] In other words, the debate in the SPC gave India the opportunity to clarify its position. It stated:

> India's views regarding the utilisation of waters of an international river were similar to those held by the majority of States. When a river crossed more than one country, each country was entitled to an equitable share of the waters

---

[41] Verghese and Iyer (n 23) [175].

[42] Iftekharuzzaman 'The Ganges Water Sharing issue: Diplomacy and Domestic Politics in Bangladesh' in B.D. Ghoshal (eds.) *Diplomacy and Domestic Politics in South Asia* (Konarak New Delhi 1996) [183]-[202].

[43] J.G. Lammers *Pollution of International Watercourses: A Search for Substantive Rules and Principles of Law* (Martinus Nijhoff Publishers The Hague 1984) [317].

> of that river. That share had to be determined by taking into account such factors as geography, the economic and social needs of the population and the availability of other resources. Each riparian State had the right to decide the priorities of use of the water to which it was entitled, although in using its share each State should take into account the manner in which the other riparian State used the water, so that there would be no clash between the use of water by all riparians. It was not, however, necessary that a particular use by a State should be subject to prior consent by the other riparian. In other words, the insistence on the continued natural flow of an international river, as asserted by Bangladesh, was inconsistent with the concept of equitable utilisation of the waters of a river.
>
> Those views did not conform to the Harmon doctrine of absolute sovereignty of a riparian State over the waters within its territory, as had been implied in the statement by the representative of Bangladesh. India, for its part, had always subscribed to the view that each riparian State was entitled to a reasonable and equitable share of the waters of an international river.[44]

The consensus resolution, which was eventually adopted in the SPC, contained nothing for Bangladesh.[45] According to Crow, 'as an attempt to mobilise support, or to obtain third-party intervention, Bangladesh's action at the United Nations was a mistake'.[46] The result was that Bangladesh was forced back into bilateral negotiations. But Bangladesh's position became weaker as 'the remedy of the last resort had been tried and found ineffective'.[47] Fortunately for it, there was a change of government in India in March 1977 with the Janata Party coming to power. 'Within weeks of the Janata government taking office, an understanding had been reached with Bangladesh on the sharing of the Ganges waters. Six months of detailed negotiations ensued before the understanding could be formalised in an agreement, but the Ganges Waters Agreement did emerge.'[48] It was signed on 5 November 1977. Both sides agreed to make certain concessions. The agreement resolved the issue of sharing dry season flows for a period of five years leaving alone the issue of how the flows could be augmented. But the issue was discussed 'intermittently' in the JRC during and after 1978.[49] The 1977 agreement expired in 1982 and was succeeded by a Memorandum of Understanding (MOU) in October of that year. The MOU was for a period of two years.

In the next phase there were discussions over the problem of augmentation with both India and Bangladesh presenting their distinct proposals. Crow has characterised the two sets of proposals thus: 'Bangladesh argued that water is best

---

44 ibid [317]-[318].
45 UN Doc A/BUR/31/SR.1.
46 Crow (n 36) [111].
47 ibid [113].
48 ibid [113]-[114].
49 Crow (n 36) [160].

transferred over time; India that it is best transferred over space'.[50] The Indian proposal consisted of a barrage across the river Brahmaputra and a canal to take water from that river to the Ganga at Farakka. Bangladesh, on the other hand, suggested that the monsoon season flow of the tributaries of Ganges be stored for use later in the year when it would most be needed. It implied that the water stored in reservoirs to be built in Nepal should be allocated for the needs of Bangladesh and of Calcutta Port.[51] What were the differences? According to Rangachari and Iyer:

> Bangladesh saw the Indian proposal as a mass transfer of water from the Brahmaputra without considering the needs of that basin which would consequently experience shortages. India considered this fallacious as the flows in the Brahmaputra are far larger than those in the Ganga considered in terms of availability per ha of cultivable land or per capita population. In its view the Indian proposal had taken into account the legitimate water needs of Brahmaputra sub-basin also. Bangladesh viewed the Ganga and the Brahmaputra as separate basins whereas India held that they were sub-basins of one vast inter-connected Ganga-Brahmaputra-Meghna system. What India held to be the optimal development of the water resources of a single large basin was considered by Bangladesh to be an inter-basin diversion inconsistent with the principles governing such transfers. Bangladesh also apprehended insurmountable problems in execution as also adverse effects from the Indian proposal, such as large-scale displacement, water logging and division of one country into two by a huge water barrier.[52]

From 1983 onwards, in a bid to try and resolve differences quickly, a 'new Bangladesh line' took shape, which separated the questions of augmentation and water sharing. Instead, it emphasised the need for a discussion of all common rivers between Bangladesh and India.[53] This line was reflected in the new MOU signed between India and Bangladesh on 22 November 1985, which was to run for a period of three years. So far as water sharing was concerned the MOU did not diverge sharply from the 1982 MOU. The new MOU however did talk of 'river water resources common to India and Bangladesh'. It also established a Joint Committee of Experts (JCE) to study the problem of augmentation and to identify mutually beneficial alternatives for the sharing of available river water resources common to both countries.[54] Between 1985-1988 in the meetings of the Joint

---

[50] ibid [163].
[51] ibid [176].
[52] Verghese and Iyer (n 23) [182].
[53] Crow (n 36) [188ff].
[54] Verghese and Iyer (n 23) [185]:
'The question may arise why a new Joint Committee of Experts (JCE) was considered necessary when there was already a Joint Rivers Commission (JRC) in existence. The JRC was not superseded; it continued in existence. However, there was a feeling in some quarters that the JRC was weighted down by the past history of positions taken, proposals put forward and disagreements expressed by the representatives of the two countries; that

Committee of Experts (JCE), and also at talks at the diplomatic levels, little progress was made. In November 1987 the life of JCE expired.[55] A new JCE was set up in August 1992 whose first meeting was held in New Delhi in November. It was however only when new governments came to power in both countries and Inder Kumar Gujral, with his insistence on non-reciprocity, became the Indian Foreign Minister that the possibilities of a new agreement on the sharing of waters emerged. The statesmanship shown by Jyoti Basu, the then chief minister of West Bengal, also played no mean part in arriving at a new arrangement. In December 1996 the Treaty between the Government of the Republic of India and the Government of the People's Republic of Bangladesh on Sharing of Ganga/Ganges Waters at Farakka (hereafter the 'Ganga Treaty') was signed.

4.3.2 The 1996 Treaty: Principal Features

4.3.2.1 Guiding principles

The preamble to the Ganga Treaty states as its objective the 'optimum utilisation of the water resources of their region' through 'finding a fair and just solution' but 'without affecting the rights and entitlements of either country other than those covered by this Treaty, or establishing any general principles of law or precedent'. Since the scope of the treaty is narrow, being confined to sharing of waters at Farakka, the basis for future agreements relating to the development of the Ganga basin, is left open. However, Article IX, which commits the respective governments to concluding water sharing agreements with regard to other common rivers, talks of being guided by 'the principles of equity, fairness and no harm to either party'. Whether this formula is shorthand for the principles of equitable utilisation and no harm is difficult to tell. The objective of sustainable development does not find a mention in the treaty or in the proposed basis for arriving at

---

the JRC had functioned not as a joint body but as a forum in which delegations from the two countries met formally across the table as two "sides" exactly as in inter-governmental negotiations; and that a new arrangement was needed under which the officials (administrators and engineers) could meet truly as a joint team and not as two sides confronting each other.'

[55] Crow (n 36) [205]:

'... India reiterated its rejection of the option of augmentation of the Ganges at Farakka through storage dams in Nepal, and insisted on the linkage between augmentation from the Brahmaputra and making an agreement for long-term sharing of the principal joint rivers. Bangladesh, for its part, argued that sharing was an immediate bilateral problem between Bangladesh and India, while augmentation was a long-term problem requiring regional co-operation. It also said that it would not consider augmentation of the Ganges from the Brahmaputra unless India guaranteed Bangladesh a share of the common rivers. In short, India would not consider sharing without augmentation from the Brahmaputra, and Bangladesh would not consider augmentation from the Brahmaputra without a guaranteed share of the principal joint rivers.'

agreements with regard to other common rivers. The treaty is to remain in force for a period of thirty years but can be renewed on the basis of mutual consent.

4.3.2.2 Water sharing formula

The Ganga Treaty establishes for a period of thirty years a new basis for the sharing of waters at the Farakka in the dry season, which runs from 1st January to 31st May. According to the formula included in the Treaty, if the Ganga flow at Farakka is 70,000ft^3/s or less, both countries will receive 50 per cent; with a flow of between 70,000ft^3/s and 75,000ft^3/s Bangladesh will receive 35,000ft^3/s and India the rest; and with a flow of more than 75,000ft^3/s India will receive 40,000ft^3/s and Bangladesh the balance (see Annexure I of the Ganga Treaty). In the event the flow at Farakka falls below 50,000ft^3/s in any ten day period the two governments are committed to enter into immediate consultations to 'make adjustments on an emergency basis, in accordance with the principles of equity, fair play and no harm to either party' (Article II(3)). Commenting on the water sharing formula Iyer writes:

> Ideally the sharing should have been based on the principle of 'equitable apportionment for beneficial uses' and carefully determined with a reference to the water needs for diverse purposes and the available options in either country; but such an approach, though sound in theory, would not have worked in practice, as there would have been no agreement either on needs or on options. Under the circumstances, the only sensible course would have been to settle for a 50:50 sharing.[56]

It is not however entirely clear as to what Iyer means by the alternative of 'equitable apportionment of beneficial uses'? Would it have led to India getting a larger share or would its deployment have been in Bangladesh's interest? A distinguishing feature of the Ganga River Treaty is 'the basis for calculating the flows of the Ganges reaching Farakka during the lean season'.[57]

Under the previous agreements, the average flow of the Ganges reaching Farakka was based on 75 per cent water availability, from observed data for the 25 year period between 1948 and 1973. Under the Treaty, the figures under the indicative schedule are based on the average total flow (and not 75 per cent availability) of the Ganges during the 40 year period between 1949 and 1988. As a result, the average total flow of the Ganges under the Treaty for each ten-day period exceeds the average flow under the previous agreements for the same period

---

[56] R.R. Iyer (n 24) [131].

[57] S.A. Salman 'Sharing the Ganges Waters between India and Bangladesh: An Analysis of the 1996 Treaty' in S.M.A. Salman and L.B. de Chazournes (eds.) *International Watercourses: Enhancing Cooperation and managing Conflict* (The World Bank Washington DC July 1998) [127]-[153].

by a margin of almost 10 per cent for each period, which means that the Treaty assumed a higher level of water availability than the previous agreements. Moreover the Treaty states '[e]very effort would be made by the upper riparian to protect flows of Farakka as in the 40 years average availability mentioned above'.[58]

Salman has compared the share of each country under the earlier agreements with the Ganga River Treaty and noted that 'the share of Bangladesh decreased from about 59 per cent under the 1977 Agreement and each of the 1985 and 1982 MOUs, to about 52 per cent under the Treaty. Correspondingly, India's share increased from about 41 per cent under the 1977 Agreement, and the 1982 and 1985 MOUs to about 48 per cent under the Treaty'.[59] But as he goes on to point out, 'although this is true, it should be noted that during most of each of the dry seasons of the eight years of vacuum between 1988 to 1996, prior to the signing of the Treaty, Bangladesh has received only 18,000 ft3/s a day'.[60] Thus, he concludes that 'Bangladesh is still far better off under the Treaty than before the Treaty'.[61]

4.3.2.3 Review clause

The treaty contains an important review clause (Article X) which provides that 'the sharing arrangements … shall be reviewed by the two governments at five years' interval or earlier, as required by either party and needed adjustments, based on principles of equity, fairness, and no harm to either party made thereto, if necessary'. This provision introduces an important element of flexibility to the Ganges treaty necessary for its effective implementation.

4.3.2.4 Dispute settlement

The treaty sets up a Joint Committee (JC), consisting of equal representatives of the two states, which is to be responsible for its implementation (Articles IV and VII). Any disputes or differences, which arise in relation to the implementation of the treaty, are to be resolved by the JC. However, if it fails to resolve the differences the matter is to be referred to the Indo-Bangladesh Joint Rivers Commission (JRC), and eventually to the two governments. Clearly, in contrast to the Mahakali Treaty, which provides for arbitration, the respective governments in this case are not in favour of compulsory and binding third party dispute settlement machinery. It may however be noted that none of the previous agreements also specified a third party compulsory and binding dispute settlement system.

---

[58] S.A. Salman (n 57).
[59] ibid [140].
[60] ibid [152].
[61] ibid.

4.3.2.5 General evaluation

According to Postel, the 1996 'agreement should greatly relieve the tensions that had persisted for so long over the Ganges water'.[62] But as she goes on to point out, 'what the treaty does not address, however, is the need for minimum flows to protect the Ganges delta'.[63] According to Salman, the Treaty is 'a major breakthrough' in attempts to resolve the long standing dispute on the sharing of waters of river Ganga.[64] He notes that this is the first time an agreement between the two countries has been called a 'treaty' and 'should be read to imply a stronger commitment on the part of the signatories'.[65] Another distinguishing feature of the treaty is the fact that it prescribes 'an actual formula for sharing the waters of the Ganges between the two countries, in addition to including an indicative schedule giving the implication of the sharing arrangements under the formula, whereas the previous agreements included a schedule for sharing the waters of the Ganges'.[66] However, Salman, like Postel, contends that:

> although the Treaty provides a fair and equitable framework for sharing the waters of the Ganges river between India and Bangladesh during the dry season, implementation of the sharing arrangements under the Treaty will depend to a large extent on the availability of sufficient water in the Ganges during such season to meet the share of each country under the Treaty, which, judging by the flow of the Ganges during the dry season in 1997, may not always be the case. Hence … an agreement on how to augment the flow of the Ganges during the dry season seems to be the most viable solution to the problem of the dry season flow.

Nonetheless, Salman concludes that 'the Treaty has created a conducive atmosphere for reaching an agreement on the issue of augmentation of the dry season flow of the Ganges, and for cooperation with regard to the other joint rivers between the two countries'.[67] Karim, on the other hand, offers a more positive valuation. He identifies the outstanding features of the Treaty from the point of view of Bangladesh.[68] First, in contrast to earlier treaties the Ganga River treaty is for a longer duration i.e., 30 years as against five years. Second, the water sharing arrangements are not contingent upon augmentation, as in the previous agreements. Third, Bangladesh cannot be (vide Article XI of the Treaty) deprived of a fair share of the waters even if the two countries were unable to arrive at an agreement at the

---

[62] Postel (n 4) [88].
[63] ibid.
[64] SA Salman (n 57) [127]
[65] ibid
[66] ibid [128].
[67] ibid [129]-[130].
[68] A.T. Karim 'The Bangladesh-India Treaty on Sharing of the Ganges Waters: Genesis and Significance' *BIISS Journal* Vol. 20 (1998) [216]-[235]. Karim was the Additional Foreign Secretary for South Asia when the Treaty was negotiated.

end of the review period.[69] Fourth, it gets a better deal under the 1996 Treaty than in the previous agreements so far as quantity of waters is concerned:

> Under the 1996 Treaty Bangladesh would have received 224,740ft^3/s of water (provided total quantity of water at Farakka was available as envisaged in the indicative schedule to the Treaty). Unfortunately, because of unprecedented drought and abnormally low precipitation, the actual quantum of water released to Bangladesh at Farakka during this period in 1997 was 207,582ft^3/s, but still more than for the corresponding period at any time under the 1977 Agreement or subsequent MOUs; under 1977 agreement Bangladesh received only 193,220ft^3/s of water.[70]

This understanding had earlier been articulated by the Prime Minister of Bangladesh at her Press Conference in Dhaka on 13 December 1996:

> According to the 1977 treaty Bangladesh received 193,220ft^3/s of water between 1 March and 10 May. The new treaty will now give Bangladesh 224,740ft^3/s. The 1977 Treaty provided us 27,600ft^3/s during the leanest period, that is, between 21 and 30 April. The 1996 treaty grants us 35,000ft^3/s in the same period.[71]

Needless to add, others in Bangladesh have questioned these conclusions. For example, Faisal, Nishat and Tanzeema argue that the Treaty 'essentially validated the status quo rather than providing Bangladesh its historic share'.[72]

According to Iyer, the Treaty is 'eminently fair to both sides'.[73] Defending the Treaty in India against the opposite charge that it gives Bangladesh water without receiving anything in return, he has aptly written: 'The question of *quid pro quo* would arise if India were doing a favour to Bangladesh: but is that the case? From the point of view of Bangladesh, the treaty merely rectifies the wrong done by the upper riparian earlier through the diversion of the natural flow of water away from

---

[69] Article XI states as follows:

'For the period of this Treaty, in the absence of mutual agreement on adjustments following reviews as mentioned in Article X, India shall release downstream of Farakka barrage, water at a rate not less than 90 percent of Bangladesh's share according to the formula referred to in Article II, until such time as mutually agreed flows are decided upon.'

[70] Karim (n 68) [233].

[71] S. Chakravarty 'Indo-Bangladesh Treaty on Sharing of Ganga Waters' *Mainstream*, 11 January 1997 [32].

[72] I.M. Faisal, A. Nishat and S. Tanzeema 'Managing Common Waters between India and Bangladesh' paper read at the *International Conference in South Asia: Resolution of Inter-State Conflicts* held at Jawaharlal Nehru University, New Delhi, 29-30 March 1999 [8].

[73] RR Iyer (n 99) [137].

the lower riparian'.[74] He also asks Indian critics to bear in mind the fact that the 50:50 formula has been arrived at after upstream uses in India.[75] It may be added that the treaty allows Bangladesh to embark on the long term planning and optimal use of its water resources. It is perhaps no accident that the Bangladesh Water Policy was adopted in 1997, that is, soon after the signing of the Ganges treaty.

4.3.3 Controversies

4.3.3.1 The problem of security of flows

One area of controversy of the Ganga Treaty is whether it ensures security of flows to Bangladesh as it does not include a guarantee clause (as in the 1977 agreement). This is not a correct charge for the Ganga Treaty does seek to offer security of flows through the following provisions: First, there is the guarantee of 35,000ft^3/s to either side in alternate 10 day segments in the period from 1 March to 10 May. Second, Article II(iii) provides that in the event that the flow at Farakka falls below 50,000ft^3/s the two countries will 'enter into immediate consultations to make adjustments on an emergency basis, in accordance with the principles of equity, fair play and no harm to either party'. In other words, the amount of water released will not be arbitrarily determined by India. Of course, it may be conceded that the emphasised words do not offer a ready formula, which could be used to resolve the problem. Nevertheless, they are strongly indicative of the just basis on which negotiations are to be carried out. Third, Article II(ii) provides that 'every effort would be made by the upper riparian to protect flows of water at Farakka...'. Fourth, Article XI states that if the reviews of the sharing arrangement provided for in Article X do not result in mutual agreement or adjustment, 'India shall release downstream of Farakka Barrage, water at a rate not less than 90% (90 per cent) of Bangladesh's share...'. Together, these clauses of the Ganga Treaty would appear to ensure the security of water flows to Bangladesh.

4.3.3.2 The 1997 lean season problem

The first signs of trouble for the Treaty came in February 1997. In the last ten days of the month Bangladesh stated that it had received only 24,559ft^3/s instead of

---

[74] ibid [136]. Even those who welcomed the Ganga River Treaty tended to believe that India had gone out of its way to help Bangladesh. Thus, for example, Chakravarty wrote that 'India has bent over backwards and tried its level best to positively respond to Bangladesh's demand for more water ...' S. Chakravarty (n 71) [32]. Likewise, Desai writes that 'by tilting the Treaty in Bangladesh's favour, the Government of India has shown its magnanimity and an effort to work towards strengthening South Asian regional cooperation' B. Desai 'Sharing of International Water Resources: The Ganga and Mahakali River Treaties' *Asia Pacific Journal of Environmental Law* Vol. 3 Issue 2 (1998) [172]-[177].

[75] ibid [134].

39,106ft^3/s stipulated in the Treaty. The situation worsened in late March. On 27 March the Ganga flow in Bangladesh recorded only 6,500ft^3/s, and by early May water availability at Farakka was only about 40,000ft^3/s, instead of the 67,351ft^3/s specified in the Treaty. Bangladesh therefore invoked Article II(iii) of the Ganga Treaty and called for immediate consultations with India, subsequent to which meetings were held in Dhaka and New Delhi. In the course of the meetings Bangladesh demanded that India should ensure that it received the 35,000ft^3/s guaranteed under Annexure I of the treaty. It may be recalled that Article II(iii) to Annexure I states that 'India and Bangladesh each shall receive guaranteed 35,000ft^3/s of water in alternate three 10 day periods during the period March 1 to May 10'. However, as would be evident this guarantee is firstly, applicable to both the Parties, and secondly, can only be implemented if 70,000ft^3/s of water is available. Absent which the share is to be 50 percent of the share of waters available. And when the flow falls below 50,000 the emergency clause in Article II(iii) comes into play.

Bangladesh also wanted to know the ways in which India was protecting the flow of water at Farakka.[76] India explained that the prevailing situation was to be attributed to the normal hydrological cycle that occurred every four to five years.[77] Fortunately for her, by mid-May unseasonal spring rains eased the crisis. In June an expert level meeting of the JRC was held in Dhaka. It led to the formation of a scientific committee to study the causes of the low flow of the Ganga during the critical period of the dry season.[78] In July the thirty-second meeting of the JRC was held at Dhaka. The Joint Communiqué which followed read:

> The two sides appreciated the need to remove the bottlenecks in implementation of the Ganga/Ganges Treaty with further negotiations. It was decided to undertake joint scientific studies in accordance with the terms of reference, which have been jointly finalised by the technical teams of the two countries.[79]

While nothing concrete emerged from these consultations, it was no small gain that the 'parties were engaged in discussions, under the umbrella of the Treaty, on how to handle the situation'.[80]

According to Swain the crisis confirmed that 'in concluding the agreement, India and Bangladesh sought a solution within the political sphere while technical risks remained poorly conceptualised ... The political nature of the 1996 agreement on Ganga water did not encompass the notion of year-to-year hydrological variations'.[81] This view is also shared by Gyawali who contends that 'given

---

[76] S.A. Salman (n 57) [145].
[77] ibid.
[78] ibid [146].
[79] Cited by Salman and Uprety (n 7) [329]-[330].
[80] Cited by Salman and Uprety (n 7) [329]-[330].
[81] A. Swain 'Reconciling Disputes and Treaties: Water Development and Management in Ganga Basin' *Water Nepal* Vol. 6 No. 1 (1998) [43]-[65].

increasing water use in the upstream reaches of Ganga, Bangladesh may have been wiser to consider in greater detail what happens in the 1996 Agreement when the flow falls below 50,000ft^3/s, as it probably will in most hydrologic years'.[82] According to Sharma, 'India seems determined not to acknowledge that developments upstream of Farakka, such as illegal lift irrigation schemes in Uttar Pradesh and Bihar, could be affecting low seasons flows substantially'. He goes on to add that 'Bangladesh appears determined to deny a reality that has prevailed now for over two decades, that Farakka or not, there is less water in the Ganga and so its plan on using water has to be modified'.[83]

But to begin with why ask Dixit and Mirza did, Bangladesh go along with the understanding that the quantum of dry season flow in Ganga, as accepted in the 1996 Treaty, would be greater by 12 percent than the figure in the 1977 Treaty? According to the JRC, the January, February and March discharges of the Ganga at Farakka were less by 8, 10, and 12 per cent respectively in the post-Farakka period (1975-1988) compared with the pre-Farakka period (1949-1973) flow.[84] The explanation offered for this reported reduced flow is:

> the increased diversion of water in upstream India for irrigation, urban and industrial use, and other purposes ... Most of the extraction of water upstream has taken place in Uttar Pradesh on the four main Ganga tributaries emerging from Nepal – the Mahakali, Ghagra (Karnali), Narayani and Kosi – which are diverted for irrigation largely in India, as they enter the plains. These irrigation schemes on or near the Nepal border all exceed the dry season flow of these rivers, which is estimated to contribute 71 per cent of the Ganga's natural lean season flow. It was quite logical, then to believe that the flow at Farakka has declined progressively over the years.[85]

It may be noted that according to newspaper reports Jyoti Basu, the Chief Minister of West Bengal, who played a crucial role in arriving at the Treaty, had observed that Bihar and Uttar Pradesh should seek permission of the Union Government before drawing water from the Ganges.[86] The Bihar government, on the other hand, has expressed the apprehension that its water rights are being curtailed in order to meet international obligations.[87] That this apprehension is not entirely misplaced is confirmed by Dixit and Mirza when they argue that if India is to meet its obligations under Article II(ii) it would call for 'severe institutional changes within India's federal structure to redefine the role of the Centre vis-à-vis

[82] D. Gyawali 'Patna, Delhi and Environmental Activism: Institutional Forces Behind Water Conflict in Bihar' *Water Nepal* Vol. 6 No. 1 (1998) [67]-[115].
[83] K. Sharma 'The Farakka fallout' *The Hindu* 29 April 1997 [12].
[84] A. Dixit and M.Q. Mirza 'Who's Afraid of Farakka's Accord?' *HIMAL South Asia* January/February [61].
[85] A. Dixit and M.Q. Mirza (n 84).
[86] *Times of India* 14 December 1996.
[87] D. Gyawali (n 82) [74].

state governments when it comes to water management'.[88] Therefore, it is pointed out, in order to appease Bihar, India signed on 9 January, 1997 an agreement with Nepal to initiate a joint Detail Project Report study for the Kosi dam. It was seen as 'an important strategic step taken by Delhi before entering into discussions mollifying Patna'.[89]

Implicit in the 'increased diversion' argument is the belief that UP and Bihar have no rights over Ganga waters.[90] This is an erroneous belief for they have legitimate rights in this regard. The vital human and socio-economic needs of their growing population cannot be disregarded, even as India cannot claim an absolute right to extract or divert quantities of water. What is called for are water conservation measures in both Bangladesh and India so that water needs of UP and Bihar as well as Bangladesh can be met:

> Considering the wasteful use of water in this subcontinent, particularly in irrigation, there is enormous scope – indeed an inescapable need – for better water management. If economy in water use and conservation of this scarce resource are given the importance they deserve, both India and Bangladesh can do with much less water. Neither Bihar nor Uttar Pradesh need have any apprehensions …[91]

Second, there is the need to restore traditional water harvesting methods in UP and Bihar, on the one hand, and in the affected districts of Bangladesh on the other to meet growing water needs. Three other points may be made here. First, it is good to remember that while India is an upper riparian vis-à-vis Bangladesh it is a lower riparian vis-à-vis Nepal. Thus it cannot afford to assume positions associated with one situation or another. Second, India has agreed to make 'every effort … to protect the flows of water at Farakka as in the 40 years average availability'. Third, the fact that there is no formula for a situation when the flow falls below 50,000ft^3/s is mainly because Bangladesh did not want it for its own domestic political reasons; it might have been used to misrepresent the contents of the treaty as being against the interests of the Bangladeshi people.

4.3.3.3 Post 1997 sharing

As it turned out, the 1997 lean season problem was an aberration: 'the 1998 dry season was the opposite of the 1997 season. Abundant rain in the upper reaches of the Ganges caused the water level, as measured at the Hardinge Bridge in Bangladesh, to reach unprecedented measurement, reaching in some ten-day

---

[88] A. Dixit and M.Q. Mirza (n 84) [62].
[89] ibid [75].
[90] See generally S.M. Hussain 'International Law and the Ganga Water Problem' *Law and International Affairs* Vol. 9 No. 2 (1986) [78]-[102].
[91] R.R. Iyer (n 24) [1515]. For a discussion of the issue of water conservation see *infra*.

periods as high as three times what was anticipated under the Treaty'.[92] In April 1999 the Indo-Bangladesh Joint Rivers Commission held its thirty-third meeting in New Delhi. The Joint Communiqué which was issued noted that:

> The sharing of the Ganga/Ganges flows during this dry season is continuing smoothly and the flows are above the historical averages. Regarding the discrepancies of flows of 1997, the Commission noted that the Joint Scientific Study Team (JSST), set up earlier, is continuing with necessary studies and is expected to be completed by 2000.[93]

There have been few problems in 1999 and 2000 as well.[94] This shows that not only the 1997 lean season problem was a temporary one. Furthermore, as Iyer has noted, some of the problems between the parties arose because of the lack of communication. Indeed, he writes that 'the greatest enemy of the treaty (and of India's own fair image) was the classification of information, i.e., the treatment of all information regarding flows and releases as secret'.[95] According to him, the shortage in the first 10 day period of April share of Bangladesh 'arose out of a concern for safety, and a prompt attempt was made to compensate for the shortfall'.[96] The threat of safety was to the feeder canal in India whose sides could collapse in the face of sudden drop in the water level. But the fear was not promptly communicated to Bangladesh.

4.3.3.4 The problem of augmentation

According to Salman, the 'real issue' is the problem of augmentation:[97]

> The dynamics of the flow of the Ganges during the dry season of 1997 has confirmed that an agreement on the augmentation of the Ganges, rather than the sharing arrangements, is the central theme to any attempt towards resolving the conflict over sharing the waters of the Ganges'.[98] In the past, as Iyer has pointed out, 'the sharp divergence between India and Bangladesh on modalities of augmentation led to an impasse on the water-sharing dispute. What the two countries needed to do was to put aside the augmentation controversy and try to reach a long-term agreement on the

---

92 S.A. Salman (n 3).
93 The text of the Joint Communiqué is reproduced in *Bhagirath* Vol. XXXXVI No. 2 (April-June 1999) [93].
94 R.R. Iyer 'Water and Security in South Asia' June 2000 (Unpublished paper on file with author).
95 R.R. Iyer (n 24) [1515].
96 ibid.
97 ibid [153].
98 R.R. Iyer (n 24). Emphasis added.

sharing of the lean-season flows on the Ganga'.[99]

But should the issue of augmentation be addressed now? Iyer writes and we quote:

> Nothing will be gained by this: we shall merely be re-enacting the disagreements of the past. Besides, we have allowed ourselves to be hypnotised by the term 'augmentation'. Assuming the questionable proposition about the inadequacy of waters in the Ganga is correct, does it follows that water should be brought from some other river and put into the Ganga for being taken out again for use? What is needed is a comprehensive study of the availability of water in all forms in that part of the sub-continent- including rivers, surface water, bodies rainfall, water needs of diverse kinds, taking into account every possibility of economy and efficient use; and on the basis of such a study, the preparation of an integrated, holistic plan for water management in this region.[100]

Unfortunately, the record of past negotiations on the issue of augmentation show that such a holistic plan for managing the waters of the region is not on the agenda of either country. The negotiations went through two distinct phases: the first phase lasted from 1977-1982 and the second phase from 1983-1987. Analysing the negotiations in the first phase Crow points to the fact that both India and Bangladesh eschewed the language of equity and rights.[101] Of the Indian proposals he writes:

> The Indian scheme was justified not as the most equitable way of sharing and developing the resources of the region, but as the only feasible method ... India might have argued that it would be more just to share the resources of the subcontinent equally between the people living in the subcontinent.[102]

On the other hand, the Bangladeshi proposal to bring in Nepal had as its objective not the resolution of the problems of the region on the basis of principles of rational water resources management but only to strengthen its bargaining position vis-à-vis India. As Crow puts it, albeit in a slightly different context, that 'the politics informing the Bangladesh Proposal was the national interest defined primarily in terms of a single goal of maximising the availability of dry season

---

[99] R.R. Iyer 'Dispute and Resolution: The Ganga Waters Treaty' [127].

[100] ibid [135]-[136]. Emphasis added. In his forthcoming book, Iyer goes further and proposes that the augmentation issue, along with development projects related to it, could be addressed 'through involving all co-riparians countries in a shared and mutually beneficial format'. R.R. Iyer 'Possibilities of Augmenting the Lean Season Flows of the Ganges' [14] (On file with the author).

[101] B. Crow (n 36) [175], [182].

[102] ibid [175], [176]. Emphasis in original.

water'.[103] To put it differently, the sub-regional level solution suggested by Bangladesh had less to do with optimal and sustainable development of the Ganges basin and more to do with correcting the power equations in the negotiations.

In the second phase, Bangladesh moved away from the augmentation proposal because it, among other things, called for trilateral negotiations, which it thought, would delay matters, and in any case, gains from any agreement would take a long time to realise given the anticipated increase in Indian irrigation consumption. Bangladesh therefore talked about permanent sharing of all common rivers[104]. Thus, the 'maintenance of national sovereignty and competition for control of a resource were, and remain, two of the more important political obstacles to the utilisation of the waters of the Ganges …'.[105] A second reason for moving away from the augmentation issue was that 'as time passed and irrigation projects came on stream [in India], the dry season flow of the Ganges was falling and, in consequence, Bangladesh's plausible claim (under the alternative legal principles of historic rights and current usage) on that flow was also diminishing'.[106] In brief, the augmentation proposal was not temporarily shelved because the idea of sustainable development had taken hold, demanding a greater focus on water conservation measures. *Albeit*, it would perhaps represent a most rational response to the water problems of the region.

We now turn to consider if the evolving international law of watercourses offers definitive solutions to the problems arising from the utilisation of international water resources.

4.4 The ILC Watercourses Convention 1997 and the Mahakali and Ganga Treaties

4.4.1 The Relevance of the Watercourses Convention

The key task in this regard is to identify the existing rules of international law applicable to the utilisation of the waters of international rivers and to see if these offer more just solutions to the disputes between Bangladesh, India and Nepal? To put it differently, both the Mahakali and Ganga treaties may be studied from the perspective of evolving international watercourses law, including trying to understand why the three States avoid the language and concerns of the Watercourses Convention whose text had been more or less settled by the time the two agreements were signed even though it was formally adopted only in 1997? Was this done to ensure that the two treaties did not possess any precedential value? But what if the Watercourses Convention were to have been the basis of the two treaties? Would it have seriously affected the rights or shares of any one of the

[103] B. Crow (n 36) [183].
[104] ibid [188ff].
[105] ibid [162].
[106] ibid [190].

participating States?

The latter questions are, in our view, unhelpful for several reasons: first, for whatever reasons, the parties consciously chose to diverge from the principles and norms codified in the Watercourses Convention. Second, India and Nepal have not ratified the Watercourses Convention. Third, the Watercourses Convention is characterised by a pervasive normative ambiguity, which makes it difficult to predict with any degree of certainty the outcome of any international negotiations over the sharing and use of international waters. Fourth, even the core rules of the Watercourses Convention cannot be considered part of customary international law and therefore binding on non-signatory member States. In the rest of the section the last two conclusions are sustained through a more detailed analysis of the Watercourses Convention.

4.4.2 Adoption of Watercourses Convention

Till 'as recently as the 1950s, there was no customary international law on the non-navigational uses of international water resources'.[107] Indeed, even today, 'for the most part the legal regime of rivers, creating rights for other riparians and non-riparian states and limiting the exercise of territorial jurisdiction for individual riparians, depends on treaty'.[108] In 1966, the International Law Association (ILA) did adopt the influential *Helsinki Rules on the Uses of the Waters of International Rivers*, and has been pointed out:

> [t]he Helsinki Rules are not an international convention. Nor are they a treaty, since they do not represent particular states' agreement among themselves to the principles expressed. The Helsinki Rules are not customary law. Insufficient state practice exists to show the Rules' widespread acceptance, and no evidence indicates that states feel bound to follow these Rules.[109]

---

[107] C.B. Bourne 'The Primacy of the Principle of Equitable Utilisation in the Watercourses Convention, 1997' [1] (on file with the author). See also I. Brownlie *Principles of Public International Law* (4edn ELBS Oxford 1990) [272].

[108] I. Brownlie *Principles of Public International Law* (4edn ELBS Oxford 1990) [272]. Till the 1950s the only major book on the subject was F.J. Berber *Rivers in International Law*; L. Caflisch 'The Law of International Waterways and its Sources' in RStJ Macdonald ed. *Essays in Honour of Wang Tieya* (Martinus Nijhoff Dordrecht 1994) [115]-[129].

[109] L.M. Jacobs 'Sharing the Gifts of the Nile: Establishment of a legal regime for Nile Waters Management' *Temple International and Comparative Law Quarterly* Vol. 7 (1993) [101]. However, according to the same observer, 'as teaching of publicists, the Helsinki Rules are a source of international law for shared watercourses'. See also J. Waterbury 'Transboundary Water and the Challenge of International Cooperation in the Middle East' in P. Rogers and P. Lydon (eds.) *Water in the Arab World: Perspectives and Prognosis* (Division of Applied Sciences, Harvard University, 1994) [39]-[65].

It may be worth pointing out that India's Nagendra Singh had even then submitted a lengthy paper rejecting the notion of equitable utilisation on the grounds that 'the ideas regarding the concept of equitable sharing are not clear' and that 'states must be free to develop their uses in accordance with their needs'.[110] But, on the other hand, according to Bourne, 'the Helsinki Rules have [...] been applied by tribunals in India in adjudicating interstate water disputes',[111] a matter discussed later i.e., whether the experience of federal India has any lessons for resolving disputes between Bangladesh, India and Nepal.

On 21 May 1997, the United Nations General Assembly adopted the Convention on the Non-Navigable Uses of International Watercourses.[112] It was negotiated in the Sixth (Legal) Committee of the General Assembly, convening for this purpose as a 'Working Group of the Whole', on the basis of draft articles adopted by the International Law Commission (ILC). The Convention remained open for signature until 20 May 2000. It is yet to enter into force; it will enter into force after 35 states deposit their instruments of ratification.

4.4.3 The Right to Adjust its Provisions

The Watercourses Convention has been aptly described as 'the first global treaty that specifically focuses on regulating the uses of international watercourses'.[113] Of great importance to the analysis of the Mahakali and Ganga agreements is its Article 3 entitled 'watercourse agreements'. Its clauses (1) and (3) state as follows:

1. In the absence of an agreement to the contrary, nothing in the present Convention shall affect the rights and obligations of a watercourse State arising from agreements in force for it on the date on which it became a party to the present Convention.
2. ...
3. Watercourse States may enter into one or more agreements, hereinafter referred to as 'watercourse agreements', which apply and adjust the provisions of the present Convention to the characteristics and uses of a particular international watercourse or part thereof (Emphasis added).

So far as watercourse agreements arrived at prior to becoming a party to the Convention are concerned the text of Article 3 paragraph (1) is unequivocal and categorical: the rights and obligations under such agreements remain unaffected.

---

[110] Cited in C.B. Bourne 'The International Law Association's Contribution to International Water Resources Law' *Natural Resources Journal* Vol. 36 No. 2 Spring 1996 [155]-[216].
[111] ibid [215].
[112] The Convention, as already noted, was adopted by 104 votes in favour, 3 against and 26 abstentions. India and Pakistan abstained while Burundi, China and Turkey voted against the adoption of the Convention.
[113] E. Hey 'The Watercourses Convention: To What Extent Does it provide a Basis for Regulating Uses of international Watercourses?' *RECEIL* Vol. 7 Issue 3 (1998) [291]-[300].

Even where future bilateral or multilateral agreements regulating to the sharing and use of international watercourses are concerned, it is clear from the text of Article 3 paragraph (3) that States have a considerable degree of freedom; the need to depart from the provisions of the Convention is anticipated and legitimised. Future watercourse agreements are allowed to adjust the terms of the Convention. In other words, even after they have become parties to the Watercourses Convention, Bangladesh, India and Nepal can modify the provisions of the Convention in any future agreements. It may be argued that the word 'apply', which precedes the word 'adjust', suggests to the contrary, but that is an untenable interpretation. Caflisch explains:

> While the verb 'apply' taken in isolation, would seem to mean that the content of future agreements has to be in line with the provisions of the Convention, the second verb 'adjust', suggests that the States concerned may also depart from those provisions. That this is so is corroborated by the words 'may enter': Whoever may conclude an agreement which applies provisions of the Convention may also do the opposite, that is, enter into an agreement which departs from those provisions ... In other words, the conventional freedom of States is fully maintained.[114]

Therefore, it is merely a hypothetical question whether any of the three States would have benefited greatly if it had relied on the Watercourses Convention. In any case, as shall be seen presently, the Convention *does not contain any formula to resolve disputes or provide any definitive answers to them.* Indeed, it is characterised by a deliberate normative ambiguity, leaving space for the disputing parties to arrive at an agreement through political compromise.

4.4.4 Deliberate Indeterminacy: the Equitable and Reasonable Utilisation Principle

Part II of the Convention (Articles 5-10) entitled 'General Principles' contains its most important provisions. Article 5 lays down the equitable and reasonable utilisation principle – the heart of the Convention. It states:

1. Watercourse States shall in their respective territories utilise an international watercourse in an equitable and reasonable manner. In particular, an international watercourse shall be used and developed by watercourse States with a view to attaining optimal and sustainable utilisation thereof and benefits therefrom, taking into account the interests of the watercourse States concerned, consistent with adequate protection of the watercourse.
2. Watercourse States shall participate in the use, development and protection of

---

[114] L. Caflisch 'Regulation of the Uses of International Watercourses' in S.A. Salman and L.B. de Chazournes (eds.) *International Watercourses: Enhancing Cooperation and Managing Conflict* (The World Bank, Washington D.C. July 1998) [3]-[17].

an international watercourse in an equitable and reasonable manner. Such participation includes both the right to utilise the watercourse and the duty to cooperate in the protection and development thereof, as provided in the present Convention.

The principle received the imprimatur of the International Court of Justice (ICJ) in the case concerning the Gabcikovo-Nagymros Project (1997). The ICJ described it as a 'basic right' of a riparian State (paragraph 78). Among other things, the principle would appear to prohibit 'unilaterally assuming control of a shared resource' (paragraph 85). The Court's view confirms 'that a regime of equitable utilisation of an international watercourse' system, together with the protection and preservation of its ecosystems, cannot be achieved *solely* through action by each riparian state in isolation; cooperation is necessary'.[115] In this context, reference may also be made to Article 8 which imposes on watercourse States a 'general obligation to cooperate' in order to attain optimal utilisation and adequate protection of an international watercourse, and it encourages the establishment of joint mechanisms and commissions.

Two points however need to be made with respect to the equitable and reasonable utilisation principle. First, it 'does not mean that each state will take an equal share of the river basin waters. Rather, it means that each state's needs are to be considered on an equal basis against the needs of other states sharing the river'.[116] On the other hand, of course, there is nothing in the Watercourses Convention to prevent States from arriving at an equal sharing formula. Second, Article 5 does not 'provide an infallible matrix for problem solving'.[117] In fact the principle of equitable and reasonable utilisation is 'highly indeterminate'.[118] In Article 6 are listed 'factors relevant to equitable and reasonable utilisation'. It provides a non-exclusive list and states that 'the weight to be given to each factor is to be determined by its importance in comparison with that of other relevant factors. In determining what is a reasonable and equitable use, all relevant factors are to be considered together and conclusion reached on the basis of the whole'. Therefore, Fuentes rightly concludes, 'the relevance of the relative weight of the different factors in the process of the establishment of an equitable regime for the utilisation of international water resources is a question that remains open'.[119] In fact, Fuentes goes on to identify certain guidelines that States and international

---

[115] S.C. McCaffrey and M. Sinjela 'The 1997 United Nations Convention on International Watercourses' *American Journal of International Law* Vol. 92 (1998) [97]-[107]. Emphasis added.

[116] L.M. Jacobs (n 109) [99].

[117] ibid.

[118] A. Nollkaemper 'The Construction of the International Law Commission to International Water Law: Does it Reverse the Flight from Substance?' *Netherlands Yearbook of International Law* Vol. XXVII (1996) [39]-[73].

[119] X Fuentes 'The Criteria for the Equitable Utilisation of International Rivers' *British Yearbook of International Law* (1996) [337]-[412].

tribunals should follow when applying the rule of equitable utilisation.[120] Nollkaemper endorses the Fuentes view. He notes that apart from the fact that the ILC lists at least 17 factors that need to be taken into account, 'these factors are not prioritised ... The weight of the factors depends upon the circumstances. Even the direction in which they have to be weighed is unclear ... The principle of equitable use justifies opposing claims from both States without offering a resolution'.[121] The Nollkaemper-Fuentes conclusion underlines the fact that the Watercourses Convention does not offer some ready-made formula, which can be applied to resolve disputes between riparian States. This may have been a deliberative move. According to Benvenisti, the fact that that the law contains a vague standard for water apportionment, rather than prescribe a clear rule, helps riparians seeks a negotiated settlement:

> A vague standard would leave room for negotiations, during which each side could develop its own interpretations of the standard, whereas clearer rules would prevent many riparians – clear winners or clear losers – from entering the negotiating room. Negotiations under the flexible standard would not only include lawyers and politicians concerned about the internal political ramifications of 'concessions' to neighbouring states; they would also include scientists from various disciplines who could suggest alternative ways of reaching optimal solutions, and whose contributions could defuse the potentially adversarial dimension of the negotiations. With the shared language of technical expertise, political constraints may be sidestepped and well-founded decisions more easily reached.[122]

Jacobs supports this understanding and states: 'because each river system is different, no one set of rules for international river systems can apply universally'.[123] In sum, the mere application of the principle of equitable and reasonable utilisation will not mean a different water regime between Bangladesh, India, and Nepal.

4.4.5 Relationship with Principle of Significant Harm: Call for Cooperation

Article 7 embodies the 'obligation not to cause significant harm'. It however contains only a best-efforts standard and places on States 'an obligation of conduct rather than an obligation of result'.[124] An important issue here is the relationship of the principle of equitable and reasonable utilisation with the principle of significant

---

[120] ibid [340].
[121] A. Nollkaemper (n 118) [44].
[122] E. Benvenisti 'Collective Action in the Utilisation of Shared Freshwater: The Challenges of International Water Resources Law' *American Journal of International Law* Vol. 90 (1996) [384]-[415]; contra A. Nollkaemper (n 118) [46].
[123] L.M. Jacobs (n 109) [100].
[124] L.M. Jacobs (n 109) [100].

harm. 'The conflict between the two principles', according to Wouters, is readily apparent. 'While the former rule might permit significant harm as a result of an equitable use of the watercourse, the latter would not'.[125] McCaffrey and Sinjela contend that the language of Article 7 attempts to 'strike a balance between the equitable utilisation and 'no-harm' rules', albeit it is conceded that it is 'reasonable to conclude that the no-harm rule would not automatically override that of equitable utilisation if they should come into conflict'.[126] Whereas, according to Bourne, 'significant harm is subordinate to equitable utilisation' in the Watercourses Convention.[127] In his view, the Convention 'does not embody the notion that a project that is admittedly equitable and reasonable, cannot be implemented if it will cause significant harm to other watercourse states; nor does it support the notion that a utilisation that causes significant harm is *ipso facto* inequitable and unreasonable'.[128] Benvenisti agrees with this view and compliments the ILC for assigning a subordinate position to the principle of significant harm:

> the ILC should be commended for the finally adopted formula, which gives priority to the equitable utilisation standard over the no appreciable harm rule and makes explicit the duty of a state that wishes to change the status quo to initiate negotiations on the legality of its acts under the equitable standard, as well as the necessary adjustments to its use and, where appropriate compensate. By refraining from assigning property rights to existing allocations, this formula emphasises the necessity of negotiation, and thus increases the likelihood of equitable, optimal and environmentally sound outcomes.[129]

---

[125] P.K. Wouters 'An Assessment of Recent Developments in International Watercourse Law through the Prism of the Substantive Rules Governing Use Allocation' *Natural Resources Journal* Vol. 36 (Spring 1996) [417]-[439].

[126] S.C. McCaffrey and M. Sinjela (n 115) [101]. Elsewhere McCaffrey has been more forthcoming in asserting that the principle of equitable utilisation prevails over the no-harm rule:

> 'In my view … paragraph 2 of Article 7 of the Convention gives precedence to equitable utilisation over the no-harm doctrine. The very existence of a second paragraph implicitly acknowledging that harm may be caused without engaging the harming state's responsibility supports this conclusion. Also indicating a recognition that significant harm may have to be tolerated by a watercourse state are the numerous mitigating clauses in paragraph 2, especially the phrase "having due regard for the provisions of articles 5 and 6"-the two equitable utilisation articles. Finally, the proposition that the "no-harm" rule does not enjoy inherent pre-eminence is supported by Article 10 of the Convention, which provides that any conflict between uses of an international watercourse is to be resolved "with reference to article 5 to 7 …". S. McCaffrey 'The UN Convention on the Law of the Non-Navigational Uses of International Watercourses: Prospects and Pitfalls' in S.M.A. Salman and L.B. de Chazournes (n 114) [17]-[29].

[127] C.B. Bourne (n 107) [19].

[128] ibid.

[129] E. Benvenisti (n 122) [404].

But perhaps McCaffrey and Sinjela are right in suggesting that 'in reality, it can probably be concluded, in the words of the *Lake Lanoux* tribunal, that 'international practice prefers to resort to less extreme solutions'. The fact and circumstances of each case, rather than any *a priori* rule, will ultimately be the key determinants of rights and obligations of the parties. Difficult cases, which are bound to proliferate in the future, will be solved by cooperation and compromise, not rigid insistence on the rules of law'.[130] This conclusion squarely applies to the water disputes between Bangladesh, India and Nepal.

4.4.6 Priority of Uses: Need for Balancing of Interests

Article 10 deals with the 'relationship between different uses'. In paragraph 1 it states that 'in the absence of agreement or custom to the contrary, no use of an international watercourse enjoys inherent priority over other uses'. However, in paragraph 2 it calls for 'special regard being given to the requirements of vital human needs'. What are these vital human needs is not indicated in the Convention, again leaving room for divergent interpretations. Furthermore, 'special regard' is to be given only in the matrix of the equitable and reasonable utilisation principle for as paragraph 2 itself clarifies, 'in the event of a conflict between uses of an international watercourse, it shall be resolved with reference to articles 5 to 7 ...'. Thus, the notion of balancing of interests comes into play and consequently offers no ready-made formula to resolve disputes between States.

4.4.7 Protection and Preservation of Ecosystems

Article 20 concerns itself with the protection and preservation of ecosystems. It states: 'Watercourses States shall, individually and, where appropriate, jointly, protect and preserve the ecosystems of international watercourses'. No definition of 'ecosystem' is offered. Thus, for example, does it include land areas adjacent to the stream? Second, 'the obligation is so generally formulated that it is difficult to know what is it actually that States would be obliged to do. The Commission [i.e., ILC] has provided few indications as to what is meant by the protection of the ecosystem of a river'.[131]

Article 21 places certain obligations in relation to 'prevention, reduction and control of pollution'. It states in paragraph 2:

> Watercourse States shall, individually, or where appropriate, jointly prevent, reduce and control the pollution of an international watercourse that may

---

[130] S.C. McCaffrey and M. Sinjela (n 115) [101]. See also S.C. McCaffrey 'An Assessment of the Work of the International Law Commission' *Natural Resources Journal* Vol. 36 (Spring 1996) [297]-[318].

[131] A. Nollkaemper (n 118) [64].

> cause significant harm to other watercourse Sates or to their environment, including harm to human health or safety, to the use of waters for any beneficial purpose or to the living resource of the watercourse. Watercourse Sates shall take steps to harmonize their policies in this connection.

It is not however clear whether even significant harm 'to human health or safety' is necessarily proscribed by the principle of equitable and reasonable utilisation. According to Nollkaemper, 'this provision too does not discard reliance on balancing of interests'.[132]

4.4.8 Evaluation

In brief, the Watercourses Convention is a 'weak convention' and therefore doubts have been expressed as to whether it can help the resolution of disputes over the uses of rivers.[133] According to Hey:

> despite the language in its preamble and the primacy of the principle of equitable utilisation over the principle of no significant harm, the Convention fails to provide the means and ways to attain sustainable water use. It does not require that states protect basic human needs, nor that they develop integrated water policies, nor indeed does it provide minimum standards that watercourse states are to further develop through cooperation among themselves.[134]

Hey also makes the significant point that because of the peculiar framework approach that the ILC adopted, 'the Convention does not offer a relatively weaker watercourse state significant protection',[135] in contrast to the Helsinki Convention, it 'does not provide minimum standards that are to be further developed by the Parties to it'.[136] At the same time, the ILC refused to acknowledge that international watercourses are 'shared property'.[137] A number of ILC members opposed the idea because they were concerned with its implications for state sovereignty and the possibility of undue restrictions on the right to use of riparian states.[138]

In any case, India abstained in the General Assembly on the vote adopting the Watercourses Convention. It noted four objections, all of which are significant

---

132 ibid [66].
133 ibid [297]-[298].
134 ibid [291].
135 ibid [293].
136 ibid.
137 E. Benvenisti (n 122) [399].
138 ibid.

from the point of view of the Mahakali and Ganga treaties.[139] First, India pointed out that Article 3 ('watercourse agreements') 'failed to adequately reflect the principle of freedom, autonomy and the right of States to conclude international agreements on the international courses without being fettered by the present Framework Convention'. Second, that Article 5 ('equitable and reasonable utilisation and participation') had 'not been drafted in a clear and unambiguous terms stating the right of the State to utilise an international watercourse for non-navigational purposes in an equitable and reasonable manner ... Article 5 in the present form is vague and difficult to implement'.[140] Third, India objected to the text of Article 32 ('non-discrimination'). It noted that Article 32 'presupposes political and economic integration among States of the region. As all watercourse regions are not so integrated, this provision will be difficult to implement in certain regions. Hence, it did not merit ... inclusion in the Convention'. Fourth, it had strong objection to Article 33 ('settlement of disputes'):

> Article 33 dealing with settlement of disputes contained in it an element of compulsion in so far as it envisages the creation of a fact-finding commission. In our view, any procedure for peaceful settlement of disputes should leave the parties to the dispute to choose freely and by mutual consent a procedure acceptable to them. My delegation is opposed to the imposition of any mandatory third party dispute settlement procedure on a State without its consent. In any case, such a provision on the fact-finding commission is inappropriate for inclusion in a Framework Convention such as this. Accordingly, in view of the particular importance India attaches to the peaceful settlement of disputes and free choice of means, my delegation voted against this provision when it was put to vote in the Working Group of the Sixth Committee. Had this Article 33 been put to vote now in the General Assembly, my delegation would again have voted against it.

These objections make it clear that India seeks to retain maximum flexibility in resolving water disputes with its neighbours, and in particular, eschew the litigation path. It is not necessarily to be faulted for this. Benvenisti has rightly argued that the Watercourses Convention sends 'politicians and lawyers the wrong signal: that litigation as a means of securing optimal and equitable uses of water resources is preferable to negotiations leading to joint management institutions'.[141] He gives the three reasons for preferring negotiations over litigation as a means to

[139] Statement made by India's Permanent Representative to the United Nations, New York (on file with the author).
[140] It further stated: 'Moreover, the Convention has superimposed the concept of sustainable utilisation on the principle of optimal utilisation without defining what is sustainable utilisation in the present context. International environmental regimes contain certain essential elements such as transfer of technology, resources and technical expertise to promote capacity building amongst developing countries. None of these elements is elaborated in the present Convention.'
[141] E. Benvenisti (n 122) [414].

resolve water-related disputes. First, the history of their resolution shows that negotiations have been more successful than litigation. Second, negotiations allow parties to exchange information and explore their divergent perceptions of the problem. Third, it promotes long-term cooperation through opening up formal and informal channels of communication. This analysis appears to justify India's stand.

Assuming that India will not ratify the Watercourses Convention do however the standards contained in it nevertheless constrain its behaviour? According to Bourne, in the face of the voting record:

> It would seem to be impossible to argue successfully that the provisions of the Convention are accepted as customary law by international community. For states not party to the Convention, therefore, its provisions will at best serve only as guidelines, assisting in determining in a particular case whether utilisation of the waters of an international watercourse is reasonable and equitable under the customary international principle of equitable utilisation.
>
> In short, then, the attempt in the ILC and the United Nations General Assembly to advance international water law beyond the flexible principle of equitable utilisation has failed'[142] (Emphasis added).

Bourne has also pointed to the 'looseness' of the language of the Convention: 'many of the crucial words in these documents lack precise meaning. Take, for example, the words "ecosystems", "environment", "optimal", "sustainable development", "protection of the watercourse", "preservation", "appropriate measures", and so forth. Words like these can mean different things to different people'.[143] More significantly, 'the intended meaning of some of the important articles can be gleaned only from the commentaries, for example, it is from the commentary on Article 21 that it is learned that the obligations under Articles 20 and 21 are ones of due diligence. Such an important qualification should have been made explicit in the body of the articles'.[144]

Caflisch also concludes that 'the law of international waterways remains a somewhat impressionistic set of rules despite the improvements made by groups such as the Institute of International Law, the ILA and the ILC'.[145] However, according to Caflisch at least two of the key principles have become part of customary international law viz., the principle of equitable utilisation and the principle of no harm.[146] This has the support of McCaffrey who would add to the list the need to notify potentially affected riparian states of planned measures on an international watercourse.[147] It may be noted that the ILC has referred in particular

---

[142] C.B. Bourne (n 107) [20].
[143] ibid [15].
[144] ibid [17].
[145] L. Caflisch (n 108) [128].
[146] ibid [124], [129].
[147] S.C. McCaffrey (n 126) [27].

to the principle of equitable utilisation as a 'well-established rule'. The commentary on Article 5.1 states that:

> A survey of all available evidence of the general practice of States, accepted as law, in respect to the non-navigational uses of international watercourses-including treaty provisions, positions taken by States in specific disputes, decisions of international courts and tribunals, statements of law prepared by intergovernmental and non-governmental bodies, the views of learned commentators and decisions of municipal courts in cognate cases reveals that there is overwhelming support for the doctrine of equitable utilisation as a general rule of law for the determination of rights and obligations of States in the field.[148]

But even if it were to be deemed a part of customary international law it does not offer, to reiterate, any ready formula to resolve disputes between riparian States. But in the first place it is difficult to firmly state that the equitable utilisation and no harm rules are part of customary international law. First, the Convention itself allows States to depart from the provisions of the Convention. Second, the content of the rules is drafted in the soft law mould; the criteria embodied merely offer guidelines for State behaviour. Third, the relationship between the equitable utilisation and no harm rules is not clearly defined. Fourth, the meaning of the terms used in the respective rules is not laid down in the Convention.

In brief, the Watercourses Convention is not of a kind which allows predictions about the possible outcome of negotiations between disputing States. It would therefore be a futile exercise to attempt to see if the application of its rules, even if were deemed binding, would have lead to a different result in the case of the Mahakali and Ganga agreements. As Postel has pointed out, 'while useful as general guidelines, these principles [i.e., adopted by ILC] are subject to widely differing interpretations, and are thus minimally helpful in practice'.[149] The problem is compounded by insufficient knowledge about the hydrological behaviour of river basins. In the words of Turan and Kut, 'given the rudimentary state of international law on transboundary watercourses and the absence of long standing international practice based a scientific understanding of the hydrological behaviour of river basins, including the relationship between groundwater and rivers, no solid ground exists for legal settlement'.[150] In this light it is perhaps more relevant to consider the internal obstacles to the goal of sustainable development of the Ganga basin. But that is another story for another time.

---

[148] See Report of the International Law Commission to the General Assembly on the Work of its Forty-Sixth Session, Doc. A/499/10 (1994) [195ff].

[149] S. Postel (n 4) [87].

[150] I. Turan and G. Kut 'Political-ideological constraints on intra-basin cooperation on transboundary waters' *Natural Resources Journal* Vol. 21 No. 2 (1997) [139]-[147]. Later they again note that 'the lack of an international legal order concerning the non-navigational uses of international waterways' [144].

4.5 Conclusion

1. Both the Mahakali and Ganga treaties, despite some problems that have arisen, represent a step forward in the water relationship between India, Bangladesh and Nepal.

2. All parties should avoid rhetoric, which creates too high expectations from the operation of the treaties. There is clearly the need for political parties to exercise restraint and not misrepresent the contents of the treaties.

3. The ILC Watercourses Convention does not offer a formula to resolve the problems of the three States. Indeed, the indeterminacy, which characterises the principal provisions of the Convention, suggests that it is not legal principles but a pragmatic approach that is best suited to resolving the problems of riparian States.

4. Sustainable development of the Ganga River calls for undertaking serious conservation measures by all three States. The constant emphasis on supply side solutions has called forth solutions that introduce disputes that are avoidable. The problem of augmentation between Bangladesh and India is a dispute that can be resolved through rational and efficient use of water resources. This calls for detailed studies of the steps taken by each to pursue the goal of sustainable development.

5. Water should be declared a human right by all three states in order to promote water rights consciousness and sustainable development.

6. Dialogue should be initiated between the three States to resolve problems that arise from time to time. The dialogue should be informed by a notion of compromise that allows common interests rather than individual national interests alone to be pursued. A diversity of actors (civil society representatives, private actor) can help the dialogic process.

Chapter 5

The Bangladesh-India Treaty on Sharing of the Ganges Water: Potentials and Challenges

Anjan Datta

5.1 Water – A Driver of Development

Availability of water and its quality are the key determinants in sustenance of life and livelihoods of people. Maintenance of biological diversity or wetland conservation is also integrally linked with water. In a situation where the supply of this crucial resource *water* is outside the control of a national government, planning and management of water for national development remains critically dependent on international agreements and protocols. Bangladesh is a clear example in this regard. Bangladesh being a lower riparian country is not in a position to design an effective water management strategy conducive for overall development without the cooperation of its neighbours. The importance of regional or international co-operation, in the case of Bangladesh lies in the fact that out of its 230 rivers, 57 are transboundary rivers (54 coming from India and 3 from Myanmar). These rivers drain a total catchment area of 1.72 million km^2, of which only 7 per cent lies within the country, and the remaining 93 per cent is beyond its territory. Therefore, regional and transboundary issues (including the management of the Himalayas – which is the prime source of fresh water for the region and therefore termed as the 'Water Towers of Asia') have serious implications for the water resources planning in Bangladesh (see Figure 5.1 for regional hydrological setting of Bangladesh). In this Chapter, I shall focus the analysis on the sharing of the Ganges water, the water that, as will be demonstrated in the sections below, has profound influences on the Bangladesh economy and society. I shall elucidate the opportunities and uncertainties of the 1996 Treaty, which the Government of Bangladesh and India signed. However, to elaborate on the prospects and problems of the Treaty, I shall provide a brief outline of the historical context, which led to the signing of the 1996 Treaty.

5.2 Sharing of the Ganges Water: A Historical Genesis

The rationale and significance of signing a water treaty with India goes back to the history of Farakka Barrage. It was in 1961 that the Indian government announced its decision to build the Barrage, and in September 1963 the site at Farakka was chosen. The construction of the 7,363 feet long barrage, designed for a maximum discharge of 765m^3/s (27,000ft^3/s) and a head regulator for diversion capacity of 1,133m^3/s (40,000ft^3/s) of flow started in the following year (1964). The Pakistan government objected to the Indian plan and used bi-lateral and other international diplomatic channels to stop this programme. But these diplomatic efforts (between 1961 and 1970) did not bring desired results. In the meantime India constructed the barrage, and Bangladesh emerged as an independent country in 1971.

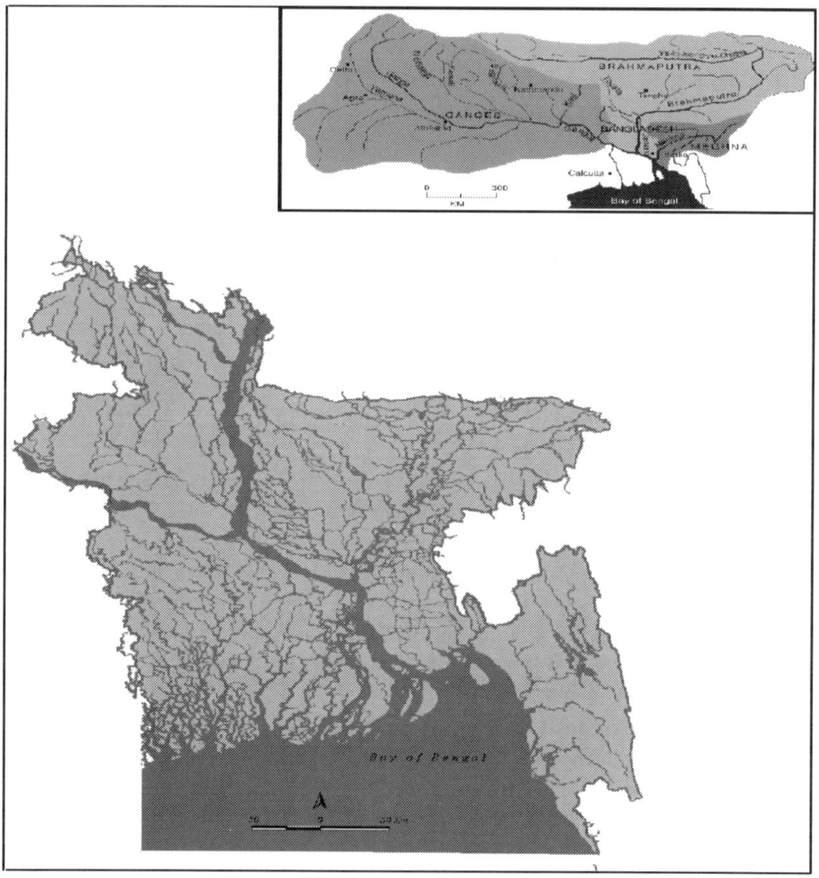

Figure 5.1: Regional hydrological setting and river systems of Bangladesh

With the independence of Bangladesh, both the governments of Bangladesh and India expressed their desires for working together in addressing the issue of water, which presents many common problems to both countries. In 1972 the Joint River Commission (JRC) was set up. The statute of the JRC among others was to harness the benefits from common river systems to both countries for the benefit of the people and to study flood control and irrigation projects so that the water resources of the region can be utilised on an equitable basis. The Farakka dispute was not specifically mentioned in the JRC's terms of reference. However, in the light of the article that 'the Commission shall also perform such other functions as the two governments may, by mutual agreement, direct to do' and the statute cited above gave the government freedom to refer the issue of Farakka to the JRC (cf. Crow et al. 1997: 99). Subsequently in May 1974, the Prime Ministers of Bangladesh and India in a joint declaration recognised that there might not be enough water to meet the needs of both countries. Therefore, as 'the fair weather flows of the Ganges in the lean months would have to be augmented to meet the requirements of the two countries' (Crow et al. 1997: 101, Adhikari et al. 2000:10), they came to a temporary agreement on the subject. Thus, with the consent of Bangladesh, a test operation of the Farakka Barrage came into place only in April 1975.

However, after the expiry of the temporary agreement (which lasted 40 days and expired at the end of May 1975), India unilaterally withdrew water until a Ganges water sharing agreement for five years was signed in November 1977. The water sharing agreement was renewed twice after the expiry of the 1977 agreement with some modification under the 'Memorandum of Understanding' (MOU) in October 1982 and November 1985, which expired in November 1987. Between 1988 and 1996, no water sharing agreement existed between the countries. India continued to divert the Ganges water unilaterally. As a consequence, the flow of water through the Ganges into Bangladesh started to fall particularly during the dry season and it reached an all time low flow (mean daily discharge of 150m^3/s at Hardinge bridge) in April 1995 (EGIS 2000: 29). The impact of this low dry season flow had many facets. One of the main consequences of this low flow was expansion of the saline frontier. Study conducted by EGIS (2000: 52-3) shows that in southwest Bangladesh, the salinity front moved some 280 km upstream of the sea-coast (see Figure 5.2), and the salinity level in the surface water increased from the pre-Farakka level of 500 micro-mhos to 29,000 micro-mhos at Khulna in April 1995, which exceeded the safe limit by some means. This high level of salinity, among others, is considered one of the important reasons for large-scale top dying of the Sundari trees in the Sunderbans – the largest mangrove forest of the country, also declared as 'World Heritage Site' by the UNESCO. All these were clear indications that the ecological balance of southwest Bangladesh and life in general were critically dependent on the flow of water through the Ganges. The people, policy makers and politicians of the country certainly realised this. Consequently, for the newly elected government of 1996, the issue of sharing the Ganges water received a new impetus.

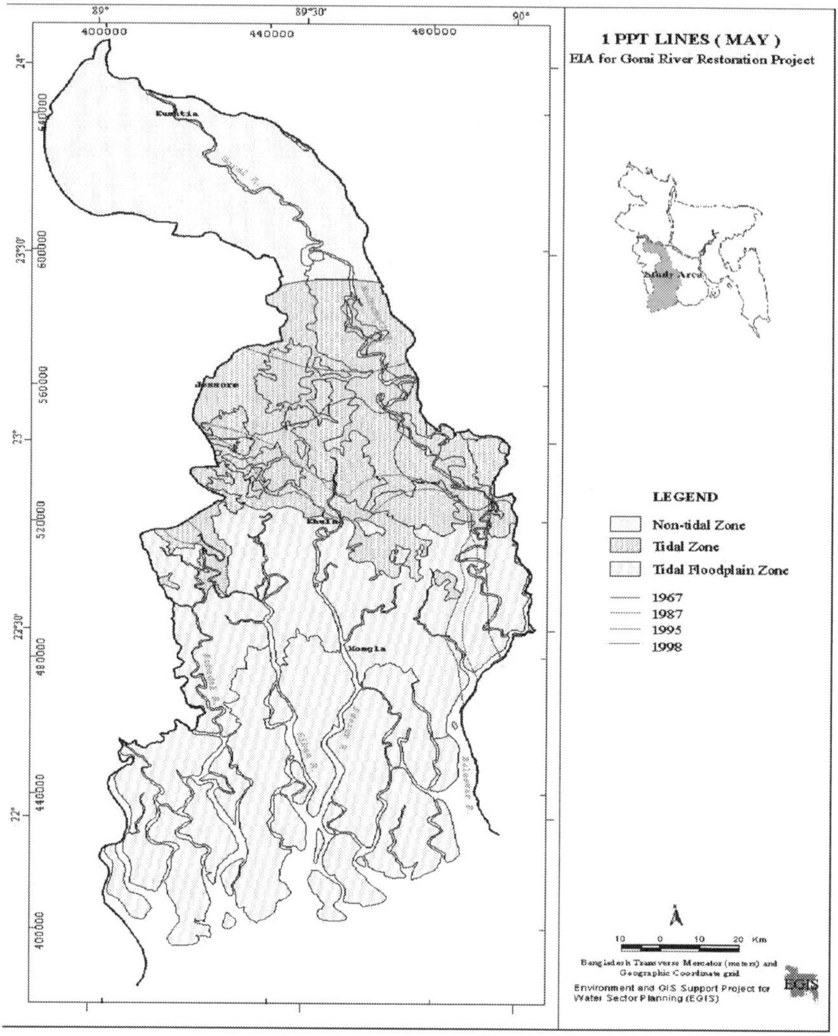

Figure 5.2

5.3 The Ganges Treaty

In 1996, renewed efforts were made to establish dialogue with India in order to reach a long-term sharing arrangement which would enable both sides to plan the utilisation of their share with a reasonable degree of security. This resulted in a treaty on the 'Sharing of the Ganga/Ganges water at Farakka', which was signed on 12 December 1996 by the two Prime Ministers, Sheikh Hasina of Bangladesh and H.D. Deve Gowda of India.

5.3.1 Core Content of the 1996 Treaty

The principal thrust of the Bangladesh-India Treaty is the determination of the amount of water to be released by India to Bangladesh at the Farakka Barrage on the Ganges for a period of 30 years (Articles I and XII). The Treaty establishes a new formula for sharing the Ganges waters at Farakka in the dry season spanning from 1 January to 31 May, further divided into ten-day periods. In sum, the new arrangement states that:

1. when the Ganges flow at Farakka is 70,000ft^3/s (cusecs[1]) or less, both countries are to receive 50 percent;
2. when the flow is between 70,000 and 75,000ft^3/s Bangladesh receives 35,000ft^3/s and India receives the rest;
3. with a flow of more than 75,000ft^3/s or more, India receives 40,000ft^3/s and Bangladesh receives the balance (Article II(i) and Annex 1 of the treaty).

However, for the situation where the flow falls below 50,000ft^3/s in any 10 day period, (Article II(iii)) of the Treaty contains a provision that 'the two governments will enter into immediate consultation to make adjustments on an emergency basis, in accordance with the principles of equity, fair play and no harm to either party'. The sharing arrangements are to be reviewed every five years and if no agreement can be reached on adjustments, India is to release at least 90 per cent of Bangladesh's share as provided by Article II.

5.3.2 A Brief Appraisal of the Treaty

The Treaty guarantees sharing of the water flowing through the Ganges over a period of 30 years. The Treaty prohibits India from withdrawing or diverting the Ganges water unilaterally through use of the barrage. Also, the Treaty provides that beyond the 30 years period, the Treaty is renewable on the basis of mutual consent.

But the question is how realistic the above assumptions are, given the flow of water particularly during the dry season in the post 1996 Treaty period. The following sections elaborate these issues based on the literature review, GoB (Government of Bangladesh) initiatives to harness the benefits of secured water flow, functioning of the JRC, and perceptions of the people whose lives and livelihoods are greatly influenced by the volume of water that flows through the Ganges.

5.3.2.1 The views and actions of the Government of Bangladesh

The security of water flow 'has opened up the opportunity of undertaking projects

---

[1] 35.3ft^3/s cusec = 1m^3 /s.

for optimum development of the Ganges water resources ... We must, and we intend to act now on the best possible option without further delay for improving the life and livelihood of our people dependent on the water of the Ganges' (GoB 1998: 20). The above words came from the Bangladesh Prime Minister when she was addressing the International Seminar on Water Resources Management and Development in Bangladesh with particular reference to the Ganges River in Dhaka on March 1998, which was attended by participants from 14 countries and representatives of 17 donor agencies.

The key papers presented in the seminar while exploring opportunities resulting from the Ganges water sharing treaty argued that having secured the water, Bangladesh got the opportunity to decide how to use the water to address environmental degradation and social problems. From this perspective the Government of Bangladesh (GoB 1998: 190) highlighted two alternative options:

1. to allow the water to remain in the Ganges river
2. to distribute some or all of it for Ganges Area Restoration.

The above clearly indicates the importance of the Treaty for long-term planning of water resources development in Bangladesh. The proposal of the GoB presented in the form of working papers was discussed and finally, the delegates agreed on a three-point action plan. These were:

1. Dredging of the Gorai to take early advantage of the opportunities provided by the Treaty, and to provide some immediate alleviation of the environmental degradation of the Ganges Dependent Area (GDA).
2. Undertaking of studies to establish the basis for optimal use of the Ganges water made available under the Treaty, and to assess the technical and economic viability of different options, including a barrage across the Ganges, for restoring the environment and promoting social and economic development in the GDA.
3. To build on the success of the Ganges Water Sharing Treaty and the Mahakali Treaty, it is desirable to continue the process of co-operation within the region over a broad range of development issues.

The above points of action were formally adopted in the seminar and received the endorsement of all co-sponsors of the seminar[2] as well as representatives of both India and Nepal (GoB 1998: 3-4). Thus the Treaty followed by a three point action plan endorsed through the International Seminar, created the opportunities for the GoB to act on issues which it could not pursue earlier. Two actions of the government deserve particular reference in this context. Firstly, following the recommendations of the FAP study on the southwestern region of Bangladesh, and the outcome of the aforementioned post-Treaty seminar of 1998, the government has undertaken the Gorai River Restoration Project (GRRP). This multi-million

[2] The Seminar was organised by the Bangladesh Government in association with the Government of Japan, the World Bank and the Asian Development Bank.

dollar project started its pilot works in 1998 with financial assistance of the World Bank and the Netherlands Government. The GRRP aims to secure the Gorai intake on the Ganges and use the water flow to restore the overall ecological balance of the region and foster social and economic development, which so far, has been adversely affected due to non-availability of water. Under GRRP, on a pilot basis, starting from the mouth of the river Gorai, a stretch of 30km has been dredged within the last couple of years. This has brought some positive impact within the pilot area as well as in the down stream of the Gorai.

The other initiative of the GoB is a study called 'Options for Ganges Dependent Area' (OGDA). It commenced in October 1999. The study aims, among other things, to investigate and 'assess the likely impact of future development on flows entering Bangladesh, and consider the implications for Bangladesh, of any changes in flows on the options for meeting the demands of the GDA' (TOR for the Consultants for the OGDA Studies, cited in Halcrow et al. 2000: 2-2). The study is also directed to explore the possibilities of augmentation, diversification and distribution of dry season flow by constructing a barrage on the Ganges to facilitate expansion of surface water irrigation and to push down the salinity which is moving upward in the whole of southwest Bangladesh. A recently published regional study offers further evidence in support of this GoB decision. The study noted that for the southwest Bangladesh, 'the strategy suggested for irrigation development was to secure the Gorai intake on the Ganges and augmentation of dry season flows by constructing a barrage on the Ganges to facilitate the expansion of surface water irrigation. It is generally agreed that since the bulk of the surface water resources is derived from the monsoon rains, these cannot be optimally utilised unless these are stored in minor, medium or large dams for multipurpose use' (Adhikari et al 2000: 15-16). However, secured water flow is one of the factors in favour of the construction of the Ganges barrage. Therefore, the GoB while formulating the terms of reference (TOR) for the OGDA studies, rightly noted that 'the effect of the operation of the Ganges Water Treaty (and, where appropriate, the Mahakali Treaty) should be studied and estimates made of likely change in flows on the Ganges and Brahmaputra' (TOR, cited in Halcrow et al. 2000: 2-2).

5.3.2.2 Views and responses of the wider civil society

Public response and reaction to the agreement has been mixed. Some claim that based on the available data, Bangladesh will receive a lower flow under the 1996 Treaty than it did under the 1977 agreement as the sharing and schedule are based on average flows. A further problem highlighted is that the Treaty makes no provision to augment the flow through regional co-operation unlike the 1977 agreement. There is also no provision for international arbitration in case of dispute. The sharing Treaty also does not take into account water quality. It is also argued that the flow agreed under the Treaty is insufficient to redress the problems of the high levels of salinity in surface water, and problems for navigability, fisheries and general deterioration of river ecosystems. The FAP study on southwest Water Resources Management indicates that Bangladesh needs a minimum flow of 1,550-1,700m^3/s during the critical period of the year (March & April) to meet the demand for water for agriculture and industrial development as well as to maintain ecology, navigability and control salinity intrusion.

The empirical evidence such as flow data during the critical months supports some of the above claims. Based on a comparative analysis of water flow data over the period 1949-70 to post 1996 Treaty, Tanzeema (1998) concluded that lean season water availability in Bangladesh did not improve. In fact what is more striking as Tanzeema demonstrated in her study is that during the critical ten day periods of March and April, the 1996 Treaty performed poorly compared to the 1977 agreement (see Figure 5.3). This according to some, is essentially a 'validation of the status quo rather than providing Bangladesh its historic share' (Faisal et al 1999: 197), although the authors recognise the fact that 'without these agreements, the situation could have been worse'.

This reduction in the dry season flow is apparently also a function of low volume of water availability at the Farakka barrage. A GoB (1998: 191-2) publication based on the average volume of water arriving at Farakka over the 5 month period January to May shows that due to increased withdrawal of water in the upper reaches of the Farakka barrage there are clear signs of decreasing trend of water availability at Farakka over the period 1949-1997 (see Figure 5.4).

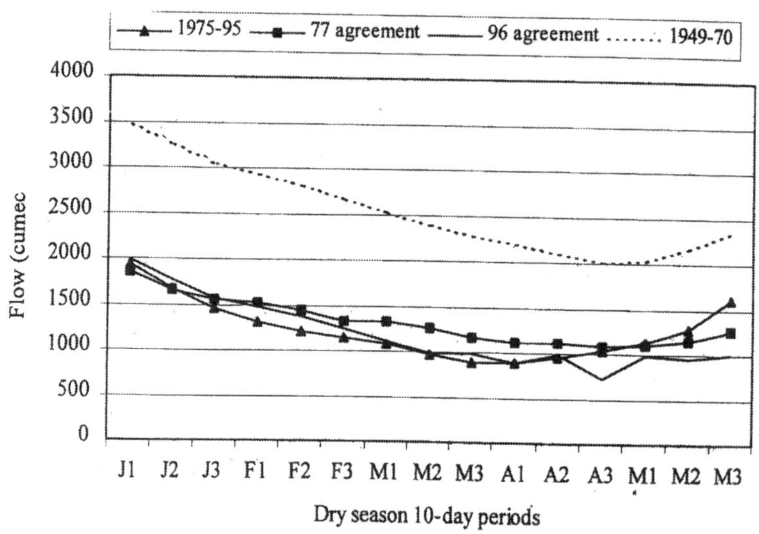

Figure 5.3: Historical and simulated flows at Hardinge Bridge. (Source: Tanzeema 1998, cited in Faisal et al. 1999: 201)

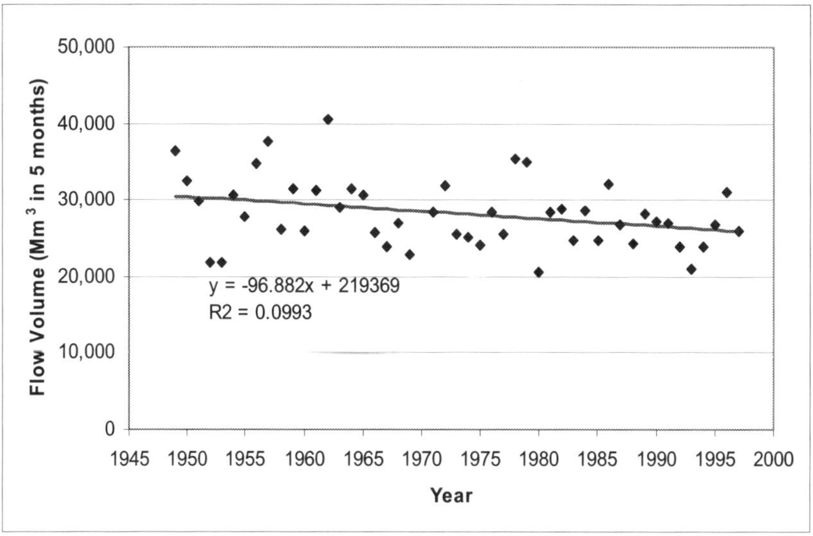

Figure 5.4: Flows arriving at Farakka (Source: GoB 1998: 192)

The opinion of the population living along the stretches of the Ganges Dependent Area echoed the same voice as the academic researches unfolded. Recently, I had the opportunity to dialogue with the people of 6 districts (Kushtia, Meherpur, Magura, Faridpur, Rajbari, Jessore) of southwest Bangladesh. One of the main reasons for this local level dialogue was to assess the social and environmental impact of the GRRP project, which the GoB had taken up for implementation in the post Treaty period. People from various professions with diverse socio-economic backgrounds participated in these local level consultations. Among the many issues discussed, one crucial issue, which came up in all these discussions, was the uncertainty of water flow. Some elderly people even came up with records of water flow that were reported in the press and questioned the very assumption of this 'ambitious' task of dredging the river Gorai to increase its off-take at the Padma-Gorai confluence. Some even argued that before making further investment, the GoB should wait and monitor for a few years, the extent and volume of water that it gets from India particularly during the critical dry periods. Otherwise, the investments may not eventually yield the desired results.

The Joint River Commission (JRC) through a Press Release in April 2001 has refuted the press reports on the flow of the Ganges water during the present dry season. The JRC stated that 'although the total flow of the Ganges is comparatively low at the Farakka point this year, Bangladesh received its due share of guaranteed 35,000ft^3/s from 11 to 20 March and 1 to 10 April. The same quantum of Ganges water is being available from 21 to 30 April, it added ... It further said that the total flow of the Ganges considerably reduced due to drought and absence of rainfall in its upstream during the dry season of this year … Although Bangladesh is getting its due share as per the agreement, compared to that of previous three years, some times its total amount is a little less' (JRC's Press Release reported in the New Nation, Dhaka April 30, 2001 [8]). In the press release, JRC could not categorically refute the claim made by the people. On the contrary, from the press release it becomes abundantly clear that availability of water at Farakka is sometimes lower than what it should be, therefore, Bangladesh received lower quantum of water than the amount stipulated in the Treaty.

In view of various contradictory data and information on flow of water, people whose livelihoods have been adversely affected due to low flow of the Ganges were keen to know whether the Treaty will ensure Bangladesh an increased and sustained flow of water, which could facilitate the restoration of the river Gorai, and its downwards channels and distributaries. Of course, the answers are not simple, but are linked to various sensitive factors much of which stem from objective situations such as gradual reduction of water availability at Farakka (see Figure 5.4), be it for natural factors such as drought or absence of rainfall as reported by JRC, and the political climate of the regions.

The views expressed by the common people are not isolated thoughts of apprehension. The non-governmental organisations (NGOs) which are actively involved in deciding the approach to development, and advocating people's right to information and participation in mainstream development activities have taken keen interest on the question of water. To ensure efficient management of the water that is expected to flow through the Ganges, the NGOs have formed an alliance called Padma Network. As yet this is a local network of twenty-eight NGOs. The Network since its formation in August 2000, met several times to review various government initiatives in the field of water management in southwest Bangladesh during the post-Treaty period. They are active in bringing the grassroot experiences and voices into the planning of water resources of the region, and working out modalities for involving people in the OGDA study.

5.4 Conclusions

The Ganges Water Treaty with India is an important milestone in the Indo-Bangladesh relationship. The Treaty has created the possibilities for Bangladesh to embark on long-term planning for optimum use of the water guaranteed under the Treaty during the lean period. In view of that, Bangladesh succeeded in mobilising regional and international support to harness the benefits of the Treaty. However, while at political level, dialogue has been established and consensus has been reached, the flow data shows that ground reality is changing very fast. This change is mainly due to intensive abstraction and continued diversion of water in the upper reaches of the Ganges. This led to the gradual decline of water availability at Farakka. This calls for corrective measures on the part of India, and at the same time taking the Treaty as the starting point for studying the potentials of basin-wide development.

The success of such an approach would entail dialogue and cooperation among the co-basin countries (including Nepal) and must draw upon experiences of the water treaties concerning the international river. It may however be noted that India being a large country, the success of such co-basin management depends largely on her. Simple enactment of rules and deliberations of mutual responsibilities will not bring much desired results. Given the growing need for water for development, and unequal power relations among the countries, often the rights and needs of both parties are not respected. This happens not only in the international context, but even within the national boundary of the same country. To illustrate the point, a recent press report on the water disputes between the two states of India (i.e., Andhra Pradesh and Karnataka) is worth noting. The Times of India on 15 May 2001 reported that:

> the Chitradurga District (located in Karnataka state – AD) Irrigation Action Committee has urged the state government to pressurise Andhra Pradesh to stop irrigation related construction activities since this would drastically affect Karnataka ... Committee president P Kodandaramaiah said Andhra Pradesh was behaving like "a bull in a China shop" by pushing ahead with projects while constantly thwarting Karnataka's efforts through legal tangles'. He continued and stated that Andhra Pradesh is diverting water from Karnataka by building feeder channel ... Whereas, according to the committee chairman 'if a state wants to do this (diversion of water, AD) it has to first have discussed with the affected state, but nothing was done ... He urged the Chief Minister S.M. Krishna to lead an all-party delegation to Prime Minister A.B. Vajpayee to impress on him the wrong doings of the Andhra Pradesh government. We need to put as much pressure on the Centre as possible to counter AP because Telugu Desam Party has a lot of clout due to the delicate position that the NDA government is in ... (and) suggested the state Government could move the High Court to obtain a stay order ... and to file an original suit in the Supreme Court since it is provided for in the Inter-State Water Disputes Act' (*The Times of India*, 15 May 2001[7], emphasis in the original).

The above report aptly demonstrates the possibilities and limitations of legal agreement and treaties when parties are competing for scarce resources and the competition is among unequal on various counts. Thus, a twin track approach,[3] in

---

[3] In the field of research on water issues this has already brought some results (see Adhikari et al. 2000). Another recent initiative is to evolve strategies to fight fundamentalism. Leading human rights activists, politicians, academics, journalists, cultural activists and many others from five South Asian countries (Bangladesh, India, Nepal, Pakistan and Sri Lanka) met in Dhaka during 1-2 June 2001. The South Asian Conference on Fundamentalism and Communalism concluded with a declaration called 'Dhaka Declaration' calling upon government and political parties in the region not to utilise fundamentalist forces for political purposes and emphasising the role of civil society in mobilising the people (cf. *The Daily Star*, 1-3 June 2001).

my opinion, seems more appropriate in addressing the problems that the countries of the region are faced with. One is continuation of dialogue at the level of the Government and the other through nurturing and strengthening the bonds of friendships, which exists among the people of the region. In the case of the latter, the researchers and advocates can certainly play a pivotal role by amplifying the voices of the people. The above tracks are indeed complementary to each other. If active debates and dialogue continue, we as a region will be in a better position to frame policies and define frameworks of cooperation for water resources planning and management with particular reference to the international rivers, to uphold the aspiration of people whose livelihoods are critically dependent on this precious resource.

References

Adhikari, K.D., Q.K.Ahmed, S.K. Malla, B.B. Pradhan, K.Rahman, R. Ragachari, K.B.S. Rasheedd and B.G.Verghese (Adhikari et al. eds.) (2000) *Cooperation on Eastern Himalayan Rivers: Opportunities and Challenges*, New Delhi: Konarak Publishers Pvt. Ltd.

Crow, B., Lindquist, A. and Wilson, D. (Crow et al.) (1997) *Sharing the GANGES. The politics and technology of river development*, Dhaka: The University Press Ltd.

Environmental and GIS Support Project for Water Sector Planning (EGIS) (2000).

Environmental Baseline of Gorai River Restoration Project, Dhaka: May.

Government of Bangladesh (1998) *Proceedings of the International Seminar on the Water Resources Management and Development in Bangladesh with Particular reference to the Ganges river*, Dhaka: Ministry of Water Resources, 8-10 March.

Faisal, I.M., Nishat, A. and Tanzeema, S. (Faisal et al.) (1999) 'Managing Common Waters between India and Bangladesh' in *The Proceedings of the regional Seminar on Conflict Management of International River Basins* jointly organized by the Bangladesh University of Engineering and Technology and UNESCO, Dhaka: 7-9 December 1999.

Halcrow et al. (2000) *Options for the Ganges Dependent Area*, Interim Report, Volume 1: Main report, Dhaka: December.

Newspaper Reports

The New Nation, Dhaka: 30 April 2001

Ganges Water – Bangladesh getting due share: JRC.

The Times of India. Hyderabad. 15 May 2001.

Chitradurga panel takes note of AP water projects.

The Daily Star, Dhaka: 1-3 June 2001.

Fight Fundamentalism in South Asia: Five-nation conference in city to evolve common strategies.

Dhaka Declaration Adopted.

Chapter 6

The Natural and Human Environment of the Ganges-Brahmaputra-Meghna Basin

Graham P. Chapman

6.1 Introduction

At the conference, which initiated this book, there was discussion about the development of institutions and case law to manage the Rhine in Europe and the Mekong in Southeast Asia, as well as the Ganges in India. What became very apparent was that these river basins were hardly comparable, and that it was very difficult to imagine viable legal frameworks of universal applicability emerging for the management of international rivers, unless at the most banal and general level. The treaties, which have developed covering international responsibilities in the Rhine, are tailored to the circumstances of that river and its nations.

The differences between these three river basins embraced levels of development and norms of governance as much as the differences in climate, geology, and flow regime. This chapter attempts to spell out those characteristics of the social, political and natural environment of the Ganges and its basin, that are the basic backdrop constraining the development of an international legal system to administer the river.

6.2 Geophysical Components of the GBM

In physical terms, the subcontinent of South Asia comes in three distinct parts, which are in continuing dynamic inter-relationship with each other. The first part is the Archaen Deccan block, one of the earth's tectonic plates, which split off from Africa more than 250 million years ago, travelled across the Indian Ocean, and bumped into the southern flank of Asia. The impact of this collision, which started 70 million years ago and which still continues, is what has made the great dent, visible on the world map, and marked by the wrinkling and pushing up of the mountains west of the Indus, north of the Ganges, and south and east of the Brahmaputra. The Deccan block is still pushing under the Himalayas at about 6cm a year and the Himalayas themselves are still rising by about the same amount, on average. This is why the whole of the northern part of South Asia is at risk from devastating earthquakes of great magnitude.

The high mountains are the second of the three major components. They are subjected to unusually high and intense levels of rainfall because of the behaviour of the Indian monsoon, which conveys far more moisture to far greater altitudes than the monsoons of East Asia. The resultant rates of erosion of the lofty young mountains are amongst the highest in the world, and naturally have led to the deposition of the alluvial sediments that have formed the world's greatest riverine flood plains. Thus the third component of the geography is comprised of the plains of the Indus, the Ganges, the Brahmaputra, and the Meghna, the silted-up trough between the first two components. These plains are being actively reworked in an unceasing process of erosion, deposition, re-erosion, re-deposition, and finally in the building of the world's largest and most active delta, in Bengal. A good example of the capacity of the rivers to choke themselves and to seek new courses is given by the behaviour of the Kosi over the last 200 years, during which, it has strayed 70km from the eastern side of its fan at the foot of the Himalayas to the western side.

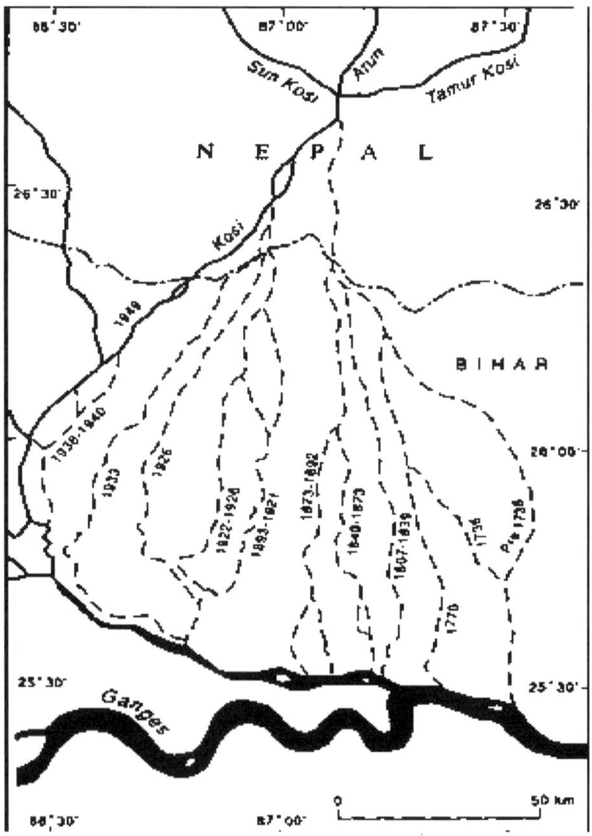

Figure 6.1: The route of Kosi River (Source: Carson 1985)

6.3 Rainfall Regimes and Seasonality

In the Rig Veda the early Aryan invaders of India describe the lands around them from the vantage of the northwest of the subcontinent. The Rig-Veda was composed about the time of their first arrival in the Punjab. From it we can get an idea of the geography of the land of the Sapta-Sindhu. (They recognised seven (sapta) rivers in the Indus where now we know the Indus and the five of Punjab (Punjab meaning Panch (five) ab (river).) It was a land of cold winters and hot summers, and unreliable rain, which could fall in either winter or summer. South lay the land of Vitra – the land of drought – the present lower Indus Valley and the Thar Desert.

To the east lay the land of both Vitra and Indra – drought and rain, or in other words quite clearly the monsoon lands of the Ganges basin. These words describe aptly the monsoon lands where somewhere around 80 per cent of the annual rainfall occurs in only three months.

The monsoon brings massively heavy rain to Bhutan and the North-East of India, and indeed Mawsynram (which has just taken the title from neighbouring Cherrapunji) in Meghalaya, has the world's highest rainfall. The monsoon in Bengal is both heavier and longer than the monsoon in the far western plains of the upper Ganga. In the area around Delhi the monsoon is much shorter, much lighter, and also less ccrtain.

The whole of the GBM is therefore characterised by the extreme seasonality of rainfall, and also by considerable spatial variation of rainfall. For millennia agriculture has perforce had to adopt to this temporal and spatial variation, so that there are rice types in Bengal which can grow at the rate of 30cm in 24 hours to match rising flood waters, and perhaps growing more than 5m high, while in the Doab north of Delhi wells have been used to protect the traditional crops of wheat and barley against drought.

6.4 River Discharge

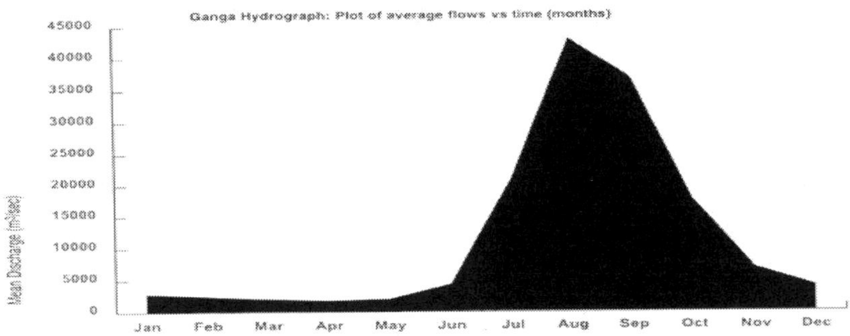

Figure 6.2: The Discharge of Ganges at Farakka (Source: Subba 2001)

Table 6.1: Comparative Indicators for Selected Major World Rivers

River	Length (km)	Basin Area ('000km^2)	Average Discharge ('000m^3)	Area (m^3/'000km^2)	Average Peak ('000m^3)	Ratio of Peak to Average Discharge
Amazon	6,516	7,180	172.00	23.96	210.00	1.22
Brahmaputra	2,900	938	20.00	21.32	73.00	3.65
Mekong	4,500	795	15.90	20.00	34.10	2.10
Ganges	2,700	1,073	14.84	13.83	70.00	4.72
Rhine	1,360	224	2.20	9.82	3.00	1.36
Congo	4,640	4,700	42.00	8.94	50.00	1.19
Yenisey	5,550	2,605	19.60	7.52	72.00	3.67
Mississippi	6,720	3,220	19.60	6.09	35.00	1.79

(Sources: Nijssen 2000, Arora 2000, http://www.rev.net/~aloe/river/)

The Ganges and the Brahmaputra are amongst the world's greatest rivers. The Amazon and the Congo have longer lengths and greater discharges, but far less seasonal variation. In terms of discharge per unit area of the basin, the Brahmaputra, the Amazon, and the Mekong are clearly in a class of their own. In terms of the ratio of average peak discharge to average annual discharge, the Ganges, the Brahmaputra and the Yenisey are in a class of their own. They are all rivers, which are both mighty and flashy. The Yenisey is however an Arctic draining river, with very little human settlement in its basin. (It is flashy because of the spring thaw.)

Some idea of the seasonality can be judged by the discharge figures for the Ganges at Varanasi – a flow of 13,454ft^3/s in the summer, and only 285ft^3/s in the winter, when the river has the appearance of a sequence of languid connected pools, or by the figures of river flow by Messerli and Hofer (1995). This huge annual variation in water flow occurs within the most extensive densely settled terrain on earth. Although other monsoon lands in East Asia have to cope with variability, nowhere else are such extremes faced.

6.5 Sediment Flux: Deposition and Erosion

Table 6.2: Sediment flux in Himalayan and other major rivers

Himalayan Rivers	**Tonnes/km²/year**
Indus	510
Brahmaputra	1,450
Ganga	1,570
Karnali	6,740
Tamur (Kosi, Ganga)	8,220
Teesta (Brahmaputra)	12,510
Non-Himalayan rivers	**Tonnes/km²/year**
Amazon	146
Mississippi	107
Nile	38
Zaire	11
Mekong	203
Huang He	1,403
Hai He	1,620

(Source: Subba 2001)

The Ganges and the Brahmaputra are also notable for the massive sediment loads they carry. The sediment loads are high because of the intense precipitation on the high and young mountains of the Himalayas, but even south bank tributaries flowing from the northern part of the Deccan block, like the Chambal, have very high sediment loads. The entrainment of sediment is not a process, which is uniform in time. The earthquakes in the hills may loosen the over-burden of soil, cause massive landslips, and dislodge tree roots. In a subsequent monsoon a new 'slug' of silt gets washed into watercourses. An earthquake in Assam may result in such a 'slug', which will take several years to work its way through the delta system downstream, causing 'extra' flooding at different points and times.

Extreme rainfall events on their own can also suddenly entrain unusually high levels of sediment. Floods in Nepal in 1993 reduced the lifespan of the Kulekhani reservoir by ten years (Hofer 1997). Detailed research suggests that deforestation in the Himalayas, to the extent that it does occur (and even that is highly disputable), cannot be blamed for the magnitude of sediment flux, nor the nature and extent of flooding in the plains and in the delta. Floods in Bangladesh seem to be principally the result of rainfall events in the Shillong block and Bhutan (Hofer 1997).

When the rivers reach the plains, as the gradient decreases and velocity diminishes, sediment is deposited. Riverbeds are elevated, and over-topping of banks occurs during the flood peak. This leads to sediment deposition on the banks and the natural construction of levees. Coarse sediment is deposited in the river bed and on the nearby banks, while the finest sediment can be deposited over the whole extent of any given flood. This finest sediment usually enhances the fertility of agricultural land. The coarser sandier sediment (chawr land) can usually only be used for agriculture after decades of manuring. As the river course becomes choked the river may breach its bank and switch to an older channel, or sometimes create a new channel, or simply meander increasing its width and eroding banks on either side. The rate of lateral movement of bigger rivers can easily exceed 100m in a year. In all parts of plains adjacent to the great rivers, local people think of the erosion and the loss of land as a greater threat than flooding, which can have beneficial as well as negative effects.

6.6 The Demographic Background

Approximately 10 per cent of the human race, more than 600 million human beings, lives in the GBM basin of South Asia. In world demographic terms the area is unique. The density of the population is about five times that of France. The reason why there is such a massive population is because of very long-term historical demographic inertia. This area was from early agricultural times and in relative terms, one of the most productive ecosystems on earth. This area was the heart of what in their day were the greatest empires on earth – the Mauryan and Gupta Empires, the Sultanate of Delhi, and the Mughal Empire.

Of the present 600 million, slightly less than 10 percent live in the hills and mountains. The hill population is, though, increasing faster than population of the plains. The hill population is less urbanised, but urbanising faster. The recent decreases in population growth rates in India have been in the areas away from the Ganges plains. In the whole GBM basin, the population growth rate for the last decade is the same as in the previous decade. The doubling time for population growing at this rate is about 30 years, so by 2031 we could expect in the GBM alone a population equivalent to the present total population of all India. It is the resource demands of this population that will more than anything drive the politics of this region.

Table 6.3: Basic Demographic Indicators for the GBM

	Total Population 1991 in '000s	Per cent Urban 1991	Annual Growth Rate of Total Population 1981-1991	Total Population 2001 in '000s	Per cent Urban 2001	Annual Growth Rate of Total Population 1991-2001	Change in Growth Rate: 1981-1991 to 1991-2001
Ganges Hills							
Uttaranchal	5,900.9	21.6	2.0	8,479.6	25.6	3.7	1.7
Himachal Pradesh	5,111.1	8.7	1.8	6,077.0	9.8	1.7	-0.1
Nepal	19,379.0	8.0	2.6	25,284.5	9.8	2.7	0.1
Total	**30,391.0**	**10.8**	**2.3**	**39,841.1**	**13.2**	**2.7**	**0.4**
Brahmaputra Hills							
Arunachal	858.4	12.2	3.1	1,091.1	20.4	2.4	-0.7
Manipur	1,826.7	27.7	2.5	2,388.6	23.9	2.7	0.2
Meghalava	1,760.6	18.7	2.8	2,306.1	19.6	2.7	-0.1
Mizoram	686.2	46.2	3.4	891.1	49.5	2.6	-0.8
Nagaland	1,215.6	17.3	4.6	1,988.6	19.6	5	0.4
Sikkim	405.5	9.1	2.5	540.5	11.1	2.9	0.4
Bhutan*	1,476.0	4	2.3	1,951.0	21.0	2.8	0.5
Total	**8,229.0**	**19.0**	**3.0**	**11,157.0**	**22.7**	**3.1**	**0.1**

** Estimates for Bhutan vary greatly. Some sources put the population at half that given here*

Table 6.3 (continued)

	Total Population 1991 in '000s	Per cent Urban 1991	Annual Growth Rate of Total Population 1981-1991	Total Population 2001 in '000s	Per cent Urban 2001	Annual Growth Rate of Total Population 1991-2001	Change in Growth Rate: 1981-1991 to 1991-2001
Ganges Plains							
Delhi	9,370.4	89.9	4.2	13,783.0	93.0	3.9	-0.3
Chandigarh	640.7	89.7	3.6	900.9	89.8	3.5	-0.1
Haryana	16,317.7	24.8	2.4	21,083.0	29.0	2.6	0.2
Bihar	86,338.8	13.2	2.1	82,878.8	10.5	2.4	0.3
Jharkhand				26,909.4	22.2		
Uttar Pradesh	133,130.0	19.8	2.3	166,052.9	20.8	2.2	-0.1
Total	**245,797.6**	**20.7**	**2.3**	**311,608.0**	**22.1**	**2.4**	**0.1**
Brahmaputra Plains							
Assam	22,294.6	11.1	2.1	26,638.4	12.7	1.8	-0.3
Total	**22,294.6**	**11.1**	**2.1**	**26,638.4**	**12.7**	**1.8**	**-0.3**

Table 6.3 continued

	Total Population 1991 in '000s	**Per cent Urban 1991**	**Annual Growth Rate of Total Population 1981-1991**	**Total Population 2001 in '000s**	**Per cent Urban 2001**	**Annual Growth Rate of Total Population 1991-2001**	**Change in Growth Rate: 1981-1991 to 1991-2001**
Bengal Delta							
Tripura	2,744.8	15.3	3.0	3,191.2	17.0	1.5	-1.5
West Bengal	67,982.7	27.4	2.2	80,221.2	28.0	1.7	-0.5
Bangladesh	107,993.0	15.7	1.9	131,269.9	20.0	2.0	0.1
Total	**178,720.5**	**20.1**	**2.0**	**214,682.3**	**22.9**	**1.9**	**-0.1**
Total Hills	38,620.0	12.5	2.4	50,998.1	15.2	2.8	0.4
Total Plains	446,812.7	20.0	2.2	552,928.7	22.0	2.2	0.0
Total	**485,432.7**	**19.4**	**2.2**	**603,926.8**	**21.4**	**2.2**	**0.0**

(Sources: Calculated from Census of India 2001, Encyclopaedia Britannica, and CIA website)

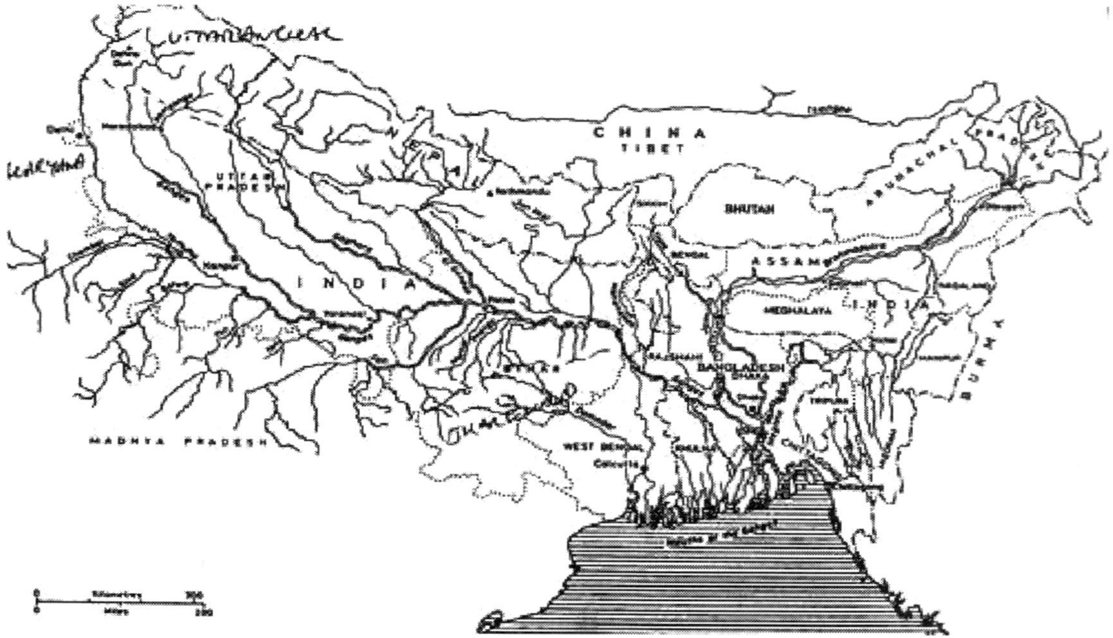

Figure 6.3: The Rivers and Political Divisions of the GBM

6.7 Water: Demand Side

As populations have grown and the demand for food has risen so have attempts to harness the rivers and the groundwater for irrigation. Such irrigation may be tried as a means to proof against the variability of rain in the main cropping season, but, since low temperatures are not a limiting condition on agriculture for much of the GBM, it may also extend cropping into different seasons. In the modern era urbanisation has seen a rise in demand for large supplies of water to be supplied to focal points on a year-round basis. Water is also needed on a year-round basis for the generation of electricity from hydro schemes.

Thus the new year-round and escalating demands for water increasingly clash with the inherent seasonality of rainfall and of the discharge of the rivers.

We will first consider the comparative positions of the agricultural and the urban sectors.

6.7.1 Water Demand from Agriculture

In the GBM somewhere near 90 per cent of total human water demand is for agriculture. This is near the average for Asia – but very substantially different from Europe, where industrial and urban development is greater (and of course the climate and terrain very different). Yet it would appear *prima facie* that economics do not justify such levels of use by agriculture. To quote Fauceys (1992):

> In a year, 1000 c^3 of water may be used either to provide water for 80 people, or to grow food for between 1.6 and 3 people. This imbalance suggests ... domestic water should win every time. It is far more economic to move food from a rain-rich area to a dry area than it is to move water.

Although the disparity of the two figures suggests that overwhelmingly the equation will work out in favour of urban water use, the equation is, of course, never this simple. The level of agricultural water demand depends on a wide range of variables, most of which are liable to substantial change.

Table 6.4: Pattern of Water Demand in Two Global Regions

	Annual withdrawal m^3 p.c.	**Withdrawal as per cent available**	**Per cent domestic**	**Per cent industry**	**Perc ent agriculture**
Asia	526	15	6	8	86
Europe	726	15	3	54	33

(Source: Chisholm in ODA 1992)

The maximum rainfall in the western wheat areas occurs during the Kharif (monsoon) season, when it is too hot and humid for wheat to grow; and the monsoon is too unreliable this far west for rain-fed rice to be a reliable staple crop. Thus the traditional farming pattern has been to grow wheat in the cooler Rabi (winter) months, using retained soil moisture from the monsoon, and irrigation from open wells where possible. The first of the major nineteenth century canal irrigation schemes, the Upper Ganga Canal, started in the 1850s, used the low winter flow of the Ganges to provide protection and security for this winter wheat crop. The arable acreage could be expanded for a while by taking new land into cultivation, but ultimately further increases could only be accommodated by increasing the cropping index (gross cultivated area/net cultivated area: indicating the extent to which a piece of land is cropped more than once a year). This of course means growing more in the second season. After Independence in 1947 the Upper Ganga Canal was modified to provide for irrigation in the monsoon period and the growing of crops such as rice and sugar cane in the Doab (interfluve between the Yamuna and Ganga). In addition, crop breeding during the Green Revolution has produced new breeds of rice, which perform better in irrigated conditions in drier sunnier areas than in the moister and cloudier conditions of the east. Given also that there is a substantial demand for rice and a price margin in its favour, in some western areas rice has become even more important than wheat. The difference in water demand between rice and wheat is substantial: therefore for this reason amongst others there has been a substantial increase in agricultural water demand in the drier western parts of the plains. There are technical, seasonal, geomorphological reasons, elaborated below, why water could not be provided in the wet season before extra investment was made-but to précis here, the principal difference is that in the low season the river water carried little silt, but in the high season silt flows are very high and can choke a canal system fast, therefore necessitating the design and construction of silt traps.

6.7.2 Urban Water Demand

Table 6.5: Suggested Urban Water Requirements in India

Purpose	Desirable litres per capita per day (lpcd)
Cooking and drinking	15
Bathing, flushing etc	40
Washing utensils and clothes	35
Total	95

(Source: GOI 1988 [294])

The current actual average water supply in urban areas for all inhabitants is at most 50lpcd (litres per capita per day). Currently perhaps a half of urban dwellers do not have flush sanitation. In most urban areas of the GBM most of the current supply comes from surface flow-though there are an unknown number of boreholes, many private, and some public. In developed European countries water usage in all sectors averages out at about 200lpcd. It may never be possible to make such a provision on a year-round basis in the GBM. However, the pressure will be to increase per capita supply as development occurs. If within 35 years the total population doubles, and the urban proportion also increases to its expected 40 percent, then that implies a quadrupling of the urban population. To this add the demands for a modest doubling of per capita consumption, then this implies an increase in urban water demand by a factor of eight times in 35 years. If this demand is to be met, it implies very significant large-scale investment and all the political decision-making that will go with the cities imposing demands on distant areas of the catchments. If it is not met, that implies an entirely different political scenario, with possibly an increase in the kind of civil disturbances already seen over water shortages.

The National Commission (of India) observes that 80 per cent of water supplied to urban areas passes through the urban area ending as sullage, sewage, or effluent of some kind. Virtually all is untreated, some is discharged simply to sink into the ground, a lot into the drainage system. Delhi alone is discharging about 4,100 million litres a day, against its supply of 5,100 million per day. During low season flows abstraction from the Yamuna upstream of Delhi is reversing the river flow – meaning that effluent discharged downstream is being taken into the water inlets.

6.8 Water: Supply Side

Surface water storage capacity covers the whole scale from a small village pond to a massive dam in the Himalayas. For some villages in India and Bangladesh such a small pond remains its main source of water throughout the dry season. The water is usually heavily contaminated by the end of this period, since it serves multiple uses for washing everything from buffalos to clothes and the village lorry. Small ponds and tanks are usually shallow, and have a large surface area in relation to the volume of water stored. They result in high evaporation losses; usually have limited irrigation potential, although they are credited with re-supply of groundwater. The extraction of water often involves lifting or pumping. By contrast, large reservoirs, usually built in deep mountain valleys, have a far smaller surface area for the volume of water stored. Since they build a head of water upstream, much of the discharge can be conveyed by gravity systems. There are, however, a myriad of problems with large schemes which detractors focus upon.

6.8.1 Big Dam Projects within the GBM Catchment

The large dams, like Bhakra and Pong, on the Sutlej and Beas, two rivers of the Indian Punjabi Indus system, are usually multipurpose. By storing monsoon rains, they can provide hydropower for much of the year. They can also provide irrigation water, and indeed millions of people in Rajasthan depend upon the flow of water from Bhakra through the Indira Ghandi Nahar. The problem is that the demands for power and the demands for irrigation releases very rarely coincide. It has also proved very difficult to get electricity charges paid from rural areas, and in many cases there is no attempt to charge farmers. This means that the electricity generating enterprises (usually state boards, but increasingly being privatised) are more sympathetic to urban than to rural needs. A further important function of these multipurpose schemes is the storage of flood peaks to protect downstream areas

The best way of managing a reservoir for flood protection is obviously to keep it as empty as possible for as much time as possible. Then, any extreme weather event may be better accommodated by the storage available. However, this is exactly the opposite of the best strategy for water management for either electricity generation or for irrigation. The experience of the management of dams in India suggests that managers will store as much water as possible throughout the monsoon from as early a date as possible, so that if later the monsoon fails, they have not wasted early chances. This means that flood peaks late in the monsoon cannot be accommodated. The dam structure may be threatened with water overtopping it, provoking an emergency release of water through the sluices. Some writers are convinced that large dams have actually increased the flood problem. The claim is made that the frequency of flooding is reduced, but when floods do occur they have a greater peak, and impact with greater suddenness, both highly damaging properties.

A further problem with large dams is that their reservoirs have an impact on the geology. The weight of water can be enough to induce an earthquake, and the pressure of water can lead to infiltration and the lubrication of fault lines. The Koyna Dam in the Western Ghats outside of Bombay caused such an earthquake the first time it was filled. Although the structure did not fail it was badly damaged. There is a suspicion that large dams in the Himalayas like the Tehri Dam being built on the Ganges, could induce earthquakes, possibly of a sufficient magnitude to cause them to fail (see Govardhan (1993) Appendix II for a list of relevant earthquake events). Their designers and geologists claim that they understand the problem well enough to design quakeproof structures. However, it has to be said that given the seismic history of the Himalayas, this is an article of faith.

Reservoirs have been known to weaken rock masses adjacent to the reservoirs, sometimes causing mass slumping of whole hillsides into the reservoir. In such events a wave is set up which can overtop the crest of the dam, and cause substantial damage downstream. A further effect of large dams includes a change in the thermal regime, with subsequent changes to downstream ecology.

Specifically in the case of the Himalayas, reservoirs silt up very fast. This means that the lifetime of some of the major projects may be well under 100 years, during which time the live storage is progressively reduced. Depending upon the calculations made, this often means that projects have a dubious economic viability.

A final critical charge made against large dams is that they displace many people from the reservoir area, and sometimes flood good woodland. It is often the case that the oustees, as they are known (or PAPs: project affected persons), do not receive adequate compensation, and join the stream of rural poor migrating to urban areas. Such displacement is highly visible, and the plight of these people has become a focal point for anti-dam protesters. It is not usually calculated against the less visible but continuous stream of people leaving rural areas, which lack irrigation, water.

In the Indian Himalayas, the Ganges is being dammed at Tehri to provide more power and more surface flow for Haryana, Uttar Pradesh and Delhi. Other good sites for mega projects are within Nepal and Bhutan. Nepal has an enormous hydro-power potential (Rasheed 1995) and Subba 2001), supposedly as much as 83,000MW (or very nearly as much as all of India's installed capacity in 2000, amounting to 98,000MW). Four major perennial rivers (the Mahakali and Karnali, which form the flood-prone Ghagara in India, the Gandak and the Kosi) offer opportunities for mega-dams that could provide huge exports of power to India, and provide flood protection possibly extending as far as Bangladesh, augment the low season flow at Farakka (see below), and provide irrigation on the plains. All of the charges levied above about the negative effects and dangers of big dams are being levied by protesters and detractors against these big schemes. But the logic that says that water should be stored in the wet season for use in the dry season never quite goes away, and it will for sure resurrect the demands for building some of these schemes. They could possibly provide Nepal with huge export earnings and all the risks of corruption that go with the size of contracts involved. Some observers believe that Nepal's young and struggling democracy could be undermined by such external pressures. The wrangles over pricing policies are critical. What are the costs to Nepal, in land submerged and people dislocated? How can the flood-control benefits in downstream India be accurately valued and monetised? What will be the price of electricity in India in, say, 2020, in a subsidised and regulated or free market? Can it be almost as high as the next best alternative – derived from coal-burning thermal stations on the plains?

Bhutan has an estimated hydropower potential of about 20,000MW (Subba 2001). It could only ever use a fraction of this for domestic purposes. Small to medium projects in the range of 300 to 1,000MW have been built or are under construction, with Indian aid and expertise, but the power demands of Assam are as yet much below those of the middle Ganges plains. Bigger projects are also entangled in the same pricing arguments as between India and Nepal.

6.8.2 Other Options: Groundwater, Inter-basin Transfer, and Recycling

Groundwater is a further alternative to surface flow. The sediments of the Ganges basin form a giant sponge, usually with a water table near the surface, and also many other aquifers in different deposits at increasing depths. The near-surface water levels do vary throughout the year, but not by as much as the seasonality of rainfall would lead one to suppose. Often the variation is measured only in a few metres. Although it seems unlikely that ground water will supply enough water for mega-cities, it seems that there are adequate resources in most of the Ganges plains to meet other envisaged local levels of demand, but on three conditions. The first is that investment is provided for an adequate number of boreholes, and secondly that there are adequate energy supplies for the extraction required, and thirdly that the water is not contaminated, or only to the extent that modest treatment will render it of adequate quality for stipulated end uses. In broad terms cheap diesel engines can be used to lift water from near-surface sources, but electric submerged pumps are needed for deep tube-wells. If the power is derived from hydro-schemes there is a complex relationship between the building of dams and the pumping of groundwater. The one does not obviate the other.

Inter-basin transfers are common in the UK and in Pakistani Punjab. However, there is very little chance of transferring water into the Ganges basin from any other adjacent basin. The water in Indian Punjab is already fully committed. The only available water resource of the North Deccan is the Narmada River, which could only be accessed with massive and costly pumping schemes, and which is in any case already committed to a scheme to transfer water to Gujarat. There are specific problems of water shortages in Bengal during the dry season. This has led to a suggestion by India of a water transfer scheme, which would require international agreement, between the lower part of the Brahmaputra and the lower part of the Ganges. We will consider this scheme in more detail below.

Internationally the idea of water recycling is accepted. In India the National Commission on Urbanisation (1988) has stressed that it is imperative to consider the potential for water recycling. In its view, recycled water may be cheaper than developing new and distant sources to augment supply. It notes that Delhi discharges almost the same amount of water as its input supply – implying that there could be a substantial increase in supply by purifying the current effluents. This needs both investment and controls on the degree of contamination in the first place. This introduces the general questions about water quality.

6.9 Water Quality

There are many purposes for which water quality may be assessed. There is no generic test, which is suitable for all purposes.

The first aspect of water quality is turbidity, which means the load of solid sediment carried. Farmers like silty irrigation water because it brings an increase in fertility to their fields. Urban water suppliers and industrial users do not like silt, which can interfere with industrial processes, and block pipe systems. In addition to the solid load, these rivers carry a load of dissolved sediment. The natural dissolved load can increase fertility, but is also implicated in damaging agricultural land. When water is spread over riverine plains by canal irrigation systems it is usual for groundwater levels to rise. When the ground water table is near enough the surface that capillary action can suck water up to the surface, then the constant dampening of the surface combined with evaporation begins a process of salt accumulation, as dissolved sediment crystallises out. Salinisation can make the ground sterile, and is expensive to correct. Tube-wells which are drilled into the ground and which are powered by either electric or diesel pumps, can keep the water table low enough for the flow to be down through the soil rather than up. They can therefore be a defence against salinisation. The balance between all of these possible movements varies considerably from system to system, soil type to soil type, and the management of natural or artificial drainage, the unsung partner of irrigation. There are some places where surface canal systems should either be lined entirely (which is very expensive), or abandoned. There are other places where farmers want the canal systems to be leaky, to recharge groundwater as much as possible, because they are pumping so much through tube wells that the water table is falling.

Organic contamination of water is not normally a problem for agriculture; indeed water polluted with sewage may be beneficial. However, from the viewpoint of drinking and bathing, clearly it is good that water has no organic contamination. The usual measure of contamination is the biological oxygen demand. This is the amount of oxygen that is necessary in the water to degrade organic matter and render it harmless. The dissolved oxygen measure indicates how much oxygen is available. Oxygen uptake is affected by absorption at the water surface, which increases with tumbling water over stones or weirs, and by the growth of oxygenating plants in the rivers. In the GBM it is naturally higher in the monsoon season and lower when the river flows are low. This means that pollutant loads are more dilute in the monsoon season and more easily mitigated. The reverse is horribly evident near urban areas in the dry season.

The organic water quality of the Ganges and its major tributaries like the Yamuna also varies enormously along the length of the system. During the dry season the Yamuna at Delhi effectively becomes stagnant. The discharge into the river of untreated sewage is such that the river is totally deoxygenated and biologically dead for much of the year. Lower downstream it recovers to some extent, but major cities along the Ganga like Kanpur or Varanasi or Patna again add massive pollution loads of their own. Near Kanpur tanneries have put heavy metal contamination into the river (chromium). The poor quality of water in this most holy of rivers induced the Government of India to undertake the Ganga Action Plan, which was something of a political flagship for Rajiv Gandhi's 'modern' India. The extent, to which control of industrial effluent and the capture and treatment of sewage effluent has improved water quality, is a matter of debate.

Table 6.6: Biochemical Oxygen Demand of the Ganga at Selected Locations 1986-1997

BOD: mg/l – (milligrams per litre)
*Values (shown in **bold**) which exceed the acceptable limit of 3 mg/l show excessive pollution loads*

	1986	*1987*	*1988*	*1989*	*1990*	*1991*	*1992*	*1993*	*1994*	*1995*	*1996*	*1997*
Rishikesh	1.7	2.8	**3.4**	1.8	1.5	1.1	1.2	1.3	2.0	1.5	1.0	1.1
Hardwar	1.8	**3.9**	**3.5**	1.9	1.8	1.1	2.0	1.4	2.1	1.7	1.1	1.8
Garhmukteshwar	2.2	2.7	**4.9**	**4.5**	**3.4**	1.6	NA	1.6	2.4	2.4	1.5	1.5
Kannuj	**5.5**	2.7	2.2	1.0	2.6	NA	2.1	2.3	2.7	2.4	2.9	**3.4**
Kannuj	NA	**5.1**	**5.6**	1.1	**3.0**	**3.0**	2.7	2.5	**3.0**	**3.2**	**3.2**	**3.7**
Kanpur	7.2	2.9	1.8	1.1	2.7	1.5	1.7	1.9	5.0	2.0	2.8	3.1
Kanpur	**8.6**	**9.7**	**13.4**	**3.5**	**3.5**	**65.8**	**25**	**24.5**	**8.5**	**5.5**	**4.1**	**5.4**
Allahabad	**11.4**	**7.0**	2.8	2.6	2.6	2.3	2.0	1.8	2.3	**4.5**	2.5	**3.3**
Allahabad	**15.5**	**8.2**	3.1	2.3	2.0	1.7	1.9	1.9	**3.6**	**3.2**	**3.3**	2.4
Varanasi	**10.1**	**4.1**	**3.3**	**3.0**	2.6	1.2	0.9	0.8	1.8	2.6	2.2	**3.1**
Varanasi	**10.6**	**4.8**	**4.3**	**4.0**	**5.9**	1.9	1.3	1.0	2.9	1.4	2.3	2.0
Patna	2.0	1.9	2.0	0.4	0.3	1.4	1.2	1.2	1.6	1.5	2.0	1.3
Patna	2.2	2.1	2.2	0.4	0.3	0.9	1.6	1.5	1.6	1.4	1.6	1.4
Rajmahal	1.8	1.6	2.0	0.2	0.3	1.0	0.6	0.7	1.9	1.7	1.3	2.1
Palta	NA	1.0	1.3	1.0	0.9	0.8	1.0	0.9	2.5	2.1	1.6	2.4
Uluberia	NA	1.1	1.1	0.9	1.0	0.8	1.0	0.9	**3.2**	2.8	2.0	NA

Note: interpretation of this data is very difficult, because time of year (or averaging), time of day, sampling site across river etc, is not given. The overall impression, clearly intended, is that the clean Ganga campaign is having an effect.

(Source: Ninth Five Year Plan, http://planningcommision.nis.in/plans/vol2/v2a8htm)

One pattern to emerge quite clearly is that people from lower middle-income brackets and upwards accept the fact that public water supplies are unlikely ever to meet drinking standards. Private enterprise provides bottled distilled ('mineral') water, and ultra-violet irradiators, which can be fitted to domestic supplies to sterilise the incoming flow. These are health-preserving options, which are still beyond the budget of the poor. However, it does suggest that there may be many different levels of solutions to different kinds of water demands, and that the European norm of providing drinking-quality water for all purposes, even cleaning the car or watering the garden, is some kind of illogical abnormality.

6.10 Conflict over Water Resources in the GBM

Conflict over the use of water within the GBM occurs at every level from within the village to between the constituent nation states. In this last section I turn to some of the larger-scale geo-politics of the GBM. Within India, water is listed in the Constitution as a state subject, and is not on the list of central subjects, nor even on the list of concurrent subjects between centre and states. Every dry season at present there are riots in Haryana or Uttar Pradesh or Delhi, quite often accompanied by police firing and the deaths of protesters, over the allocation and abstraction of water from the Yamuna. [In the south there is an equally bitter and violent clash between Karnataka and Tamil Nadu over the waters of the Kaveri (Cauvery).] These are not events which get mentioned in the Nepali or Bangladesh press – even though clearly there has to be an implication for resource politics within the wider GBM.

Given these kinds of pressures, and the proportion of the GBM population that is resident on the plains of India, it is almost inevitable that the federal government of India will see its first interest in using whatever water resources are available for the perceived advantage of its own population. In addition to this factor, and no doubt better remembered by its neighbours than by itself, India has in the past used water as an international political pressure point on Pakistan. In 1948, following independence in 1947 and the disaster of Partition, India and Pakistan were locked in an undeclared war over Kashmir, the source of so much of Punjab's water. On April 1st 1948 India, alleging Pakistani intransigence over re-signing a standstill agreement, shut off the water flowing from the Firozpor (Ferozepore) headworks into Pakistan's Dipalpur Canal (Michel 1967). Eight percent of Pakistan's culturable command area (of the country, not just of this scheme) was deprived of water; so too was the city of Lahore. In addition hydroelectric power supplies were cut. Observers flying over the two Punjabs had no doubt where the border lay: to one side the seedlings of the new kharif crops were ready for the monsoon, to the other was a brown and barren land. India claimed that the waters in the rivers originating in her territory were hers, something that had never been suggested in the Radcliffe award, which demarcated the new borders in Punjab and Bengal. Indeed, Radcliffe could see no hope but for the schemes spreading over the two halves of Punjab to be managed cooperatively as an integrated whole as suggested by (Coupland 1943 Pt III: 86). The flow was later restored pending the negotiation of the Indus Waters Treaty (1960), which, with American financial backing, provided for the complete severance of the integrated schemes into two independent halves. It was a kind of vivisection, necessary because of political hostility.

There are a myriad of trans-border problems in Bengal between India and Bangladesh, about environmental management connected with flow augmentation, river training, flood prevention, and the minimisation of saline bores. However, there is one headline issue, which dominates all others, the Farakka barrage built in India on the Ganges just upstream of the Bangladesh border. It is this project, which we examine here.

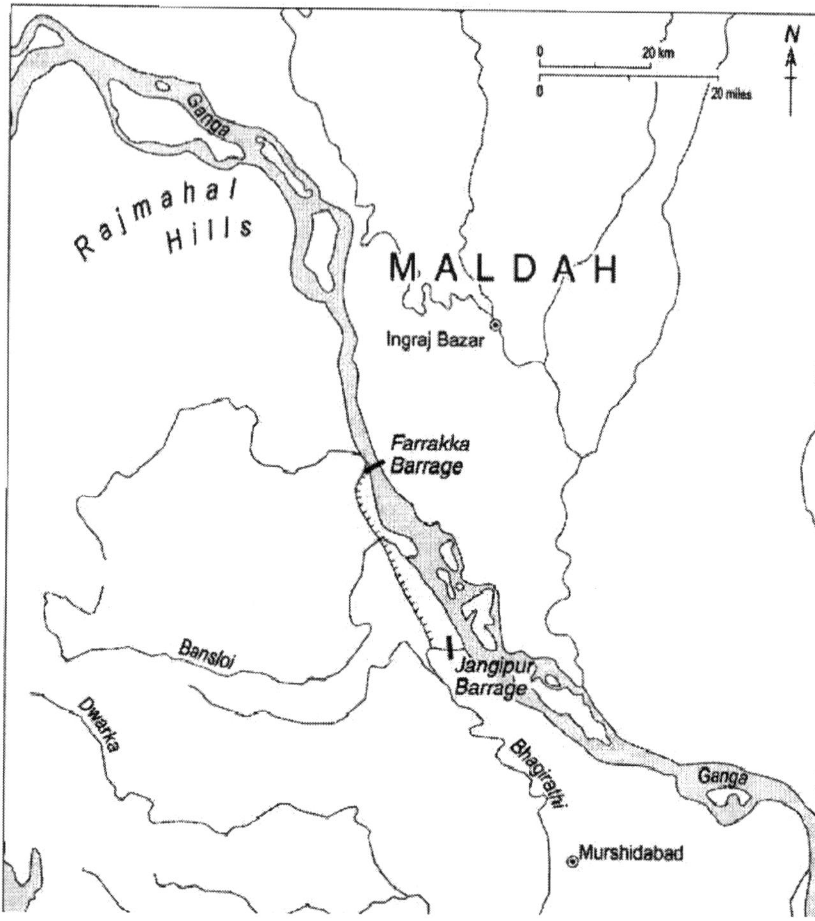

Figure 6.4: The Bhagirathi Feeder Canal at Farakka

Because the Bengal delta is so active, the geomorphology and hydrology of the area is constantly changing. Very roughly speaking, since the British first established their ocean port city of Calcutta 120 miles up the Hugli, one of the western distributaries, the flow of the rivers has been shifting more and more to the eastern distributaries. The mouths of the western distributaries are now known as the moribund delta – here the mangrove forests are thick. The eastern shore is very different, with bald new islands emerging from beneath the seas.

Calcutta was for long India's largest and most important port and manufacturing centre. It is still overwhelmingly the most important port for the whole of east and northeast India. Its population, for the urban agglomeration, is given as more than 13 million in the 2001 Census. Since its foundation, whether or not the port can maintain good communications with the open sea has been a matter of prime economic and strategic concern. So, whether the navigability of the Hugli to the sea has been deteriorating over time or not, has been a matter of anxiety and observation for much more than the last century. In all this time that the anxiety has been expressed, and the experts have delivered their reports, there has been neither an unambiguous nor a unanimous conclusion about exactly how the condition of the river is changing. As a 'minor' distributary in the delta it has stretches where shoals form, and the navigable channel can get too shallow. For many decades dredging has been used to deepen the channels where necessary. But this does not constitute unambiguous evidence. Over time, sea-faring ships have got bigger, and their draughts deeper. And, as in any river, shoals can shift from place to place.

Table 6.7: Use of Ganges Water: Flow at Farakka (in millions m^3)

	Dry Season	**Wet Season**	**Total (November to May)**
Total Flow	61,674	397,181	458,855
Requirements			
Bangladesh	51,806	7,400	59,207
India	20,969	14,801	37,004
Nepal	not calculated	not calculated	37,000
Excess/deficit	-11,101	374,978	325,639

(Source: recalculated from Abbas 1982)

An 'obvious' tempting solution is to build a barrage across the Ganges, to divert low-season flow down the Bhagirathi-Hugli to 'flush' the river. The barrage at Farakka in India was conceived to do just this when Bangladesh was East Pakistan. No consultation took place with East Pakistan over the proposal. The barrage also had and still has a strategic significance, replacing a lost bridging point (the Hardinge Bridge in Bangladesh) between Calcutta and Assam.

Thus the barrage has been built, even though the answers to the following questions cannot be given unambiguously:

1. has the discharge of the Bhagirathi linking the Ganges to the Hugli (Hooghly) been declining over time, particularly in the low season?
2. have tidal bores increased in the Hugli, bringing greater salinity further north?
3. do tidal bores bring greater sedimentation with them?
4. will augmentation of the fresh water flow in the Hugli 'flush' the port of Calcutta and keep the Hugli open?

5. will it be cheaper than other options (e.g. new ports downstream or more dredging)?
6. what impact will water abstraction have downstream of the barrage in East Pakistan/Bangladesh?

A public announcement was made of the intention to build the barrage in 1961, and the project was completed by 1975. It can take up to 40,000ft^3/s from the Ganges, which at some periods of the dry season in low rainfall years is almost a majority of the flow. From the Bangladesh viewpoint the diversion of water in the dry (low-water) season has a number of deleterious effects. Those most commonly cited are a loss of water for irrigation and urban use. Over the last few decades, as population has grown fast and the green revolution has taken off, the demand for good irrigation water from the rivers has grown substantially. In Bangladesh the reduced low season flow also allows saline bores to penetrate much further upstream in many rivers than hitherto, again reducing irrigation potential, and also possibly harming ground water. Table 6.7 shows the figures given by Abbas (1982), to demonstrate that there is already a deficit in the dry season, without taking into account the future needs as population increases and development occurs in the region, in particular increasing demands for irrigation water upstream in the Ganges plains. The government of, first Pakistan, and then Bangladesh, as the downstream and smaller party, has struggled to sign a treaty for the equitable sharing of the Ganges. Crow (1995) divides the history of negotiation into four phases. (i) From 1951 to 1971 the project was discussed and planned. Pakistan protested but was impotent. (ii) From 1971 to 1975 the barrage was built and implemented, without international agreement: attempts were made to sign a treaty sharing the waters between India and Bangladesh, but failed. (iii) In 1977 a short-term agreement was signed between India and Bangladesh over the allocation of low season flows, running for five years. During this time it was imagined that the negotiation would broaden to encompass not just the Ganges but water sharing in the whole delta. The idea was for international co-operation in the management of both the Brahmaputra and the Ganges-which would enable water from the former to augment the latter. This would have been a westward shift of water a bit reminiscent of the eastward shift of water in the Punjab in 1905. But the Indus Waters Treaty of 1960 severed the scheme along the lines of political sovereignty. Bengal is now divided along lines of political sovereignty, and yet they were proposing to run an integrated scheme regardless of these borders. In the event there has been serious difficulty in reaching an agreement, hence there have been a number of ad-hoc extensions of the 1977 agreement in the form of Memoranda of Understanding (MOU) pending a new 'final' solution. (iv) From 1983 the emerging 'reality' is that a treaty dividing permanently all the waters of all the common rivers of Bengal will enable both countries to develop 'their' share on their own territory as they best see fit. This then replicates the 'reality' of what happened in Punjab over the Indus Waters.

Stage (iv) has not been completed. The MOU ran out, although its provisions continued to be respected. But the core issue of Farakka has, for the time being, apparently been settled. In 1996 India and Bangladesh signed a Ganges Water Treaty, for the sharing of water at Farakka. The new arrangement is as follows: if the Ganges flow at Farakka is 70,000ft^3/s or less, both countries are to receive 50 per cent; with a flow of between 70,000 and 75,000ft^3/s Bangladesh receives 35,000ft^3/s and India receives the rest; with a flow of more than 75,000ft^3/s or more India receives 40,000ft^3/s and Bangladesh receives the rest. Further provision is made for the situation where the flow falls below 50,000ft^3/s, but this is much less clear.

In the first year following the treaty itself, the dry season of 1997, the inflow hit a low of 46,000ft^3/s raising a question mark on sharing. No one knew who under the treaty would sort out the 'special' situation. Calcutta got its share of 35,000ft^3/s for 10 days and stood to get just 11,000ft^3/s for the next 10 days. Then common sense prevailed, and each got 50 per cent of the flow. This amount did not satisfy the Calcutta Port Authorities. At this level of flow they predict that Calcutta will silt up and the port die. There are other ways of increasing the low season flow – through storage dams in the catchment – and diverting water from the Brahmaputra.

Figures 6.5 and 6.6 broadly summarise the conflicting strategies of Bangladesh and India in the early 1980s. Bangladesh wanted many storage dams in the Ganges basin, the biggest on the Nepalese border, to augment the low season flow during phase (iii) identified above. (It would also allow a new navigation canal to link the new port of Mongla with Nepal, though crossing a neck of Indian land.) At various stages Bangladesh attempted to initiate tri-lateral talks with all three countries, although India resisted, insisting that it would be the vehicle through which the downstream-upstream issues could be discussed. The Indian proposal was to augment the flow at Farakka by diverting flow from the Brahmaputra. This is the inter-basin transfer noted above, which would involve a canal half a mile wide right across Bangladeshi territory, with both of the significant control points in Indian hands. This was and still is unacceptable to the Bangladeshis.

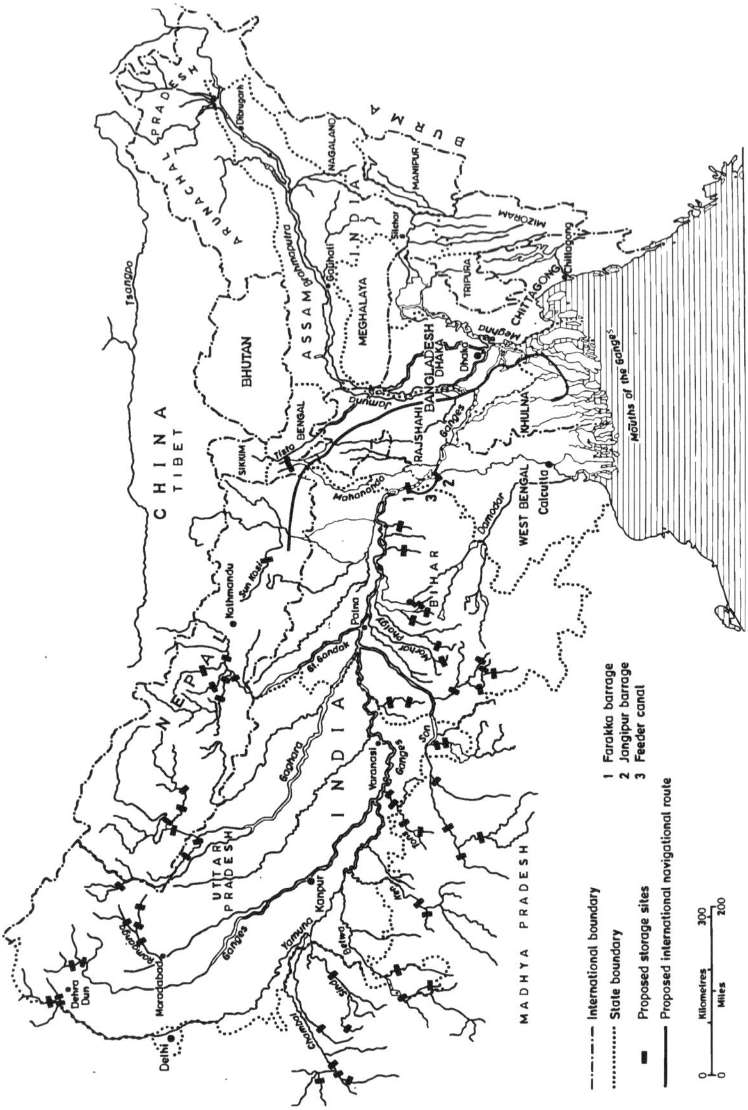

Figure 6.5: A Bangladeshi Proposal for Augmenting Low Season Flow.

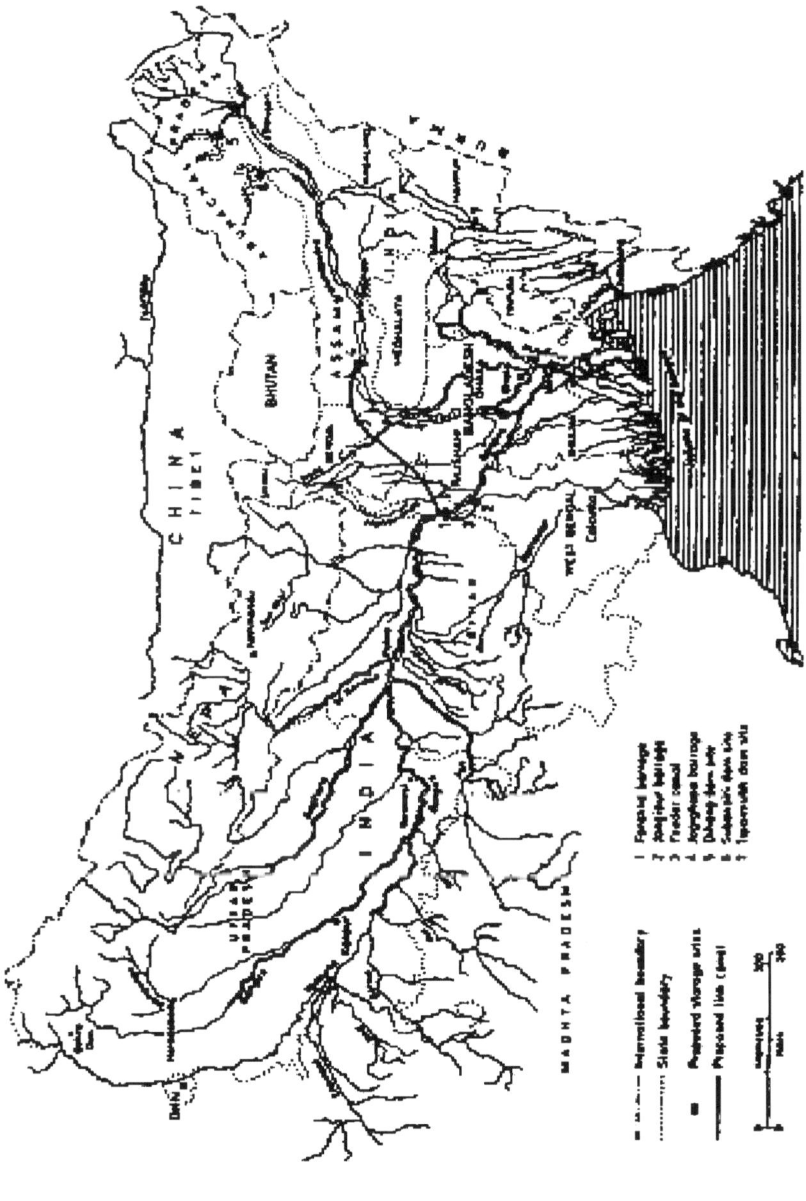

Figure 6.6: The Indian Proposal for Inter-basin Transfer

6.11 Conclusion

The GBM is a huge region, which embraces many great rivers with highly seasonal flow characteristics. The area is also the home to a very great percentage of the world's population, albeit one of the world's poorest and most deprived segments. The management of development, of water supply to town and country, of flood, of drought, of erosion, even locally, is complicated, paradoxical and ambiguous.

At the scale of the whole GBM basin, the management of development, of water supply to town and country, of flood, of drought, of erosion, is beyond rational observation and rational calculation. If any expert group wielded sufficient power, like once the Politburo did in the USSR, to attempt a basin-wide management scheme, they would almost certainly come up with mega-projects that would be economically and environmentally disastrous, and because of that, never actually completed.

An alternative extreme is complete laissez-faire of all individuals and parties, with no regulation and no planning, allowing economic markets to dictate outcomes. The problem with this kind of Adam Smith hidden hand is that economics takes no account of the externalised environmental costs of development, and, for example, has nothing to say about the pollution of the Ganges when tannery owners are creating wealth and employing people. Nor does it have anything to say about saline intrusions into Bangladeshi rivers if low season flows are diverted down the Bhagirathi. Nor does it have anything to say about the intrinsic value of biodiversity in the rivers, nor the expectation of being able to bathe in the Sangam without risk to health.

As a third-way, a rights-based approach to management has its attractions. Rights and duties presumably can be enshrined within legal systems, but the complexity of the issues here is daunting. Do downstream farmers have the right to sue upstream irrigators if the frequency of flooding and fine-silt deposition *lessens*? Do downstream farmers have the right to sue the owners of dams for reducing the flux of silt? Should irrigation departments have the right to zone land within a command area for water-intensive or water-conservative crops? When ground water levels change and cause an accompanying change in levels of *natural* heavy metal contamination, who sues whom for what? So much of what can be thought of as right or wrong depends on ephemeral ideas about ephemeral technologies and ephemeral political and economic trends.

In the end, the over-riding factors are likely to be political. Never before in its history has Bengal been divided into separate polities. It is one ecosystem, with one culture and one language. But it has been divided because for the first time in its history in 1947 people were given the chance for self-determination. With classic myopia, the idea of being Bengali was taken for granted, and the idea of self turned on local difference. So 'self' in Bengal rested on the idea of religious community. But, if the reader follows through the above account of Farakka, it is clear that this '*new conception of self in a new political system, not the technologists' plan, is the defining moment allowing and requiring the construction of the Farakka barrage*'.

So it will be with other major GBM issues. It will be the idea of self-interest within weak democracies that defines what happens. Already the problems over the mega dams in the Nepalese mountains are credited with putting the kingdom's fledgling democratic institutions under intolerable strain.

One thing is certain. The introduction to this chapter outlined the long-term dynamic nature and the huge scale of the fundamental forces at work in this region. Heterogeneous human society comprised of individuals with microscopically short life spans is unlikely ever to produce the kind of consensus of knowledge, values and aspiration to 'manage' the GBM in any comprehensive sense. Thus, I conclude that implementable legal frameworks will have to tread a path of acute local political sensitivity.

References

Abbas, B.M. (1982) *The Ganges Water Dispute*, New Delhi.

Arora, V.K. and Boer, G.J. (2002) 'The effects of simulated climate change on the hydrology of major river basins' available at http://www.cccma.bc.ec.gc.ca/~varora/papers/impact_report_for_wgne.pdf.

Brammer, H. (2000) 'Flood Hazard Vulnerability and Flood Disasters in Bangladesh' Ch. 6 pp 100-115 in Parker, D.J. (ed.).

Carson, B. (1985) 'Erosion and Sedimentation Processes in the Nepalese Himalayan', *ICIMOD Occasional paper*, No. 1, Kathmandu.

Chapman, G.P. (1983) 'Underperformance in Indian Irrigation Systems: the Problems of Diagnosis and Prescription' *Geoforum* Vol. 14 no 3 pp.267-275.

Chapman, G.P. (1999) 'Water and the Urban Future of the Ganges Plains' Ch. 25, pp. 444-454 in Chapman, G.P., Dutt, A.K. and Bradnock, R.W. (eds.).

Chapman, G.P. (2000 and 2003) *The Geopolitics of South Asia: from Early Empires to the Nuclear Age*, Ashgate, Aldershot.

Chapman, G.P. and Rudra, K. (2002) 'Bengal's Millennium Flood', *MSS* pp.44, Dept. of Geography, Lancaster University.

Chapman, G.P. and Thompson, M. (eds.) (1995) *Water and the Quest for Sustainable Development in the Ganges Valley*, Cassell, London.

Chapman, G.P., Dutt, A.K. and Bradnock, R.W. (eds) (1999) *Urban growth and Development in Asia: Vol. I: Making the Cities*, Ashgate Publishing, Aldershot UK.

Coupland, R. (1943), *Report on the Constitutional Problem in India, Pt III The Future of India*, Oxford University Press.

Crow, B., Lundquist, A. and Wilson, D. (1995) *Sharing the Ganges: the Politics and Technology of River Development*, Sage, New Delhi.

Fauceys, R. (1992) 'Domestic Water Use: Engineering, Effectiveness and Sustainability' in ODA (1992).

GOI (1988) 'Water and Sanitation' Chapter 14 pp 293-301 in *Government of India: Report of the National Commission on Urbanization,* Vol. II, New Delhi.

Govardhan, V. (1993) *Environmental Impact Assessment of the Tehri* Dam, Ashish Publishing, New Delhi.

Hofer, T. and Messerli, B. (1997) *Floods in Bangladesh: Process Understanding and Development Strategies*, Institute of Geography, University of Berne, Switzerland.

Michel, A.A. (1967) *The Indus Rivers: A Study in the Effects of Partition*, Yale University Press, New Haven and London, p. 595.

Nijssen, B., O'Donnell, G., Lettenmeier Dennis P., Lohman, D. and Wood, E.F. (2000) 'Predicting the discharge of global rivers', *Journal of Climate Change.*

ODA (1992) *Proceedings of the Conference on Priorities for Water Resources Allocation and Management Natural resource Engineering Advisors'*

Conference, Southampton July 1992, Overseas Development Administration, London.

Parker, D.J. (ed.) (2000) *Floods*, Vols. I and II Routledge, London and New York.

Rasheed, S. (1995) 'Nepal's Water Resources: The Potential for Exploitation in the Upper Ganges Catchment' Chapter 5 in Chapman, G.P. and Thompson, M. (eds.).

Subba, Bhim (2001) *Himalayan Waters: Promise and Potential: Problems and Politics*, Panos South Asia, Kathmandu.

Thompson, M. (1995) 'Disputed Facts: A Countervailing View from the Hills' Chapter 6 in Chapman, G.P. and Thompson, M. (eds.).

Verghese, B.G. (1990) *Waters of hope: integrated water resource development and regional cooperation within the Himalayan-Ganga-Brahmaputra-Barak Basin*, New Delhi: Centre for Policy Research.

Acknowledgements

I am grateful for the cooperation of research colleagues Dr Emma Tomalin and Mr Julian Crandall Hollick. I am grateful for financial support to attend the conference in Middlesex University, provided by Independent Broadcasting Associates Inc.

PART III:

COMPARATIVE PERSPECTIVES: EXPERIENCE OF OTHER REGIONS

Chapter 7

The Evolution of the Regime for the River Rhine

André Nollkaemper[1]

7.1 Introduction

In the last decades, the riparian states of the River Rhine have attempted to achieve nothing short of a miracle: the return of healthy runs of salmon in the River Rhine. The return of the salmon should symbolise the fundamental transformation from the historically prevailing situation where the river was free for all, to a situation in which riparian states accept limitations on their uses for the purpose of ecosystem protection.

This transformation finds its origin in 1986, when an accident in the Sandoz factory near Basel, Switzerland, caused a massive escape of chemicals into the Rhine.[2] In an overnight moment of enlightenment, the ministers responsible realised their historic failure to manage the Rhine properly. They adopted the ambitious Rhine Action Program that was to end the history of the over-development of the Rhine basin and to rehabilitate the ecosystem of the river. Riparian states now attempted to undo 'the wrongs caused by earlier generations doing what they thought was right'.[3]

What ensued was a paradigm shift. The riparian states sought to end the era of the free development of the basin, legitimised by legal doctrines of free apportionment and optimum use. They also aimed for the end of the period of fragmented and ineffective attempts to regulate few individual pollutants witnessed in the seventies and early eighties. Increasingly, the law was to be based on, and sought to contribute to, ecologically sustainable development of the Rhine basin. The Rhine water that has been used to bolster urban and agriculture development is

---

[1] This chapter is an expanded and updated version of 'The River Rhine: from Equal Apportionment to Ecosystem Protection' published in 5 *Review of European Community & International Environmental Law* (1996) [152]-[160].

[2] See H.U.J. d'Oliveira 'The Sandoz Blaze: The Damage and the Public and Private Liabilities' in F. Francioni and T. Scovazzi (eds.) *International Responsibility for Environmental Harm* (Graham and Trotman 1991) [429]-[445].

[3] Quoted from M. Reisner *Cadillac Desert. The American West and Its Disappearing Water*, (Revised edn Viking Penguin New York 1993) – making this observation with regard to comparable developments in water policy in the United States.

now to be a component of the maintenance of the ecosystem of the river basin. This legal development has found its temporary conclusion in the signing of the 1999 Convention on the Protection of the Rhine.[4] The riparian states attempted to draft a modern convention that would function as a role model in international water management.[5] In several respects it has succeeded in doing so.

This Chapter examines the model of the regime for the Rhine River. It is divided into the following sections: Sections 7.2 and 7.3 contain an overview of the development of the Rhine basin and the traditional liberties of international water law; Sections 7.4 and 7.5 discuss recent developments in the management of the river pertaining to pollution control and ecosystem protection respectively and Section 7.6 examines the legal translation of these developments in the 1999 Convention and related instruments.

7.2 Development of the Rhine Basin[6]

With a length of 1,248km, the Rhine is the longest river in Western Europe. It is the only Alpine river that drains into the North Sea. A fan of tributaries drains a 325km span of the Alps, from Lake Geneva eastwards into Austria. The main stream flows through Switzerland, France, Germany and the Netherlands. Its tributaries run through Austria, Liechtenstein, Luxembourg and Belgium. One cannot talk about the Rhine as a river – it is a river system or a drainage basin in the true sense of these terms.

Before the Middle Ages, the Rhine was a healthy, free, wildly meandering Alpine river. Since the early Middle Ages, man made its presence felt through dams, dikes, locks and pollution. Major drainage and channelling works that transformed it from natural state to a human vision of what it ought to be like were completed on the Rhine in the eighteenth and nineteenth centuries. Dikes limited the flood plains, to protect villages built on shifting riverbanks and farmers who had converted river meadows to arable fields. The 'new' Rhine was also to become more convenient for navigators. Further work made the upper Rhine accessible for navigation and made the river take the shortest path to sea.

These modifications achieved their purposes as perceived at the time. They paved the way for the booming industrial cities along the Rhine in the nineteenth and twentieth centuries. The drainage basin of the Rhine now covers the highest

---

[4] Convention on the Protection of the Rhine, signed on 12 April 1999 in Bern, reproduced as Annex to the Proposal for a Council Decision concerning the Conclusion, on behalf of the Community, of the new Convention for the Protection of the Rhine, COM(2000) 6 final.

[5] Conference of Rhine Ministers, *State of the Rhine, yesterday – today – tomorrow*, 29 January 2001, Strasbourg at <http://www.iksr.org/Zustand%20des%20Rheins%20e.doc>; Letter from the Minister for Foreign Affairs of the Netherlands submitted in connection with the approval of the Convention by Parliament, K. I/II 2000-2001, 27511, nr. 114 and 1 [1]

[6] This section is in part based on T.H. Elkins 'The Rhine Basin: A Geographical Introduction' in *Regional Management of the Rhine. Papers of a Chatham House Study Group* (Chatham House London 1975) [7]; and F. Pearce *The Damned. Rivers, dams and the coming of the world water crises* (The Bodley Head London 1992) [36]-[40].

concentration of industry of all rivers and links directly or indirectly, for example, Ludwigshafen, Mannheim, Frankfurt, Köln, the Ruhr area and Rotterdam. The river is also a source of drinking water for about 20 million people along the Rhine. The river became one of the underpinnings of the economy of Western Europe.

These benefits, however, came with a price: in the form of floods, pollution and the loss of the ecosystem. The reconstruction works carried out in the nineteenth and twentieth centuries reduced the length of the river by about 100km and more than halved the time taken for the peak of the winter flood to flow from the Alps to the Netherlands. Today, with 90 percent of the natural flood plain of the Rhine cut off from the river behind dikes; the river is more prone to flooding than it ever has been.[7] The major floods in 1993-1994 and 1994-1995, when hundreds of thousands of people in Germany and the Netherlands were forced out of their homes, were largely man-made.

The channelling of the river also degraded the ecosystem. The high flow velocity scoured the river bed drop and lowered the water-table in the alluvium along the flood plain: for several kilometres on either side of the river, fields and ancient forests of oak and elm and willow dried out.[8] The pre-existing eco-system of the Rhine is gone. The upper Rhine of today is an almost entirely engineered channel with giant locks and a series of hydroelectric plants. The construction of dikes and the straightening of the river's course have cut off meanders, tributaries and river-meadows. Many animals and plants formerly living in the Rhine basin have either reduced in number or disappeared altogether. The most greatly affected victims were the migratory fish that once populated the Rhine. Effects of over-fishing were temporary and could have been reversed; the effects of dams, weirs and locks are permanent. The adaptation of the river destroyed resting places and spawning grounds. In 1885, the number of salmon caught in Germany and the Netherlands was about 250,000; by the 1940s the species was extinct.[9]

Pollution of the Rhine contributed to the degradation of the ecosystem. Power plants, industries, households, farmers and drinking water companies took water from the river and returned it after having added heavy metals, pesticides, heat, nitrogen and other undesirable elements. The effects of pollution on the ecosystem became worse since the river had been cut off from its natural cleansing mechanisms. Marshlands, swamps and gravel beds have been reclaimed and can no longer filter the waters. The situation reached its nadir in the mid-seventies when the river was cut off from its surrounding ecosystems, migration routes for fish were blocked, and the river became an open sewer. The ecosystem of the river was virtually dead.

---

[7] F. Pearce *The Damned. Rivers, Dams and the Coming of the World Water Crises* (The Bodley Head London 1992) [36]-[40].
[8] ibid.
[9] International Commission for the Protection of the Rhine against Pollution *Ecological Master Plan for the Rhine 'Salmon 2000'* 3 (1991) Koblenz.

7.3 The Liberties of International Water Law

International law did little to prevent all this. The historic function of international law applicable to the Rhine was to protect the objective of optimum development – as defined at the time by the riparian states. The law allowed and facilitated the destruction of the ecological integrity of the Rhine. Riparian states did not approve of all development projects carried out by other riparians, but the small conflicts that emerged undermined no State's fundamental freedom to use the Rhine. The 1886 Salmon Treaty[10] ended the Netherlands' practice of taking most of the salmon before they started their run upstream. The 1925 Franco-German frontier treaty recognised that the polluting effects of industrialisation and agricultural activities had to be controlled,[11] yet, to the same extent that the former treaty failed to save the salmon, so did the latter treaty fail to reduce pollution.

While documented statements of any principle underlying the behaviour of the riparian states are rare, it would seem that for centuries the use of the Rhine was governed by the principle of equal apportionment. This principle, deeply entrenched in international water law, holds that each riparian state has an equal right to use the river. In the event of a conflict of interests, this principle is accompanied by the indeterminate sharing rule known as the principle of equitable use. For most of the history such rules of sharing appeared not to play an explicit role. Legal rules that put limits to the equal (in practice: free) use of the river were few and far between. There were, for instance, no laws that designated salmon as an endangered species and thus that could have halted some of the development projects. Similarly, until the mid-seventies there were no legal rules banning the use of the water as a dumping medium for mercury, cadmium and other harmful substances.

7.4 Development of Laws for the Prevention of Pollution

Concern on the part of the Netherlands and Germany about the effects of pollution on human health and agricultural interests provided the stimulus for a revision of the regime for the Rhine that only now, fifty years later, has stated to show its true benefits for the river. In 1950, the riparian states created the informal International Commission for the Protection of the Rhine against Pollution (hereafter: ICPR) that was to study the causes and effects of pollution. In 1963, they concluded a treaty to formalise the ICPR and endowed it with a permanent secretariat.[12] 'The history of international legal developments relating to the continued pollution of

---

[10] Legislative Series of the Netherlands, Stb. 1886 No. 118.

[11] Reproduced in UN Doc. ST/LEG/SER.B/12 [657]-[658].

[12] Agreement on the International Commission for the protection of the Rhine against pollution (Bern 29 April 1963) 994 UNTS 3.

the river Rhine, as that has proceeded since the existence of the ICPR has been told and retold.'[13] Here only the main recent developments are discussed.

7.4.1 The 'Definite Solution' for the Salinisation Problem

Salinisation of the Rhine has been the main source of disputes between the riparian states. Chlorides are discharged from many small and a few large sources in all riparian states. The largest contributions (between one third and one half) originate from the *Mines Domaniales de Potasse d'Alsace* (MDPA) in France. The salinisation harms German and the Netherlands' drinking water interests and agriculture and horticulture in the Netherlands, as well as contributing to the pollution of the sediment in the port of Rotterdam. Because of apparent difficulties in controlling small sources, regulatory efforts have attempted to get the MDPA to reduce its discharges.

The issue of chlorides problem illustrates how difficult it has been for riparian States to agree that certain uses of the river are illegal. The Netherlands first introduced the issue in negotiations in 1946. It took thirty years to agree on the 1976 Convention on the Protection of the Rhine caused by Chlorides.[14] This treaty only minimally reduced chlorides loads. It took another 15 years to agree on further steps to reduce salinisation. In 1991, the riparian states signed the Additional Protocol to the 1976 Convention. The Protocol entered into force in 1994. This agreement appears to have solved the problem to the satisfaction of the states; the Netherlands accepted the protocol as the 'definite solution' to the problem.[15]

The Protocol's solution consisted of two parts. First, the French mines are to stop discharges once the chloride concentration gets above 200mg/l. The remainder of the salt is temporarily to be stored on land.[16] The Protocol envisaged that in 1998, the first mines would close and the production of salt would decrease. After a reduction in salt production, the salt that was stored on land could, under certain conditions, as yet be dumped in the Rhine.[17] Second, the Netherlands would reduce the salt-concentration of the IJsselmeer (a major source of drinking water) by discharging the salt seepage water from the Wieringermeer polder into the Wadden Sea, rather than, as was previous practice, into the IJsselmeer. This would accelerate the reductions that are necessary upstream. The riparian states

[13] e.g. J.G. Lammers *Pollution of international watercourses: a search for substantive rules and principles of law* (Nijhoff Publishers The Hague 1984) [166ff]; see also 'The Rhine: Legal Aspects of the Management of a Transboundary River' in W. Verwey (ed.) *Nature Management and Sustainable Development* (IOS Press 1989) [440]-[457].

[14] Convention on the Protection of the Rhine by chlorides 16 ILM [265].

[15] Dutch Treaty Series 'Protocole additionel à la Convention relative à la protection du Rhin contre la pollution par les chlorides' 25 September 1991 Brussels, reproduced in French in Trb. 1992 [3].

[16] Article 1(1).

[17] Article 2.

apparently appear to consider this to be a more cost-effective and probably also a more equitable solution than exclusive reliance on reductions in France. The costs of both parts of the Protocol were to be allocated in conformity with the formula of the 1976 Chlorides Convention: Germany, the Netherlands and Switzerland pay respectively, 30, 34 and 6 per cent.[18] Note that the Netherlands not only contributes to the storage of the salt after 1991, but has also agreed to pay for the dumping of salt into the Rhine after 1998. This is remarkable given that the Protocol will not guarantee safe drinking water: after the conclusion of the Protocol, the Netherlands Government estimated that the threshold of 200mg/l would be exceeded 26 per cent of the time.[19]

The fundamental international legal questions underlying the chlorides problem are complex. Salinisation in the Netherlands arises only from upstream discharges. The natural background concentration of salt is extremely high due both to the seepage of sea water and to the Netherlands' policy of maintaining a deep, open connection with the North Sea. Fresh water with a low salt concentration is essential in compensating for the consequences of that policy and in making the Rhine useful for agriculture and drinking water. The question is whether under international law a natural salt concentration, which is deliberately kept high, is to be taken into account by upstream states. The solution chosen suggests that the riparian states answer this question in the affirmative, and consider that this legitimises calls for compensation by the Netherlands in its role as a downstream state. The Additional Protocol does not support the construction that often has been propagated: that significant upstream pollution is *per definition* inequitable and thus unlawful.[20]

Some members of Parliament of the Netherlands expressed misgivings about the solution and argued that the Additional Protocol violates the 'polluter pays' principle. The Netherlands Government disagreed. Without discussing the legal status of the principle, it considered that the Additional Protocol does conform to the 'polluter pays' principle.[21] This position may be contrasted with its own views in 1967. At that time, the Netherlands strongly objected to the idea that she should contribute to the cleansing of the water of the Rhine and took the view that 'no country may permit itself to pollute water which flow to countries downstream in such a way it causes a nuisance'.[22] However, at what may be the end of an almost 50 year process, neither the Netherlands nor any other riparian state aspired to deal

[18] Article 4.

[19] TK 1992-1993, 22 971 nr. 5 [3].

[20] S.C. McCaffrey 'The Law of International Watercourses: Some Recent Developments and Unanswered Questions' 17 *Denver JIL & Policy* (1989) [505]-[526]. See further discussion in A. Nollkaemper 'The Contribution of the International Law Commission to International Water Law: Does it Reverse the Flight from Substance?' in 27 *Netherlands Yearbook of International Law* (1996) [39]-[73].

[21] K. II 1992-1993, 22971 nr 5 [3].

[22] Bijl. Hand. II 1967/68-7884 No. 5 [7] (translation in J.G. Lammers 'International Cooperation for the Protection of the Waters of the River Rhine Against Pollution' 5 *Netherlands Yearbook of International Law* 1974 [59]-[110]).

with the issue in doctrinal terms. All states appeared happy to close the dossier in the thought that they had reached a pragmatic and definite solution.

The solution provided for by the 1991 Protocol has largely been implemented. In the period between 1991 and 1998, France stored 960,000 tons of chlorides on land. This is only about 20 per cent of the amount that had been envisaged in 1991, mainly due to the relatively high volume of river flows. In recent years, the norm of 200mg/l at the German-Dutch border was only rarely exceeded.[23] The Netherlands, furthermore, implemented its part in discharging the salt seepage water from the Wieringermeer polder into the Wadden Sea.[24] The financial arrangements have not been solved entirely to the satisfaction of the riparian states, however, and have been submitted by the Netherlands and France for arbitration.[25] The case concerned a conflict concerning the interpretation of Article 4.2.1. Annex III of the Protocol concerning financial modalities. Both France and the Netherlands proposed a method of auditing with respect to the storing of waste salt in France. The Tribunal, after taking into consideration the various instruments of treaty interpretation as embodied in the VCLT, decided in favour of the Dutch proposition to audit on the basis of flat-rate amount rather than on the basis of real cost units, as proposed by France.

7.4.2 The Problems of Chemical Pollution and Nutrients

The Rhine was always prone to falling victim to pollution by chemicals and other undesired substances due to the concentration of industry and agriculture near the river. Direct discharges and accidents have taken a severe toll on the river. Agriculture contributes to pesticides and nutrients. While these problems have not created as much controversy as the chlorides issue, a satisfactory legal solution has proven difficult to achieve – partly because of the economic interests underlying the emissions, and also of the fact that emissions from such a wide variety of sources are notoriously difficult to control.

The Netherlands put chemical pollution on the agenda of the International Rhine Commission in the early seventies.[26] In 1976 this led to the adoption of the Chemical Pollution Convention.[27] However, it soon became clear that this treaty was a regulatory failure. The Convention envisaged development of limit values for individual 'black list' substances. Few of such limit values were established, because there existed too intricate a mix of scientific uncertainty (the Convention failed to specify limits in influencing the regulation of a substance), competitiveness concerns (Germany preferred to regulate industries in the

---

[23] RIVM Bouwstenen foor het NMP4 (2001) [20].

[24] ibid.

[25] The case is listed on http://pca-cpa.org/RPC/#Netherlands/France.

[26] J.G. Lammers 'International Cooperation for the Protection of the Waters of the River Rhine against Pollution' 5 *Netherlands Yearbook of International Law* 1974 [59]-[110].

[27] Convention on the Protection of the Rhine against Chemical Pollution 16 *ILM* 242 (1976).

European Community) and a lack of political will. When the 8th Ministerial Conference adopted the Rhine Action Programme (RAP) in 1987, the Chemical Pollution Convention was virtually a dead letter. Devoid of practical relevance, it survived until the entry into force of the 1999 Convention.

The RAP, a non-legally binding document, proved to be much more effective. Indeed, it is probably was the most successful instrument in the history of the Rhine. In addition to measures to improve the physical and biological condition of the river (see below), the RAP aimed to reduce pollution by, initially, 27 identified priority substances. It achieved its best record with regard to point sources. Riparian states were to prescribe state of the art technology for the responsible industries 'with a view to reducing drastically (by around 50 per cent) the total quantity of discharges of priority substances between 1985 and 1995'.[28] When the 11th Ministerial Conference evaluated progress in 1994, it could with satisfaction note that for about two-thirds of the priority substances, this target had been achieved. In 2001, the ICPR could note that, for instance, emissions of trichloromethane, chloroaniline and AOX had been reduced by more than 90 per cent.[29] While it cannot be ascertained whether this is due to the spirit of the times, to social and political pressures, or indeed to the RAP, the fact remains that the quality of the water of the Rhine has improved dramatically over the past decade. The results of the pollution era will long be felt, though. Decades of pollution are clenched in sediments that pose a continuing threat to the ecosystem. Sediments polluted with PCBs, lindane and hexachlorbenzol can only with great difficulty and at great cost be cleansed.

A range of other (diffuse) sources of pollution proved more difficult to tackle, particularly those from agricultural uses. The 1976 Rhine Chemical Pollution Convention failed completely to address diffuse sources. The RAP did indeed recognise the problem,[30] but prescribed neither specific nor demanding measures. The 2001 Ministerial Declaration had to recognise that while the majority of substances no longer pose a problem in the Rhine, 'Efforts to reduce the inputs of diffuse sources have been less successful and, as a consequence, the share of diffuse nutrient and heavy metal inputs in the total inputs has risen'.[31] The targeted 50 per cent reduction of nitrogen by 1995 had failed. The reduction that has been achieved was due almost totally to a reduction of point source inputs: by implementing measures in industry and improving denitrification in sewage treatment plants. Diffuse nitrogen inputs from leaching and drainage via groundwater has remained almost unchanged so that the overall reduction target has not been achieved.[32] It will take several more years before the adverse side effects of decades of agricultural development on the borders of the Rhine can be reversed.

---

[28] ICPR, RAP, Strasbourg, 1987, para 3.1.
[29] Conference of Rhine Ministers (n 5).
[30] ICPR (n 28) para 3.1.B.6.
[31] Conference of Rhine Ministers *Ministerial Declaration* 29 January 2001, Strasbourg at http://www.iksr.org/pdf/communique_iksr_e.pdf.
[32] Conference of Rhine Ministers (n 5).

The development of EC law will help the riparian states. For instance, reduction of the use and inputs of pesticides that still enter the Rhine will largely have to be achieved through the implementation and amendment of EC Directives 91/414 and 94/93 concerning the placing on the market of plant protection products.[33]

7.5 Rehabilitation of the Ecosystem

For years, riparian states have restricted their cooperation in the prevention of pollution. Issues such as salmon recovery and flood plain protection were not in the minds of the drafters of the 1963 Convention on the ICPR or the 1976 Conventions. With the adoption of the RAP this has changed. Protection of the Rhine ecosystem now became the basis for a water protection policy. This has come to fruition, since now, except for the Eel, fish from the Rhine are again edible. Today, 63 fish species live in the Rhine. Thus the former species composition has almost been re-established, with only the sturgeon missing.

7.5.1 Rehabilitation of Salmon and the Rhine Ecosystem

The most ambitious element of the rehabilitation of the ecosystem is the attempt to bring back in the Rhine salmon and other migratory fish, including sea trout, allice shad, sea lamprey and sturgeon. The RAP set the objective that by the year 2000, the ecosystem of the Rhine 'must become a suitable habitat to allow the return to this great European river of the higher species which were once present here and have since disappeared, such as salmon'.[34] To implement this objective, in 1994 the Ministerial Conference adopted the Ecological Master Plan for the Rhine, titled 'Salmon 2000'.[35]

Bringing back salmon is a difficult if not impossible task. It requires not only the reduction of pollution loads, but also hydrological, biological and morphological improvements. These include new spawning grounds, clean and oxygen-rich nurseries in the upper reaches of the river, and the construction of fish ladders and locks to enable migrating species to pass artificial obstacles.[36] The main stream of the Rhine and its tributaries contain many obstacles that impede

[33] Council Directive 91/414/EEC of 15 July 1991 concerning the placing of plant protection products on the market, OJ 1991, L 230/1; Council Directive 94/93/EC of 27 July 1994 establishing annex vi to Directive 91/414 concerning the placing of plant protection products on the market, OJ 1994, L 227/31.

[34] ICPR (n 28) para 2.1.

[35] International Commission for the Protection of the Rhine against Pollution (n 9).

[36] ICPR (n 28) para 2.4.

free migration.[37] According to first estimates from 1991, costs for the necessary modification would amount to DM 110,000,000.[38]

By the end of 2000, about 600 mature salmon had returned to the Rhine. Several parts of the Rhine system had now been made accessible as the result of new fish passages. In 2001, the ICPR could report that the Rhine 'is slowly developing towards a salmon river', but had to add that 'many more efforts must be made before salmon may reach Switzerland'.[39] By the beginning of 2003, over 1,910 salmons have returned to the Rhine system. Since not all of them are recorded by controls when returning to their home rivers, the number of specimen having actually returned will be much higher. In the sole Iffezheim fish passage opening mid 2000, 286 salmon and more than 1000 sea trout have so far been registered. The salmon programme will continue until the target of a self-sustaining Rhine salmon population has been reached.[40]

Bringing back salmon to the Rhine is indeed an end in itself and a trigger for political and public support, but it is not the only objective. It is part of what should become a much broader recovery of the main stream of the Rhine and connected banks and alluvial areas. In several riparian states promising projects have been initiated.[41] These include new passages through in summer dikes, recovery of natural vegetation, removal of 'armoured' defences to enable migration of natural elements from and to the bed, dynamic and increasing flooding of floodplains, and compensating farmers for leaving farmland to the river.[42] By 1986 the Netherlands had initiated the 'Stork plan'. This aims to liberate nature from agricultural domination, especially in floodplains; to use river meadows as nature areas; to tear down some summer dikes so as to achieve natural flooding; to allow natural grazing and, as a symbolic target, to bring back the black stork as a breeding bird in floodplain forests.[43] The World Wide Fund for Nature has initiated some spectacular projects that accelerate ecological rehabilitation of the Rhine ecosystem in the delta and envisage reintroduction of roe deer, beaver, elk and the European sea eagle.[44] The 2001 Ministerial Conference supported further implementation of

---

[37] International Commission for the Protection of the Rhine against Pollution (n 9).
[38] ibid [9].
[39] Conference of Rhine Ministers (n 5).
[40] ibid.
[41] e.g. G.J. Gerritsen 'Ecological Rehabilitation of the River Ijssel' in International Commission for the Hydrology of the Rhine-basin 'Contributions to the European Workshop Ecological Rehabilitation of Floodplains' Report II-6 1992 [79].
[42] H. Havinga 'Floodplain Restoration: A Challenge for River Engineering' in International Commission for the Hydrology of the Rhine-basin 'Contributions to the European Workshop Ecological Rehabilitation of Floodplains' Report II-6 1992 [95].
[43] E.H.R.R. Lammens and E. Marteijn 'Ecological Rehabilitation of Floodplains, The State of the Art' in International Commission for the Hydrology of the Rhine-*basin* 'Contributions to the European Workshop Ecological Rehabilitation of Floodplains' Report II-6 1992 [183].
[44] G.J.J.M. Litjens 'World Wildlife Fund Reanimates Delta of Rhine' in International Commission for the Hydrology of the Rhine-basin 'Contributions to the European Workshop Ecological Rehabilitation of Floodplains' Report II-6 1992 [105].

such projects and envisaged new projects when it adopted the Rhine 2020 Programme on the Sustainable Development of the Rhine.[45]

None of this is yet firmly established. Costs are high and competing interests (flood control, agriculture, and navigation) remain strong. However, while it is very easy to criticise slow progress, the more appropriate perspective is to acknowledge that present practices constitute a radical break away from the pre-existing history of over-development of the river basin and towards a more sustainable use of the Rhine.

7.5.2 The Floods

The reconstruction of the ecosystem received a further stimulus in the aftermath of the massive floods of 1993-1994 and 1994-1995. These were intimately related to the ecological degradation of the river basin in previous centuries. While the unavoidable direct reaction to the floods was to strengthen the dikes, the matter did not, this time, end there: riparian states realised that flood protection could be combined with conservation by giving back to what was left of the flood plain its former role as flood retention reservoir.

A stream of measures followed. The 11th Ministerial Conference on the Rhine (1994) took a cautious step in that direction by stipulating that riparian states should protect the remaining flood retention areas approximately 20 per cent of the earlier flood plains, and restore other areas to the extent that that can be combined with interests of flood control and navigation.[46] On 4 February 1995, the Ministers of the riparian states adopted the Declaration of Arles. This underlined that measures are required not only in the field of water management, but also in the fields of spatial planning and land use, example, in connection with agriculture and forestry, nature protection, development of settlements and recreational use.[47] On 22 January 1998, the 12th Conference of Rhine Ministers adopted the 'Action Plan on Flood Defence' in Rotterdam.[48] Key principles include recognition that water is part of the natural ecological cycle of all surfaces and of land use and must be taken into account by all fields of policy; that the water must be stored in the catchment area and along the Rhine as long as possible; that the river must be expanded so that the runoff may be slowed down without danger, and that integrated and concerted action in the entire catchment area is a prerequisite for the success of the Action Plan.

These reactions to the recent floods build on and strengthen the ecosystem approach of the RAP, and differ fundamentally from previously prevailing reactions to build a greater number of stronger and higher dikes. The new approach

---

45 Available at http://www.iksr.org/Rhine%202020%20-%20e.doc.

46 Kommunique über die 11. Ministerkonferenz zum Schutze des Rheins, Bern, 8 December 1994, reproduced in IKSR, Tätigkeitsbericht 1994, para V.7.

47 See http://www.iksr.org/icpr/11uk.htm.

48 ibid.

is unfinished, though. The 2001 Ministerial Declaration refers as one of the remaining challenges in the Rhine catchment range the interlocking of flood prevention and ecosystem improvement.[49]

7.6 The Legal Translation of the Revised Paradigm

The traditional question in international water law has been the extent to which how much a state could maximise its use (example, by introducing pollutants) before the rights of downstream states were infringed. Today, this question appears to play a much less prominent role. The above development has transformed the nature of cooperation between riparian states. The present cooperation regarding pollution control and ecosystem rehabilitation shows only few traces of the previously dominant maxim of equal apportionment. States' current use of the river is strongly determined by joint management among all riparian states. All states accepted equal levels of commitment to reduce pollution loads and to undertake projects to rehabilitate the ecosystem. Practice has evolved into the direction of what might be called an ecosystem paradigm. Present activities, whether they concern floods, urbanisation or agriculture on the riverbanks, or discharges, are examined from the point of view of their compatibility with the protection of the Rhine ecosystem.

This paradigm shift lacked express legal direction when it initially occurred. Eventually, though, the paradigm shift was translated into, and thereby supported by, law. This was achieved in three steps: the 1992 Helsinki Convention, the 2000 Directive establishing a framework for Community action in the field of water policy, and most significantly, the 1999 Convention for the Protection of the Rhine.

7.6.1 The 1992 Helsinki Convention

The 1992 Helsinki Convention on the Protection and Use of Transboundary Watercourses and International Lakes[50] contains the obligatory principles that states shall take all appropriate measures to prevent, control and reduce pollution of waters causing or likely to cause transboundary impact and that they shall ensure that transboundary waters are used in a reasonable and equitable way.[51] In several respects, however, the Convention goes beyond these maxims and recognises the developments in the management of international watercourses that we have witnessed in the Rhine basin. The Convention gives ecologically sound water management, conservation of water resources and environmental protection the highest priority. Riparian states are to ensure conservation and, where necessary,

---

[49] Conference of Rhine Ministers (n 31).
[50] The Convention is in force since 6 October 1996. All riparian states of the Rhine as well as the European Community are party to the Convention.
[51] Article 2.

restoration of ecosystems.[52] In addition, they shall promote sustainable water resources management, 'including the application of the ecosystems approach'.[53]

These principles and obligations apply directly to the riparian states of the Rhine. In that respect, it can be said that at least since the entry into force of the Helsinki Convention, the changes in the management of the river, as discussed above, are explicitly translated into legal principles. The true significance of the Convention, however, is that it envisages that riparian states of international watercourses conclude bilateral and multilateral agreements, in order to apply and to amend the Convention in the context of particular watercourses. Article 9 provides that:

> The Riparian Parties shall on the basis of equality and reciprocity enter into bilateral or multilateral agreements or other arrangements, where these do not yet exist, or adapt existing ones, where necessary to eliminate the contradictions with the basic principles of this Convention, in order to define their mutual relations and conduct regarding the prevention, control and reduction of transboundary impact. These agreements or arrangements shall embrace relevant issues covered by this Convention, as well as any other issues on which the Riparian Parties may deem it necessary to cooperate.

It is not immediately obvious that the existing Rhine conventions contained 'contradictions' with the principles of the Convention. A more accurate assessment would be that the new principles simply were not provided for in the 1963 and 1976 Rhine Conventions. Nonetheless, the riparian states have acknowledged that the existing conventions had to be adjusted and updated and brought them, whether or not as a matter of legal obligation, largely in line with the Helsinki Convention (VI.C below).

7.6.2 The EU Framework Directive

A second legal development that translates the developments in the Rhine river basin into law thereby providing a legal basis for their implementation and further development in the Rhine basin is the adoption of the EC framework directive for Community action in the field of water policy.[54] This Directive seeks to contribute to the implementation of Community obligations under the Helsinki Convention. At least indirectly, this will also affect the management of the Rhine.

The key principles of the Directive have direct relevance to the development in the Rhine system. The Directive aims at establishing a framework for the

---

[52] Article 2.

[53] Article 3(1)(i).

[54] Directive 2000/60/EC of the European Parliament and of the Council of 23 October 2000 establishing a framework for Community action in the field of water policy Official Journal L 327.

protection of, *inter alia*, transboundary watercourses, which protects and enhances the status of aquatic ecosystems and related terrestrial ecosystems, promotes sustainable water use and aims at reduction of discharges,[55] including pollution from diverse sources of pollution.[56] Member States are to produce 'international river basin management plans' for international river basins such as the Rhine.[57]

The 2001 Ministerial Conference for the Rhine recognised the relevance of the Framework Directive. It considered that the programme on the sustainable development of the Rhine which had been adopted at the same Conference sets aims similar to those of the framework directive and would therefore appear to constitute a river basin management plan as envisaged by the framework Directive. The Conference also noted that the riparian states would, together with the European Commission, continue to co-ordinate activities in implementing the directive.[58] Also in 2002, one of the main points of discussion of the ICPR Plenary Assembly was the implementation of the EU framework directive on water policy in the Rhine basin. As far as the aspects of overriding importance applicable to the Rhine and its complete international watershed are concerned, the ICPR furthers the implementation of this directive. Since large parts of the new ICPR working programme 'Rhine 2020' overlap with the contents of the framework directive on water policy, working structures have now been co-ordinated or combined with a view to using exiting resources and to avoid duplicating work.

7.6.3 The 1999 Convention for the Protection of the Rhine

One could plausibly argue that it did not really matter whether the ecological rehabilitation of the Rhine since 1987 has been undertaken on the basis of the non legally binding RAP or on the basis of a treaty, or even that progress was possible precisely because of the non-legally binding nature of the RAP, yet, the 11th Ministerial Conference deemed it desirable to lay down achievements in law and called for the preparation of a new treaty. Arguably, the Helsinki Convention induced that modernisation. The new Convention was negotiated between 1994 and 1999, when it was signed in Berne.[59] It entered into force 1 January 2003, substituting the Bern Convention of 1963.

The Convention writes into law several principles that either expressly or implicitly had been adopted and implemented by the riparian states since the adoption of the Rhine Action Programme in 1987, and incorporates principles included in the 1992 Helsinki Convention. The main innovations include the following:

---

[55] Article 4.
[56] Article 10.
[57] Article 13.
[58] Available at http://www.iksr.org/Kommunique-WRRL-e.doc.
[59] It is not yet in force. France and Germany have not ratified it; (Suisse) Département Fédéral des Affaires Etrangères, Notification aux Gouvernements des Etats signataires de la Convention du 12 avril 1999 pour la Protection du Rhin, P.655.20-RHEIN 5, 2 février 2001.

The geographical scope of the 1999 Berne treaty is to include the aquatic and terrestrial ecosystems that directly interact with the Rhine.[60] This is a significant step forward compared to the current Rhine treaties. It no longer excludes the flood plains from the river regime. It also brings it within the scope of the ICPR (that presumably will be renamed); to engage in land-use measures relating to the Rhine ecosystem.

The Convention pursues the aim of sustainable development of the Rhine ecosystem. It contains obligation pertaining to pollution control, both in regard to point sources (example, industry and municipalities) and diffuse sources (example, agriculture and traffic). It also envisages the maintenance and restoration of the natural function of the waters, including the conservation, protection and reactivation of alluvial areas as natural floodplains. Natural habitats for wild fauna and flora in the water, on the riverbed and banks and in adjacent areas are to be restored, living conditions for fish are to be improved and their free migration is to be restored. The Convention also calls for general flood prevention and protection, taking account of ecological requirements. None of these objectives was (fully) provided for in the existing treaties. They indicate that the regime has moved far beyond the traditional principle of equal apportionment to a set of principles that above all are characterised by protection of the ecosystem of the river.

The ICPR continues to exist, but receives a new legal basis under article 6 of the Convention. Contracting Parties shall pursue their cooperation within the Commission. The Commission is to prepare international measuring programmes and studies of the Rhine ecosystem, make proposals for individual measures and programmes of measures, and evaluate the effectiveness of the actions decided upon. In view of the broad objectives of the Convention, the mandate of ICRP is also extended. The new treaty contains a sufficiently flexible mandate that, for instance, allows the Commission to respond to the by no means hypothetical challenges imposed by climate change.

7.7 Conclusion

The regime for the Rhine has undergone a fundamental transformation. Its underlying principle of equal apportionment has been exchanged for the principle of sustainable development. The river is no longer free for all and is no longer an exclusive material for economic progress. Ecosystems (including aquatic and terrestrial ecosystems that interact with the Rhine) have to be protected and restored, pollution to be minimised and any development (including flood control, energy, navigation, and developments in the river basin) has to be assessed against the fundamental objective of the protection of the system. Moreover, the regime no longer consists of a set of obligations to which riparian states must adhere in different ways depending on whether they are upstream and downstream states. It

---

[60] Article 2(c).

contains similar obligations for the protection of the ecosystem for all states – largely irrespective of their being upstream or downstream states.

The change is radical, so radical that the question may be asked whether the riparian states are ready for the full implementation of the new Convention. Will states accept that they must clean up sediments, reduce the discharge of nitrogen or build the necessary fish traps? Will they be willing to restore the natural flood plains? The answers to these questions will determine whether international law can play a more prominent role in resolving the conflicts between economic development and ecosystem protection in the Rhine basin than it has done in the past decade. Even if full implementation takes its time, as it must, the new Convention in any case succeeds in providing a model for other international watercourses.

Chapter 8

International Watercourses Law: The Experience of the Mekong River Basin

Bantita Pichyakorn*

8.1 Introduction

The Mekong River, with a length of 4,200km, is the twelfth longest river in the world and the longest river in South East Asia.[1] There are two upper riparian states, China and Myanmar, and four lower riparian states, Thailand, Laos, Cambodia and Vietnam sharing the waters that run from the northwestern edge of the Tibetan plateau in China. The mainstream races through deep gorges and reaches the joint Myanmar-Laos-Thai boundary in an area, which has become known as the 'Golden Triangle'. It also constitutes the frontier between Laos and Thailand for some distance before veering into Laos and becoming the Laos-Thai boundary river before crossing into Cambodia. Just below Phnom Penh, the capital of Cambodia, the river divides itself into two branches before emptying into the South China Sea in Vietnam.

The Mekong development project was initiated in 1957 by the Economic Commission for Asia and the Far East (ECAFE), which was renamed the Economic and Social Commission for Asia and Pacific (ESCAP)[2] in 1974. One of

* I would like to express deep gratitude to Prof. Patricia W. Birnie for her long compassionate support over the last four years, to Prof. Surya. P. Subedi for his encouragement and opportunity to present an earlier version of this Chapter at the conference and to Mr. Jethro F. Marsh and my family for their faith in me.

[1] The Mekong Secretariat *The Mekong Committee: A Historical Account (1957-1989)* (The Mekong Committee Secretariat Bangkok 1989) [3]. In terms of annual discharge, its ranks the tenth as it release water at about 475,000 million m^3. Its drainage basin covers 795,000km^2. However, the starting point of the lower Mekong basin is at Km 2,382 at the confluence of the Nam Ruak (a Mekong tributary between Thailand and Myanmar) and the Mekong where the Golden Triangle is located.

[2] After World War II, there was a concern within the UN to restore social and economic conditions in the countries, which had suffered economically from the War. The UN therefore created the Economic and Social Commission for Asia and Pacific (ECAFE) as a subsidiary organ to be responsible for restructuring and reforming the economic situation of these countries. Five sub-commissions were further established to be responsible for this matter in five different regions worldwide. They included the Economic Commission for

its mandates[3] was to assist the countries in the Asian and Pacific regions, which suffered economically from World War II in the restoration and development of their economic situation. It implemented its mandate by originating many development programmes, one of which was a study of international rivers and flood control. This was aimed at re-establishing the economic development of the states concerned by developing their water resources. For this purpose, the Bureau of Flood Control was established in order to be responsible for conducting research on international rivers. The Bureau selected the Mekong River as a case study rather than elsewhere[4] because the flooding there was so severe and the riparian states were very supportive of the project and willing to co-operate fully with ECAFE.[5] The first study, prepared by the Bureau in 1952, discovered that the Mekong River basin had potential for resource development, particularly in irrigation and generating hydropower.[6] The Bureau also suggested the four riparian

---

Europe (both headquarters located in Switzerland, see www.unece.org), the Economic Commission for Africa (head office situated in Ethiopia, see www.un.org/Depts/eca), the Economic Commission for Latin American and Caribbean (headquarters based in Chile, see www.eclac.cl), the Economic Commission for Western Asia (head office located in Lebanon, see www.escwa.org.lb), and the Economic Commission for Asia and the Far East (its headquarters are situated in Thailand, see www.unescap.org). ECAFE originally comprised four regional and six non-regional members, namely China, the Philippines, India and Siam (Thailand), Australia, France, the Netherlands, USSR, the UK and the USA respectively. Initially, full membership was restricted to full members of the UN. The first four states, as full members of the UN in that region, therefore, became members of the Commission. France, the UK, and the Netherlands became members by virtue of their colonial possessions in the region. Due to their interest in the region's problems, Australia as well as the USA and USSR, became members of ECAFE. ECAFE has currently 51 member states and nine associate members and was renamed the Economic and Social Commission for Asia and Pacific or ESCAP in 1974 in order to reflect both the economic and social aspects of development and the geographic location of its member countries. For further details of ESCAP, see www.unescap.org.

[3] Full details of the mandates of ESCAP, ibid.

[4] This was because the political situations in the riparian states of other international rivers would not be supportive of such research. For example, in the Indus and Ganges regimes, the states concerned were in dispute. The Yangtze River is located in China, which at that time did not have the open door policy to open itself to the world and outsiders; therefore, it was not possible to conduct research within its territory.

[5] The four riparian states supported this project since they expected to benefit from it. Economically, this project would improve the flow of money into the region because a large sum of money would be invested and spent on many local projects, labour, and equipment. Politically, this project would bring the Mekong region to international attention, which would give a positive impression of the regime. At the very least, this would provide an opportunity for the four riparian states to be known by international community.

[6] The Bureau of Flood Control 'Preliminary Report on Technical Problems Relating to Flood Control and Water Resources Development of the Mekong – an International River' (1952). ECAFE was initially interested in the water resources' problem, in particular flood control. The Bureau of Flood Control was therefore called upon in 1951 to do further study on the Mekong River. According to the Preliminary Report on Technical Problems Relating to Flood Control and Water Resources Development of the Mekong – an International

states jointly evolve their resources under a co-operative regime.[7] The same conclusion was also reached when the Bureau of Reclamation of the US Development of Interior conducted research on the Mekong basin and suggested that the four riparian states should however develop their potential resources individually (not jointly as recommended by ECAFE).[8]

The positive results of the above reports convinced ECAFE, with the support and approval from the four riparian states, to pursue further studies on the Mekong River basin. ECAFE later recommended that the four states should establish their own framework by concluding an agreement. Consequently, in 1957, they later adopted[9] the first Statute for Co-ordination of Investigation of the Lower Mekong Basin[10] (the Mekong Statute) which established the Committee for Co-ordination of Investigations of the Lower Mekong basin, better known as the Mekong Committee (MC).

In addition, the four riparian states concluded three further agreements, viz. the 1975 Joint Declaration of Principles for Utilisation of the Waters of the Lower Mekong Basin[11] (continuing the MC), the 1978 Declaration concerning the Interim Committee for Co-ordination of Investigations of the Lower Mekong Basin[12] (replacing the MC with the Interim Mekong Committee (IMC)), and the 1995 Agreement on the Co-operation for the Sustainable Development[13] of the Mekong

---

River, published by ECAFE's Bureau of Flood Control, revealed the Mekong River's possibilities for further development, particularly in irrigation and generating hydropower.

[7] It was suggested that the Mekong River, at full capacity could be used to irrigate up to 4.3 million ha of land and generate 130,000kWh/year from 24,000MW installed capacity.

[8] The US participated in this region partly because it was alerted by the spread of communism of which China was the major supporter in the region and wanted to balance its political power in this region. They therefore initiated a project to conduct a reconnaissance study of the Mekong basin in order to play a more political role in the region. See also, L Singh *The Politics of Economic Co-operation in Asia* (University of Missouri Press Columbia 1966). D Wightman *Towards Economic Co-operation in Asia* (Yale University Press New Haven 1963) and also The United States Bureau of Reclamation 'Reconnaissance Report – Lower Mekong River Basin' (1955).

[9] The 1956-1957 Annual Report of the Economic Commission for Asia and the Far East (15th February 1956 - 25th March 1957) E/CN.11/454.

[10] The draft of the Statute was prepared in 1957 by an *ad hoc* Secretariat established for the Development of Water Resources in the Lower Mekong Basin, ECAFE/L.119. Text in UN, Legislative Texts and Treaty Provisions concerning the Utilization of International Rivers for Other Purposes than Navigation, (ST/LEG/SER. B/12) (1963) [267].

[11] Unpublished, on file with the author.

[12] Unpublished, on file with the author.

[13] The concept of sustainable development has been increasingly accepted and applied in many areas of international law, including the protection of the global atmosphere, global desertification, biodiversity, and water resources. Its definition was firstly found by the WCED. It stated that 'humanity has the ability to make development sustainable-to ensure that it meets the needs of the present without compromising the ability of future generations to meet their own needs. World Commission for Environment and Development *Our Common Future* (OUP Oxford 1987) [8].

River Basin[14] (replacing the IMC with the Mekong River Commission (MRC)).

It is worth noting that the 1995 Mekong Agreement has adopted an increasingly accepted principle of international law, the concept of sustainable development, therein. It is therefore of great interest to consider whether and to what extent this notion is applied and implemented in this region. The purpose of this chapter, therefore, is to review and analyse the main features of the 1995 Mekong Agreement and compare them with those of the 1996 Treaty on Sharing of the Ganges Waters at Farakka. This chapter argues further that although the concept of sustainable development has been increasingly adopted as a principle of international law in many international watercourse agreements[15] and by international tribunals,[16] this tendency does not guarantee that it will be interpreted in the same way and render sustainable result to every regime. The practice of the Mekong regime illustrates this well, as the 1995 Agreement does not elaborate this concept as was hoped by the Rio Declaration.[17] The developmental concern is obviously promoted much more than the environmental one.

Nevertheless, the Mekong experience is a good example for other regimes, including the Ganges River basin, as it demonstrates the way in which the concept of sustainable development is applied in international watercourse law. Its practice illustrates many weak points they have encountered over the last six years since the Agreement was concluded. The role of the MRC is also examined in considering to what extent it plays a supportive role in promoting this concept. To date, it is far from clear that the MRC has performed progressively because they lack needed resources, for instance, knowledge, technology, financial resources, and competent staff. Public participation and precautionary measures have played a less active role, becoming non legal-binding regional policies. Therefore, it is of great interest how far the Mekong Member States can achieve sustainable development of the basin whilst their local communities and their domestic law are not ready for this revolution and their people are concerned only with the utilisation of their water rather than the preservation of its quality.

Before embarking on the purpose of this Chapter, a short history and development of the Mekong co-operation and the overview of the 1995 Mekong Agreement will be presented. The focus of the instrument, particularly the concept of sustainable development, and the role of the Mekong River Commission will be discussed. The four riparian countries and their roles will be analysed and to what extent they might be able to effectively implement the obligations adopted in the

---

[14] 34 ILM (1995) [864].

[15] For instance, the 1998 Convention on the Protection of the Rhine, the 1994 Agreement on the Establishment of a Permanent Okavago River Basin Water Commission, the 1994 Convention on Co-operation for the Protection and Sustainable Use of the Danube River, the Protocol on Sharing Watercourse Systems in the Southern African Development Community (SADC) Region, and the 1987 Agreement concerning the Utilisation of the Zambezi River.

[16] For example, the *Gabcíkovo-Nagymaros* (Hungary/Slovakia) case, see the details of the decision of the International Court of Justice (ICJ) at http://www.icj-cij.org/icjwww/idocket/ihs/ihsframe.htm.

[17] See Principle 2 of the Rio Declaration.

Mekong Agreement in practice. The Mekong and Ganges River basins will then be compared from the legal perspective. The conclusions will be drawn afterwards.

8.2 History of the Mekong Cooperation

According to the long history of the Mekong co-operation and the changes that occurred within the Southeast Asia continent, its development shall be divided into four main periods, viz. 1957-1975, 1975-1978, 1978-1995, and 1995-present.[18]

8.2.1 Period between 1957 and 1975

Between 1957 and 1975, the Mekong riparian states attempted to get the Mekong project established. The Mekong Committee (MC) mainly originated the activities initiated in that period.[19] The most successful action of the MC was the introduction of the Mekong development project at international level as many countries and international organisations donated a large amount of funding.[20]

---

[18] For this particular period, see III. The 1995 Mekong Agreement.

[19] According to Article 4 of the Statute, the MC was mandated to promote, co-ordinate, supervise and control the planning and investigation of water resource development projects. The Committee may, however, perform four other functions, which included:

(a) prepare and submit to participating governments plans for carrying out co-ordinated research, study and investigation;

(b) make requests on behalf of the participating governments for special financial and technical assistance and receive and administer separately such financial and technical assistance, and take title to such property, as may be offered under the technical assistance programme of the United Nations, the specialised agencies and friendly governments, or other organisations;

(c) draw up and recommend to participating governments criteria for the use of the waters of the main river for the purpose of water resources development;

(d) employ on behalf of the participating governments, personnel to assist the Committee in the performance of its functions.

[20] These included Japan, USA, Canada, Germany, the Netherlands, France, UNDP and UNESCO. The Mekong Committee Annual Reports published during 1958-1962 revealed that those countries financially supported some important programmes, including, for instance, the first aerial survey that was completed in 1958 with financial assistance from the Canadian government. The Japanese government supported the first reconnaissance survey of the Mekong tributaries that was undertaken in 1959, see The Mekong Reconnaissance Team organised by the Government of Japan produced a *Comprehensive Reconnaissance Report on the Major Tributaries of the Lower Mekong Basin*, Tokyo, 1961. The US government funded and donated computers for collection and examination of hydrologic data and also donated equipment for the hydrometeorological stations in Laos and Thailand. For various reasons these countries donated and invested money in order to play active roles in this region; e.g. France wanted to evidence its power in this continent because Vietnam was a colony of France. The US also wanted to pursue its anti-communism policy whereas China, the upstream riparian state, had fallen under communist rule in 1950. The four

Several surveys and researches were initiated and conducted in order to explore the basic data of the basin. Among those significant projects, the 'Preliminary Report on Technical Problems Relating to Flood Control and Water Resources Development of the Mekong – an International River',[21] a report prepared by the United States Bureau of Reclamation,[22] a Ford Foundation study,[23] and the 'Indicative Basin Plan'[24] are worth mentioning as they all provide important information and reveal previously unknown potentials of the Mekong basin. As far as the plan for using and sharing the water flow was concerned, the Mekong Committee did not formulate it until 1972 when the US offered to assist it in drafting rules for water utilisation. A project to draft the so-called 'Water Charter'[25] was initiated and completed in 1975. The four riparian states later adopted the Water Charter as the 1975 Joint Declaration to replace the 1957 Mekong Statute.

---

member countries did, however, fund and contribute their own shares in this project but with relatively much smaller amounts because of their economic situation For example, the budget of the Mekong Committee in 1973 was at about 270 million US$. This was funded by three major groups of contributors, including the four riparian states at about 37 per cent (Cambodia 4 per cent, Laos 5 per cent, Thailand 65 per cent and Vietnam 15 per cent), other donor countries at approximately 52 per cent, and international organisations at roughly 9 per cent. *The 1973 Mekong Committee Annual Report* [117].

[21] The Bureau of Flood Control and Water Resources Development (n 6). This report considered the possibility, in particular hydropower of the Mekong River Basin for further development. The Bureau also suggested the four riparian States to jointly evolve their resources together under a co-operative regime.

[22] US Bureau of Reclamation (n 8). This study reached the same conclusion as the one prepared by the Bureau, but advised each riparian to act separately.

[23] G. White, E. De Vries, H. Dunkerley and J. Krutilla *Economic and Social Aspects of Lower Mekong Development* (Bangkok 1962). This study focused on the need for studies on market factors and natural resources and on basic education and training. Its recommendations were very practical. It pointed out for example such basic needs as strengthening the Mekong Committee staff, and expanding the Committee's services.

[24] The Mekong Committee 'Report on Indicative Basin Plan: A Proposed Framework for the Development of Water and Related Resources of the Lower Mekong Basin' (1970). This project was the first skeleton plan for the development of the basin between 1970 and 2000. During the drafting of the Plan, there were a number of projects submitted by the four governments for consideration, for example, Thailand and Laos proposed the issue concerning generating power that they were very much concerned; Cambodia nominated multipurpose project studies in Tonle Sap area, whereas Vietnam was concerned about flood control and irrigation projects in the Mekong delta area. The final version of the Plan therefore came up with a long-term plan for irrigation, power generation, flood control, agriculture development, navigation and water transport for the benefit of the whole Mekong River basin.

[25] The 1973 Mekong Committee Annual Report [28].

8.2.2 Period between 1975 and 1978

The Joint Declaration, adopted in January 1975, was one of the most important legal instruments concluded in this region as it contained many current legal principles of international watercourses law, which were the obvious influences of the 1966 Helsinki Rules during the 1970s. The concepts such as the equitable utilisation and the duty to prevent pollution were accepted for the first time. In addition, the Joint Declaration formulated another three sets of regulations governing the utilisation of: (a) 'the mainstream's water', (b) 'the tributaries' water', and (c) 'other water resources'. These rules represented the development of international watercourse law in this region as it incorporated for the first time the need to maintain the water flows as well as the need to prevent misuse, waste and water pollution.[26] In addition, several regulations were also adopted concerning the use of the mainstream waters that reflected the need to control and preserve the quantity and quality of the water. These included, for instance, the concept of equal sharing, which was introduced to the allocation of the water of the mainstream. However, it did not mean the equal division of the quantity of the water.[27] All the development projects carried out along the Mekong mainstream were also required to conduct and present the results of the environmental impact assessment.[28]

However, it was unfortunate that the above arrangement was never put into practice because of the political disruption in Cambodia (April), Laos (November) and Vietnam (April) in 1975. Their failure to appoint plenipotentiary members to the MC forced it to cease its operation in the same year. As a result, the financial assistance from other countries was later dropped in 1976.[29] Thailand was the only member, which escaped from the invasion of communism and was trying to revive the Mekong co-operation. It was not until April 1977 that Laos, Thailand, and Vietnam agreed to conclude a new agreement, the 1978 Declaration concerning the Interim Committee for Co-ordination of Investigations of the Lower Mekong Basin and established the Interim Mekong Committee (IMC) to replace the MC.

---

[26] The same concept was also developed in the 1995 Mekong Agreement, see Articles 3, 5, 6 and 7 for the new direction of this approach that was adopted under the concept of sustainable development. See below for details.

[27] Article X of the 1975 Joint Declaration. Compare this with the interpretation of the term 'equal share' reached by the US Supreme Court in the following cases. *Kansas v. Colorado* 185 U.S (1902) 125, 46 L. ed. 838; 206 U.S (1907) 46, 51 L. ed. 956 and *New Jersey v. New York* 238 U.S (1931) 336, 75 L. ed. 1104.

[28] Article XVII, which laid down an obligation to conduct an environmental impact assessment was the first environmental preventive measure ever adopted by the Mekong regime. Compared this with its new status as a non legal-binding policy that was introduced by the Mekong regime after the 1995 Mekong Agreement was adopted. Details, see below.

[29] The UNDP financial support dropped sharply from US$5.6 million in 1973 to US$60,000 in 1975 and to nil in 1976. During this period, the Committee had to rely on other sources of funding, e.g. by the government of the Netherlands which funded US$6.2 million for studies and US$9.5 million for construction. UNDP resumed their funding in 1977 at US$240,000 and up to US$950,000 in 1978. The Mekong Secretariat (n 1) [51].

8.2.3 Period between 1978 and 1995

As far as the international watercourse law is concerned, this instrument may be regarded as the interruption of the development of law as it abandoned all the principles and related practices adopted earlier in the 1975 Joint Declaration. It made no mention of any legal concepts concerning the usage or sharing of water because it was no longer intended to carry out any joint project with Cambodia. It however re-adopted the vague outdated framework of the 1957 Statute with the purpose to continue the Mekong project and all the ongoing projects in order to maintain the financial support from outsiders.[30]

Nonetheless, the activities of the IMC during 1978-1995 were of great interest. Although most of the projects were small plans conducted in Laos, Thailand, or Vietnam, the IMC was active in promoting the environmental protection in those countries in order to deal with the degradation of water and other related problems. A large number of environmental programmes,[31] such as the Environmental Impact Assessment (EIA) and water quality monitoring network were created for the first time and have become one of the most effective water quality controls continuously operative to date.[32]

The three riparian states at the same time expressed their hope that Cambodia would soon resume its participation in the IMC as the UN was assisting Cambodia to arrange the first election in 1990. The National Council of Cambodia (SNC), the official government of Cambodia formed from that election, put forward a proposal to resume its membership and reactivate the Mekong Committee.[33] The other three members welcomed its request. They then realised that the 1978 Declaration was outdated and needed revision because a number of new legal issues had arisen in the interim none of which was taken into account before. With major support from

[30] In the writer's opinion, there were three reasons why the three Mekong states had to do so. Firstly, some regulations of the 1975 Joint Declaration, for example, the rules for using water from the Mekong mainstream, became impossible to be implemented because Cambodia was not a member, therefore, the three Member States could not carry out any development project on the mainstream. The three states concerned then had to find a new regime that would benefit only three of them since the projects outside Cambodia's territory could only be carried out. Secondly, the three riparian states hoped that Cambodia would solve its problems and rejoin the Mekong co-operation soon, as Principle 3 stated that the MC would be activated once 'all members' of the MC decided to do so. Thus, adopting the old scheme of the 1957 Statute as a temporary measure seemed the best option since they were all so familiar with it and they did not have to spend time to draft a new regime. Lastly, in such an urgent situation, the three states were forced to establish a new regime as soon as possible in order to keep all the ongoing programmes and studies in operation and to maintain confidence of the donor countries in the Mekong project. Thus, the re-adoption of the old scheme of the 1957 Statute was the best alternative.

[31] For details, see the annual reports prepared by the Interim Mekong Committee during the period between 1978 and 1992.

[32] For current development of these environmental activities, see *Mekong River Commission's Annual Reports* of 1995 to date.

[33] *The 1991 Interim Mekong Committee Annual Report* (1991) [11].

UNDP, the four states subsequently set up a working group to draft a new agreement. It took twenty-one months to complete the draft and the new Agreement on the Co-operation for the Sustainable Development of the Mekong River Basin was later concluded in 1995. This agreement immediately established the Mekong River Commission (MRC) as a new joint organisation to promote co-operation between the four countries and has been in operation ever since.

8.3 The 1995 Mekong Agreement

The Agreement on the Co-operation for the Sustainable Development of the Mekong River Basin has six chapters and the most important are Chapters III, IV, and V which lay down the objectives and principles of co-operation. Among those legal concepts, the most significant is the concept of sustainable development to the effect that the contracting parties agreed to co-operate and make every effort to use their natural resources in a manner in which the environment and ecological balance of the river is also conserved and maintained.[34]

According to the provisions of the Mekong Agreement, the concept of sustainable development is interpreted as a balance reached between the maintenance of the 'adequate quantity' and the preservation of 'good quality' of water. To do so, the concept of equitable utilisation (Articles 5) and maintenance of water flow (Article 6),[35] and the obligation to protect the environment and water resources of the Basin (Articles 3 and 7) are applied in order to establish particular practice for the use of the Mekong water in every season. A remedial clause was also introduced requiring the Member State, which causes substantial damage to one or more riparian states from its use of and/or discharge to waters of the Mekong River, to pay compensation to the suffering states. Freedom of navigation[36] along the Mekong mainstream is endorsed and the duty to notify and consult is affirmed.[37]

With regard to the structure of the new Mekong joint organisation, the composition of the Mekong River Commission (MRC) was reformed. It now comprises of three new bodies, the Council, the Joint Committee, and the Secretariat,[38] all of which are mandated to perform more functions than those of

---

[34] Preamble of the 1995 Mekong Agreement.

[35] Article 5 sets out procedures for the use of water in both dry and wet season, whereas Article 6 requires all the Member States to maintain the flows of the mainstream even in the flood season.

[36] For the purpose of this Conference, the issue of navigation is not discussed because its main objectives are reaching the most appropriate solution for the Ganges River Basin in relation to the use and protection of the water resources.

[37] Article 10 requires the Member States to notify and consult directly with the parties concerned if they become aware of any special water quantity or quality problems which requires an immediate response.

[38] Compare this with the previous two Mekong organisations, the Mekong Committee and the Interim Mekong Committee. Both of them had the same organisational structure, viz. each committee was comprised of one representative from each country. The post of

their predecessors.[39] Dispute resolution is one of its new mandates, as the MRC is required to take a decision on any difficulties or issues arising from this Agreement.[40]

8.3.1 How Does This Agreement Work to Achieve Sustainable Development?

As stated above sustainable development in this regime means the balance reached between the adequate amount and the good quality of the waters, to what extent it can be achieved however depends on the effectiveness of putting Article 5[41] and Article 6[42] (for the quantity of water), and Article 3[43] and Article 7[44] (for the

---

Chairman of the Committee was held only for a one-year term and rotated in turn among the members of the Committee.

[39] The MC and IMC had very similar mandates. Article 4 of 1957 Mekong Statute (n 19). See also Article XXVII of the 1975 Joint Declaration, and Article 4 of the 1978 Declaration.

[40] In the case that the MRC is unable to resolve the conflict, it must be referred to the governments concerned to negotiate through diplomatic channels. For further details, see Article 35 of the Mekong Agreement.

[41] Article 5 reads:

> To utilise the waters of the Mekong River system in a reasonable and equitable manner in their respective territories, pursuant to all relevant factors and circumstances, the Rules for Water Utilisation and Inter-basin Diversion provided for under Article 26 and the provision of A and B below:
> A. On tributaries of the Mekong River, including Tonle Sap, intra-basin uses and inter-basin diversions shall be subject to notification to the Joint Committee.
> B. On the mainstream of the Mekong River:
> 1. During the wet season:
> a) Intra-basin use shall be subject to notification to the Joint Committee.
> b) Inter-basin diversion shall be subject to prior consultation, which aims at arriving at an agreement by the Joint Committee.
> 2. During the dry season:
> a) Intra-basin use shall be subject to prior consultation which aims at arriving at an agreement by the Joint Committee
> b) Any inter-basin diversion project shall be agreed upon by the Joint Committee through a specific agreement for each project prior to any proposed diversion. However, should there be a surplus quantity of water available in excess of the proposed uses of all parties in any dry season, verified and unanimously confirmed as such by the Joint Committee, an inter-basin diversion of the surplus could be made subject to prior consultation.

[42] Article 6 reads:

> To co-operate in the maintenance of the flows on the mainstream from diversion, storage, releases, or other actions of a permanent nature; except in the cases of historically severe droughts and/or floods:
> A. Of not less than the acceptable minimum monthly natural flow during each month of the dry season;
> B. To enable the acceptable natural reverse flow of the Tonle Sap to take place during the wet seasons; and,
> C. To prevent average daily peak flows greater than what naturally occur on the average during the flood season.

quality of water) into practice. Then two possible scenarios may arise:

1. If Articles 5 and 6 as well as Articles 3 and 7 are effectively implemented, the potential scenario would be: the adequate quantity of water is assured and its quality is preserved in certain good standard: or
2. If Articles 5 and 6 are effectively implemented whereas Articles 3 and 7 are not so well put into practice, the possible scenario would be: the adequate quantity of water is ensured but in bad quality.

Articles 5 and 6 are quite rigid and likely to guarantee that the amount of water will be used equitably inasmuch as the flows are well maintained. The duty to notify, and arrange prior consultation ensure that the use of the quantity of the water will be monitored by all the four countries. For instance, if the Member States would like to divert water between intra-basin[45] in the dry season, they must arrange a prior consultation, which aims at arriving at an agreement by all members of the Joint Committee, or they are required to reach a specific agreement with the Joint Committee if they wish to conduct inter-basin development project.

However, it should be noted that the above relevant provisions might be misused for political reason. In particular, Article 5, which requires a condition to conclude an agreement for the diversion of water between inter-basins in the dry season? The project in question might be put permanently on hold if any member of the JC votes against such a project. The proposing states have no freedom to

---

The Joint Committee shall adopt guidelines for the locations and levels of the flows, and monitor and take action necessary for their maintenance as provided in Article 26 (*sic*).

[43] Article 3 reads:

To protect the environment, natural resources, aquatic life and conditions, and ecological balance of the Mekong River basin from pollution or other harmful effects resulting from any development plans and uses of water and related resources in the basin.

[44] Article 7 reads:

To make every effort to avoid, minimise and mitigate harmful effects that might occur to the environment, especially the water quantity and quality, the aquatic (eco-system) conditions, and ecological balance of the river system, from the development and use of the Mekong River basin water resources or discharge of water and return flows. Where one or more states is notified with proper and valid evidence that it is causing substantial damage to one or more riparians from the use of and/or discharge to water of the Mekong River, that states or states shall cease immediately the alleged cause of harm until such cause of harm is determined in accordance with Article 8.

[45] Intra-basin diversion means the use of water between the basins that has geographical linkage with the Mekong River basin, so the diverted waters will be at some point returning to the watershed area. On the contrary, the inter-basin diversion represents the diversion of water from the Mekong mainstream to other river basins that are not geographically linked with the Mekong watershed. Such amount of water will never return to the Mekong mainstream. Therefore, it is clear why this Mekong Agreement has laid down very rigid requirements upon the states, which aim to operate inter-basin projects.

proceed at their own risk or even have no chance to re-submit the less harmful alternative or make an appeal to the IMC or other tribunal for a final decision.[46] It is unfortunate that this provision does not provide such an opportunity and represents the curtailment of rights in exploiting the resources on which all the riparian states share common interests.

As for the preservation of the quality of the water, Articles 3 and 7 are quite flexible as they provide an opportunity for the Member States to use and cause harmful effects to the waters as long as they do not cause substantial damage. It is however doubtful to what extent the environment of the Mekong River will be effectively protected and to what extent the first scenario can be achieved. This is because firstly, it is unclear what the term 'substantial damage' really means, as it is not defined elsewhere in the Agreement. Many possible questions may also be raised; for example, who would decide whether such 'damage' is substantial? What are the relevant criteria for such consideration? Particularly, the flexibility of Article 7 seems not so convincing that it would successfully preserve the good quality of the Mekong's water because it requires the Mekong Member States to 'minimise' the harmful effects and cease its operation only when proper and valid evidence is found. This implies that the Member States are allowed to cause 'insignificant harm'[47] or in other words, it allows the Member States to use and pollute water up to the level where their activities do not cause substantial effects to the river.[48]

Secondly, it is quite unfair that Article 7 puts a burden of proof and duty to notify upon the states suffering from environmental damage. In addition, the

---

[46] Compare with Article 20 of the 1990 ILC's Draft Article, UN Doc. A/CN.4/428 where the operator was allowed to re-propose another alternative project that produced less harm in the case that the state of origin refused the operation of the original project. See also A Boyle 'Codification of International Environmental Law and the International Law Commission: Injurious Consequences Revisited' in A. Boyle and D. Freestone (ed.) *International Law and Sustainable Development* (OUP Oxford 1999) [81].

[47] At this point, it is interesting to note that the Mekong Agreement makes no mention of the definition of 'substantial damage' therein. So, it is doubtful how Article 7 (it deals with prevention and cessation of harmful effects) really works in practice because no one knows at what level a particular damage should be deemed substantial and its operation must be ceased. Furthermore, before such damage would be considered substantial, should any state or body step in to declare that ecological harm is caused? According to the Mekong Agreement, there is no provision referring to this situation, which means there is a gap left for the Member States to pollute water resources legally as long as their activities have not yet produced substantial damage. Compare this requirement with the relevant provisions and Annexes of the 1972 Convention for the Prevention of Marine Pollution by Dumping of Waste and Other Matter in which some substances listed therein are permissible to be dumped in the sea. The similar provision is also found in Article 21(3)(c) of the 1997 UN Convention on Non-Navigational Uses of International Watercourses as it requires the establishment of lists of substances that must be prohibited, limited, investigated or monitored.

[48] It should also be noted that in practice the MRC also applies the measure to assess environmental impact to development projects initiated within the basin; however, it is not a legally binding obligation.

burden should be imposed on the states that cause environmental harm with 'proper and valid evidence' in order to curb such activities. These requirements are questionable as to who would decide whether the evidence is 'proper and valid'? What would happen if the suffering sates intentionally turn a blind eye on[49] or do not have the advance technology to detect such harm? Would such substantial damage last forever or should the MRC step in and take any action for the interests of the rest of the Member States? It is unfortunate that the Mekong Agreement provides no solution and makes no mention of the competent body to deal with these conceivable problems.

Nonetheless, it is worth noting that the Mekong Agreement provides an indication of the closer integration between the issues of water quantity and water quality, as they are in fact inseparable. Article 6 illustrates the possibility of the combination between the preservation of the ecological balance through the requirement to maintain minimum water flows[50] of the Mekong River because the amount of water supports the diversity of the natural resources of the basin. This reflects that Article 6 can be implemented not only for the purpose of flood control, but also for the purpose of preserving the biodiversity of the Mekong basin as was mentioned by the ILA at its 2000 Conference in the Campione Consolidation.[51]

8.4 THE Mekong River Commission (MRC)

Compared with its predecessors, the structure of the MRC was reformed in order to facilitate and promote the implementation of the Mekong Agreement more effectively. It now comprises three bodies, the Council, the Joint Committee, and the Secretariat, which are responsible for different tasks. The Council is the

---

[49] This circumstance may arise if the two states concerned agree to allow environmental harm to occur and none of them would raise this because they assist and benefit each other on some other matters.

[50] The original purpose of this provision is to prevent the salt-water intrusion in the Mekong Delta in Vietnam in the dry season – the Delta is known as the most important floodplain in which rice and other food are produced for the population of Vietnam, and, or to secure the natural reverse flow of Tonle Sap – Tonle Sap or the Great Lake is located in Cambodia. Tonle Sap is a branch of the Mekong River that supplies an enormous amount of water to the Mekong mainstream, particularly during the dry season. Geographically speaking, it has its own unique characteristic as its headwater starts from the northwest of Cambodia and runs down to the south and joins the Mekong mainstream at Phnom Penh. During the wet season, the water in the Mekong mainstream that flows down from Laos and Thailand border would divide itself into two branches at Phnom Penh. One would run southwards to the Mekong Delta in Vietnam and the other would interestingly run up to the north and be stored in the Tonle Sap that serves as a natural reservoir. Tonle Sap would then release the water and alleviate the shortage of water during the dry season when the water in the mainstream runs below its average level. Tonle Sap supplies a great amount of water to the downstream countries like Cambodia and Vietnam and this explains why the Member States are so concerned and want to maintain the natural reverse flow of the Tonle Sap during the wet season.

[51] *The 2000 Report of the ILA*, the Committee on Water Resources Law [2].

supervisory body and consists of one member from each state at Ministerial or Cabinet level. It also has decision-making power which basically involves establishing policies and plans at basin level, including the Basin Development Plan (BDP)[52] and the Rules for Water Utilisation and Inter-Basin Diversion (WUP), making other decisions to implement the Agreement, and resolving any disputes referred to it. Its Chairman serves its post only for a term of one year and the position rotates among its members.

The Joint Committee (JC) is an executive body of the organisation, comprised of one member from each participating country at no less than Head of Department level. Its Chairman serves only for a year term. The JC is the most important and active organ in the MRC as it is mandated to perform many significant functions, including, to implement the decision and policies of the Council, to formulate the BDP, the Rules, and other development plans, and to resolve the disputes referred to it.

With regard to the formulation of the BDP, the JC is the key body and has been working on this project since 1999 and divided this project into three phases.[53] The first phase or BDP1 would carry on for five years with five different stages.[54] The second phase consists of a medium-term plan covering years six to ten during which the selected model (from phase I) would be implemented. The last phase consists of a long-term plan, which would provide the blueprint for years eleven to twenty.[55] At present, it is the period of the first stage, which will last until 2003. It is then quite doubtful to what extent the completed version of the BDP will effectively respond to the current situation and the problems of the basin because the factors and situation of the basin do change regularly.

In addition, the JC is formulating the Rules for Water Utilisation and Inter-Basin Diversion[56] which is known as the 'Water Utilisation Programme or WUP'

---

[52] The BDP is elaborated in Chapter II of the Mekong Agreement as 'a general planning tool and process that the JC would use as a blueprint to identify, categorise and prioritise the projects and programmes to seek assistance for and to implement the plan at the basin level'.

[53] The MRC 'Formulation of the Mekong Basin Development Plan (Basinwide)' (1999) [18].

[54] Stage 1, the integrated development of water and related resources at a 'sub-area' of a cluster of sub-basins will be the basis for analysis. Potential problems in the 'sub-area' will be assessed. Stage 2, once Stage 1 has been assessed, some scenarios for its development will be formulated. Stage 3, Preparation of the Management and Development Strategy for the waters systems based on the proposed scenarios (from Stage 2) will be formulated. Stage 4, the agreed projects and programmes can be concluded to be candidates (long list) for next Stage. Stage 5, consideration of the long list and decision concerning the 'short list' projects, viz. those which are of high priority, great importance and meet basinwide interests. For details see the MRC (n 33) [18]-[19].

[55] ibid [18].

[56] The MRC Secretariat *Water Utilisation Programme: Project Implementation Plan* (MRC Secretariat Phnom Penh 1999). This recent report explains the MRC's objectives in its ongoing work concerning that drafting of the Rules (according to Article 26). These are to (a) assist the MRC to put in place a mechanism to promote and improve coordinated water management in the basin and among the riparian countries, (b) promote reasonable and

within the Secretariat. Two Sub-Committees are established, one on Rules for 'Water Quantity' and the other one on 'Water Quality', to work separately on these two discrete issues. However, it seems that many difficulties, such as the different levels of economic and technological development,[57] and in particular technical skill of the staff and people concerned with the project[58] are the main obstacles delaying the whole progress of the project. Though the World Bank has recently approved its support to the MRC by providing legal experts and funding for consultation and training, the future of WUP remains uncertain because the governments, NGOs, and the local community of the states concerned do not seem to be aware of the urgent need to have the Rules established.[59] This may be because they lack the education and access to the fact that their water resources are degrading both in terms of quantity and quality.

The MRC Secretariat is the permanent office, which has consultative power to render technical and administrative services to the Council and the JC, and assist both in the implementation and management of projects and programmes.[60] The Chief Executive Officer (CEO) is the head of the Secretariat, which is appointed by the Council. The head office of the Secretariat is now located in Cambodia after it was situated in Thailand for more than 40 years.[61] This is because other Member States would like the MRC Secretariat to be situated in their countries. The conclusion was reached in the second meeting of the Council when Thailand and Vietnam withdrew their nominations[62] and left Cambodia and Laos to offer their capital cities for the location of the Mekong Secretariat. The four states eventually agreed to relocate the MRC Secretariat between Cambodia and Laos every five years[63] and the first relocation was to Cambodia. An Agreement on the Establishment of the Headquarters of the Mekong River Commission in Cambodia was signed between the Government of Cambodia and the Mekong River Commission on 20 February 1998.[64] The Secretariat moved to Laos in 2003.

---

equitable water utilization by the countries of the Basin, and (c) enhance the protection of the environment, aquatic life and the ecological balances of the basin.

[57] The MRC Secretariat 'WUP Information Bulletin No. 1' October 2000 (unpublished) [1]

[58] The MRC Secretariat 'WUP Information Bulletin No. 2' January-February 2001 (unpublished) [8].

[59] ibid [2].

[60] Articles 28-33.

[61] The reason for adoption this provision is to provide an opportunity to Cambodia, Laos, and Vietnam to have permanent offices of international or regional organisations located in their countries. This is to prove that the political situations in these three countries are positively settled after a long period of domestic wars and the invasion of communism. As a result, the MRC Secretariat has been relocated to Phnom Penh, Cambodia in 1998. However, this office will be moving to Laos in 2004.

[62] Minutes of the Second Meeting of the Council, MRC, 30-31 January 1996 [5]. The reasons for the withdrawal were however never disclosed.

[63] *The 1996 Mekong River Commission Annual Report* (1996) [3].

[64] The 1998 Agreement on Headquarters of the Mekong River Commission, concluded on 20 February 1998 (unpublished) on file with the author.

This situation is controversial since it is doubtful whether such rotation is beneficial towards the operation of the MRC and the riparian states. Firstly, it is inevitable that moving the Secretariat will cause disruption to all the ongoing projects of the MRC, not only because of the unnecessary administrative upheaval and transfer of books, paperwork and officials, but also it stirs the mentality of the staff. Secondly, this will consequently not only delay the completion of projects and affect their quality, but that very delay is surely likely to disintegrate the confidence of donors and any funding they may be likely to offer. Lastly, the execution of each rotation absorbs a large sum of money. A considerable amount has to be spent on the re-decoration of the building, transportation and other related works, e.g. packing all the documents and training new staff, etc. Therefore, relocation every five years may well result in doubling the budget, which seems a waste of money, time and effort.[65]

8.5 Potential of Each Member State in Implementing the Mekong Agreement

It is too early to analyse how and to what extent the four riparian states will effectively implement the Mekong Agreement, particularly since the BDP and the Rules (WUP) are still in the developing stages. This section would rather discuss the potential of the four Member States in implementing the obligations set out in the Mekong Agreement.

Thailand is the most active and has the best potential among the members to implement the Mekong Agreement. A number of Thai domestic laws concerning the use and preservation of water resources do exist and have been in force for quite some time. Among the important ones are:

1. The 1992 Enhancement and Conservation of National Environment Quality Act
2. The 1992 Factory Act
3. The 1992 Hazardous Substances Act
4. The 1992 Energy Conservation Act, and
5. The 1992 Public Health Act.

These laws reflect that Thailand is very enthusiastic in this matter and has a long experience in promoting environmental concern. These Acts pay more attention on regulating, controlling, and preserving the quantity and quality of water resources. In addition, its population is far better educated than that of the other three riparian countries. The political and economic situations are comparatively more settled as well, and the technology is far more developed. Thus, Thailand has better potential to implement the Mekong Agreement effectively compared with the other members.

Vietnam also has better potential than Laos and Cambodia, as it has been

---

[65] This should be compared to the moving of the EC parliament between France and Luxembourg.

increasingly enthusiastic in law reform after the civil war between the Northern and the Southern governments, which ended in the 1980s.[66] The Vietnamese government has been concurrently working on formulating a new draft of Water Law.[67] Several environmental regulations were also adopted in early 1990s. These include, for example, the 1993 Environmental Protection Law, and the 1995 Vietnamese Criteria for Environment, compiled by the Ministry of Science, Technology and Environment (MOSTE).[68]

In terms of human resources, Vietnam still has some difficulties in building and developing their capacity. This is because, for political reason, a large number of skilled professionals were kept and trained during the period between 1975 and late 1980s in the re-education camp. Their education was thus interrupted. As a result, the education of their people is comparatively 15 years behind that of Thailand.

Nonetheless, Vietnam has actively developed its economic situation to become an industrialised country. A large number of western companies have invested a lot of money during the last ten years because labour costs in Vietnam are comparatively cheaper than other developing countries. Its economy has developed into a more market-based economy where the export industry is dramatically promoted. However, it is likely that environmental issues will become one of the most controversial topics in the near future because Vietnam still lacks effective environmental regulations. More pressure is put on, as Vietnam has become a party to some important environmental agreements.

For example, the 1987 Montreal Protocol on Substances that Deplete the Ozone Layer, the 1989 Basel Convention on the Control of Transboundary Movements of Hazardous Wastes and their Disposal, the 1992 Climate Change Convention, and the 1992 Biodiversity Convention. These agreements require it to implement the environmental obligations adopted therein in the future.

Cambodia[69] and Laos[70] share a similar situation, as both are unlikely to

---

[66] For the history of Vietnam, see D.J. Duncanson *Government and Revolution in Vietnam* (OUP Oxford 1968); R.B. Smith *An International History of the Vietnam War* (Macmillan London 1983); P.B. Davidson *Vietnam at War: the History 1946-1975* (OUP Oxford 1991) and M.B. Young *The Vietnam Wars 1945-1990* (Harper Collins New York 1991).

[67] B. Boer, R. Ramsay and D. Rothwell *International Environmental Law in the Asia Pacific* (KluwerLaw International The Hague 1998) [205]-[209].

[68] T.V. Truong 'Water Quality Management in Vietnam' a paper presented to the seminar on Integrated River Basin Development and Management held in Thailand, 13-16 May 1997 (unpublished).

[69] For Cambodian history, see D.P. Chandler, B. Kiernan (ed.) *Pol Pot Plans the Future: Confidential Leadership Documents from Democratic Kampuchea, 1976-1977* (Yale Centre for International and Area Studies New Heaven 1988); D. Bull *The Poverty of Diplomacy: Kampuchea and the Outside World* (Oxfam Oxford 1983) and M. Osborne *Politics and Power in Cambodia, the Sihanouk years* (Longman Camberwell 1973).

[70] For Laos politics, see G.C. Gunn *Politics Struggles in Laos, 1930-1954: Vietnamese Communist Power and the Lao Struggle for National Independence* (Duang Kamol Bangkok 1988); H. Toye *Laos: Buffer State or Battleground* (OUP Oxford 1968); J.J. Zasloff and L. Unger *Laos: Beyond the Revolution* (St. Martin's Press New York 1991); M. Stuart-Fox *A*

effectively implement the Mekong Agreement in the near future. It is obvious that they are comparatively much more backward and very slow in terms of their economic, legal and political development. As for the former, it had long suffered from an uncertain political situation during 1970s-1980s when the Pol Pot regime took isolationism as the country's political ideology.

As a result, Cambodia separated itself from the outside world, including the Mekong Member States. Though the new Cambodian government proposed to resume its membership in the Mekong co-operation, it seems that Cambodia is much far too behind its neighbour countries like Thailand and Vietnam. The only positive sign is the drafting of a new environmental law, 'Law on Environmental Protection and Enhancement Authority', which is now under consideration.[71] However, Cambodia still lacks the human resources and finance capacity to manage its environmental protection system. It might take a long period of time and a large amount of funding to educate and train its people to understand how they should promote this Agreement as it will provide with them positive results in the long term.

As for the latter, Laos is a landlocked country, forested and biologically very diverse. Economically speaking, Laos however relies only on exporting timbers and electricity to other countries. As a result, it has suffered from the effect of environmental degradation, including deforestation and changes in water quality.[72] The aftermath of the civil war that carried on for over 30 years also caused severe environmental damage to Laos. The Laotian government has thus initiated projects to reform the law, and establishes the Science, Technology and Environmental Organisation (STENO) to especially deal with environmental matters.

The 1996 Water Resources Law was later drafted to set out regulations for the preservation of water resources in order to ensure that the quantity and quality of the water is preserved for its domestic consumption.[73] Nonetheless, lack of competent and skilled manpower as well as financial support reflects the uncertain future of putting these regulations into practice. The same situation is likely to be found when Laos implements the obligations adopted in the Mekong Agreement.

History of Laos (Cambridge University Press Cambridge 1997) and D.J. Arthur *Conflict in Laos: the Politics of Neutralisation* (Pall Mall Press London 1964).

[71] This law was prepared by a UNEP consultant in 1994, See also B. Boer (n 67) [205].

[72] The large important hydropower dams that cause effects to the population and environment of Laos include, for example, the Nam Theun I and II that export electricity to Thailand.

[73] 'Legal and Institutional Conditions for Land and Water Resources Development in Lao P.D.R. and Vietnam' a paper presented to the Workshop Proceedings held on 3-14 March 1997 in Vietnam and Lao (unpublished) on file.

8.6 The Mekong and the Ganges River Basins

The Mekong and the Ganges River Basins[74] share certain characteristics. For example, they run through developing countries that are more concerned with promoting their economies through the development of the water resources than conserving the quality of their resources for future uses. The increase in their population forces them to divert and use more water whereas the waters run either at the same amount or in some seasons may run less than the previous year. As a result, the most important problem of these two regimes is a shortage of water. The riparian states of both basins have been therefore attempting to set out new schemes for water sharing that satisfy and fulfil the needs of all the riparian states. To solve such problems, India and Bangladesh thus recently concluded in 1996 a new Treaty on Sharing of the Ganges Waters at Farakka[75] (the Ganges Treaty),[76] whereas the four Mekong riparian states adopted the Agreement a year earlier.

8.6.1 Allocation of Water

According to the objectives of these two instruments, it is clear that the Mekong and Ganges River basins have different goals to achieve. The former has a broader purpose as the riparian states of the Mekong River attempt to deal with the problems concerning the quantity and quality of the water at the same time through the concept of sustainable development. To do so, they aim to (a) control the utilisation of water, and (b) promote the conservation of the water, in order to reach a balance between the multiple-use of water and the minimisation of the harmful effects. The latter however has a narrower objective. It aims to solve the problem of augmenting the flows of water, particularly during the dry season when the water normally runs below the average level. India and Bangladesh then adopted a scheme for water sharing, but this makes no mention of the need to preserve and conserve the quality of the water resources.

As far as the water utilisation is concerned, the Mekong riparian states have established a scheme requiring that the water must be shared equitably and those

---

[74] India and Bangladesh are the main riparian States, which play key important roles in allocating and sharing the water of the Ganges River. Nepal and some part of China are also the riparian states but did not enter into this 1996 Agreement. Full text; see 36 ILM (1997) [519]. Also, see the Mahakali River Commission (India and Nepal), 36 ILM (1997) [531]

[75] This Treaty has superseded the previous Agreements concerning sharing of water of the Ganges river, concluded among India and her neighbours. For further analysis on this Treaty, see S.M.A. Salman 'Sharing the Ganges Waters between India and Bangladesh: An Analysis of the 1996 Treaty' in S.M.A. Salman et al. *International Watercourses: Enhancing Co-operation and Managing Conflict (World Bank Technical Paper No. 414)* (World Bank Washington DC 1998) [127]; B. Chow *Sharing the Ganges – The Politics and Technology of River Development* (1995); B.M. Abbas *The Ganges Water Dispute* (1982).

[76] Prior to the 1996 Treaty, India and Bangladesh entered into three international instruments, the 1977 Agreement, the 1982 and 1985 Memorandum of Understanding (MOU).

water development projects must be formulated in conformity with a long term Basin Development Plan and the Rules (WUP). Some procedural obligations are introduced, including the duty to notify the MRC or arrange prior consultation.[77] This is to provide opportunities to all the Member States to control and monitor the activities of each other via the MRC. It is worth noting that the flexibility and unclear characteristics of the concept of equitable utilisation become problematic. This is because the Mekong riparian states firstly need to define what equitable utilisation really means in the Mekong context. Under Article 5, this concept must be interpreted and applied pursuant to three related factors, viz. (a) all relevant factors and circumstances, (b) the Rules for Water Utilisation and Inter-basin Diversion (the Rules are known as WUP within the Mekong River Commission Secretariat), and (c) the provisions of A and B of Article 5 of the Mekong Agreement.[78]

The delay in drafting the Rules or WUP gives rise to the delay in implementing the equitable utilisation as the Rules is a part of the criteria that the Mekong states must consider if a particular use of water should be deemed equitable or not. As a result, the concept of equitable utilisation has not yet been effectively applied. Its experience has yet to contribute any example of putting this notion into practice.

The Ganges River regime however establishes a more rigid formula to control each state's activities as India and Bangladesh agree to share the exact amount of water on the basis of equity.[79] According to Article II and Annexure I, the share between them will be 50:50 if the water available at Farakka is at 70,000ft^3/s or less. If the water runs more than 70,000ft^3/s, the apportionment will then be allocated otherwise.[80] The question then arises to what extent this rigid scheme could be effectively put into practice. Both the riparian states must have adequate water monitoring stations and effective measuring equipment in order to ensure

[77] For more detail, see note 76.

[78] This first element has not been defined in this Agreement. However, some indications may be found in Article VI of the 1975 Joint Declaration, which included, for instance, the geography of the basin, the economic and social needs of each basin states, and the past utilisation of the waters of the basin. These factors are crucial to the interpretation of the principle of equitable utilisation because they are the basic elements declaring the different level of needs and imperatives that each Member States require by referring to their own fact and certain circumstances. Therefore, a country like Thailand, for example, which has more population and industrial activities than Cambodia, might be allocated water more than the latter.

[79] Article IX of the Treaty.

[80] The details regarding availability of water at Farakka and the respective shares of India and Bangladesh have been affirmed (Annexure I) and can be tabulated, as it is done below:

Availability at Farakka	Share of India	Share of Bangladesh
70,000ft^3/s or less	50%	50%
70,000 –75,000ft^3/s	Balance of flow	35,000ft^3/s
75,000ft^3/s or more	40,000ft^3/s	Balance of flow

This arrangement is subject to revision every five years to assure that it will be updated and the water will be shared equally, fair, and creates no harm to either party.

that the data is appropriately collected. In addition, in the case of the availability of water dropping below 50,000ft^3/s, what would the state parties do? What would the share between India and Bangladesh then be? Would it still remain at 50:50? The answer is unclear because no criteria for the situation resulting from such circumstance have been specified in the Treaty. Article II(iii) of the Treaty declares only that if the water falls below 50,000ft^3/s, in any 10 day period, the two governments will enter into immediate consultation to make adjustments on an emergency basis, in accordance with the principles of equity, fair play and no harm to either party. This situation arises because during the period up to and during the drafting of this Treaty, the water at Farakka never dropped below 50,000ft^3/s.[81] The two states concerned, therefore, did not perceive any appropriate solution. This may lead to unexpected conflict in the future if a drop in water does occur.

The same principle is applied to the sharing of the water between India and Nepal of the Mahakali River.[82] The preamble of the Mahakali Treaty recognises that the treaty is based on 'equal partnership' and Article 3 reaffirms the 'equal entitlement' of the parties in the utilisation of the water of the Mahakali River. Article 3(2) reaffirms this concept in stating that the benefits generated from the two power stations shall be shared equally between the parties. The concept of 'equity' is interpreted in Article 3 of the Mahakali Treaty, which provides that it is subject to the condition that this is 'without prejudice to their respective existing consumptive uses of water of the Mahakali River'.

This approach is not new but it has been accepted in some watercourse basins, such as the 1946 Agreement concerning the utilisation of the rapids of the Uruguay River in the Salto Grande Areas that set out the net amount of water that Argentina and Uruguay would share from the river, which was 85:15 respectively. The sharing of the water between Austria and Bavaria was also solved by referring to this concept, as each of them was entitled to exploit half of the volume of the waters.[83] The above examples illustrate that each basin has unique characteristics that in some cases the principle of equitable utilisation, as widely adopted in many river basins, including the Mekong regime, may not be able to serve all those differences appropriately. This explains why the rigid concept, such as the equal share of water, is still being accepted and applied in some regimes, though the equitable utilisation concept has been increasingly adopted. This is because it can guarantee the exact percentage of water shared between the states concerned and it does not require those states to set up criteria to determine whether a particular use is equal or equitable, as the precise percentage of water shared between them is already fixed. The clear and firm characteristic of this concept is very promising

[81] S.P. Subedi 'Sharing of International Water Resources in International Law: The Experience of the River Ganges' a lecture given at The Institute of Advance Legal Studies 3 November 1999.

[82] The Mahakali Treaty (n 74).

[83] Austrian statement of principles regarding successive rivers, in 'Legal aspects of hydroelectric development of rivers and lakes of common interest' E/ECE/136-E/ECE/EP/98/Rev. 1 (1952) [49]

and the Mekong regime might consider adopting a clearer framework like that of the Ganges basin in the future.

It is worth noting that the Ganges Treaty clarifies the starting period of conflict whereas the Mekong Agreement does not. According to Article II of the former, the period of dry season starts from the 1st of January to the 31 May every year.[84] The similar clarification can also be found in Articles 1 and 2 of the 1996 India-Nepal Treaty concerning the Integrated Development of the Mahakali River[85] where the 'dry season' runs from 16 October to 14 May and the wet season from 15 May to 15 October.[86] The effect caused by the lack of definition for the seasons in the Mekong Agreement gives rise to the delay in implementing the instrument because it is still unclear when the dry, wet, and flood seasons begin and end.[87]

8.6.2 The Joint Committee

Both the Ganges and Mekong regimes established the joint river committees to facilitate and manage needed matters on behalf of and for the benefit of all the states concerned. Compared with the Ganges Joint Committee, the Mekong River Commission plays a far more active role as it is mandated to perform many important tasks, including taking decisions, drafting development plans, and implementing those plans. The three bodies of the MRC[88] have decisional, executive, and operational powers, and are required to assist each other in promoting the effectiveness of the implementation of the Mekong Agreement. The Ganges Joint Committee, however, has more limited functions, as it is mainly required only to perform administrative functions. These include submitting all data collected at the four monitoring stations[89] and preparing an annual report for the two governments,[90] and resolving differences and disputes arising in this

---

[84] The text of the Agreement is confusing and vague, in addition, there has no document written about this point. From the writer's point of view, this Article intends to declare that the dry season starts 'by ten days from 1 January and last until 31 May every year', which means it may start either from the 1, 2, 3 or (the latest) 10 January but will finish on 31 May. If the Agreement aims to mean so, the terms 'by' ten days … should be replaced by 'within' ten days …

[85] Article 1 of the Treaty clearly indicates that Nepal shall have the right to a supply of 28.5m^3/s (1,000ft^3/s) of water from the Sarada Barrage in the wet season (i.e. from 15 May to 15 October) and 4.25m^3/s (150ft^3/s) in the dry season (ie from 16 October to 14 May). Article 2 also defines a certain amount of water, which should be supplied from the Tanakpur Barrage during both the wet and dry seasons, to which Nepal is entitled.

[86] During the wet season, Nepal is guaranteed a right to a supply of 28.34 m^3/s (1,000ft^3/s) of water from the Sarada Barrage and 4.25 m^3/s (150ft^3/s) in dry season.

[87] To date, there is no evidence in any Annual Reports declaring the exact period of the dry, wet, and flood seasons.

[88] See the MRC above.

[89] These include Farakka barrage, Hardinge Bridge, Feeder Canal, and the Navigation Lock.

[90] Article VI of the Ganges Treaty.

regard.[91] A question then arises as to whether the Ganges Joint Committee should have been mandated to deal with any urgent water problems, such as a diversion of water that must be made in order to prevent possible flooding in the lower riparian country or the immediate shortage of water. To whom should such issues be entrusted? The Ganges Joint Committee, or should it be other authorities? This point is doubtful since this Treaty makes no mention of the possibility of such emergencies or circumstances.

8.6.3 The Ganges Treaty and the Way to Achieve its Objectives

According to the purposes and objectives of the Ganges Treaty, this instrument aims to 'solve the long-term problem of augmenting the flows of the Ganges River, particularly for the dry season'. It is however doubtful whether the provisions adopted therein provide effective measures to achieve this.

The provisions of the Treaty explain this well as there are no provisions or principles adopted therein aimed at augmenting the flows of the Ganges River. Rather they were adopted to 'control the amount of water to be shared between the two countries'. For example, the concept of equity is adopted to ensure that the water will be shared equally but does not further lay down any obligation that in doing so the riparian states must also take measures to increase or at the very least maintain the quantity of water. The same is also true for the obligation to review the sharing arrangement every five years (Article X), which does not guarantee that by the time of the next revision the Ganges Treaty would provide an effective measure for this matter.

As far as the role of the Ganges Joint Committee is concerned, its mandates do not promote the augmentation of the Ganges River's water. Its functions mainly focus on administrative functions. However, there is a possibility that the Ganges Joint Committee would become more involved and promote the issue of the augmentation of the water flows as at the very least it already serves India and Bangladesh as a bilateral forum that in the future might lead to a conclusion of a new agreement that contains more serious requirements on this matter.

8.7 Conclusion

There is no doubt that the concept of sustainable development has played an increasingly active role in the international watercourse context as many watercourse co-operations have adopted it in their agreements.[92] The Mekong regime is one of those, which also believes that this concept would provide positive results and solve the problems of the basin where the shortage of water and the degradation of the quality of water have become more serious. They therefore set

[91] Article VII of the Ganges Treaty.

[92] See note 15.

out a new legal model to deal with both issues in order to achieve the sustainable water quantity and water quality of the basin.

The first question is thus raised whether or not the Mekong model should also be applied to the Ganges River regime. If so, to what extent should it be applied? Considering the main problems of the Ganges River, namely the shortage of water and the need to augment the quantity of water are playing dominant roles and have become the most imperative issues between India and Bangladesh, the duty to maintain the water flows adopted in the Mekong model is worth considering. This is because this duty guarantees that at the very least the acceptable natural water flows of the Ganges River will be maintained. A certain level of water should thus be available for sharing between India and Bangladesh and the conflict between them should also be to a certain extent alleviated. However, in order to achieve the augmentation of the water flows, the two countries need additional requirements: for example, the requirements of any water development projects must be planned in such a way that it will return the water to the mainstream of the Ganges River. The water flows will then be augmented or at the very least maintained at the average level.

What should be urgently promoted in the Ganges River regime, however, is the mechanism to protect the quality of the water. The mechanism applied in the Mekong regime is flexible but should be practical for the Ganges River[93] because it allows the riparian states to use the water whilst making every effort to minimise and mitigate environmental effect or avoid causing 'substantial damage' to the basin.[94] This issue is imperative because the Ganges Treaty makes no mention of this matter and it is likely that India and Bangladesh will encounter the serious problem of water degradation in the near future, although there would an adequate amount of water to share between them. This issue will obviously become another major conflict between them if it is not tackled at an early stage. Unlike the Mekong regime, the Ganges scheme should not lay the 'duty to notify with proper and valid evidence of the substantial damage' upon the state, which suffers from environmental harm because it is unfair that they also be required to find such proper and valid evidence to cease the projects which cause them harm.

An additional environmental preventive measure may also be adopted in the future when both countries are ready (both financially and technologically) to carry out more expensive mechanism that can prevent harmful effects from the outset. The environmental impact assessment is one of those practical procedures that the

[93] The above mechanism may be adopted for the time being since it leaves the riparian states feeling not too committed to environmental obligation. Other environmental preventive measures, such as the environmental impact assessment might be introduced in the future when both countries are ready (financially and technically) to apply an additional preventive measure, which can prevent environmental harm from the outset.

[94] Although the absence of the definition of 'substantial damage' is controversial but it at the very least provides opportunities to the contracting parties to pursue their own development policies but at the same time to ensure that the quality of the water will be maintained at a certain level.

Ganges regime should consider. Like the Mekong riparian states,[95] India and Bangladesh may initially adopt it as a non legally binding policy because they would not feel too committed to it and would be more willing to implement it more effectively. Whether this duty would be developed to become a legally binding obligation however depends on the two countries' decision in the future.

The role of the Ganges Joint Committee should be promoted. Like the MRC, the Ganges Joint Committee is mandated to operate at administrative level, i.e. to collect, submit and report all the data collected at water stations to the relevant governments, however, it lacks the authority to perform at decisional and executive levels. To promote closer co-operation between India and Bangladesh, the consultation and exchange of information need to be added to the mandates of the Ganges Joint Committee, as they would promote closer co-operation and transparency between the higher levels of the two countries.

As has been stated above, the Mekong Agreement is the first and only international watercourse agreement in which the contracting parties are developing countries and aims to deal with both the problems of the quantity and quality of water under the concept of sustainable development.[96] The experience of the Mekong riparian states illustrates that putting this concept into practice is a very complicated task because sustainable development is a vague notion and its definition varies from basin to basin. Additional principles are also needed to be adopted in order to interpret and define a clearer meaning of this concept in a particular regime. These principles include not only the legal concepts, such as the notion of equitable utilisation, the duty to maintain the water flows, and the obligation to protect water resources, but also the procedural obligations including the duty to notify and arrange prior consultation. The 'Mekong balance'[97] is then reached as the definition of sustainable development under this regime.

More importantly, the Mekong balance cannot be achieved if the states concerned are unwilling and fail to wholeheartedly co-operate in the regime. They must accept that adopting the principles such as the equitable utilisation concept or the duty to protect the environment of the basin alone cannot provide sustainable development of the basin. They must however co-operate and implement them sufficiently and effectively. The long history of conflict between them must be left behind as the new challenge of the basin's development depends on the future vision of the four countries, which have agreed to move forward towards the concept of sustainable development. The issues of water quantity and water quality

---

[95] The reason for this may be the Mekong riparian states fear of being committed to those that would, to a certain extent, force them to slow down their rapid economic growth. The MRC 'Details Planning Phase for Formulation of the Mekong Basin Development Plan (Final Report: Part II)' (1999) [25].

[96] Unlike the 1999 Rhine Convention or the 1998 Danube Convention that also adopted this concept, but aim to apply it only to promote the conservation of water resources.

[97] This means the Mekong riparian states may use the water up to a certain level and at the same time are required to maintain the water flows and cease their uses if they cause substantial damage to other riparian countries. See details in III The 1995 Mekong Agreement.

are integrated much more closely as the Mekong Agreement confirms that they should not be treated separately.[98] However, it is too early to consider the effectiveness of this integration. It is expected that within the next 5 years, its practice would be worth revisiting because by that time the Basin Development Plan and the Rules for Water Utilisation and Inter-Basin Diversion should be completely formulated.[99] The application of these two important instruments would make crucial contributions to the process of the integration of these two issues and to the capability of international watercourse law in adopting the concept of sustainable development into regional practice.

---

[98] It is clear that the main obligations adopted in the Mekong Agreement aim to deal with these two issues at the same time. See Articles 3, 5, 6 and 7.

[99] These two instruments are also the factors that the four riparian states consider how to apply and implement the concept of equitable utilisation, the duty to maintain the water flows, and the obligation to protect the water resources in order to achieve sustainable development of the basin. See *supra.*

PART IV:

THE NATIONAL PERSPECTIVES

Chapter 9

The Legal Regime on Water Resources in Nepal

Surya Nath Upadhyay

9.1 Introduction

Nepal is bestowed with abundant and unique water resources. There are around 6,000 rivers, small and large, which carry about 225 billion m^3 of water annually.[1] However, Nepal faces a water stress situation during the dry season. When a country has 1,000-1,667m^3 of annual water availability per person, it is considered to be in stress.[2] During the dry season, the per capita availability in Nepal falls below 1,600m^3. Similarly, all the regions of the country are not equally blessed with this resource. The four largest rivers, the Koshi, the Narayani, the Karnali and the Mahakali, have between them 89 per cent of the flow and remaining scattered pocket areas in the Terai have 2 per cent of the total flow.[3] As regards groundwater availability, data indicates that over 13.2 billion m^3 of groundwater is exploitable out of 63 billion m^3 available annually, and this can be replenished on a continuous basis.[4] The groundwater is largely available in the Terai region, which is a surface water stress area. However, groundwater irrigation is not economically feasible. Hence, on the one hand the country has abundant water resource if calculated on the basis of total availability on an annual basis, while on the other hand it is in a stress situation in terms of time and space. This situation from a policy perspective calls for integrated management and from the legal perspective poses a challenge to balance the conflicting claims for various uses.

---

[1] BB Thapa and BB Pradhan *Water Resources Development – Nepalese Perspectives* (Konark Publications New Delhi 1995) [22].
[2] R Engelman and P LeRoy *Sustaining Water* (Population Action International 1993) [50]–[54].
[3] A Dixit et al. *The Political Economy of Water in South Asia, Policy Problems and Proposals* (Nepal Water Conservation Foundation 1997) [13].
[4] Department of Hydrology and Meteorology 'Study on Nationwide Hydro-Meteorological Data Management Project (JICA)' (1993).

9.2 Historical Development of Law on Water Resources

Before the unification of the country by King Prithvi Narayan Shah, Nepal was ruled by many small principalities. The systems of governance in those principalities were deeply rooted in their own traditions. The Kiratas, the Lichhavis, the Mallas and the Shahs all had provisions for regulating their behaviour in the use of water – especially for irrigational use, as was only natural in an agrarian economy. Annual repair and maintenance of canals, rights to drinking water and irrigation on a first-come-first-served basis, fines for cutting down trees around water sources and regulations specifying that petty cases relating to water should be settled at the local level were some of the important provisions for managing water in those times.[5] These arrangements were developed over a long period of time in different principalities in different ways. However, the first unified national code for the dispensation of justice came into existence only in 1853.[6] This code, among many other things, provided for rights over water as incident to ownership of land. Later on, in 1964, this code was amended, improvements were made and a new national code was introduced.[7] The chapter of the code on land cultivation provided *inter alia* that:

> No person shall get water unless the person who has constructed the ditch [kulo] gets the water first. After the upstream field is filled with water, the owner of the field further downstream may take water to his field. In case any obstruction is caused to the upstream landholder, the person next to him may take water and plant rice.
>
> A new system may be constructed in the upstream provided it will not diminish water for the existing use downstream.
>
> Where water is shared traditionally, it should be maintained as per the share agreed upon previously.
>
> An unhindered right to construct an irrigation system is granted to all the riparian owners of land.

The application of the national code in practice strongly favoured the prior appropriation right. Case studies of some of the farmer-managed irrigation systems in the districts of Tanahu, Sindhupalchowk and Chitawan indicate that the farmers from the upper reaches have persisted in their claims for water by taking advantage of their geographical position at the upper end of the river. Farmers in the upper

---

5 R. Pradhan et al. (eds) *Water Rights, Conflicts and Policy* (International Irrigation Management Institute 1997) [15]–[16].

6 Ministry of Law and Justice *National Code* (in Nepali) (Law Books Management Committee 1965) [21].

7 Ministry of Law and Justice *National Code* (in Nepali) (Law Books Management Committee 1964) chapter on Land Cultivation.

reaches have been found to be reluctant to share water with downstream farmers.[8] At the same time, in a number of cases district courts have upheld prior appropriation rights over water for irrigation. In *Kaluram v. Bucks* (2025 BS, 1968) the District Court of Chitawan held that a new canal might not be constructed upstream, which would diminish water for an existing canal.[9] As the cropping patterns and agrarian technology of the country were by and large traditional in nature, there could be no rational use of water. It was not anticipated that with the growth of the population, people would face a water stress situation.

Conflicting demand for water started to surface over time. The government began to intervene by way of investing resources to expand the system and include the new farmers in the existing command areas. The farmers cooperated, and the system of irrigation moved toward more rational use and inclusion of new farmers. It has also been found that on many occasions farmers have, on their own initiative, had recourse to informal discussions and conflict management procedures for water allocation and distribution.[10]

9.3 The Statutory Law versus the Traditional Law

This law on water resources governed Nepali society for a long time, largely based on riparian right and the recognition of existing use. However, in 1967 for the first time a system of licensing in the use of water resources was introduced. The Canal Electricity and Related Water Resources Act 2024 (1967) (CERWA) provided that licence is required to be obtained for the use of such water, which is designated under the law for the said purpose. The reason for introducing such a law seemed to have emanated from the increasing pressure on the demand for water, which led the state to intervene and regulate it properly. The law was to be applicable to designated bodies of water only. However, it is curious to find that until 2045 BS (1989) not a single body of water was designated. During the period between 2024 and 2045 BS (1964-1989) this statute remained dormant and inoperative, meanwhile, the national code seemed to continue to govern the use of water, based simply on recognition of the traditional rights and uses for irrigation purposes.

During the same period the courts also recognised the customary users' rights over water resources. One case among many may be cited. A dispute arose when a petitioner constructed a boundary wall preventing access for others to the well on her land. The action resulted in shortage of drinking water for the people of that locality. On receiving a complaint, Kathmandu Municipality pulled down the newly constructed wall and made the well accessible to the local people. A writ petition was filed with the Supreme Court against the Municipality's action. The

---

[8] Government of Nepal *Water Resources Strategy Formulation Phase II Study, Legal and Institutional Cooperation* (His Majesty's Government of Nepal, Water and Energy Commission Secretariat Kathmandu 1965) Annex 12, [4].

[9] ibid.

[10] ibid [5].

respondent, the Municipality, contended that it had pulled down the wall to make drinking water available to the local people. The Supreme Court held the action of the Municipality unlawful, but ruled that the local people should be given access to the well because they had been dependent on it for a long time.[11] This sets an example of customary users' rights recognised by the court. Such a user's right could also be created for water bodies lying within an individual's property.

Later, in 1988, Irrigation Regulation 2045 was introduced under CERWA. This regulation was introduced for the primary purpose of making the traditional water-user group of the farmers a corporate body, and defining their rights and duties in managing their external and internal affairs. This regulation also provided for new ideas for participatory management of irrigation systems and handing over irrigation systems to farmers. Being a country based on an agrarian economy there are numerous farmer-managed irrigation systems, popularly known as FMIS. These FMIS are managed by informal groups of farmers. They have their own informal rules of acquisition, allocation and distribution of water as well as provisions for mobilisation of resources and the maintenance of irrigation systems.[12]

With the growing population in the country the stress on water started increasing; subsequently, it was felt necessary to regulate even this informal use so that it could be made more efficient and reasonable. At the same time the FMIS needed help with strengthening their institutional framework and addressing the various associated needs of their agricultural practices, such as the need for fertilisers, seeds, pesticides etc. In order to address these issues, they needed resources – which could only be obtained through the banks or other institutions if they had a corporate existence. Besides, in those systems that were built by the government, farmers were to be organised in groups and a system of participation between the government agency and the beneficiaries was to be developed. These institutional requirements could only be met by according corporate status to the FMIS. Hence, the existing laws on the registration of associations were used for registering the FMIS, whereas a new set of rules for governing the irrigation system was introduced under CERWA. Such corporate legal status was accorded to the informal FMIS largely due to the requirements of the several loan agreements entered into by the government with the lending agencies.[13] This, however, was only a partial application of the statutory law on water resources, leaving several aspects of water regulation to customary and traditional practices and unwritten

---

[11] *Ram Bahadur Tamang and others v. Krishna Raj Lama* Nepal Law Report 2043 [465]–Code No. 034.

[12] P. Pradhan 'Patterns of Irrigation Organisation in Nepal' – A Comparative Study of 21 FMIS (1989).

[13] Such loan agreements were made with the World Bank for irrigation lines of credit in 1988; the concept was further carried forward by various other agreements with the Asian Development Bank and the World Bank.

understandings among the users of water that, in times of conflict, were used to define the rights and obligations of individuals.[14]

9.4 The Prevalent Laws on Water

Water has multifarious uses and its management has numerous aspects, ranging from conservation to quality control and replenishment. It thus naturally touches upon various natural and human behaviours and hence is regulated by several laws. Attempts have been made in some countries to have a unified code on water resources, yet no water code has been so comprehensive as to cover every single aspect of water resources regulation. In the case of Nepal the Water Resources Act 2049 (1992) is such an attempt to introduce a general law. This is a landmark in the history of water resources law in Nepal. It has attempted to cover many aspects, yet there are many other laws which are applicable to water resources regulation. These laws may be categorised as follows:[15]

General Law on water

The Constitution of the Kingdom of Nepal 2047 (1990)
Water Resources Act 2049 (1992)
Local Self-Governance Act 2055 (1998)
Water Resources Regulation

Use-related Acts

Irrigation Regulation 2053 (1996)
Drinking Water Regulation 2055 (1998)
Electricity Act 2049 (1992)
Electricity Regulation 2050 (1993)
Trekking and River Rafting Regulation 1984
Forest Act 1992
Aquatic Animal Protection Act 1960
Vehicle and Transportation Management Act 1992
Industrial Enterprises Act 1992

Pollution control, protection and conservation-related laws

Environment Protection Act 2053 (1996)
Environment Protection Regulation 2054 (1997)
Soil and Watershed Conservation Act 2039 (1982)
Soil and Watershed Conservation Regulation 2042 (1985)
Mines and Minerals Act 2042 (1985)
Mines and Minerals Regulation 2056 (1999)

---

[14] Government of Nepal (n 8).

[15] The laws referred to in this chapter are published first in the *Nepal Gazette* and subsequently by the Law Books Management Committee of His Majesty's Government of Nepal in book form. Such books have been divided into several volumes. Volume 7 contains laws relating to water resources and the environment.

This categorisation and enumeration of water-related laws is not exhaustive: indeed, one may find some provisions related to water resources in many other laws on various subjects.

The chapter now deals with some basic issues on water resources law.

9.4.1 Ownership of Water Resources

The constitution of the Kingdom of Nepal in its directive principles of state policy holds that the state shall pursue a policy of mobilising the natural resources and heritage of the country in a manner that might be useful and beneficial to the interest of the nation. In consonance with this provision of the constitution, Section 3 of the Water Resources Act provides that the ownership of the water resources available in the Kingdom of Nepal vests in the state. This means that private ownership of water resources is not allowed. Section 4 provides for licensing: an individual is only entitled, except for certain kinds of uses, to make use of water resources under a licence. 'Water resource' under this Act is defined as the water that is available in the Kingdom of Nepal in the form of surface water, underground water or water in whatsoever form. This means that even the water that is found in or on the land of any person would not be under the ownership domain of the person to whom such land belongs. This, however, is in conflict with the concept of 'private water' as defined in the Aquatic Life Protection Act 2017 (1960). This Act defines 'private water' as being a pond, land, reservoir etc. situated in land belonging to an owner. The owner of such a water body is entitled to harvest the aquatic life in any manner as is deemed fit except by using poison.

There is yet another problem with the concept of vesting the ownership of water in the state. The Local Self-Governance Act 2055 (1998) has a very different concept of ownership so far as water resources are concerned. This Act has established various local bodies like village development committees (VDCs), district development committees (DDCs) and municipalities. Each of these local bodies has been entrusted with responsibilities related to the use of water resources. It has the responsibility to plan, execute and maintain water development projects, impose a natural resources tax on the use of water, issue licences for such use, impose service charges and adjudicate water-use conflicts concerning the water belonging to that local body. According to Section 68 of the Act, the VDC shall have full rights over the natural resources lying within its territory, which, of course, includes water resources. Similarly, Section 134 of the same Act establishes the rights of the municipality over the natural resources, including water resources, lying within its territory. The local bodies according to the said Act are corporate autonomous entities with perpetual succession. Now, conceptually, there is an incompatibility as to who owns the resource – is it the state as the WRA provides, or the local bodies established under the Local Self-Governance Act? If someone wants to make use of the water falling under the jurisdictional area of a local body, should that person or entity get the permission of the local bodies or the government authorities, as is currently the case? What should be the procedure for getting a licence if it is to be issued by the local bodies? Similarly, who is to impose royalties on the use of water resources? Which royalty is to be applicable? Is it the VDC's royalty or the royalty as imposed by Electricity Act for the use of water?[16]

9.4.2 Right to Use Water Resources

As mentioned above, an individual may under the WRA use a water resource by obtaining a licence. Section 4(1) states: 'No person shall be entitled to utilise the water resources without obtaining a licence under this Act.' Such a provision, however, is very impractical and difficult to implement, thus it is subject to several exceptions. A licence is not required for:

1. one's own drinking, domestic or irrigation use on an individual or collective basis
2. running a water mill or water grinder as a cottage industry
3. plying a boat on a personal basis for local transportation
4. use of water found within one's own land, in a manner as prescribed by the rules.

These exceptions have been made taking into account the use of water resources by people at various levels in the country. An analysis of this provision leads to a conclusion that a commercial use of water for any purpose may only be made under a licence. Similarly, a formal use of water on an institutional basis may only be made under a licence.

The WRA places further conditions on water use. It provides that the user must use it in a beneficial manner and without causing any harm to others. These conditions of beneficial use and no harm to others put practical limitations on the water-use licence holder. The licence is to be issued by a district water resources committee formed under the chairmanship of the administrative chief of the district and the representatives of various water-use agencies of the government acting as members. In cases where the work involved in utilisation of water resources is related to more than one district water resources committee, a joint committee of all the district water resources committees shall act as one such committee under the Act and perform its responsibilities. The WRA also makes a provision that all those who are utilising water resources at the time of the commencement of the Act are required to apply for a licence within one year if such use could only be made by obtaining a licence under the WRA.

These provisions of licensing have, in fact, some inherent and impractical deficiencies. Firstly, the district water resources committee is not a full-time committee with a separate secretariat of its own. Moreover, the delineation of a

---

[16] S.N. Upadhyay 'Legal regime of water resources use in the light of the Self-Governance Act 2055' in Water and Energy Commission Secretariat 'Water and Energy Commission Secretariat Annual Report 1999'.

district has been made on administrative considerations. Water, being a fluvial substance, is not limited to land boundaries. It travels along the watershed and its physical course. Therefore, the management and regulation of water should have been institutionally organised on the basis of watersheds and river basins. In the absence of a watershed and river basin concept, the regulation becomes much more prone to conflicts of interest rather than harmonious integrated planning and management. Secondly, going by the nature of the district water resources committee, it is simply not practical and functional. The committee must have the requisite data and other information relating to the water which it purports to manage, such as an inventory of existing uses, planned measures, future requirements, potential for development etc. In fact, the committees do not have any of these. By the very nature of the district water resources committees and the meagre resources at their disposal, it is not possible to regulate the water resources under their domain. The current situation on the ground is that out of 75 districts in the country, only in a very few districts has such a committee been formed. What is more, existing users need to obtain a licence within one year of the commencement of the Act if such use of water can only be made by obtaining a licence under the existing law. This provision has also not been implemented in practice. Hence, there is a need to rethink the existing institutional mechanisms and the licensing system of the law on water resources in the country.

9.4.3 Dispute Settlement

One of the important functions of law is to settle disputes arising out of conflicting claims. The use of water is perhaps the most dispute-prone subject in our social life. It has local, regional, national and international dimensions depending on the magnitude and nature of the dispute. Claims and counterclaims are made even before a full-blown dispute erupts. Quite often, differences and claims are settled by using informal mechanisms such as negotiation, mediation, examination, discussion etc. In many cases, as is found in Nepal, the FMIS have their own written or unwritten codes for settling such differences or claims. When such remedies do not prove to be effective and are exhausted, only then do people take recourse to the general court. According to the WRA the licence holder has to make beneficial use of the water that has been licensed, and in doing so cause no appreciable harm to others. The WRA has also prescribed priorities for the use of water. It has also, for the first time, introduced a separate mechanism, of a committee, for making enquiries and examining disputed cases, and making awards as to whether a claim could be sustained or not. In making such a decision, the committee takes into account various relevant factors associated with the claim, such as the population dependent on water, the nature and efficiency of its use, etc. Such a decision is supposed to be final. The committee empowered to make these decisions consists of representatives of the Ministry of Water Resources, the DDC and the National Planning Commission.

The procedure for settling disputes is such that even the rights acquired under a licence may sometimes be in question. A use that is legitimate and valid at present may not be so in future. Hence, a very specific provision should have been included in the law itself. What is more, even the mechanism that has been provided in the existing law has not been properly implemented. So far, very few cases have been referred to the committee. Differences and claims are settled by resorting to informal discussions and negotiations. The provisions of the law seem to be overlapping in their jurisdiction, thereby creating confusion for the decision-makers. In the case of imposition of royalties, the formation and functioning of the committee empowered to make decisions overlaps between general water use and drinking use. The reason for this overlap is not clear.

So far as agreements between Nepal and India are concerned, discussion, negotiation and arbitration procedures have been adopted to settle the differences or disputes between the two parties.

9.4.4 The Quality Aspects of Water Regulation

Quality is a relative term in the case of many daily consumer goods. It is essentially a subject of economics. However, it cannot be seen in the same manner when it comes to the quality of air and water. Water is the essence of life, and thus the deterioration of water quality is directly related to the very survival of life. But being a poor country, Nepal has not accorded quality of water the priority it deserves in its overall management. The result is that thousands of people die yearly of waterborne diseases in Nepal. So far as the legal regime on the quality of water is concerned, Section 18 of the WRA provides that the government may, by a notification, fix the quality standard of water resources for various uses. Such a notification has not yet been issued. Besides the WRA, several other laws mentioned above provide for pollution control or the quality aspect of water in the country. Various institutions like the Ministry of Environment, Ministry of Water Resources, Department of Industry, Department of Standards, Department of Water Supply and Sanitation and the Water Supply and Sewerage Corporation all have their jurisdiction over the issue. Some of these institutions have separate regulations. These regulations and institutions have overlapping provisions with regard to the quality of water, and this has created jurisdictional confusion. In fact, the laws on the municipal water supply system and the laws on industry are supposed to take care of drinking water quality and effluent discharge into water respectively. However, they have been poorly implemented. On the other hand, the law on the environment is supposed to regulate the quality of water for all kinds of uses, but in this respect no substantial work has been done.

9.5 Sustainable Development and Conservation

The biggest challenge for water resources in our modern times is their sustainable development. As the population of the world, and more particularly of the developing countries, is increasing, the demand for water is also bound to increase. Many countries are already facing water stress situations. In the case of Nepal, the population growth rate is 2.08 per cent per annum,[17] while the forests and watersheds are already diminishing due to human encroachment. The present deforestation rate – particularly in the Teri, where most of the forestland of the country is found – has been estimated to be 1.25 per cent per annum.[18] This phenomenon is contributing to the occurrence of annual floods, landslides and many other related problems. Every year tonnes of sediment loads are washed away. This has contributed enormously to the degradation of fertile land. The soil erosion process that mainly occurs in hill areas is raising the riverbeds of the country by 15-30cm annually, which has been a major cause of the incidence of floods.[19]

Hardly any attention has been paid to the sustainable development and conservation of water resources. The legal regime on water resources is very much oriented towards aspects of the use of the resources. It provides, in detail, the rights, obligations and procedures for making use of water resources, but it does not impose any obligations to ensure that the banks of rivers would be protected, that boulders and sand and other materials would not be extracted without observing strict conditions, etc. The Soil and Watershed Conservation Act 2039 (1982) has provided certain conditions for the use of land to ensure the non-degradation of land and soil. It is believed that such activities would help the conservation of watersheds. However, the law has been made applicable only to designated areas, and the area so designated is very small.[20] The Environment Protection Act 2053 (1998) includes several provisions to ensure that any developmental activities would not degrade the environment. Primary environmental examination and environmental impact assessment procedures have been introduced for that purpose. These provisions of law may sound adequate, but their implementation has been far from satisfactory; furthermore, the implementation of such laws touches upon the institutional capacity of the implementing agencies as well as upon the capacity of the general public. On both these fronts, unfortunately, Nepal seriously lags behind. But there is no way forward other than to continue pursuing a policy of sustainable development and building capability to implement such a policy.

9.6 Development of Water Use on a Private Basis

Nepal is blessed with a huge potential for hydropower development. The very nature of the steep mountains fed by some perennial rivers means there is a wide

[17] Government of Nepal *Statistical Pocket Book Nepal* (His Majesty's Government of Nepal, Central Bureau of Statistics 1994).

[18] MOPE *State of the Environment of Nepal* (His Majesty's Government of Nepal, Ministry of Population and Environment Kathmandu 1998) [27]–[29].

[19] Government of Nepal (n 17) [39]–[40].

[20] It has been made applicable on the Shivpuri watershed area, located north of the Kathmandu valley.

availability of dam sites, contributing to this potential. Studies have shown that the theoretical potential of hydropower development is 83,280MW, whereas the established potential capacity of 29,761MW could be economically exploited.[21] The installed capacity by the year 2002 will reach only about 600MW,[22] while the huge potential remains almost untapped. Both Nepal and also a large part of northern India across the border clamour for energy. The installed capacity in India at the end of 1992 was of the order of 70,000 MW while the available load forecast projects a capacity requirement of 180,000MW for 2005.[23] Hence it was felt necessary that the legal regime be developed in such a way that direct private finance could be attracted for the development of hydropower resources. The Electricity Act 2049 (1992) was introduced for that purpose. Other associated laws on investment protection, regulation of foreign investment and technology, industrial enterprises, etc. were enacted. These laws give various incentives to foreign investors. Some private investment has been attracted and a few power projects (Bhote Koshi – 36MW, Chilime – 20MW and Khimti – 60MW) have been started on a private basis.[24] However, all of them are intended for domestic consumption, and their energy cost to the consumer and their impact on foreign exchange has not been very encouraging.

No project has yet been constructed with the sole purpose of exporting power to India, although licences to some power projects under the existing law have been granted for that purpose. One such project for which a licence has already been granted is West Seti (760MW). The licence was granted some six years back, but no power purchase agreement has been established between the exporting and importing parties. Besides hydropower some drinking water processing and bottling plants have been established; beyond these two uses, no particular private use of Nepal's water on a commercial basis has been made.

9.7 Legal Regime on Cooperation with Neighbouring Countries

All the rivers of Nepal drain into India and form part of the Ganges system. During the monsoon period some 71 per cent of the total runoff of the Ganges basin passes from Nepal to India. Nepal, on an average, contributes 41 per cent of the total annual flow of the Ganges.[25] Given the size of the country and the part of the Ganges basin that lies in Nepal this is a significant contribution. As there have been difficulties in the past in Nepal-India cooperation on water resources (mostly due to the implementation of various projects), there exists serious doubt as to whether cooperation between the two countries can be achieved on water resources. There

[21] D. Gyawali *Water in Nepal* 1989 Paper No. 8 [79].
[22] Government of Nepal (n 8) Annex 5.
[23] Q.K. Ahmad et al. (eds.) *Converting Water into Wealth* (Institute of Integrated Development Studies 1994) [40].
[24] Government of Nepal (n 8) Annex 5 [11].
[25] S.N. Bastola *Water Resources Development* (Publisher Sunil Bastola 1994) [70].

seems to be no general meeting ground between them, at least in principle, about the harnessing of this resource.[26] Hence in 1992 when a new constitution was being written after the scrapping of the Panchayat system of government, the drafters introduced Article 126, which provides for the ratification of treaties relating to the sharing of natural resources and their use by a majority of two-thirds of the members present at a joint sitting of both Houses of Parliament.[27] However, treaties, which are ordinary and do not affect the nation extensively, seriously or on a long-term basis may be ratified by a simple majority of the House of Representatives.

This provision has much room for interpretation. First, how would one define 'sharing of natural resources' and their use? Should an agreement for the sale of timber or boulders be considered as falling within its ambit? Should a hydroelectricity sale agreement entered into by a Nepalese utility with an Indian utility come under the purview of this article? The article seems to have assumed that any treaty concerned with the sharing of natural resources and their use may only be entered into between the two countries. However, over the years the concept has changed: now even for the exploitation of natural resources private financing has started to come to the fore. Legal regimes have been developed to support this concept, but time alone will reveal how they are going to be interpreted by the courts in the future.

The problems have already started to emerge. There has not been any progress on the sale of electricity to India by private financing. The important issue that is being faced is how one can account for the water that is regulated through a dam or reservoir for producing power at the private level under a licence. Can there be an agreement between two private parties on the issue of huge and extensive use of water downstream in India associated with the production of power? How would

---

26 In the past, three agreements were entered into between Nepal and India: the first was in 1920 through an exchange of notes on the construction of a barrage at Banbasa on the Mahakali River; the second was the Koshi Project Agreement in 1954 regarding the Koshi River; and the third was an agreement on the Gandak Irrigation and Power Project in 1959. The first project did not create many problems, although on the same river, upstream of the project, the construction of the Tanakpur Power Project created a big bone of contention, which later subsided when the countries entered into a treaty in 1996 on the integrated development of the Mahakali River. The second and third agreements were revised in the wake of protests and demonstrations in Nepal. The first agreement was amended in 1966 while the second agreement was amended in 1964. From 1966 to 1996 no agreement could be reached between the two countries on any project. Numerous meetings were held, a joint commission was established, studies were made separately by Nepal and India on some possible projects and several committees were formed for various projects. However, all these efforts did not yield any tangible result until 1996. The record of discussions reveals that even the implementation of the existing agreements has not been satisfactory. As recently as last year the agenda of the discussion between the two countries concerned the proper implementation of the existing agreements.

27 Government of Nepal *The Constitution of the Kingdom of Nepal* (English translation) (His Majesty's Government of Nepal, Law Books Management Committee 1990).

one calculate and share the downstream benefit to India in the form of irrigation, flood control, etc.? In the light of these problems and issues it seems that private power production may at best be possible in the case of a run-of-the-river project – i.e. a project which does not change the water release pattern and quantum downstream in India. But when it comes to the issue of reservoir projects, the provision of the constitution comes in and a treaty between the two countries becomes inevitable.

This article of the constitution, however, was once interpreted at a time when a memorandum of understanding was entered into between India and Nepal on the construction of a barrage at Tanakpur on a border river, the Mahakali. The Mahakali serves as a boundary in some places, while elsewhere it meanders to and fro across the Nepal-India border. Back in 1920 during the British India period, an agreement through an exchange of letters was made between the two countries whereby some land was made available to India for the construction of a barrage to divert water for India. In lieu of this India was to give some water to Nepal free of charge through the barrage. Later on, at a certain distance upstream in the same river, India constructed a second barrage on its territory where the river at that point flows in India. The afflux bund of the barrage was to be tied to the high ground on the Nepalese side of the border. A Nepalese delegation led by the Prime Minister agreed to make available to India the required land for that purpose, in lieu of which Nepal was to get some power produced in the powerhouse in India on the basis of the water diverted through the barrage and also to get some water for irrigating Nepalese land. This was agreed through a memorandum of understanding.

A big issue was made of this understanding, and the question was whether the memorandum of understanding was a treaty and whether it should have been ratified by a two-thirds majority of the joint session of both Houses of Parliament. The court interpreted it as a treaty and said that it needs to be ratified.[28] On the issue of whether it should be ratified by a simple majority or a two-thirds majority in Parliament, the court simply said that the government should evaluate its effects and decide whether it would cause long-term, serious and extensive impact, and on that basis it may be decided as to whether it needs a simple majority or a two-thirds majority under Article 126 of the constitution. The court declined to make any specific decision or observation on that issue at that time, but went on to say that on making such a determination, if it was contended, the court reserved its right to make a judgment on the issue.

Later on, a treaty was entered into between the two countries on the integrated development of Mahakali River.[29] This treaty included the present arrangements on the utilisation of the water of that river at Banbasa. The arrangements made through the memorandum of understanding and the future plan to build Pancheshwor high dam were also included in the treaty. This treaty was ratified by

---

[28] D.B. Baral et al. *Tanakpur – From the Beginning to the End* (in Nepali) (Pairabi Prakashan 1992).

[29] The text of the treaty is to be found in ILM Vol. XXXVI No. 3 May 1997 [533]–[546].

a two-thirds majority of a joint session of the House of Representatives and the National Assembly. The ratification was not easy. Sharp differences emerged within the political parties on the issue of ratification, and one political party split completely on the issue. The treaty is a framework relating to the construction of future projects.

A detailed project report is being prepared to reach further agreement on the construction of Pancheshwor high dam. The preparation of the report is taking much longer than is stipulated in the treaty, and thus the time prescribed for the preparation of the report has been extended. There are already differences of opinion on the claim of 'existing consumptive use' by one of the parties. The Parliamentary Committee of Nepal among other things has tied the finalisation and later conclusion of an agreement under the treaty for the Pancheshwor high dam to the solution of a border demarcation dispute between the two countries at the point of the source of Mahakali River. There are differences on border demarcation between the two countries, and Nepal has been claiming that 372km^2 of land belonging to Nepal is being occupied by India.[30] The resolution passed by the Nepalese Parliament cannot be binding on the Indian party. In the bilateral treaty, as is obvious, no reservation could be made and the treaty was ratified by Nepal. The resolution passed by the Parliamentary Committee could at best be guidance to the Nepalese authorities for reaching agreement on Pancheshwor. It seems clear that the road to agreement on Pancheshwor is still very difficult.

While the Pancheshwor project is in imbroglio, the legal regime that Nepal has created purportedly for facilitating private power development with a view to exporting power to the Indian market has not produced any result. In 1997 Nepal and India entered into an agreement for power trading between the two countries. This agreement tried to establish a commitment between the two parties for facilitating within their respective countries the development of power production by private entrepreneurs with a view to exporting it to other countries.

Unfortunately, the agreement could not be ratified by Nepal and at present stands in limbo. In the meantime problems of flooding of Nepalese land have occurred in several places because of the construction of civil structures in India to use or obstruct the water flowing from Nepal. India may have its reason for doing this, but it has contributed to further distrust of cooperation between the two countries.

9.8 The Road Ahead

Many lessons have been learnt from the experience of creating and implementing a legal regime on water in Nepal. These lessons are pertinent to the conservation and development of the resource within the country, and at the same time contribute to

[30] B.N. Shrestha *Boundary of Nepal* (in Nepali) (Bhumi Chitra (Mapping) Kathmandu 2000) [544].

the strengthening of cooperation between Nepal and India. In this regard, certain conclusions are apt.

The legal regime of Nepal on water resources is a good start to looking at the resource in a comprehensive way. The WRA has made an attempt in this direction. However, the lack of institutional capability and the overlapping, contradictory, repetitive and concurrent jurisdictions contribute to confusion and has marred progress on the implementation of the legal regime. Furthermore, its lacunae and the partial implementation created lopsided development. Hence there is a need to look at this more closely, and start first to strengthen the institutional capability and second to implement the provisions of the law. While doing so, those provisions, which are overlapping and contradictory, need to be harmonised and the gaps in the law need to be filled.

With regard to the legal regime relating to cooperation between Nepal and India, it should take a more realistic approach. The provisions of the constitution of the Kingdom of Nepal seem to indicate clearly that in the matter of water resources cooperation, it is necessary to develop a consensus between the political parties in the respective countries themselves. In the absence of in-house understanding within each country, no cooperation between Nepal and India can materialise. For such an understanding, two important elements are necessary: firstly an understanding of the compulsions, and secondly appreciation of the fact that the overall national interest is above any political party interest. The problem lies initially in Nepal itself, and the country must come out with a firm Nepalese perspective. Recently, some initiatives have been taken in this direction. A strategy for water resources development is in almost its final shape and the hydropower development policy has been prepared. This naturally entails urgent amendments being made to the existing laws.

As far as India is concerned, there seems to be a willingness to cooperate. However, there needs to be an understanding of the Nepalese perspective, which is currently seen by India as negative. As a matter of fact such a perspective is mainly attributable to the improper implementation of existing treaties on the one hand and creation of small irritants like inundation of land on the Nepalese side of the border on the other hand. It may be worthwhile to reach a comprehensive treaty on water resources between Nepal and India, laying down some basic principles, and start implementing in good faith one or two projects. Mahakali is a good start. The sooner it is implemented, the better it is for both countries to set an example.

Chapter 10

The Policy and Law of Bangladesh Concerning the Utilisation of her Water Resources

Mohammad Humayun Kabir

10.1 Introduction

Bangladesh is a low-lying flood plain in the northeast of the South Asian sub-continent, with innumerable rivers, tributaries, distributaries, streams and creeks criss-crossing its small, deltaic territory of about 144,000km^2. It is a Least Developed Country (LDC), with all the implications that are associated with this status, although it is now showing several positive signs that have the potential to take it out of the poverty trap and is gaining in international profile. Although services and industries sectors are growing, agriculture remains the mainstay of the country's economy. While it has achieved remarkable success in population control, the aggregate number is still staggering and that builds up pressure to increase food production and ensure adequate protein supplies. Irrigation facilities and fish production thus need to increase considerably.

Ensuring safe drinking water is a problem in Bangladesh, particularly in view of the extent of the arsenic contamination of ground water in a good part of the country. The importance of navigation in riverine Bangladesh can hardly be over-emphasised, not least because waterways are the cheapest mode of transportation in the country. Increasing urbanisation, driven by acute land-man ratio and quest for economic opportunities, often creates environmental hazards and causes the ground water table to fall alarmingly. Bio-diversity and environment in Bangladesh has also been affected for a variety of reasons.

Clearly, water is central to the way of life in Bangladesh. Being a resource-strapped country, water is the single-most important resource for the well being of its people. The country's development as well as the sustenance of its natural environment largely depends on this natural resource. But contrary to popular perception in riverine and water-dependent Bangladesh, water is not an infinite bounty of nature. As such, how to address the issues of exploration, management and use of water resources in a comprehensive, integrated, equitable and sustainable manner are crucial questions for the country and its people. An attempt to understand these and other related issues is, therefore, a worthwhile exercise.

The aim of this Chapter is to discuss the water policy of Bangladesh and the legal regime that exists in the country in relation to the development and utilisation of its water resources. The first objective of this Chapter is to highlight the salient features of the water policy of Bangladesh and the most pertinent laws governing the utilisation of her water resources. And the other objective is to underscore the problems facing Bangladesh in implementing its water policy. It is argued in the chapter that management and development of the water resources of Bangladesh may not be possible by means of its unilateral efforts and that it would require sincere and long-term cooperation from the upper riparian states. The Chapter argues on that Bangladesh, the lower-most riparian state in the River Ganges basin, is likely to immensely benefit from international watercourses law.

The Chapter is divided into five sections, including this introductory one. The second section deals with the water resources system of Bangladesh, including the geopolitical setting of international watercourses entering the country. The third section focuses on the water policy of Bangladesh, while the fourth concerns itself with the laws of Bangladesh concerning the utilisation of her water resources. And some concluding remarks are made in the last section.

10.2 Water Resources System of Bangladesh

Here, the main characteristics of the water resources system of Bangladesh will be highlighted. These characteristics are due to the country's geographical setting and hydrological situation. Bangladesh is one of the largest deltas in the world, situated between the Himalayas in the north and the Bay of Bengal in the south, and bounded on the west, north and east by India and on the southeast by Myanmar.

Rainfall and surface water flows are the two major sources of water in Bangladesh. Availability of water from both these sources is variable, both spatially and seasonally. Bangladesh experiences heavy rains in the monsoon, recording water surplus with about 80 per cent of the total rainfall only in five-six months from May. It does not rain much in the dry period during the rest of the year. Water is deficient, sometimes acutely, in the dry season. Of the total available water in the country throughout the year, eighty four percent comes as surface flow through 3 major rivers – the Ganges, the Brahmaputra and the Meghna. Their maximum monthly flows are in August and the minimum in February. While flows in the dry winter months in the major rivers fall sharply, most small rivers are seen to dry up.

Bangladesh is prone to frequent flooding, in the wet season, due to its low-lying flat topography and heavy rainfall. Most of the areas of the country lie less than 20m above mean sea level. It is a floodplain with the riverine floodplain covering much greater land area than the coastal floodplain. While comparing Bangladesh with the Netherlands, one eminent Dutch water expert states that floods in Bangladesh have more, and often conflicting, functions. Agriculture and fisheries, for example, are intrinsically related to different stages of flood. These not only depend on the peak and duration of the floods, but also on the onset and recession of floods, while their requirements are different.[1]

Regional variations are also found in Bangladesh's relief pattern as well as in its hydrological characteristics. There are five hydrological regions in Bangladesh identified on the basis of the characteristics of rivers, intensity of flooding, salinity condition, etc. These are northwest, northeast, southwest, south-central and southeast regions. The northwest elevated (12m to 90m) region is prone to low rainfall and high water deficiency, while the country's northeast is dominated by the Meghna depression or the Sylhet basin that is only 3m to 6m above the sea level. The southwest region is characterised by low gradient, poor relief and salinity condition, while the level of salinity concentration is low in the south-central region due to availability of enormous volumes of water from the combined flow of the Ganges, the Brahmaputra and the Meghna. The southeast region is geographically different from the rest of the country, having generally elevated relief and being independent in terms of hydrological response from the major rivers. The rivers of this region, that are mainly non-deltaic in nature, originate in the hill ranges of Tripura and Assam of India and empty directly into the Bay of Bengal.[2] As Bangladesh is an active delta, most of its rivers are in an active stage of siltation, and localised physiographic changes keep taking place either by erosion and/or by deposition every year.

A paradox is too glaring to miss – abundance of water during the monsoon and its scarcity in the dry season. So the task is to control and mitigate floods and guarantee supply of water in both quantitative and qualitative terms.

There are as many as 57 rivers in Bangladesh, including the three major river systems – the Ganges, the Brahmaputra and the Meghna – whose headwaters are located outside its territory. The primary surface water development potential in the country remains with the perennial or major rivers. Significantly, the inflow of waters from India into Bangladesh constitutes about 92 per cent of the total surface flow, while only about 8 per cent are generated within the country. As such, Bangladesh, being the lowermost riparian country, has hardly any control over the common rivers.

Apart from the problems inherent in the country's hydrological characteristics, relief patterns and the geopolitical setting of the common rivers, there are other problems that are encountered in the management and utilisation of her water resources. These are meeting the ever-expanding water needs of a growing economy and population, halting massive river sedimentation and bank erosion, ensuring water quality, maintenance of the eco-system, satisfying multi-sector water needs, promoting efficient and socially responsible water use, delineating public and private responsibilities, and decentralising state activities where appropriate. And the other constraints are borne of the difficulties of

---

[1] R. Koudstall 'The water resources systems in Bangladesh and the Netherlands' *The Daily Star*, Dhaka 30 April 2001 [18].

[2] N.I. Nazem and M.H. Kabir 'Indo-Bangladesh Common Rivers and Water Diplomacy' *BIISS Papers*, Dhaka, No. 5, December.

managing the deltaic plain and the virtual absence of unsettled land for building water structures in Bangladesh.

It is in this context that the water policy of Bangladesh needs to be examined.

10.3 Water Policy of Bangladesh

The Water Policy of Bangladesh was adopted in 1997. It is a comprehensive document, including sectoral policy, institutional policy and emphasis on the need for a legislative framework.[3]

10.3.1 *Objectives of National Water Policy*

The National Water Policy of the Government of Bangladesh aims to provide direction to all agencies working with the water sector, and institutions that relate to the water sector in one form or another, for achievement of specified objectives. Broadly, these objectives are:[4]

1. To address issues related to the harnessing and development of all forms of surface water and ground water and management of these resources in an efficient and equitable manner.
2. To ensure the availability of water to all elements of the society, including the poor and the underprivileged, and to take into account the particular needs of women and children.
3. To accelerate the development of sustainable public and private water delivery systems with appropriate legal and financial measures and incentives, including delineation of water rights and water pricing.
4. To bring institutional changes that will help decentralise the management of water resources and enhance the role of women in water management.
5. To develop a legal and regulatory environment that will help the process of decentralisation, sound environmental management, and improve the investment climate for the private sector in water development and management.
6. To develop a state of knowledge and capability that will enable the country to design its future water resources management plans by itself with economic efficiency, gender equity, social justice and environmental awareness to facilitate achievement of the water management objectives through broad public participation.

---

[3] This section heavily draws on the *National Water Policy*, Ministry of Water Resources, Government of Bangladesh, Dhaka, 1999.

[4] ibid.

10.3.2 Water Policies

Here sectoral policies are given. The sectors/areas are given below:

1. River Basin Management
2. Planning and Management of Water Resources
3. Water Rights and Allocation
4. Public and Private Involvement
5. Public Water Investment
6. Water Supply and Sanitation
7. Water and Agriculture
8. Water and Industry
9. Water and Fisheries and Wildlife
10. Water and Navigation
11. Water for Hydropower and Recreation
12. Water for the Environment
13. Water for Preservation of Haors, Baors, and Beels
14. Economic and Financial Management
15. Research and Information Management, and
16. Stakeholder Participation

Not all but only some of these policies are discussed below.[5]

10.3.2.1 River Basin Management

The policy of the Government of Bangladesh, in the short and intermediate term, for fostering international cooperation in water management is to:

1. Work with co-riparian countries to establish a system for exchange of information and data on relevant aspects of hydrology, morphology, water pollution, ecology, changing watershed characteristics, cyclone, drought, flood warning, etc., and to help each other understand the current and emerging problems in the management of the shared water sources.
2. Work with co-riparian countries for joint assessment of all the international rivers flowing through their territories for better understanding of the overall basin potentials.
3. Work jointly with co-riparian countries to harness, develop, and share the water resources of the international rivers to mitigate floods and augment flows of water during the dry season.
4. Make concerted efforts, in collaboration with co-riparian countries, for management of the catchment areas with the help of afforestation and erosion control for watershed preservation and reduction of land degradation.

---

[5] This section heavily draws on the *National Water Policy*, Ministry of Water Resources, Government of Bangladesh, Dhaka, 1999.

5. Work jointly with co-riparian countries for the prevention of chemical and biological pollution of the rivers flowing through these countries, by managing the discharge of industrial, agricultural and domestic pollutants generated by human action.
6. Seek international and regional cooperation for education, training, and research in water management.

10.3.2.2 Planning and Management of Water Resources

In this regard, the policy of the Government is as follows:[6]

1. The Water Resources Planning Organisation (WARPO) will delineate the hydrological regions of the country, based on appropriate natural features, for planning the development of their water resources.
2. The WARPO will prepare, and periodically update, a National Water Management Plan (NWMP) addressing the overall resource management issues in each region and the whole of Bangladesh, and providing directions for the short, intermediate and long runs.
3. The NWMP and all other related plans will be prepared in a comprehensive and integrated manner, with due consideration for the interest of all water-related sectors. The planning methodology will ensure co-operation across sectors and people's participation in the process.

Within the macro framework of the NWMP:

1. The Bangladesh Water Development Board (BWDB) will implement all major surface water development projects and other FCDI (Flood Control, Drainage and Irrigation) projects with command area above 1,000 hectares. The Local Government will implement FCDI projects having a command area of 1,000 hectares or less after identification and appraisal through an interagency Project Appraisal Committee.
2. The participation of all project affected persons, individually and collectively, will be ensured in the planning, design, implementation and operation and maintenance (O&M) of publicly funded surface water resources development plans and projects. Local Governments (Parishads) will be the principal agencies for coordinating these efforts. Community level self-help groups (private) and Non-Government Organisations will also be relied on to assist in the participatory process.
3. The Government will further make social and environmental assessments mandatory in all plan development

[6] This section heavily draws on the *National Water Policy*, Ministry of Water Resources, Government of Bangladesh, Dhaka, 1999.

10.3.2.3 Water Rights and Allocation

The ownership of water does not vest in an individual but in the state. The Government reserves the right to allocate water to ensure equitable distribution, efficient development and use, and to address poverty. Rules for water allocation will be developed for in-stream needs (ecological, water quality, salinity control, fisheries and navigation) during low-flow periods; for off-stream withdrawal (irrigation, municipal and industrial, power), and for groundwater recharge and abstraction. Allocation for non-consumptive use (e.g. navigation) would imply ensuring minimum levels in water bodies used for that purpose.

10.3.3 Institutional Policy

It is the policy of the Government that:[7]

1. The Government will formulate a framework for institutional reforms to guide all water sector related activities.
2. The National Water Resources Council (NWRC) will coordinate all water resources management activities in the country and oversee the implementation of the National Water Policy.
3. WARPO will be the exclusive government institution for macro-level water resource planning. It will also serve as the Executive Secretariat of the ECNWRC (Executive Committee of the National Water Resources Council).
4. The Government will lead the effort towards developing grassroots institutions, in conjunction with the civil society, for managing water resources at community levels.
5. Public water projects will include a training component for transfer of knowledge and technology to the users that will be monitored by the executing agency at every stage of the project work.

10.3.4 Legislative Framework

Setting the appropriate legislative framework is fundamental to effective implementation of the water policy. This policy will be given effect through a National Water Code encoding specific provisions of the water policy to facilitate its implementation. Let us now turn to the laws of Bangladesh concerning the utilisation of her water resources.

---

[7] This section heavily draws on the *National Water Policy*, Ministry of Water Resources, Government of Bangladesh, Dhaka, 1999.

10.4 Laws of Bangladesh Concerning Utilisation of her Water Resources

This section outlines the domestic legal regime of Bangladesh concerning the regulation of use of water, control of pollution, sustainable development of water resources of the country, etc. Although the National Water Code is not yet in place, the following are some of the water sector legislation that currently exists in the country:[8]

Legislation enacted in English

1876	The Irrigation Act	1972	Bangladesh Water and Power Development Boards Ordinance
1882	Transfer of Property Act	1982	The Acquisition & Requisition of Immovable Property Ordinance
1908	Registration Act	1983	Local Government (Union Parishads) Ordinance
1950	The State Acquisition and Tenancy Act	1983	Irrigation Water Rate Ordinance
1952	Embankment and Drainage Act	1985	Groundwater Management Ordinance
1958	Inland Water Transport Authority Ordinance		

Legislation enacted in Bangla

1990	Land Management Manual (Settlement of Khas Land, Water Estates and Rivers / Riversides)	1992	Water Resources Planning Act
		1996	Water Supply and Sewerage Authority Act

10.4.1 Water Resources Act/National Water Code

The existing legislation needs to be supplemented in a number of key areas. The National Water Policy requires that a National Water Code be enacted to revise and consolidate the laws governing ownership, development, appropriation, utilisation, conservation, and protection of water resources. The NWMP will identify where legislation needs to be reviewed and will make recommendations for change, or new legislation, where considered necessary. In addition to the NWMPP effort, the

---

[8] This section draws on Water Resources Planning Organisation, Ministry of Water Resources, Government of Bangladesh, *National Water Management Plan, Draft Development Strategy*, Vol. 7, August 2000, Dhaka [107]-[113].

Water Policy Advisory Group (which reports to the Secretary, Ministry of Water Resources) is engaged in reviewing existing legislation to ensure effective implementation of the National Water Policy.

The purpose of the National Water Code must be to establish the Government's obligation to manage and administer the country's water resources. As a code it should take precedence over all former legislation and replace the Water Resources Act of 1992. It should promote the rational management and use of water by providing a legislative framework that would amend and replace existing legislation, as appropriate.

10.4.2 International Dimension

In addition to the above pieces of legislation, there are several other laws that are pertinent to our purpose here. These are laws on maritime water of Bangladesh and laws on international water of which Bangladesh is a party. Maritime Water Laws are The Territorial and Maritime Zones Act, 1974 (Act No. XXVI of 1974) and The Territorial Waters and Maritime Zones Rules, 1977. The Act of 1974 deals with the issues of Territorial Waters, Contiguous Zone, Economic Zone, Conservation Zone and Continental Shelf, and also the issue of preventing and controlling marine pollution and preserving the quality and ecological balance in the marine environment. The Rules of 1977 regulate the conduct of foreign ships in the Territorial Waters, construction of installations, etc by the Government in the Economic Zone, conduct of persons there, etc.[9] The International Water Laws concerning Bangladesh are the Statute of the Indo-Bangladesh Joint Rivers Commission, 1972, and the Indo-Bangladesh Treaty on Sharing the Ganges River Waters, 1996.

10.5 Concluding Remarks

What is clear from the preceding exposition is that there is at long last an unmistakable recognition in Bangladesh of the fact that water is not an infinite bounty of nature, and that it is not only a techno-economic and strategic resource it is also an issue of social preference. The concept of stakeholder has not only been accepted, its rights and role also are visible in the management and utilisation of water resources alongside the national and local governments. Both institutional and participatory approaches have been adopted, encompassing a wide variety of

---

[9] See for details, M. Farooque and S.R. Hasan 'Laws Regulating to Environment in Bangladesh' Bangladesh Environmental Lawyers Association (BELA), Dhaka, 1996 [310]-[333]. Also see for details of the Environment Conservation Act 1995, Act 1 of 1995, Law Enacted for Conservation, Improvement of Quality Standard, and Control and Mitigation of Pollution of the Environment, Abdus Sattar Syed, *Introduction to Environmental Laws of Bangladesh*, Ace Data Products, Dhaka, 1998.

sectors of national development on the basis of conjunctive use of surface and ground water. The policy, therefore, has been for a comprehensive, integrated, equitable, decentralised and sustainable development, management and utilisation of the water resources of Bangladesh.

However, there are several constraints for Bangladesh in regard to the utilisation of her water resources. These are locational, management-related, technical-legal, financial, and the lower-most riparian status. While the National Water Policy and the concomitant legal framework would eventually redress some of these problems, those have not yet been put into operation. Indications were made regarding basin-wide planning for water resources management and utilisation. This would require long-term solution to common river water sharing disputes, cooperation among the co-basin states in the eastern Himalayan sub-region on harnessing and utilisation of their water resources, and unequivocal adherence to the Convention on the Law of the Non-Navigational Uses of International Watercourses and the other pertinent international legal instruments.

Chapter 11

Equitable Utilisation of Nepalese Water Resources: Bilateral and Regional Perspectives

Trilochan Upreti

11.1 Introduction

This chapter aims to discuss the water resources in Nepal, their significance for the overall socio-economic development as an economic tool and associated legal issues from the perspective of international law. Furthermore, issues inextricably intertwined with transboundary freshwater resources, ranging across hydrological, geographical, political, socio-economic, legal and technical fields also will be dealt with in the light of existing legal principles and practices. At the same time, the issues of bilateral Indo-Nepal co-operation and of regional cooperation with Bangladesh and Bhutan will also be covered, and water resources issues, in particular, will be analysed according to the letter and spirit of international law. On the basis of the findings, a conclusion will be drawn as to how to overcome the problems related to the maximisation of the benefits for Nepal and its bilateral and regional partners.

11.2 Nepal – Water Abundant

There are about 6,000 rivers and rivulets in Nepal, having a total drainage area of 194,471km^2, 45.7 per cent of which lies in Nepal. There are 33 rivers, whose drainage area exceeds 1,000km^2. The total average annual runoff into Nepal's rivers is estimated to be 200,000 million m^3 originating from areas within the country; the catchments area from Nepal alone make up about 45 per cent of the long-term average annual flow of the Ganges basin and contributes over 70 per cent of the Ganges flow during the driest months.[1]

Numerous studies suggest that Nepal theoretically has 83,000MW of hydropower potential, more than the combined total produced by the United States,

---

[1] His Majesty's Government, Water and Energy Commission Secretariat, (HMG/N-WECS) *Water Resources Strategy Nepal*, Kathmandu, WECS, (2002) [14].

Canada and Mexico, of which about 43,000MW is presently considered economically viable to harness.[2] Despite the abundance of water resources, only about one third of the population has got access to safe water, and only 42 per cent of the net calculated land has been irrigated so far.[3]

11.3 Potential for Nepalese Watercourses

Nepal is endowed with immense water resources potential, which, if utilised properly would be a boon both for itself and for countries further downstream. The benefits could be applied to several spheres, including hydropower, irrigation, and particularly navigation, which is crucial for the landlocked countries of Nepal and Bhutan and the north-eastern Indian states which could access the sea via Bangladesh. Moreover, benefits from flood control, and industrial, recreational and other areas are possible.[4] Due to the nature of these rivers and the geography of the area, the optimum site for a barrage might be in one state (e.g. Nepal), but the benefits could be accrued in other states, (e.g. India and Bangladesh) and such benefits could be shared by yet more states.[5]

The concept of 'drainage basin'[6] or 'watercourse'[7] has been developed for these reasons and also the concept that a watercourse should be regarded as a single unit regardless of political borders.[8] In the bilateral sphere, the successful model of co-operation between USA and Canada with regard to the Columbia River Treaty has been repeatedly put forward as a basis for other such co-operative models. Hence, Indo-Nepal water resources offer opportunities and challenges for overall development.[9]

The case of Nepalese water resource development is unique in comparison with other countries; Nepal has huge resources available with a tiny land area requiring irrigation and a very low requirement for hydroelectricity. Conversely, India has got a huge territory but very little water, and no water during the dry season either for herself or for Bangladesh.

Fundamental benefits could accrue to Nepal, in particular, from co-operation over navigation facilities, giving access to the sea, an essential requirement for Nepal's trade.[10] In order to maximise the benefits, an integrated and holistic

---

[2] C.K. Sharma *A Treatise on Water Resources of Nepal* (Kathmandu Nepal 1999) [118].
[3] His Majesty's Government (n 1).
[4] B. Crow, A. Lindquist and D. Wilson *Sharing Ganges: The Politics and Technology of River Development* (Saga Publication New Delhi 1995) [218]-[237].
[5] ibid [204]-[210].
[6] Article 1 Helsinki Rules in Report of the ILA held at Helisinki 1966 [484]-[532].
[7] Article 1 of the 1997 UN Convention in 36 ILM 1997 [721].
[8] H.A. Smith *The Economy Use of International River* (P.S. King & Son London 1931) [121].
[9] B.C. Upreti *Politics of Himalayan River Waters* (Nirala Publication New Delhi 1993) [84]-[88].
[10] C.K. Sharma *Water and Energy Resources of the Himalayan Block* (Sangeeta Sharma Kathmandu 1983) [377].

approach needs to be undertaken in Nepal, e.g., in watershed management, and afforestation in the Siwalik and in the hills of the Himalayas, which would significantly reduce the silt and sediment that causes tremendous loss and damage to territory downstream. As a result of these, all nations involved would benefit.[11] An example of this is the Indo-Bhutan co-operation in the Chukha project, which enormously benefited both nations.[12] Additionally, there are several projects under review for implementation; primarily, the hydroelectric projects: the (1,020MW) Tala Project on the Wangchu downstream of Chukha, Chukha II, Sunkosh High Dam Project (1,525MW), Chukha III (900MW) and the Mannes High Dam project (2,800MW), and apart from these India's strategy to divert the Brahmaputra into rivers in Bhutan is also under planning.[13] Due to the income of Chukha I, a 336MW project, Bhutan is emerging as one of the wealthiest nations, in terms of per capita income, in South Asia.[14]

11.4 Indo-Nepal Co-operation on Water Resources

Nepal's water resource development dates back to 1920 when it agreed to transfer 4,093 acres of its land on the east bank of the Mahakali so that India could build the Sarada Barrage to regulate waters for irrigation. In exchange, Nepal received an equal amount of land elsewhere. India agreed to provide Nepal with a supply of up to 460ft^3/s of water and, provided surplus was available, a supply of up to 1,000ft^3/s from the Sarada canal should cultivation expand at any time in the future.[15] This project was initially undertaken to provide irrigation facilities at her own cost and initiative, and was natural for India to accrue benefits for herself. However an assessment of the treaty provision seems to indicate that much of the benefits went to India inequitably, such arrangements are rarely encountered in international water case law elsewhere.

Another water resource project involving Indo-Nepal co-operation, was the Kosi Project Agreement.[16] By 1954 it was considered urgent to implement the

---

[11] B.G. Verghese *Waters of Hope* (Oxford & IBH Publishing New Delhi 1990) [347].

[12] B.G. Verghese and R.R. Iyer (eds.) *Harnessing the Eastern Himalayan rivers: Regional Co-operation in South Asia* (Konark Publishers New Delhi 1994) [199]-[200]: the 336MW hydropower project jointly undertaken by means of Indo-Bhutan co-operation provides a good example, in which India provided 40 per cent amount of the project cost as assistance to Bhutan and remaining 60 per cent as an investment on 50/50 ownership of the joint investment project. The electricity generated is being exported to India as a result of which a huge amount of money, 40 Crore annually, has accrued to Bhutan as revenue from which her economy has benefited.

[13] B. Subba 'Tapping Himalayan Water Resources: Problems, Opportunities and Prospects from a Bhutanese Perspective' in *Water Nepal* Vol. 4 No. 1 1994 [210], also see R.S. Kharat *Bhutan in SAARC: Role of a Smaller State in a Regional Alliance* (South Asian Publication New Delhi 1999) [97]-[99].

[14] B. Subba *Himalayan Waters* (Panos South Asia Kathmandu 2001) [204].

[15] B.C. Upreti (n 9) [94]-[95]. Also see B.G. Verghese (n 11) [201].

[16] B.G. Verghese (n 11) [201].

project in order to control the devastating effect of the Kosi floods during the monsoons. For the project, embankments were constructed on both sides of the river extending for about 130km downstream, to ensure flood protection of approximately 280,000ha of land; and a diversion structure was also built for a network of canals to provide irrigation to a total of 1,150,000ha of land.[17] The project was criticised in all levels in Nepal, the complaint being that it was a sell out of national property for India's benefit. Eventually, India agreed to reconsider,[18] and a revised agreement was signed in 1966. Based on the assurance of the then Indian Prime Minister Lal B. Shastri, Nepal agreed to resume work on the project. Some agreements were changed to assure Nepal's benefit.[19]

Despite the revised agreement and its execution, the intention to bring these benefits to Nepal has not fully materialised. The Chatra Inundation Canal, which was proposed to irrigate 66,000ha of land in Nepal, has in the event only led to the irrigation of 10,000ha.

The Gandak Project Agreement (1959) is the third agreement that was executed for India's benefit, i.e. flood control, irrigation and hydropower. On the Gandak, a barrage was constructed on a reach of the river, which forms the boundary between India and Nepal. The project was to provide irrigation to a gross command area of 1,340,000ha in Bihar, 500,000ha in Uttar Pradesh (both Indian States), and 63,000ha in Nepal. Utilising the head available on the main western canal, a hydropower plant of 15MW was also provided for in the project as a secondary benefit.[20] The agreement was heavily criticised within Nepal. Subsequently both parties agreed to revise this agreement to pass on more benefits to Nepal. However, it has been argued that in those projects India had invested large amounts of resources, and that it was therefore natural that it should accrue more benefits than Nepal.[21]

Nepal's concerns are understandable, as the promise made in these treaties were never fulfilled by India, i.e. the Chatra canal under the Kosi agreement, and the navigation facility as stipulated in the Gandak agreement, were never undertaken. Similarly, the hydro generation from the Kosi project was never carried out. Furthermore, India objected to Nepalese projects such as Kanakai Multipurpose Project (38MW) with Asian Development Bank assistance, the Maulghat 38MW hydropower project, the Sikta, Babai and Rapti irrigation projects, stating that they would affect its existing consumptive rights.[22] On the other hand, India developed several irrigation projects, damming the rivers along

---

[17] T. Prasad *Comprehensive Water Resources Development in Indo-Nepal Region: Perspective and prospects* presented at a conference on the Large Scale Water Management held in Kathmandu, October 1997 [18].

[18] ibid, also see B.C. Upreti (n 9) [100]-[101]: Indian Power and Irrigation Minister, K.L. Rao who had assured the revision of the Treaty in 1962-63 during his Nepal visit and in 1965, during Prime Minister Lal B. Shastri's visit it was again assured.

[19] B.C. Upreti (n 9) [100]-[102].

[20] ibid [102]-[108].

[21] ibid [107].

[22] C.K. Sharma (n 10) [341]. Also see D.R. Pandey *Nepal's Failed Development: Reflections on the Mission and the Maladies* (Nepal South Asia Centre Kathmandu 1999) [340]

the Nepal border without providing the requisite information; consequently these projects have largely submerged Nepalese territory.[23] These activities were sufficient to aggravate Nepalese grievances. Furthermore, donors willing to lend money to Nepal to develop a water project required Indian consent, whilst in the case of India; they never asked for Nepalese consent or even furnished any information of above projects.[24] From a legal standpoint, Nepal's entitlement to 'equitable and reasonable use' has been explicitly denied in these treaties, contrary to the principles of Article IV and V of the Helsinki Rules and Article 5, 6 and 7 of the 1997 UN Convention of the IWC. For example, Nepal's share of irrigation was less then 3 per cent of the total area watered by the Kosi and the Gandak Scheme.[25]

A fourth Treaty is the 1996 Treaty concerning the Integrated Development of the Mahakali River including Sarada Barrage, Tanakpur and Pancheswar Project. This is the first treaty to accommodate, in principle, the interests of both nations equally and equitably. The first two projects have already been executed by India at Mahakali on the Indo-Nepal border at its own cost. For its contribution to the Tanakpur Barrage, Nepal was provided with a supply of 1,000ft^3/s of water in the wet season and 300ft^3/s in the dry season and a annual supply of 70 million KW's of energy on a continuous basis, free of cost. India is to construct the head regulator and the waterways as well as the transmission line up to the Nepal border. The waters of the Mahakali River from the Sarada canal and from the Tanakpur Barrage have been incorporated in this treaty, replacing all such previous agreements.[26] However, the Mahakali treaty has not yet been implemented and the criticism is made that the intention of India was never to execute the Pancheswar project, but rather to ensure the continuity of the defunct Sarada benefits and legalise the contentious Tanakpur project, which was constructed entirely for Indian benefit, ignoring Nepal's legitimate half-entitlement with respect to such a boundary river.

The provision of this treaty constitutes the first time India's willingness to join hands with Nepal in the development of water resources for the common benefit of its people, and according to the principles of equity. Nevertheless, due to disputes over the interpretation of the Article 3 of the said treaty, which provides for existing consumptive use, Nepal's consumptive use has been specifically defined in the treaty, whilst India's consumptive use was not defined, and in later stages was disputed, against the spirit of the treaty. Thus, the finalisation of the Detail Project Report (DPR) could not be agreed upon, irrespective of numerous meetings. Although the DPR was estimated to be completed in 6 months it is now

---

[23] B.G. Verghese (n 11) [340]-[341].

[24] Staff, 'the World Bank discriminates us', *The Kathmandu Post* 6, 2002; stated that the World Bank had lent money to the Indian state of Uttar Pradesh to develop an irrigation project but did not provide even notice or information to Nepal; on the contrary, on the other hand, it has sought Indian, Bangladeshi and Chinese consent for lending money to a Power Development Fund in Nepal. Later, US$80 million fund was provided and no objections were made.

[25] B. Subba (n 14) [192]-[193].

[26] 36 ILM 1997 [533]-[535].

expected to take 10 years to finalise, a fact which demonstrates the complexities associated with it.

However, it has been argued that the treaty has attempted to follow a model based on the principle of 'equitable utilisation' and 'no harm' principles. Nonetheless, whether these concepts are clearly embodied is not clear, due to the ambiguity reflected in Article 3 and 5(1) as well as paragraph 3 and 6 of the exchange of letters of the Mahakali treaty. The contentious fact is the wording of 'respective consumptive use' of the waters of the Mahakali River without actually specifying the nature of the use. At the same time the letter, in paragraph 3(b) contains some restrictions as to the notion of equal entitlement, whereas Article 5.1, which states that the water requirements of Nepal are to be given prime consideration, contradicts the other provisions and creates ambiguity. It is obvious that India's consumptive use is higher than Nepal's which may impact on Nepal's plans to forgo part of its water entitlement in return for bearing a proportionately lower share of the costs of non-hydro components.[27] That is to say, the treaty provides that the cost of the project will be shared proportionately to the benefits; if India is able to define maximum existing use, the remaining water use cost will be lower; this is the obvious reason for the wrangling over the definition of consumptive use. However, Article V of the Helsinki Rules and Article 6 of the 1997 UN convention on the IWC, both state that existing use is only one of the factors to be considered in determining whether or not any specific use is equitable. Thus it seems, however, that the emphasis on defining more water in terms of consumptive use may not serve India's interests as well as might have been considered.

It can be concluded that the water resources of Nepal, which are in abundant excess, if developed in an integrated manner, could lead to the entire region, including Nepal, becoming as Kuwait is to the Middle East, with water being, as it were, the oil. The other point is that if the former treaties, as described above, are not addressing Nepal's interests, or are not being implemented as per treaty provisions, they should be renegotiated for their better implementation, or otherwise abrogated. If they are against the principles of the 1997 UN Convention and Articles 64 of the Vienna Convention on the Law of Treaties 1969, such treaties can be abrogated or may be declared to have automatically come to an end.[28] There are several examples of this kind of abrogation, renegotiation and conclusion of new treaties in the international arena as well as in interstate practice.

The Nile treaty 1929 was annulled by Sudan and a new treaty was concluded in 1959.[29] However, the ICJ declared Hungarian termination of a 1977 treaty with Czechoslovakia pertaining to the sharing of benefits from the Danube river waters illegal.[30] Similarly, Pakistan has unilaterally repudiated the May 4 1948 agreement with India, regarding the payment of compensation for getting continued flow of waters from the former stating that this agreement was concluded on such a

---

[27] B.G. Verghese (n 11) [344]-[345].

[28] *ILM* 1969 [679].

[29] *Year Book of ILC* 1974 [65].

[30] 37 *ILM*, 1998 [162]-[202].

compulsion that the former could not have refused.[31] From the point of state practice and the view of international law, if an agreement is not serving the interest of one party, due to changed circumstances, or in other similar situations, there is a way of enabling the negotiation of a new agreement or revising an existing one. Furthermore, from the point of view of treaty law it is the states concerned who conclude a treaty, and if it no longer seems good for them, the state has every right to renegotiate a new one. However, Article 3 of the UN IWC Convention 1997 suggests that the state may harmonise existing agreements and Article 3(1) suggests that states should enter into new agreements in which they can adjust the provisions of the convention. However, as argued by Lucius Caflisch, this provides states complete freedom in the matter.[32]

11.5 Bilateral Relations with India

The nature of Indo-Nepal relations is unique.[33] Nepal is between the giant states of Asia, described perfectly by the late King Prithvi Narayan Shah, as 'a yam between two boulders'. The Himalayas have since the time of the British Raj, been regarded as a second frontier and used to keep Nepal within the sphere of influence of India. For these reasons, India has used a variety of measures, including the granting of transit facilities (the provisions of services and facilities to export and import through its territory, and free access to and from the sea) as a political tool and as leverage, to ensure that Nepal remains within the broader Indian security framework.[34]

At times the special relationship has deteriorated and serious conflict has arisen, particularly during the trade and transit impasse in 1989.[35] India virtually imposed an economic blockade in 1989 by closing all but two of the 21 trade routes, and 13 of the 15 transit routes used by Nepal for trade under the 1978 transit treaty. It is worth mentioning that March 1989 was the time when Nepal's 1978 trade and transit treaty was about to expire; and when renewal of the treaty was unexpectedly refused by India only days before the appointed date.

---

[31] R.K. Baxter 'The Indus Basin' in A. Garrison, R.D. Hayton and C.J. Olmstead *The Law of International Drainage Basins* (Oceana Publications New York 1967) [456]-[457]. Also see Lucius Caflisch 'Unequal Treaties' in *German YB of International Law* Vol. 35 1992 [520].

[32] L. Caflisch 'The Use of International Waterways: The Contribution of the United Nations' in M.I. Glassner (ed.) *United Nations At Work* (Praeger Westport, CT 1998) [1]-[25].

[33] S.D. Muni *Foreign Policy of Nepal* (National Publishing House New Delhi 1973) [67]-[96].

[34] S.P. Subedi 'Indo-Nepal Relations: the Causes of Conflict and Their Resolution' in SK Mitra and D Rothermund (eds.) *Legitimacy and Conflict in South-Asia* (South Asia Institute, Manohar Publishing New Delhi 1997) [220].

[35] ibid [220]-[241]: in Indo-Nepal bilateral relations, it was only in 1978 that India agreed for a separate transit treaty for 10 year period, which expired in 1988; at the last moment India rejected to continuation of the earlier arrangement, alleging that Nepal was not complying with the provisions of the 1950s Peace and Friendship Treaty and its subsequent Letter of Exchange.

The reasons advanced by India for its reluctance were many.[36] Nepal in relation to these allegations had explicitly rejected them as baseless and untrue and pointed out that India's action with regard to economic blockades and its reluctance to continue the utilisation of existing trade and transit facilities was a blatant violation of customary international law.[37] The conflict continued for over a year, but after the change of the political system in 1990, when a multi-party democracy was restored in Nepal, followed by the installation of a new government, the two governments agreed to restore the *status quo ante* of April 1987 in matters of trade and transit.[38]

11.6 Negotiations on Water Resources Projects

To grasp the opportunities afforded by its water resources, Nepal alone does not have the capacity economically, technologically, or in skilled manpower nor even the consumer demand to absorb such huge benefits. On the other hand, neither India alone can utilise these resources without meaningful co-operation from Nepal, because Nepal offers an ideal location for project construction. Such a unique location offers tremendous benefits in mitigating flood hazards, the augmentation of water flows in the dry season, hydropower, irrigation and navigation facilities.[39] The water talks between the two countries have always been dominated by their political relationship. Whenever the general atmosphere of political relations between the two countries has not been encouraging, the water talks did not yield any result, but rather intensified bitterness instead of enhancing progress. On the one hand, Nepal is very suspicious of India's attitude; on the other hand India is alleging that Nepal is not really interested in developing those vast resources for the mutual benefit of their people.[40]

11.7 Associated Multi-Disciplinary Complications

The completion of water projects takes a long time and huge investment, and several other issues must be dealt with simultaneously, including environmental aspects, seismic evaluation, socio-economics, rehabilitation and resettlement. In the Nepalese scenario, the first question that confronts the planner and policy

---

[36] S.P. Subedi 'Transit Arrangement between Nepal and India: A Study in International Law' in D. Hodder, S.J. Lloyd and K. McLachlan (eds.) *Geopolitics and International Boundaries* (Volume 2, Frank Cass London 1997) [175].
[37] ibid [175]-[176].
[38] S.P. Subedi (n 34) [221].
[39] B.C. Upreti (n 9) [92]-[94].
[40] C.K. Sharma (n 10). C.K. Sharma, an eminent scholar, has pointed out that the current situation (after Kosi and Gandak agreement) is such that no politician or bureaucrat will ever dare to stake his career or fame in dealing with the sensitive issue of water resources which involves the question of sharing between and among riparians.

maker is who will purchase the electricity. India is the sole buyer so far and without her agreement Nepal cannot export to Bangladesh or Pakistan. Evidently, potential market such as China must be researched. The other issue is whether by building a dam in the upper riparian country, the flood problem can be reduced and low water flow increased for irrigation benefit of the lower riparian country. The upper riparian state must be paid by this beneficiary proportionately on the basis of benefits from the construction of a dam and basin management, similar to the case of the Columbia River Treaty.[41] It should be noted that through building a dam, the upper riparian country may obtain hydropower benefit, but will submerge her land and lose other wealth, flora, fauna, fish stocks, and biological diversity; and there will be a need for rehabilitation and resettlement of the peoples etc. Moreover, after about 50 years such sites will be unable to give benefits as a result of the sedimentation, and any chance to reuse them is lost forever.[42]

The position of the lower riparian country, however, will be different to that of the upper one; she will be more concerned about regulating and increasing low flow, about flood control, and extra irrigation costs. For example, in the case of the KMP, India is refusing to share flood control benefits, stating that she had already constructed complete flood protection along the Karnali by building and maintaining embankments on either side of the river at huge cost.[43] However, in practice, these embankments are not able to eliminate or check flood damage.[44]

11.8 Problems and Prospects of Nepalese Water Resources

In Nepal, it is a known fact that the development of the country depends upon the utilisation of its vast water resources and tourism. It is also known that in the past, whatever development projects were carried out in co-operation with India, Nepal was not adequately benefited. It was reported by an author, B.C. Upreti that King Birendra of Nepal once remarked that his country had been cheated by India in the case of Kosi and Gandak.[45] In the political election in Nepal, water issues were always a 'hot potato'. It was evident that after the conclusion of the Memorandum of Understanding (MOU) in connection with the Tanakpur Barrage, the Nepali Congress Government became the target of much political criticism from within Nepal. The dispute was referred to the Supreme Court, which declared that the said MOU was a kind of treaty which dealt with the sharing and allocation of national

41 B.C. Upreti (n 9) [284].
42 Ibid.
43 C.K. Sharma (n 10) [345]. See also BC Upreti (n 9) [284].
44 A.B. Thapa 'Kosi Floods' in *Spotlight, Nepal*, 22-29 September 2002.
45 H.A. Smith (n 8) [110].

resources; hence it fell within the provisions of the constitution of the kingdom of Nepal, 1990, Article 126, and needed to be ratified accordingly.[46]

It is clearly envisaged in the Ninth Plan (1997-2002) as well as the tenth Plan (2003-2008) that poverty eradication and infrastructure development will both be accomplished by means of the effective and efficient utilisation of water resources. Furthermore, bilateral and regional co-operation will be enhanced in order to achieve these goals; small and medium hydroelectric projects should be carried out to meet domestic needs, whereas mega projects will be undertaken to export power to the neighbouring countries with other downstream benefits being shared.[47] The Nepalese government adopted policies and made laws in this context,[48] and also adopted a water resources strategy recently.[49] The strategy sets out in detail the proposed use of these resources for poverty alleviation and infrastructure development, by exporting hydroelectricity from the mega projects, alongside domestic consumption from medium and small projects, and implementation of these resources in the spirit of bilateral as well as regional co-operation.[50]

Under the existing arrangement between India and Nepal, up to 100MW of electric power may be traded (in either direction) between the two countries according to requirements. Nepal is willing to increase this figure to 150MW; by including power generated from the Kali Gandaki A project.[51] However, the major obstacle to Nepal's export potential is the noncooperative attitude of the buyer and the expense of electricity generation.[52] If it cannot be harnessed at a competitive price, the chances of export are nil. Private sector involvement may be required in order to achieve efficiency and competitive targets.[53] Even Pakistan has paid the

---

[46] Judgement of the Nepalese Supreme Court in the case of *B. K. Neupane v His Majesty's Government*, Nepal, including the Council of Ministers and the Ministry of Water Resources and this copy is with the author.

[47] His Majesty's Government, Nepal, *The Ninth Plan*, Kathmandu, Nepal [89]-[92]; also see NK Sharma *Planning and Development in Nepal and the Tenth Plan* (Paribi Pub. Kathmandu 2003) [119].

[48] Hydropower Development Policy 2049, irrigation Policy 2054, Industrial Policy 2049, membership of MIGA and the Convention for the Enforcement of the Foreign Arbitral Awards (the New York Convention) etc.

[49] His Majesty's Government (n 1) [36].

[50] His Majesty's Government (n 47) [115]: From the private sector involvement Khimti (60MW), Bhotekosi (36MW) projects were implemented; and west Seti (750MW) which is an export oriented project has also been in implementation stage. They are finalising the details of export conditions with Indian companies.

[51] The MD of NEA put forth a plan for exporting 150MW of hydropower to India, The Kathmandu Post, 16 August 2002.

[52] B. Subba (n 13) [179]: the cost per KW of installing mini hydro plants varies from a low of around US$350 in Pakistan to a high of US$2,000 in Nepal. Also see D. Gyawali 'Himalayan Waters: Between Euphoric Dreams and Ground Realities' in K. Bahadur and MP Lama (eds.) *Nepal Perspectives on Indo-Nepal Relations* (Har-Anand Publication New Delhi 1995) [253].

[53] ibid.

IPPs 6.5US cents/kWh and is not able to export to India at the same price. Therefore, the pricing policy needs to be radically reviewed.[54]

Keeping all the above facts in view, together with the rising demand for electricity in northern India due to rapid industrialisation there, with an approximate deficit of 30,000MW predicted for the year 2005, Nepal would benefit if hydropower could be generated and exported to the power-hungry regions of that country. Steps should be considered to enable the extraction of economic benefits from the export of power and the provision of irrigation and navigation facilities to India and Bangladesh.[55]

India has utilised almost every drop of available water for irrigation, beyond the Nepal-India border, by constructing huge reservoirs and systems of irrigation networks, concerning which she has never provided Nepal with the requisite information. Such reservoirs have virtually submerged Nepalese land in several areas,[56] namely Banke, Rapti, Dang, Rupandehi, Rautahat, Mahotarri and Mahendranagar. Except for taking a few mitigatory steps in some areas,[57] she has neither compensated Nepal nor given assurances that she will not repeat such harmful projects in the years to come. In essence, she never follows the principle of 'equitable utilisation' and the 'no harm rule'; rather, she has always behaved against the notion of these norms, and also against the existing trend currently adopted even in interstate disputes within India.[58] Several diplomatic initiatives have been made by Nepal and notes have been sent to India; also negotiations were held to wipe out such illegal acts, but no tangible result has so far been achieved.

India's non-cooperation and the significance of bilateral or regional support is well explained by V.G. Verghese, an eminent Indian scholar, who asserted that delay is tantamount to denial:

> ... Nepal would be unwise to rehearse ancient grudges, some of them exaggerated, for little purpose and India would do well to be less over-bearing on occasion and to deal with Nepal in a more relaxed and understanding fashion.[59]

---

[54] S.B. Pun 'The Evolving Role of the Public and Private Institutions in the Nepalese Power Sector' in Annual Report of Water and Energy Commission Secretariat, Adm./060799/1/1, Seq. 041 [38]-[49].

[55] ibid [498]-[499].

[56] C.K. Sharma (n 10) (pandey) [340].

[57] *National Water Policy*, Ministry of Water Resources, Government of Bangladesh, Dhaka, 1999: In relation to submergence of 16 VDC in Banke District with the effect of Laxmanpur barrage both governments have undertaken mitigation efforts, such as embankment in the affected areas. Moreover such work so far seems ineffective to avert or mitigate the inundation caused by the barrage.

[58] B.R. Chauhan *Settlement of International and Interstate Water Dispute in India* (N M Tripathi Pvt. Ltd. Bombay 1992) [313]-[316].

[59] B.G. Verghese (n 11) [351].

11.9 The Tanakpur Controversy

In 1983, India completed the technical study for a 120MW hydroelectric project on the Mahakali, to be built upstream of the Sarada barrage, on land which was swapped with Nepal in 1920. In the downstream area of the project, the Mahakali Irrigation Project in Nepalese territory was already in operation, which could have suffered adverse effects from such an upstream diversion. Without giving either due notice or any technical information to Nepal, India carried out this project almost as if on a war footing, irrespective to obvious adverse effects. Nepal voiced her concerns about the proposed project, but they were not heard or the corrections were implemented until the 1992 Joint Communiqué between the Prime Ministers of both countries, contrary to the rules of 'equitable utilisation' and 'no harm'. Only in the Joint Communiqué, was it agreed that the Tanakpur tailrace waters should be discharged upstream of the Mahakali barrage so as not to affect existing consumptive use in Nepal.[60] The Tanakpur barrage, a *fait accompli* once constructed, aggravated situations already controversial in Nepalese political circles and serious questions were asked about the future of Indo-Nepal relations. The 120MW hydroelectric project lies below the proposed Pancheshwar dam site and little above the old Sarada barrage at Banbasa. A short 577m long afflux bund (embankment or causeway in India and Pakistan) (occupying some 2.9ha of land) has been constructed, with the consent of the Nepalese government (consent which was only sought retrospectively), tying the barrage to high ground in Nepal as a flood protection measure. The afflux bund is in Nepal and remains under Nepalese sovereignty.[61] However, as no amendments or corrections were made to address Nepalese concerns and interests, no further co-operation was possible; it was a case of the dichotomy of perceptions between two states. After a long dispute and general outcry in Nepal, several negotiations were held and finally an agreement was concluded, with the Mahakali treaty of 1996.

As a result of the conclusion of a new treaty and the inclusion of Tanakpur in it, Nepal has benefited from the project in several ways. She is being provided with 150ft^3/s of water (from a 1,000ft^3/s capacity). Additionally, Tanakpur had a regulator constructed in order to irrigate some 4,000 to 5,000 hectares of land in Nepal; an annual 20 million units of energy 'free of charge'[62] was provided and a road link was built from the barrage to connect with Nepal's east-west highway at Mahendranagar. It should be possible for India to divert a full 1,000ft^3/s supply to satisfy Nepal's desire for water from this project (in contrast to the initial diversion of 150ft^3/s), once the Pancheshwar storage dam is completed.

---

[60] S.C. McCaffrey *The Law of International Watercourses* (OUP Oxford 2000) [348], also see D. Gyawali and O. Schwank 'Interstate Sharing of Water Rights: An Alps-Himalayan Comparison' in Water Nepal Vol. 4 [234].

[61] B.G. Verghese (n 11) [207].

[62] ibid [208]: the word 'free of charge' does not seem appropriate for Nepal's entitlement.

11.10 Issues of Downstream Benefits

Water diplomacy is indeed a very sensitive issue in the entire region of south Asia; Nepal has come to understand that water resources have become both a symbol of national identity and pride, and a source of economic potential. A precise definition of downstream benefits upon which all are agreed cannot be found; however, if any water resources project activities in the upper reach of an IWC yield any type of benefits to the lower reach of a catchment area or downstream country, these are call 'downstream benefits'.[63] In principle and in practice, such benefits must be shared equally and equitably.

There are numerous practices in bilateral relations, which cover similar issues without necessarily using the same practices or procedures. Professors Bourne, McCaffrey and Utton hold the view that:

> There is support for the existence of a principle of downstream benefits in customary international law. Under the concept of equitable utilization, watercourse states are entitled to a reasonable and equitable share of the benefits of an international watercourse. It would seem to follow, therefore, that when a watercourse state does or refrains from doing an act that confers a benefit on another state sharing the watercourse, the latter state is under an obligation to share the benefit equitably with the former. The treaty practice of states supports the existence of this principle of sharing benefit. As it is well known, the principle of downstream benefits is dealt with explicitly in the Columbia Treaty.[64] And many other treaties provide for the return, either in kind or in cash, of a share of the benefits received as a result of the acts done in another state.[65]

It would be worthwhile to have a brief look at the Columbia treaty. The damming and storage of flood and snow fed waters in the Canadian territory made it possible to augment and regulate an enormous volume of water, from which a series of hydropower stations were constructed to harness power in US territory. Furthermore, flood damage was controlled, and substantial harm was thereby prevented. In addition, the regulated flow of the waters was substantially used for irrigation in US in times of need to increase agricultural productivity. However, a huge chunk of Canadian territory was submerged by these reservoirs and forests, flora and fauna were extinguished; also a big amount of money was spent in order to construct these structures. The United States agreed to pay US$64 million for

---

[63] T. Upreti 'A Perspective on Downstream Benefits' in the Kathmandu Post 25 June 2000 [10].

[64] 542 UNTS [244].

[65] Report on the Panel on Nepal's International Rivers, comment on '*A Position Paper on The Rights, Duties and Obligations of Upper and Lower Riparian Countries for Sharing Water Resources*' a position paper of Nepal submitted to the Nepalese Parliament by a team headed by the author in 1998 Annex-2 [2]-[5].

downstream benefits accrued in their territory as a result of Canadian storage; the power generated by these augmented waters was divided equally with Canada, and the Canadian share was later bought by the US at an agreed price of US$254 million.[66] The benefits accruing from these works were classified as power, flood control and irrigation and were each shared equally. However, it took almost twenty years to convince the United States about these benefits and conclude this treaty.

Bourne, McCaffrey and Utton have given a few instances of downstream benefits from the several treaties concluded between riparian states. Those practice show that the concept was practised from the early nineteenth century, and has been widely recognised; as a result of such practice, it has become the rule of customary law.[67] Moreover, as further argued by the above group of professors:

> While treaty practice can be invoked in support of the principle of downstream benefits where the act or the omission to act that confers the benefits was done or not done at the request of the downstream state, treaty practice does not exist to support the wider proposition that a downstream state is obliged to share benefits that it receives from the acts or omissions of an upstream state that it has not asked for or otherwise agreed to. The obligation to share downstream benefits, however, may exist under customary international law even when these benefits have not been solicited or agreed to. Logically, the obligation would seem to be implicit in the principle of equitable utilisation; for, if benefits are to be shared equitably, it should not matter whether or not they were sought by the beneficiary. Furthermore, a failure to share windfall benefits would seem to be a case of unjust enrichment. This is not to say, however, that there may not be a difference between a case in which a downstream state has asked for a benefit and one in

---

66 R.W. Johnson 'The Columbia Basin' in A. Garrison, R. Hayton and C. Olmstead *The Law of International Drainage Basins* (Oceana Publications New York) [228].

67 Report on the Panel on Nepal's International Rivers (n 65): The authors refer to six examples: i) the 1919 Treaty of Versailles gave France the exclusive right to use the Rhine for power production in return for paying Germany one-half the value of the energy produced; ii) the 1921 Barcelona Convention provides for sharing downstream benefits, though where a state is required to improve or maintain a river, it is entitled to a reasonable contribution of costs; iii) a 1926 agreement between South Africa and Portugal allowed South Africa to make diversion works on the Kunene River in Angola but required it to compensate Portugal (a 1969 treaty between the parties also provided for a sharing of benefits from the construction of a dam); iv) the 1977 Rhine Chlorides agreement states that the Netherlands is to pay a share of the cost to France of disposing of waste salts in a manner other than discharging them into the river (the authors note that 'this is a particularly striking example since it could be argued that France had a duty to avoid significant pollution harm to the Netherlands apart from the treaty'); v) the Lesotho Highlands Project treaty requires South Africa to pay a significant share of construction costs for works undertaken in Lesotho in return for downstream benefits; vi) the 1977 treaty between Czechoslovakia and Hungary (which was the subject of the *Gavcikovo-Nagymaros case*) provides for a dam and hydro plant to be located in Czechoslovakia (now Slovakia) with Hungary to receive power and flood control benefits.

which it has not so asked; in the latter case, equity might dictate that the downstream state not pay as much as it would have to in the former case.[68]

Another example is provided by the Owen Falls Dam in Uganda, where Egypt has developed and supplied hydropower to Uganda at her own cost; however, the water augmented in the reservoir was exclusively for her own use. In order to supervise the water and power arrangements, a resident Egyptian engineer was provided for in the agreement between the two states; in addition, electricity was produced for Uganda, and reparation for resettlement paid to her, at Egypt's expense, as a downstream benefit (accruing in this case to the upstream country).[69]

Besides this, in India, even in the sphere of inter-state relations, the states of UP and Bihar, agreed to share both costs and benefits in proportion, in the jointly developed Muskhand Dam Project.[70] The interesting fact about this project is that central government intervention was required in order to conclude this agreement. Later, the states of Gujarat and Rajasthan also concluded another agreement on cost sharing in the Bajaj Sagar Dam Project in 1966, in which Rajasthan agreed to pay an amount to Gujarat for work undertaken by the latter and the benefit was shared by the former.[71] In another dispute between Gujarat and Madhya Pradesh (MP) (both Indian states), over Narmada waters in the Narmada Sagar dam, the Narmada Tribunal applied this principle and as a result MP obtained downstream benefits from Gujarat.[72]

Moreover, there is a further interesting example of sharing downstream benefits with another sovereign state. India is planning to construct the Dihang Dam in its far east, which, she claims, would bring down the flood level by one metre, with Bangladesh substantially benefiting from the mitigation of the flood damage. Dubey, a former foreign secretary of the GOI, has questioned how India can deny Nepal payment for downstream benefits resulting from Nepalese work whilst India is simultaneously bargaining with Bangladesh over this project.[73]

In order to share the downstream benefits co-operation is essential. The prerequisite for achieving or sharing these kinds of broader benefits are co-operation, good neighbourly relations, and good faith between the riparian states. That is to say, in the absence of any investment of money, effort or technology by the lower riparian country, if hard work and investment is put into any water resources project in a boundary or transboundary watercourse, and such work yields any benefit to the downstream country (e.g. augmentation of water, flood

[68] Report on the Panel on Nepal's International Rivers (n 65) [4].
[69] D.A. Caponera 'Legal Aspects of Transboundary River Basin in the Middle East: The Al Asi (Orontes), The Jordan and The Nile' (1993) in 33 NRJ [654].
[70] B.R. Chauhan (n 58) [313]-[314].
[71] ibid [314]-[315].
[72] B.G. Verghese (n 11) [323]-[324].
[73] M. Dubey 'Some Reflection on Indo-Nepal Relations' in L.R. Baral *Looking to the Future: Indo-Nepal Relations in Perspective* (Anmol Publication New Delhi 1996) [51]-[57]; also see R. Paisley 'Adversaries into Partners: International Water Law and the Equitable Sharing of Downstream Benefits' (2002) in 3 MJIL [280]-[300].

modernisation, navigation, power generation, recreation, fisheries), benefits must be paid for by the beneficiary in proportion to the cost and benefits. Avoided cost theory (a method of allocating costs and benefits in water projects) will be helpful in assessing benefits; as a case in point, it seems that Nepal is willing to sell power to India at the alternative thermal or nuclear replacement cost, plus generation cost.[74]

This issue has been recognised in India in principle as well as in practice. For example the Indian River Act of 1956, Section 15(4), has recognised the downstream benefit concept. This Act provides that in the preparation and execution of schemes by the Board it shall take into account the costs likely to be incurred in constructing and maintaining such works; and the costs shall be allocated among the interested governments in such proportion as may be agreed or, in default of agreement, 'as may be determined by the Board having regard to the benefits which will be received from the scheme by them'.[75] In addition, a committee constituted by the Government of India has recommended that such benefits must be shared between the states concerned; this report was submitted to the Indian government in 1961.[76] Furthermore, it seems that the Indian government has practised the idea of sharing the benefits proportionately in the interstate sphere of India. The Ministry of Irrigation and Power wrote to all state Governments on April 17, 1967, stating that the cost of multipurpose river valley projects should normally be allocated only to three functions: irrigation, power and flood control. The letter recommended the 'facilities used' method of allocation of joint costs in preference to the 'alternative justifiable expenditure' or 'separable costs, remaining benefits' methods.[77]

In the United States of America, the principles of downstream benefits have also been practiced in the interstate sphere. For example, Section 10(f) of the Federal Power Act, 1935, imposes on the Federal Power Commission the duty to determine the benefits to downstream plants from upstream storage, and assess charges against those downstream plants.[78] In fact, the United States has remained fertile land for the enunciation of the principle of equitable apportionment, which is

---

[74] B.G. Verghese (n 11) [282].

[75] ibid.

[76] ibid [323]: The Yadav Mohan Committee was appointed by the Government of India in 1961 to examine the levy of charges for utilisation of water on a downstream project. The committee recommended as follows: 'when an upstream project is constructed later than an existing downstream project, the latter shall be liable to pay for the benefit obtained from an upstream project irrespective of the period that has elapsed after its construction; but when the downstream project is constructed after the upstream project, the downstream project need pay for the benefits received only if it is conceived within 20 years of completion of the upper project. In either case the charge will be borne only if it is clearly established that the downstream project has been benefited by the changes in flows or otherwise by the construction or operation of the upstream project. The lower project will bear the cost to the extent that the actual additional benefits are made available to it and as and when these benefits accrue'.

[77] ibid [324].

[78] ibid.

considered the foundation of the principle of equitable utilisation. Furthermore, being an indispensable part of equitable utilisation, the issues of sharing the costs and benefits in a shared river, lake or stream, has been dealt with in several resolutions of conflicts between states.[79]

Nepal and India have agreed in principle to share the cost in proportion to the benefits in the Mahakali River Treaty, 1996. Article 3(3) states:

> The cost of the project shall be borne by the Parties in proportion to the benefits accruing to them. Both the Parties shall jointly endeavour to mobilize the finance required for the implementation of the Project.[80]

This arrangement entails the acceptance of the principle that must be applied in future co-operation in the area of water resources development between two states. Besides this, two projects, namely the Gandak and the Kosi projects were implemented by India at her own cost. These projects do not provide examples of downstream benefits. However, they are instances of providing some irrigation and hydroelectric benefits for Nepal as a matter of Nepal's entitlement to such shared resources.[81]

Nonetheless, putting the theory into practice is a very complicated task, as experience shows, which suggests that without co-operation between the riparian countries concerned, the task is not feasible. The real issue in the development of Nepalese water resources is the sharing of costs and benefits with her lower riparian states. Evidently, the sharing and allocation of benefits from Nepalese water resources is not only bilateral in nature: it has crossed over into the sphere of regional management. The fact is that Bangladesh would, like India, benefit from water works in Nepal.

From experience in the international arena, downstream benefits could be categorised as follows:

---

[79] G.W. Sherk *Dividing the Waters: The Resolution of Interstate Water Conflicts in the United States* (Kluwer Law the Hague 2000) [60].

[80] 37 *ILM* (1997) [700].

[81] Article 5 of the Gandak project states '(iii): the Government of India agrees to provide locking arrangements for facility of riverine traffic across the barrage free from payment of any tolls whatever, provided that this traffic will be regulated by the project staff in accordance with the rules mutually agreed upon between His Majesty's Government and the Government of India. Similarly Article 7 provides irrigation facilities to Nepal at their cost. The Kosi project agreement Article 4 provides that Nepal would be entitled to 50 percent of electricity generated from the project and that a huge irrigation network would be provided at India's cost, and that some irrigation benefits would also be provided. These benefits would also be provided as a share of Nepal's ownership in the resources.'

11.10.1 Power Benefits

These should be evaluated by comparison with other alternatives available for generating power. This obviously sets the maximum price that Nepal might seek for the cost of generation and transmission to the Indian border, i.e. the average of the two 'costs', and if it goes on to other countries adjoining India, some of the costs for such facilities could be paid by Nepal to India. It is understood that Nepal has suggested to India that her current thermal replacement cost, plus the Karnali generation cost, divided by two, would lead to a fair price. That could provide a basis for negotiation, but it should not be forgotten that there could be a cut-off price which India would not be willing to exceed, as she would then find it prudent and economic to develop her own hydroelectric, thermal or nuclear options.[82] The Columbia River Treaty has provided a method for calculating flood benefit, and also regulated flow in the downstream state for extra generation of power.[83] Likewise, the Yacyreta and Itaypu Project in the Border River Panarma, the Columbia River experience, and the Laos-Thailand experience on the Mekong basin have furnished good examples of the sharing of border resources. Several hydroelectric projects in Canada which sell power to the USA provide examples of methods of the sale of power; this is generally on the basis of 80 percent of alternative generation cost, or sometimes its cost of generation and sale of power shared by two.[84] However, India persistently advocates the plus price principle based on the price of generation plus a certain percentage as profit.[85]

11.10.2 Irrigation Benefits

An augmented flow of water could provide extended irrigation and cropping downstream, and the potential for increasing productivity to feed 240 million people of a growing population in North India, and 10 million in Bangladesh.[86] It is argued from technical experience that the life of a dam or reservoir is normally 50 years and the benefits should be taken within this period. It appears (in Indo-Nepal water diplomacy), that this issue remains much more complicated than expected. Nepal asserts that the waters augmented in a reservoir or dam can be used in times of scarcity during the dry season, increasing crop yields and even permitting the growing of different types of more beneficial crops. Hence, those benefits should be calculated and duly paid to Nepal. The other benefit is the control of silt and sedimentation, which significantly reduces or even prevents flood devastation and other damage; this too must be shared. In this sphere, international experience

---

82 B.G. Verghese (n 11) [344]-[345].

83 R.W. Johnson 'The Columbia Basins' in A.H. Garretson, et al (eds.) *The Law of International Drainage Basins* (Oceana Pub. New York 1967) [167]-[241].

84 B. Crow, A. Lindquist and D. Wilson (n 4) [339].

85 D. Gwawali *Water in Nepal* (Himal Books Kathmandu 2001) [53]-[65].

86 B. Subba (n 14) [225].

could be shared and meaningful co-operation from India is to be expected, to enable a breakthrough.[87]

11.10.3 Flood Control Benefits

These could be calculated on the basis of the value of people and property in the lower reaches of the catchment area saved from damage. There are numerous reports prepared by the Government of India and international organisations, which suggest that the annual damages from the recurrent floods from Nepalese rivers could form a basis for negotiation. Billions of dollars could be saved by flood modernisation programmes alone. Take, for example in Bihar State, the Kosi River flood in 1987: out of 39 districts, 33 were severely flooded, and an estimated Rs1200 Crore worth of property was damaged; such huge potential benefits should be shared on an equal basis.[88]

11.10.4 Navigational Benefits

Much emphasis has been given to the basic need for Nepal's existence, and this remains a crucial element of Indo-Nepal relations. If this issue were appreciated by India, Nepal could enjoy navigational facilities via rivers down to the sea. This is a problem for Nepal that should be sorted out, and we should note here that its resolution is pivotal in the solving of the wider problems of Indo-Nepal water sharing and allocation. Navigation on the Gandak and Kosi, via the Mahananda and the Koroyota and thus into the lower Ganga-Brahmaputra system, has been proposed by Bangladesh. If the Gandak-Kosi-Mahananda schemes were to be consented to by India, or works were carried out pursuant to the Indo-Nepal Gandak agreement of 1959, which provides for a lock in the Gandak barrage, or if other potential for navigation at the Kosi or Karnali rivers were expedited by India as a gesture of goodwill, a big impediment for Nepal would finally be removed.[89]

In the case of India herself, she has declared National Navigational Route No 1 to be from Allahabad to Kolkotta; if proper arrangements could be made up to Nepal, she also would benefit from these services. There are similar problems in relations between India and Bangladesh. India has persistently resisted a former proposal for Ganga flow augmentation and related reservoir construction in Nepal, asserting that the Ganga is an Indian river not an international river, contrary to the precepts of IWL, particularly in view of the judgment rendered by the PCIJ in the *River Oder case*.[90] While India rejected Bangladesh's proposal of augmentation of

---

[87] B.G. Verghese (n 11) [344]-[346].
[88] B.C. Upreti (n 9) [116].
[89] B.G. Verghese (n 11) [347]; see B. Crow, A. Lindquist and D. Wilson (n 4) [177]; also see B.G. Verghese and RR Iyer (n 12) [208]-[209].
[90] PCIJ Reports (1937) [221]-[222].

dry season flow in the Ganges, Bangladesh similarly refused to accept the Brahmaputra-Ganga link canal proposal.[91]

It is technically viable for boats to travel from the Hooghly (in India) on the Ganges (which emerges in Bangladesh), via Farakka and Kanpur in India to the following points in Nepal: Bhardaha on the river Kosi, Narayanghat on the Gandak, and Chisapani on the Karnali; however, the economic and technical feasibility, and other implications, need to be studied further.[92] Furthermore, Water Resources Ministers of Nepal and India constituted a joint study team to investigate the possibilities of navigation on the Kosi, Karnali and Gandak rivers, in 1997. It is understood that the studies have not been not completed so far,[93] but it is expected that once the technical feasibility has been endorsed, both states can expect to execute projects for navigation. The experience gained by Austria and Paraguay in the area of inland waterways and access to and from the sea can be of significance in the Nepalese context.[94]

11.11 Regional Cooperation

There are several views on how to maximise benefits from these huge resources. As indicated earlier, the issues have several aspects: two riparian countries involvement, in Indo-Bangladesh co-operation; trilateralisation of the issues that include Nepal-India and Bangladesh, even inviting Bhutan in, as conceived in the SAARC Quadrangle concept, and the possibility of adding China to this group. Finally, internationalisation of the issue by involving multilateral organisations, e.g. the World Bank, GEF, UNDP, UN or indeed any influential and resourceful western government; it is noteworthy that the UK and the USA have already shown an interest.[95] These institutions are capable of making a breakthrough in issues of this magnitude, in terms of economics, technology and politics.[96]

India has persistently maintained that Ganga[97] is an Indian river, disregarding Nepal's legitimate demand for navigational rights over the river access to the sea.

---

[91] B. Crow, A. Lindquist and D. Wilson (n 4) [203]-[210].

[92] B.G. Verghese and R.R. Iyer (n 12) [208]-[209].

[93] *Annual Report of Water and Energy Commission Secretariat 1999* [13]-[14].

[94] A.B. Thapa 'Landlocked Austria's Lesson for Nepal' in 22 Spotlight 27 Sept.-3 Oct. 2002 [1]-[3].

[95] M.R. Josse 'The Case For New Thinking' in *Water Nepal* Vol. 4 1994 [260]: The US President Jimmy Carter and the British Prime Minister James Callaghan have made separate statements in January 1978 offering their 'country's technical and financial support to any regional water development project that India, Nepal and Bangladesh may put up' which was not liked by India.

[96] Ministry of Water Resources, His Majesty's Government, Nepal, *Water Resources Development in Nepal*, March 1985 [128].

[97] J.G. Lammers *Pollution of International Watercourses* (Martinus Nijhoff The Hague 1984) [313]-[317], see B.G. Verghese, R.R. Iyer, P.K. Ahmad, B.B. Pradhan and S.K. Malla (eds.) *Converting Water into Wealth: Regional Co-operation in Harnessing the Eastern Himalayan Rivers* (Konark Publishers New Delhi 1994) [122].

It was once demanded that Ganga is declared 'an international river of South-Asia' and Nepal is considered a co-riparian partner along with India and Bangladesh, for the purpose of sharing its waters and benefits. This specific proposal was made by Hiranya Lal Shrestha, an expert on Nepalese foreign policy, who has pointed out that it cost Nepal Rs66 million to transport 100,000 tonnes of freight from Kolkotta to Kathmandu against just Rs6.7 million if the goods were moved by inland waterways. He concluded that a navigational outlet to the sea is Nepal's birthright.[98] There are two other alternatives for Nepal in terms of routes to access the sea: the Kosi-Gandak link canal to Mahananda- Koroyoka in Bangladesh; and a 16km long tunnel-link between the Jhapa district of the eastern part of Nepal, passing through India at a depth of 3,000m, and coming out at the western border of Bangladesh. Both of these alternatives require multilateral consent and co-operation. If a spirit of co-operation is established, technical and financial assistance is easy to obtain; examples include the Eisenhower tunnel in US and Tunnels below the sea in Japan and Hong Kong.[99] Several tunnels are already in Switzerland, which have proved this technology.

Bangladesh, from the time of its emergence in 1971 has persistently demanded Nepalese involvement in the augmentation of the dry season flow of the Ganges. It is evident that without Nepal's involvement in building huge reservoirs in her own territory, this is not feasible and India, for her part, has repudiated the idea. On the contrary, India demanded the construction of a Brahmaputra-Ganges link canal, 324km long, one third within Bangladesh's territory and joining the Ganges above Farakka, although this was explicitly rejected by Bangladesh. In order to increase the Ganges flow, the diversion of the Brahmaputra through the Arun valley in Nepal is also recommended; if this were implemented, the chronic problems between India and Bangladesh would definitely be sorted out.[100] But broader co-operation is still the key.

Moreover, navigation services and business-trade links can be established through India, while coal and gas could be imported from Bangladesh; these are the potential benefits of a multilateral arrangement.[101]

There are general guidelines for and examples of co-operation, and allocation of the benefits from an IWC, by following these practices and learning from these experiences, states of this region can accrue maximum benefits.[102] Every aspect is

---

[98] B.G. Verghese (n 11) [209]; A.B. Thapa 'Kosi Navigational Canal' in *Water and Energy Commission Secretariat bulletin* B.G. Verghese (n 11) Vol. 8 Kathmandu [5]-[7]. The experience shows that the shallow draft inland water transportation can be about 5 times cheaper than railway, 21 times cheaper than road transportation and 63 times cheaper than air transportation [5].

[99] B.C. Upreti (n 9) [134].

[100] H.M. Shrestha and L.M. Singh 'The Ganges-Brahmaputra System: A Nepalese Perspective in the Context of Regional Cooperation' in A.K. Biswas and T. Hashimoto (eds.) *Asian International Waters From Ganges – Brahmaputra to Mekong* (OUP Oxford 1996) [81].

[101] *Supra* note 2. p. 361.

[102] B.G. Verghese (n 11) [326]-[328]; also see J.S. Mehta 'Opportunity Costs of Delay in Water Resources Management between Nepal, India and Bangladesh' in D.J .Eaton (ed.)

closely linked to equity, which takes each one's interests into consideration. The new potential afforded by the involvement of a third party to enhance and facilitate regional or bilateral co-operation is one result of recently emerging creative thinking. It is recognised that India's predominant role in the region, in terms of her size, economic and military power, technological status and political stability, has made other smaller and weaker neighbours feel vulnerable and suspicious. In turn, India is also afraid of these neighbours ganging up against her, or taking other hostile attitudes.

In order to enhance the idea and implement regional co-operation, several initiatives have been undertaken, both in unofficial and official spheres; for example, under the auspices of United States Agency for International Development (USAID), the US government is implementing a project called the South Asia Regional Initiative (SARI) with a view to promoting sub-regional co-operation in the fields of energy and trade (among others) is also considered to be a watershed. Furthermore, regular meetings of experts are taking place, and a common electricity grid for these nations is expected very soon.[103] Further, the Asian Development Bank (ADB) has given the green signal for providing financial assistance to develop a series of three Arun hydropower projects, of 1,050MW total capacity in Nepal, enhancing regional co-operation. It has initiated another project namely, Regional Technical Assistance (RETA), being implemented to enable the South Asia Growth Quadrangle (SAGQ) nations to share and trade off the available energy benefits available between themselves.[104]

In a recent development, India is now undertaking a study investigating linking 37 rivers in a region extending from the Himalayas to the southern peninsula of India and bringing water from where there is a surplus to areas of water deficit by constructing a network of dams and reservoirs and a network of canals. In order to implement this ambitious project, riparian co-operation from Bhutan, Bangladesh and Nepal is essential. Unfortunately India seems determined to implement this project unilaterally and complete the vast amount of work involved by 2016; starting in 2006 (she expects to complete the chains of studies before 2006).[105] After successful negotiation with riparian states, which would be hard, but will yield a definite outcome, the grievances and bitterness of the past would be removed, and everyone's interests would be taken into consideration. However, this project will only happen given a spirit of regional co-operation.

The Ganges-Brahmaputra Basin: Water Resources co-operation between Nepal, India and Bangladesh (Lyndon B. Johnson School of Public Affairs University of Texas, Austin 1992) [12].

[103] Staff, SAARC Common Grid, *The Kathmandu Post* 10 January 2002.

[104] Staff, Regional Cooperation, *The Kathmandu Post* 26 December 2001; also see *The Kathmandu Post* 4 September 2002.

[105] S. Aiyer 'Changing the Course' in *XXVII India Today*, 20 January 2003 [28]-[32]; also see R.R. Iyer 'Making of a Subcontinent Fiasco' in *Himal South Asian* [1]-[8]; also H. Thakkar 'Flood of nonsense: How to Manufacture Consensus for River-Linking' *Himal South Asian*, August 2003 [1]-[5]. Also see 'Bangladesh Concerned over India's Proposed River-Linking Project' at html://www.internationalwaterlaw.org.html.

11.12 Conditions for Funding Imposed by the World Bank and Other Donors

The implementation of water projects is a costly business, involving huge amounts of money with a long gestation period before the completion of the project. The WB has been financing trans-boundary water projects since 1949 like the El Salvador's Rio Lempa Hydroelectric Project and again in Rhodesia in 1956, where there was no riparian dispute. On the other hand, the Bank refused to finance the Bhakra Nangal Project in India in 1949, the Lower Sind Barrage in Pakistan in 1950, the Aswan Dam in Egypt 1955, the Roseries Project in Sudan in 1987, and the Three Gorges project in China. All of these refusals were linked with adverse effects and riparian objections.[106]

From its experience the Bank first drafted its operational policy memorandum in 1956 for its own staff to use; it revised it in 1964 and in 1985. In 1993 the Bank adopted an Operational Manual and Operational Policies O.P. 750, 'Project on International Waterways' (Annex 2. O.P. 750, 1994), and bank procedures 'Project on International Waterways'. All these documents are based on the philosophy of 'no harm' rules because, supposedly, the concept of 'equitable utilisation' contains abstract ideas, vagueness and lack of clarity.[107] These rules are against the core principle of IWL, equitable utilisation, and it should be amended to reconcile to this principle, because international institutions can no longer operate against the rules of IWL. It is illegimate not only from the legal point of view but also from the political point of view.

Before 1980 little attention was given to the environment and sustainable development; as a result of which, the WB and other multilateral funding agencies had received pointed criticism.[108] Consequently the WB has changed its policy to take environmental issues into consideration, and several new rules have been enacted. These measures have been adopted by regional development banks, UN agencies and bilateral donor countries as well, particularly the EU and G7 countries. Furthermore, in order to preserve and protect several aspects of the environment, numerous funds have been created since 1990, e.g. the World Heritage Fund, Wetlands Fund, Montreal Protocol Multilateral fund, Global Environment Facility and so on.[109] These instruments set out conditions to be complied with in order to qualify for a loan or assistance. Consistent with these

---

[106] R. Krishna 'The Evolution and Context of the Bank Policy for Projects on International Waterways', in B.J. Ridley and C.H. Schofield (eds.) *The Peaceful Management of Transboundary Resources* (Graham & Trotman/Martinus Nijhoff Dordrecht 1995) [31]-[43].

[107] ibid; also see D. Goldberg 'World Bank Policy on International Waterways in the context of Emerging International Law and the Work of International Law Commission' in *The Peaceful Management of Transboundary Resources* (Graham & Trotman/Martinus Nijhoff Dordrecht 1995) [153]-[165].

[108] P. Sands *The Principle of International Environmental Law* (Manchester University Press Manchester 1995) [731]. The construction of the Polonoreste dam in Brazil has resulted in significant environmental damage at national and international level.

[109] ibid [730]-[736].

institutions regulations, a state that is looking for a loan for developing a water project requires riparian consent in order to proceed; in the case of international watercourses, riparian states are required to exchange information regarding a particular project.[110]

Under such an arrangement, the poorer state cannot develop any water projects in her watercourses whilst a wealthy state can develop any project of her own. The reason for this situation is that the wealthy country can undertake a water project in an IWC, ignoring other riparian interest, only taking into consideration her own maximum benefit; this frequently happens. The argument is that although IWL is universal, its application varies. That is to say, one country with resources can develop a project as they wish, even to the detriment of others and no one can stop them; but if you have no resources you have to borrow the money, and only if riparian states concerned are in favour can the project be developed. The wealthy nations have not adhered to the law, whereas the developing nations can do nothing except agree with all the preconditions of the donor, which constitutes an inequitable arrangement in this area. Special favourable clauses to the less developed states have been written into the instruments by numerous institutions, such as GATT, the WTO, the UNCTAD, and the LOSC Convention. Moreover, the third United Nations conference on the Least Developed Countries held in Brussels, 14-20 May 2001 and the Debt Relief Scheme adopted for the assistance of least developed countries. Such favourable rules are absolutely essential to a vulnerable state.[111]

The Bank has also been blamed for dictating on the adoption of economic and other policies, thus exploiting developing states and retarding their development. As a result, it is argued that drawing loans from the WB amounts to a surrender of economic sovereignty.[112]

11.13 Conclusions

The issue of water resources development from the standpoint of bilateral and regional co-operation has been dealt with, in which it has been seen that national effort alone cannot yield holistic results without bilateral and regional involvement.

---

[110] The World Bank Operational Manual: Operational Policies; Project on International Waterways. The WB annex 2.A.O.P. 750 October 1994 [193]-[200].

[111] J.R. Crook and S.C. McCaffrey 'The United Nations Start Work on a Watercourse Convention' in 91 AJIL 1997 [374]-[377]: Article 125 of the Law of the Sea provides right of access to and from the sea and is also regarded as a customary rule of international law especially to the land-locked and geographically handicapped nations. Similar arrangements could have been made for such nations whilst applying and interpreting the provisions of Article 5 of the 1997 UN Convention. Also see S.C. Vasciannie *Land-Locked and Geographically Disadvantaged States in the International law of the Sea* (Clarendon Press Oxford 1990) [187]-[196].

[112] S.R. Chowdhury 'Intergenerational Equity: Substratum of the Right to Development' in S.R. Chowdhury, E. Denters and P. de Waart (eds.) *The Right to Development in International Law* (Martinus Nijhoff Publishers Dordrecht 1992) [350]-[359].

The necessity of the co-operation is not only necessary from the point of view of money and technological capability, but also, because of the requirements of a watercourse itself, in order to maximise benefits. There is too much water causing havoc in the wet season, but there is not a single drop of water in the dry season, which in turn causes devastation, hunger and famine. This observation leads to the conclusion that the characteristics of developing states are obviously found in the SAARC region, namely, the scarcity of water and associated issues: water conflicts only remain in developing states, whereas developed states have already settled such issues.[113]

It appears that without settling major existing political problems in the bilateral sphere, water resources co-operation cannot make the progress that might be expected. Thus, major changes are needed in government outlook regarding how to develop relations with neighbouring countries, how to utilise these immense water resources for the common benefit, and how to face the challenges arising from the riparian problems, for which purpose a summit of the leaders of this region has been suggested.[114] Indeed, the key to the resolution of all national water resource problems lies in bilateral and regional co-operation. Nepal is relatively weaker than India. Thus, according to the principle of equitable utilisation enshrined in Articles 5 and 6 of the UN Convention of 1997, India should give a high priority to Nepal's development with a magnanimous attitude.

A suitable model, particularly in the Indo-Nepalese sphere, is the Columbia River Treaty arrangement between the USA and Canada, which could be the ideal point of reference.[115] According to the current energy trends, India has enough fossil fuel reserves for forty years, Bangladesh for thirty years and Pakistan for about twenty years. After these periods have elapsed, each country will be compelled to turn to water resources.[116] The co-operation between Bhutan and India shows that both states accrue tremendous benefits. The same approach is proving successful in the Mekong Basin, in which Thailand guaranteed a loan on behalf of Laos from the world capital market and provided some amount in advance for the purchase of the hydropower, which is being developed. Laos is commissioning these projects purely for export purposes, for which a regional grid has already been constructed to deliver the hydropower to Thailand. It was constructed by the Mekong Commission with the money provided by the WB and the UNDP.[117] There are other similar models: Itaipu (Paraguay and Brazil) and

---

[113] R. Clarke *Water: the International Crisis* (Earthscan Publications London 1991) [91]-[92].

[114] B.G. Verghese, R.R. Iyer, P.K. Ahmad, B.B. Pradhan and S.K. Malla (eds.) *Converting Water into Wealth: Regional Co-operation in Harnessing the Eastern Himalayan Rivers* (Konark Publishers New Delhi 1994) [130].

[115] L. Teclaff 'Harmonising Water Use and Development With Environmental Protection' in A. Utton and L. Teclaff (eds.) *Water in Developing world: The Management of a Critical Resources* (West View Press Colorado 1978) [104]-[105].

[116] R.D. Joshi 'Nepali Hydropower and Regional Energy Needs' in *Water Nepal* Vol. 4 [156].

[117] P. Chomchai 'Management of Trans boundary Water Resources: A Case Study of the Mekong' in M.I. Glassner (ed.) *The United Nations at Work*, New Port, CT (1998) [254]-

Yacyreta (Paraguay and Argentina).[118] Any of the above models are suitable for south Asia and can be followed. However, the problem does not lie in the area of knowledge, technology or even finance; the real impediment is the lack of political will of the leaders of the region. This can be resolved according to the norms of equity, the Himalayan waters will be at their disposal, and this could obviate the misery of poverty.

---

[255]. The Nam Ngum Hydro project 150MW was completed in 1991 and numerous projects for export purposes are underway.

[118] H. Dhungel 'Risks and Rewards of Mega Projects: The Political Economy of Paraguayan Hydropower' in *Water Nepal* Vol. 7 1999 [25]-[26].

Conclusions and Recommendations

Surya P. Subedi

The River Ganges basin is going through a rapid process of industrialisation and population growth and both of these activities are putting pressure on the whole ecological balance of the area. Nepal has abundance of water but due to poor irrigation network the country is not able to produce enough food for the growing population. Once Nepal was known for exporting rice but now the country has become dependant on the import of grain from other countries. Nor has it got the ability to generate hydroelectric power to export to India. Nepal does not have any other known significant source of natural resources. India needs not only every drop of water during the dry season but also the economical and perhaps more environmentally friendly form of energy – hydropower. Bangladesh sitting on the other end of the stick suffers in both ways – from the monsoon floods during the wet season and the scarcity of water during the dry season, but is helpless to do much about it. The situation prevailing in this part of the world would make it a convincing case for closer sub-regional cooperation in the interests of all three countries. However, the political leaders of these countries seem to be lacking in foresight and wisdom to achieve meaningful cooperation in the area.

As seen in the preceding chapters, a number of treaties have been concluded between both India and Nepal as well as between India and Bangladesh either to harness the waters of a river or to devise a formula for sharing the waters. The irony is that none of the treaties is designed to deal with the longer-term crisis facing the region. The approach has been a piecemeal one rather than a comprehensive one. The intention of the parties seems to be to regard each of the individual treaties concluded as *sui generis* and to leave everything else to the political goodwill of the governments of the day. For instance, the Ganges Treaty is a narrow treaty in its scope and is confined mainly to the sharing of available water between the two countries. It has no provision for the management of the water resources of the River Ganges Basin. The element of the conservation of water, the protection of the ecosystem or aquatic life and the concept of sustainable use or exploitation do not figure in the treaty. The concept of development of water resources in the River Ganges Basin is missing in the Treaty. It does not contain any provision concerning the control of pollution of the river either.

There is no certainty that whatever quantity of water Bangladesh receives will be of the quality required for its different types of uses. It should be borne in mind that the Ganges is already one of the most polluted rivers in the world and the level of pollution is likely to increase with the massive process of industrialisation that is under way in northern India. There is no provision for the judicial settlement of disputes between the parties. Some of the obligations are couched in vague terms and some of the provisions providing the formulae for water sharing are contradictory. All in all, it is a treaty with a narrow vision and fraught with a number of difficulties.

The same is true of the Mahakali River Treaty. The elements of sustainability or environmental impact assessment or public participation with regard to the development of the Pancheswar Multipurpose project are missing from the Treaty. The requirement of the international law of watercourses is not only to share the water resources in an equitable and reasonable manner but also to develop, conserve and manage the water resources in a sustainable manner. However, the perception in both the Mahakali River and the Ganges River Treaties seems to be to regard water as an economic good to be shared and used here and now as optimally as possible rather than as a vital resource to be developed, managed and conserved for greater benefits in the future. Both of these treaties take little account of the developments taking place in the field of the environment.

Unlike the regional or sub-regional arrangements that exist in other parts of the world with regard to the shared international watercourses of the region, there is no sub-regional, regional or basin-wide approach adopted in these treaties to the broader water or environmental problems facing the region. Owing, *inter alia*, to deforestation in the hills of Nepal and northern India, the capacity of the topsoil to preserve water has diminished. Consequently, all rains drain quickly into the Ganges and ultimately into the Bay of Bengal during the monsoon season, creating floods and havoc on the plains of Nepal, India and Bangladesh. While such is the case during the wet season, there is a shortage of water both in Bangladesh and India during the dry season.

However, none of the treaties has any provision concerning either flood control during the wet season or augmentation of the flow of water during the dry season. Thus, the States of the River Ganges Basin have still a long way to go to develop a framework designed to utilise the waters of the basin in a sustainable, equitable and reasonable manner and to address the water and related environmental problems facing the River Ganges Basin as a whole. It would be better for these States to conclude a comprehensive basin-wide treaty defining the principles governing the utilisation of the waters of the River Ganges basin on the basis of the extant and evolving norms of general international law in general and international watercourses law and international environmental law in particular. Compared to the other regions of the world, South Asia is lacking very much in regional and sub-regional mechanisms to promote cooperation and the water sector is one of them. Not only the international river basins located in the developed part of the world such as the Rhine, but also the initiatives taken by the States of some regions in the developing world such as the Mekong and Southern African region, i.e. the SADAC region, are much more progressive and conducive to regional cooperation than the situation in South Asia. The time has come for the leaders of the States of the River Ganges Basin to demonstrate vision, wisdom and far sightedness by moving in the direction of closer co-operation through regional and sub-regional mechanisms to utilise the waters of the Basin in an equitable, reasonable and sustainable manner for the benefit of the people of the region.

One of the factors that is hindering any meaningful cooperation among the States of South Asia is that these States have not been able to resolve bilateral disputes that exit among them. This is one the reasons why the regional organisation, South Asian Association for Regional Cooperation (SAARC) has not been able to achieve much since bilateral matters are excluded from the agenda of this regional body. Therefore, it seems imperative for the States of the region to resolve their bilateral disputes, at least in the area of water, in order to conclude a regional or sub-regional arrangement. While India is viewed by both Bangladesh and Nepal as a giant hegemonic neighbour intent on securing deals favourable to it at the expense of her smaller neighbours, India views the politicians of her neighbouring countries as so paranoid by nationalist sentiments that they were incapable of striking sensible deals with New Delhi. There is obviously a degree of mistrust between India and her neighbours. This mistrust should be removed by demonstrating farsightedness and wisdom by the political leaders of the region. For instance, the Mahakali River Treaty was concluded between India and Nepal in 1996, but not much has been done to implement the treaty. There are a host of other bilateral issues, which require a forward-looking approach in order to resolve them in an amicable manner. Similarly, the conclusion of the Ganges Treaty between Bangladesh and India was a step in the right direction but there are a number of other water issues that have hindered further cooperation between these countries.

Neither the 1997 UN Convention on the Non-Navigational Use of International Watercourses nor any other international instrument offer a ready formula to resolve the outstanding issues between these three countries. However, a satisfactory resolution of the problem could be found by relying on the extant and evolving principles of international environmental law in general and international watercourses law in particular. Indeed, the Berlin Rules on Water Resources, 2004, adopted by the International Law Association on the recommendation of its Water Resources Committee contain a helpful set of principles and rules for those States willing to enter into a regional cooperation mechanism for the conservation, development and utilisation of the water resources of a watercourse. The ILA Berlin Rules, which include the expanded and revised versions of the Helsinki Rules, 1966, represent the most comprehensive set of rules on the use of international watercourses.

As stated by Chimni in Chapter 4 of this volume, even if a full scale co-operation was not achievable at this stage, these countries could consider establishing a tripartite water commission for exchange of data and information as a first step towards the eventual basin-wide mechanism to promote cooperation in the water sector among the three basin States of the River Ganges. There is a great deal of confidence building to be done in this region and such an initial step would facilitate greater co-operation in the future. There are already bilateral high level water commissions in existence between India and Nepal and India and Bangladesh and the setting up of a tripartite one would enable these three countries to exchange information and date necessary to predict what course of action each of them could take to minimise the risks of adverse conditions and maximise the benefits for each of them.

APPENDICES ON TREATIES

Appendix I

The 1954 Agreement on the Kosi Project (as revised in 1966)

Amended agreement between His Majesty's Government of Nepal (hereinafter referred to as 'HMG') and the Government of India (hereinafter referred to as the 'Union') concerning the Kosi Project.

WHEREAS the Union was desirous of constructing a barrage, headworks and other appurtenant works about three miles upstream of Hanuman Nagar town on the Kosi River with afflux and flood banks, and canals and protective works on land lying within the territories of Nepal for the purpose of flood control, irrigation, generation of hydro-electric power and prevention of erosion of Nepal areas on the right side of the river, upstream of the barrage (hereinafter referred to as the 'Project').

AND WHEREAS HMG agreed to the construction of the said barrage, headworks and other connected works by and at the cost of the Union, in consideration of the benefits arising therefrom and a formal document incorporating the terms of the Agreement was brought into existence on the 25th April, 1954 and was given effect to;

AND WHEREAS in pursuance of the said Agreement various works in respect of the Project have been completed by the Union while others are in various stages of completion for which HMG has agreed to afford necessary facilities;

AND WHEREAS HMG has suggested revision of the said Agreement in order to meet the requirements of the changed circumstances, and the Union, with a view to maintaining friendship and good relation subsisting between Nepal and India, has agreed to the revision of Agreement.

NOW, THEREFORE, THE PARTIES AGREE AS FOLLOWS:-

1. DETAILS OF THE PROJECT: (i) The barrage is located about 3 miles upstream of Hununman Nagar town.

(ii) The general layout of the barrage, the areas within afflux banks, flood embankments, and other protective works, canals, power house and the lines of communication are shown in the amended plan annexed to this agreement as Amended Annexure A.[1]

(iii) Any construction and other undertaking by the Union in connection

---

[1] Not reproduced here.

with this Project shall be planned and carried out in consultation with HMG,

Provided that such works and undertakings which, pursuant to any provision of this Agreement require the prior approval of HMG shall not be started without such prior approval;

And further provided that in situation described in Clause 3(iii) and Clause 3(iv) intimation to HMG shall be sufficient.

(iv) For the purpose of Clauses 3 and 8 of this Agreement the land under the ponded areas and boundaries as indicated by the plan specified in sub-clause (ii) above, shall be deemed to be submerged.

2. INVESTIGATIONS AND SURVEYS:- (i) Whenever the Chief Engineer of Kosi Project, Government of Bihar may consider any survey or investigation to be required in connection with the said Project, HMG shall, if and in so far as HMG has approved such survey or investigation, authorise and give necessary facilities to the concerned officers of the Union or other persons acting under the general or special orders of such officers to enter upon such land as necessary with such men, animals, vehicles, equipment, plant, machinery and instruments as necessary to undertake such surveys and investigations. Such surveys and investigations may comprise aerial and ground surveys, hydraulic, hydrometic, hydrological and geological surveys including construction of drill holes for surface and sub-surface exploration, investigations for communications and for materials of construction; and all other surveys and investigations necessary for the proper design, construction and maintenance of the barrage and all its connected works mentioned under the Project. However, investigations and surveys necessary for the general maintenance and operation of the Project, inside the project area, may be done by the Union after due intimation to HMG.

In this Agreement, the 'Project Area' shall mean the area acquired for the Project.

(ii) The provisions of sub-clause (i) of this clause shall also apply to surveys and investigations of storage dams or detention dams on the Kosi, soil conservation measures, such as check dams, afforestation, etc., required for a complete solution of the Kosi problems in the future.

(iii) The surveys and investigations referred to in sub-clauses (i) and (ii) shall be carried in co-operation with HMG.

(iv) All data, maps, specimens, reports and other results of surveys and investigations carried out by or on behalf of the Union in Nepal pursuant to the provisions of this clause, shall be made available to HMG freely and without delay. In turn, HMG shall, upon request by the Union, make available to the Union all data, maps, specimens, reports and other results of surveys and investigations carried out by or on behalf of HMG in Nepal in respect of the Kosi River.

3. AUTHORITY FOR EXECUTION OF WORKS AND USE OF LAND AND OTHER PROPERTY:- (i) Provided that any major construction work not envisaged in the amended plan (Amended Annexure–A) referred to in clause 1(ii) shall require the prior approval of HMG, HMG shall authorise the Union to proceed with the execution of the said project as and when the project or a part of

the project receives sanction of the said Union and notice has been given by the Union to HMG of its intention to commence work on the respective constructions and shall permit access by the Engineer and all other officers, servants, and nominees of the Union, with such men, animals, vehicles, plant, machinery, equipment and instruments as may be necessary for the direction and execution of the respective constructions, to all such lands and places, and shall permit the occupation, for such period as may be necessary, of all such lands and places as may be required for the proper execution of the respective constructions.

(ii) The land required for the purposes mentioned in Clause 3(i) above shall be acquired by HMG and compensation thereof shall be paid by the Union in accordance with the provisions of clause 8 hereof.

(iii) HMG shall, upon prior *notification*, authorise officers of the Union to enter on land outside the limits or boundaries of the barrage and its connected works in case of any accident happening or being apprehended to any of the said works and to execute all works which may be necessary for the purpose of repairing or preventing such damage. Compensation, in every case, shall be tendered by the Union through HMG to the owners of the said land for all accidents done to the same in order that compensation may be awarded in accordance with clause 8 hereof.

(iv) HMG will permit the Union to quarry the construction materials required for the project from the various deposits at Chatra, Dharan Bazar or other places in Nepal.

4. USE OF WATER AND POWER:- (i) HMG shall have every right to withdraw for irrigation and for any other purpose in Nepal water from the Kosi River and from the Sun-Kosi River or within the Kosi Basin from any other tributaries of the Kosi River as may be required from time to time. The Union shall have the right to regulate all the balance of supplies in the Kosi River at the barrage site thus available from time to time and to generate power in the Eastern Canal.

(ii) HMG shall be entitled to obtain for use in Nepal any portion up to 50 per cent of the total hydro-electric power generated by any Power House situated within a 10-mile radius from the barrage site and constructed by or on behalf of the Union, as HMG shall from time to time determine and communicate to the Union:

Provided that:-

HMG shall communicate to the Union any increase or decrease in the required power supply exceeding 6,800 KW at least three months in advance.

(iii) If any power to be supplied to Nepal pursuant to the provisions of this sub-clause is generated in a power house located in Indian territory, the Union shall construct the necessary transmission line or lines to such points at the Nepal-Indian border as shall be mutually agreed upon.

(iv) The tariff rates for electricity to be supplied to Nepal pursuant to the provisions of this clause shall be fixed my mutual agreement.

5. LEASE OF THE PROJECT AREAS:- (i) All the lands acquired by HMG under the provisions of clause 3 hereof as of the date of signing of these amendments shall be leased by HMG to the Union for a period of 199 years from

the date of signing of these amendments at an annual Nominal Rate.

(ii) The rent and other terms and conditions on which lands for Western Kosi Canal shall be leased by HMG to the Union pursuant to this Agreement shall be similar to those as under sub-clause (i).

(iii) The rent and other terms and conditions of any other land to be leased by HMG to the Union pursuant to this Agreement shall be fixed by mutual agreement.

(iv) At the request of the Union, HMG may grant renewal of the leases referred to in sub-clauses (i), (ii) and (iii) on such terms and conditions as may be mutually agreed upon.

(v) The sovereignty rights and territorial jurisdiction of HMG, including the application and enforcement of the law of Nepal on and in respect of the leased land shall continue unimpaired by such lease.

6. ROYALTIES:- (i) HMG will receive royalty in respect to power generated and utilised in the Indian Union at rates to be settled by agreement hereafter:

Provided that no royalty will be paid on the power sold to Nepal.

(ii) HMG shall be entitled to receive payment of royalties from the Union in respect of stone, gravel and ballast obtained from Nepal territory and used in the construction and future maintenance of the barrage and other connected works at rates to be settled by agreement hereafter.

(iii) The Union shall be at liberty to use and remove clay, sand and soil without let or hindrance from lands leased by HMG to the Union.

(iv) Use of timber from Nepal forests, required for the construction, shall be permitted on payment of compensation. Provided that no compensation will be payable to HMG for such quantities of timber as may be agreed upon by HMG and the Union to be necessary for the use in the spurs and other river training works required for the prevention of caving and erosion of the right bank in Nepal.

Provided likewise that no compensation will be payable to the Union for any timber obtained from the forestlands leased by HMG to the Union.

7. CUSTOMS DUTIES:- HMG shall charge no customs duty or duty of any kind, during construction and subsequent maintenance, on any articles and materials required for the purpose of the Project and the work connected therewith.

8. COMPENSATION FOR LAND PROPERTY AND FOR LAND REVENUE:- (i) For assessing the compensation to be awarded by the Union to HMG in cash:-

(a) Lands required for the execution of various works as mentioned in clause 3(ii) and clause 9(i); and
(b) Submerged lands will be divided into the following classes:-
    1. Cultivated lands.
    2. Forest lands.
    3. Village lands and houses and other immovable property standing on them.

4. Waste lands.

All lands recorded in the register of lands in the territory of Nepal as actually cultivated shall be deemed to be cultivated lands for the purpose of this clause.

(ii) The Union shall pay compensation:-

(a) to HMG for the loss of land revenue as at the time of acquisition in respect of the area required, and

(b) to whomsoever it may be due for the lands, houses and other immovable property acquired for the Project and leased to the Union.

The assessment of such compensation and the manner of payment shall be determined hereafter by mutual agreement between HMG and the Union.

(iii) All lands required for the purposes of the Project shall be jointly measured by the duly authorised officers of HMG and the Union respectively.

9. COMMUNICATIONS:- (i) HMG agrees that the Union may construct and maintain roads, tramways, railways, ropeways, etc., required for the Project in Nepal and shall provide land for these purposes on payment of compensation as provided in clause 8. Provided that the construction of any roads, tramways, railways, ropeways, etc., outside the Project area shall require the prior approval of HMG.

(ii) Any restrictions, required in the interest of construction, maintenance and proper operation of the Project, regarding the use of the roads, etc., referred to in sub-clause (i) by commercial or private vehicles may be mutually agreed upon. In case of threatened breach or erosion of the structures on account of the river, the officers of the Project may restrict public traffic under intimation to HMG.

(iii) HMG agrees to permit, on the same terms as for other users, the use of all roads, waterways and other avenues of transport and communication in Nepal for *bona fide* purposes of the construction and maintenance of the barrage and other connected works.

(iv) The bridge over Hanuman Nagar barrage shall be open to public traffic. With prior approval of HMG, the Union shall have the right to close the traffic over the bridge temporarily if an in so far as required for technical or safety reasons. In such cases, the Union shall take all measures required for the most expeditious reopening of the bridge.

(v) HMG agrees to permit installation of telegraph, telephone and radio communications in Nepal for the *bona fide* purposes of the construction and maintenance of the Project:

Provided that the Union shall agree to the withdrawal of such facilities, which HMG may in this respect, provide in future.

Further provided that the Union agrees to permit the use of internal telephone and telegraph in the Project area to authorised servants of HMG for business in emergencies provided such use does not in any way interfere with the construction and operation of the Project.

10. NAVIGATION RIGHTS:- All navigation rights in the Kosi River in Nepal shall rest with HMG. Provision shall be made for suitable arrangements at or

around the site of the barrage for free and unrestricted navigation in the Kosi River, if technically feasible. However, the use of any watercraft like boast, launches and timber rafts within two miles of the barrage and headworks shall not be allowed on grounds of safety, except by special permits to be issued by the competent authority of HMG in consultation with the Executive Engineer, Barrage. Any unauthorised watercraft found within this limit shall be liable to prosecution.

11. FISHING RIGHTS:- All the fishing rights in the Kosi River in Nepal shall continue to rest with HMG. However, no fishing shall be permitted within two miles of the barrage and headworks except under special permits to be issued by the competent authority of HMG in consultation with the Executive Engineer, Barrage. While issuing the special permits within two miles, HMG shall keep in view the safety of the headworks and the permitholders.

12. USE OF NEPALI LABOUR:- The Union shall give preference to Nepali labour, personnel and contractors to the extent available and in its opinion suitable for the construction of the Project but shall be at liberty to import labour of all classes to the extent necessary.

13. CIVIC AMENITIES IN THE PROJECT AREA:- Subject to the prior approval of HMG, the Union may, in the Project area, establish schools, hospitals, water-supply systems, electric supply systems, drainage and other civic amenities for the duration of the construction of the Project. On completion of construction of the project, any such amenities shall, upon request by HMG, be transferred to HMG, and that, in any case, all functions of public administration shall, pursuant to the provisions of clause 5(v) be exercised by HMG.

14. ARBITRATION:- (i) Any dispute or difference arising out of or in any way touching or concerning the construction, effect or meaning of this Agreement, or of any matter contained herein or the respective rights and liabilities of the parties hereunder, if not settled by discussion shall be determined in accordance with the provisions of this clause.

(ii) Any of the parties may by notice in writing inform the other party of its intention to refer to arbitration any such dispute or difference mentioned in sub-clause (i); and within 90 days of the delivery of such notice, each of the two parties shall nominate an arbitrator for jointly determining such dispute or difference and the award of the arbitrators shall be binding on the parties.

(iii) In case the arbitrators are unable to agree, the parties hereto may consult each other and appoint an Umpire whose award shall be final and binding on them.

15. ESTABLISHMENT OF INDO-NEPAL KOSI PROJECT COMMISSION:- (i) For the discussion of problems of common interest in connection with the Project and for the purposes of co-ordination and co-operation between the two Governments with regard to any matter covered in this Agreement, the two Governments shall at an early date establish a joint 'Indo-

Nepal Kosi Project Commission'. The rules for the composition, jurisdiction, etc., of the said Commission shall be mutually agreed upon.

(ii) Until the said Joint Commission shall be constituted the 'Co-ordination Committee for the Kosi Project' shall continue to function as follows:-

(a) The committee shall consist of four representatives from each country to be nominated by the respective Governments.

(b) The Chairman of the committee shall be a Minister of HMG, and the Secretary shall be the Administrator of the Kosi Project.

(c) The committee shall consider among other such matters of common interest concerning the project as land acquisition by HMG for lease to the Union, rehabilitation of displaced population, maintenance of law and order.

(iii) As soon as the said Joint Commission shall be constituted, the Co-ordination Committee for the Kosi Project shall be dissolved.

16. (i) This present Agreement shall come into force from the date of signatures of the authorised representatives of HMG and the Union respectively and thereafter, it shall remain valid for a period of 199 years.

(ii) This present Agreement shall supersede the Agreement signed between the Government of Nepal and the Government of India on the 25th April, 1954 on the Kosi Project.

IN WITNESS WHEREOF the undersigned being duly authorised thereto by their respective Governments have signed the present Amended Agreement.

Done at Kathmandu, in quadruplicate, this day, the 19th of December, 1966

For the Government of India	For His Majesty's Government of Nepal
SHRIMAN NARAYAN Ambassador of India in Nepal	*Y. P. PANT* Secretary, Ministry of Economic Planning and Finance

Appendix II

Agreement between His Majesty's Government of Nepal and the Government of India on the Gandak Irrigation and Power Project, Kathmandu, December 4, 1959

PREAMBLE: - WHEREAS His Majesty's Government of Nepal and the Government of India consider that it is in the common interests of both Nepal and India to construct a barrage, canal head regulators and other appurtenant works about 1,000 feet below the existing Tribeni Canal head regulator and of taking out canal systems for purposes of irrigation and development of power for Nepal and India (hereinafter referred to as 'the Project').

AND WHEREAS in view of the common benefits, His Majesty's Government have agreed to the construction of the said barrage, canal head regulators and other connected works as shown in the Plan annexed[1] to this Agreement to the extent that they lie within the territory of Nepal, by and at the cost of the Government of India.

NOW THE PARTIES AGREE AS FOLLOWS:-

1. INVESTIGATION AND SURVEYS:- His Majesty's Government authorise the Project Officers and other persons acting under the general or special orders of such officers to move in the area indicated in the said Plan with men, material and equipment as may be required for the surveys and investigations in connection with the Project, before, during and after construction, as may be found necessary from time to time. These surveys include ground, aerial, hydraulic, hydrometric, hydrological and geological surveys; investigations for communication and for the alignment of canals and for materials required for the construction and maintenance of the Project.

---

[1] Not reproduced here.

2. AUTHORITY FOR THE EXECUTION OF WORKS AND THEIR MAINTENANCE:- (i) His Majesty's Government authorise the Government of India to proceed with the execution of the Project and for this purpose His Majesty's Government shall acquire all such lands as the Government of India may require and will permit the access to, the movement within and the residence in the area indicated in the Plan of officers and field staff with labour force, draught animals, vehicles, plants, machinery, equipment and instruments as may be necessary for the execution of the Project and for its operation and maintenance after its completion.

(ii) In case of any apprehended danger or accident to any of the structures, the officers of the Government of India will execute all works which may be necessary for repairing the existing works or preventing such accidents and/or danger in the areas indicated in the Plan. If any of such works have to be constructed on lands as may be necessary for the purpose. In all such cases the Government of India shall pay reasonable compensation for the lands so acquired as well as for damage, if any, arising out of the execution of these works.

3. LAND ACQUISITION:- (i) His Majesty's Government will acquire or requisition, as the case may be, all such lands as are required by the Government of India for the Project, i.e., for the purpose of investigation, construction and maintenance of the Project and the Government of India shall pay reasonable compensation for such lands acquired or requisitioned.

(ii) His Majesty's Government shall transfer to the Government of India such lands belonging to His Majesty's Government as are required for the purpose of the Project on payment of reasonable compensation by the Government of India.

(iii) Lands requisitioned under paragraph (i) shall be held by the Government of India for the duration of the requisition and lands acquired under sub-clause (i) or transferred under sub-clause (ii) shall vest in the Government of India as proprietor and subject to payment of land revenue (Malpot) at the rates at which it is leviable on agricultural lands in the neighbourhood.

(iv) When such land vesting in the Government of India or any part thereof ceases to be required by the Government of India for the purposes of the Project, the Government of India will reconvey the same to His Majesty's Government free of charge.

4. QUARRYING:- His Majesty's Government shall permit the Government of India on payment of reasonable royalty to quarry materials such as block stones, boulders, shingle and sand required for the construction and maintenance of the Project from the areas indicated in the said Plan.

5. COMMUNICATIONS:- (i) His Majesty's Government shall allow the Government of India to construct and maintain such portion of the main Western Canal which falls in the Nepal territory and to construct and maintain communications for the construction and maintenance of the Project. The roads will be essentially departmental roads of the Project and their use by commercial

and non-commercial vehicles of Nepal will be regulated as mutually agreed upon between His Majesty's Government and the Government of India.

(ii) The bridge over the Gandak Barrage will be open to public traffic, but the Government of India shall have the right to close the traffic over the bridge for repair, etc.

(iii) The Government of India agree to provide locking arrangements for facility of riverine traffic across the Barrage free from payment of any tolls whatever, provided that this traffic will be regulated by the Project staff in accordance with the rules mutually agreed upon between His Majesty's Government and the Government of India.

(iv) His Majesty's Government agree to permit installations of telegraph, telephone; and radio communications as approximately indicated in the Plan for the *bona fide* purpose of the construction, maintenance and operation of the Project.

(v) The Government of India shall permit the use of internal telegraph, telephone and radio communications as indicated in the Plan to the authorised servants of His Majesty's Government in emergencies, provided such use does not interfere with the construction, maintenance and operation of the Project.

6. OWNERSHIP, OPERATION AND MAINTENANCE OF WORKS:- Subject to the provisions of sub-clause (v) of clause 7, all works connected with the Project in the territory of Nepal will remain the property of and be operated and maintained by the Government of India.

7. IRRIGATION FOR NEPAL:- (i) The Government of India shall construct at their own cost the Western Nepal Canal including the distributary system thereof down to a minimum discharge of 20 ft3/s for providing flow irrigation in the gross commanded area estimated to be about 40,000 acres.

(ii) The Government of India shall construct the Eastern Nepal Canal from the tail end of the Don Branch Canal up to river Bagmati including the distributary system down to a minimum discharge of 20 ft3/s at their own cost for providing flow irrigation in Nepal for the gross commanded area estimated to be 103,500 acres.

(iii) His Majesty's Government shall be responsible for the construction of channels below 20 ft3/s capacity for irrigation in Nepal but the Government of India shall contribute such sum of money as they may consider reasonable to meet the cost of construction.

(iv) The Nepal Eastern Canal and the Nepal Western Canal shall be completed, as far as possible, within one year of the completion of the barrage.

(v) The canal systems including the service roads situated in Nepal territory except the main Western Canal shall be handed over to His Majesty's Government for operation and maintenance at their cost.

8. POWER DEVELOPMENT AND RESERVATION FOR NEPAL:- (i) The Government of India agree to construct one Power House with an installed capacity of 15,000 KW in the Nepal territory on the Main Western Canal.

(ii) The Government of India also agree to construct a transmission line from the Power House in Nepal to the Bihar border near Bhaisalotan and from Sagauli to Raxaul in Bihar in order to facilitate supply of power on any point in the Bihar Grid up to and including Raxaul.

(iii) The Government of India shall supply power to His Majesty's Government at the Power House and/or at any point in the Grid up to and including Raxaul to an aggregate maximum of 10,000 KW up to 60 per cent load factor at power factor not below 0.85. The charges for supply at the Power House shall be the actual cost of production, and on any point on the Grid up to Raxaul it shall be the cost of production *plus* the cost of transmission on such terms and conditions as may be mutually agreed upon.

(iv) His Majesty's Government will be responsible for the construction at their own cost of the transmission and distribution system for supply of power within Nepal from the Power House or from any point on the Grid up to and including Raxaul.

(v) The ownership and management of the Power House shall be transferred to His Majesty's Government on one year's notice in writing given by them to the Government of India after the full load of 10,000 KW at 60 per cent load factor has been developed in Nepal from this Power House.

(vi) The ownership of the transmission system constructed by the Government of India at its cost shall remain vested in the Government of India, but, on transfer of the Power House, the Government of India shall continue the arrangements for transmission of power, if so desired by His Majesty's Government, on payment of the cost of transmission. Provided that His Majesty's Government shall have the right to purchase the transmission system from the Power House to Bhaisalotan situated in the Nepal territory on payment of the original cost *minus* depreciation.

(vii) The Government of India shall be free to regulate the flow into or close the Main Western Canal Head Regulator temporarily, if such works are found to be necessary in the interest of the efficient maintenance and operation of the Canal or the Power House, provided that in such situations the Government of India agree to supply the minimum essential power from the Bihar Grid to the extent possible on such terms and conditions as may be mutually agreed upon.

9. PROTECTION OF NEPAL'S RIPARIAN RIGHTS:- His Majesty's Government will continue to have the right to withdraw for irrigation or any other purpose from the river or its tributaries in Nepal such supplies of water as may be required by them from time to time and His Majesty's Government agree that they shall not exercise this right in such manner as is likely, in the opinion of the parties hereto prejudicially to affect the water requirements of the Project as set out in the schedule annexed hereto.

10. PRO RATA REDUCTION OF SUPPLIES DURING PERIOD OF SHORTAGE:- Whenever the supply of water available for irrigation falls short of the requirements of the total area under the Project for which irrigation has to be provided the shortage shall be shared on *pro rata* basis between the Government of

India and His Majesty's Government.

11. SOVEREIGNTY AND JURISDICTION:- Nothing in this Agreement shall be deemed to derogate from the sovereignty and territorial jurisdiction of His Majesty's Government in respect of lands acquired by His Majesty's Government and made available to the Government of India for investigation, execution and maintenance of the Project.

12. ARBITRATION:- (1) Any dispute or difference arising out of or in any way touching or concerning the construction, effect or meaning of this Agreement, or of any matter contained herein or the respective rights and liabilities of the parties hereunder, if not settled by discussion, shall be determined in accordance with the provisions of this clause.

(2) Any of the parties may by notice in writing inform the other party of its intention to refer to arbitration any such dispute or difference mentioned in sub-clause (1) and within 90 days of the delivery of such notice, each of the two parties shall nominate an arbitrator for jointly determining such dispute or difference and the award of the arbitrators shall be binding on the parties.

(3) In case the arbitrators are unable to agree, the parties hereto may consult each other and appoint an Umpire whose award shall be final and binding on them.

13. This Agreement will come into force with effect from the date of signatures of the authorised representatives of His Majesty's Government and the Government of India respectively.

IN WITNESS WHEREOF the undersigned being duly authorised thereof by their respective Governments have signed the present AGREEMENT in Nepali, Hindi and English in duplicate, all three texts being equally authentic, at Kathmandu this 19th day of Magh Sambut 2016 corresponding to December 4, 1959. For purposes of interpretation the English text shall be used.

For the Government of India
For and on behalf of the
PRESIDENT OF INDIA

On behalf of
HIS MAJESTY'S
GOVERNMENT OF NEPAL

BHAGWAN SAHAY,
Ambassador of India

SUBARNA SHAMSHERE,
Deputy Prime Minister

Appendix III

Treaty between His Majesty's Government of Nepal and the Government of India concerning the Integrated Development of the Mahakali River, including Sarada Barrage, Tanakpur Barrage and Pancheshwar Project

His Majesty's Government of NEPAL and the Government of INDIA (thereinafter referred to as the 'Parties'),

Reaffirming the determination to promote and strengthen their relations of friendship and close neighbourliness for the co-operation in the development of water resources;

Recognizing that the Mahakali River is a boundary river on major stretches between the two countries;

Realizing the desirability to enter into a treaty on the basis of equal partnership to define their obligations and corresponding rights and duties thereto in regard to the waters of the Mahakali River and its utilization;

Noting the Exchange of Letters of 1920 through which both the Parties had entered into an arrangement for the construction of the Sarada Barrage in the Mahakali River, whereby Nepal is to receive some waters from the said Barrage;

Recalling the decision taken in the Joint Commission dated 4-5 December, 1991 and the Joint Communiqué issued during the visit of the Prime Minister of India to Nepal on 21st October, 1992 regarding the Tanakapur Barage which India has constructed in a course of the Mahakali River with a part of the eastern afflux bund at Jimuwa and the adjoining pondage area of the said Barrage lying in the Nepalese territory;

Noting that both the Parties are jointly preparing a Detailed Project Report of the Pancheshwar Multipurpose Project to be implemented in the Mahakali River;

Now, therefore, the Parties hereto hereby have agreed as follows:

Article 1

1. Nepal shall have the right to a supply of 28.35 m3/s (1000 ft3/s) of water from the Sarada Barrae in the wet season (i.e. from 15th May to 15th October) and 4.25m3/s (150 ft3/s) in the dry season (i.e. from 16th October to 14th May).

2. India shall maintain a flow of not less than 10 m3/s (350 ft3/s) downstream of the Sarada Barrage in the Mahakali River to maintain and preserve the river eco-system.

3. In case the Sarada Barrage become non-functional due to any cause:

   (a) Nepal shall have the right to a supply of water as mentioned in Paragraph 1 of this Article, by using the head regulator(s) mentioned in Paragraph 2 of Article 2 herein. Such a supply of water shall be in addition to the water to be supplied to Nepal pursuant to Paragraph 2 of Article 2.

   (b) India shall maintain the river flow pursuant to Paragraph 2 of this Article from the tailrace of the Tanakpur Power Station downstream of the Sarada Barrage.

Article 2

In continuation of the decisions taken in the Joint Commission dated 4-5 December, 1991 and the Joint Communiqué issued during the visit of the Prime Minister of India to Nepal on 21st October, 1992, both the Parties agree as follows:

1. For the construction of the eastern afflux bund of the Tanakpur Barrage, at Jimuwa and tying it up to the high ground in the Nepalese territory at EL 250 M, Nepal gives its consent to use a piece of land of about 577 metres in length (an area of about 2.9 hectares) of the Nepalese territory at the Jimuwa Village in Mahendranagar Municipal area and a certain portion of the No-Man's Land on either side of the border. The Nepalese land consented to be so used and the land lying on the west of the said land (about 9 hectares) up to the Nepal India border which forms a part of the pondage area, including the natural resources endowment lying within that area, remains under the continued sovereignty and control of Nepal and

Nepal is free to exercise all attendant rights thereto.

2. In lieu of the eastern afflux bund of the Tanakpur Barrage, at Jimuwa thus constructed, Nepal shall have the right to:

   (a) a supply of 28.35 m3/s (1000 ft3/s) of water in the wet season (i.e. from 15th May to 15th October) and 8.50 m3/s (300 ft3/s) in the dry season (i.e. from 16th October to 14th May) from the date of the entry into force of this Treaty. For this purpose and for the purposes of Article 1 herein, India shall construct the head regulator(s) near the left undersluice of the Tanakpur Barrage and also the waterways of the required capacity upto the Nepal-India border. Such head regulator(s) and waterways shall be operated jointly.

   (b) a supply of 70 millions kilowatt-hour (unit) of energy on a continuous basis annually, free of cost, from the date of the entry into force of this Treaty. For this purpose, India shall construct a 132 Kv transmission line up to the Nepal-India border from the Tanakpur Power Station (which has, at present, an installed capacity of 120,000 kilowatt generating 448.4 millions kilowatt-hour of energy annually on 90 percent dependable year flow).

3. Following arrangements shall be made at the Tanakpur Barrage at the time of development of any storage project(s) including Pancheshwar Multipurpose Project upstream of the Tanakpur Barrage:

   (a) Additional head regulator and the necessary waterways, as required, up to the Nepal-India border shall be constructed to supply additional water to Nepal. Such head regulator and waterways shall be operated jointly.

   (b) Nepal shall have additional energy equal to half of the incremental energy generated from the Tanakpur Power Station, on a continuous basis from the date of augmentation of the flow of the Mahakali River and shall bear half of the additional operation cost and, if required, half of the additional capital cost at the Tanakpur Power Station for the generation of such incremental energy.

<u>Article 3</u>

Pancheshwar Multipurpose Project (hereinafter referred to as the 'Project') is to be constructed on a stretch of the Mahakali River where it forms the boundary between the two countries and hence both the Parties agree that they have equal entitlement in the utilization of the waters of the Mahakali River without prejudice to their respective existing consumptive uses of the waters of the Mahakali River.

Therefore, both the Parties agree to implement the Project in the Mahakali River in accordance with the Detailed Project Report (DPR) being jointly prepared by them. The Project shall be designed and implemented on the basis of the following principles:

1. The Project shall, as would be agreed between the Parties, be designed to produce the maximum total net benefit. All benefits accruing to both the Parties with the development of the Project in the forms of power, irrigation, flood control etc., shall be assessed.

2. The Project shall be implemented or caused to be implemented as an integrated project including power stations of equal capacity on each side of the Mahakali River. The two power stations shall be operated in an integrated manner and the total energy generated shall be shared equally between the Parties.

3. The cost of the Project shall be borne by the Parties in proportion to the benefits accruing to them. Both the Parties shall jointly endeavour to mobilize the finance required for the implementation of the Project.

4. A portion of Nepal's share of energy shall be sold to India. The quantum of such energy and its price shall be mutually agreed upon between the Parties.

Article 4

India shall supply 10 m3/s (350 ft3/s) of water for the irrigation of Dodhara-Chandani area of Nepalese Territory. The technical and other details will be mutually worked out.

Article 5

1. Water requirements of Nepal shall be given prime consideration in the utilization of the waters of the Mahakali River.

2. Both the Parties shall be entitled to draw their share of waters of the Mahakali River from the Tanakpur Barrage and/or other mutually agreed points as provided for in this Treaty and any subsequent agreement between the Parties.

Article 6

Any project, other than those mentioned herein, to be developed in the Mahakali River, where it is a boundary river, shall be designed and implemented by an agreement between the Parties on the principles established by this Treaty.

Article 7

In order to maintain the flow and level of the waters of the Mahakali River, each Party undertakes not to use or obstruct or divert the waters of the Mahakali River adversely affecting its natural flow and level except by an agreement between the Parties. Provided, however, this shall not preclude the use of the waters of the Mahakali River by the local communities living along both sides of the Mahakali River, not exceeding five (5) percent of the average annual flow at Pancheshwar.

Article 8

This Treaty shall not preclude planning, survey, development and operation of any work on the tributaries of the Mahakali River, to be carried out independently by each Party in its own territory without adversely affecting the provision of Article 7 of this Treaty.

Article 9

1. There shall be a Mahakali River Commission (hereinafter referred to as the 'Commission'). The Commission shall be guided by the principles of equality, mutual benefit and no harm to either Party.

2. The Commission shall be composed of equal number of representatives from both the Parties.

3. The functions of the Commission shall, inter alia, include the following:

    (a) To seek information on and, if necessary, inspect all structures included in the Treaty and make recommendations to both the Parties to take steps which shall be necessary to implement the provisions of this Treaty,

    (b) To make recommendations to both the Parties for the conservation and utilization of the Mahakali River as envisaged and provided for in this Treaty,

    (c) To provide expert evaluation of projects and recommendations thereto,

    (d) To co-ordinate and monitor plans of actions arising out of the implementation of this Treaty, and

(e) To examine any differences arising between the Parties concerning the interpretation and application of this Treaty.

4. The expenses of the Commission shall be borne equally by both the Parties.

5. As soon as the Commission has been constituted pursuant to Paragraphs 1 and 2 of this Article, it shall draft its rules of procedure, which shall be submitted to both the Parties for their concurrence.

6. Both the Parties shall reserve their rights to deal directly with each other on matters, which may be in the competence of the Commission.

Article 10

Both the Parties may form project specific joint entity/ies for the development, execution and operation of new projects including Pancheshwar Multipurpose Project in the Mahakali River for their mutual benefit.

Article 11

1. If the Commission fails under Article 9 of this Treaty to recommend its opinion after examining the differences of the Parties within three (3) months of such reference to the Commission or either Party disagrees with the recommendation of the Commission then a dispute shall be deemed to have been arisen which shall then be submitted to arbitration for decision. In so doing either Party shall give three (3) months' prior notice to the other Party.

2. Arbitration shall be conducted by a tribunal composed of three arbitrators. One arbitrator shall be nominated by Nepal, one by India, with neither country to nominate its own national and the third arbitrator shall be appointed jointly, who, as a member of the tribunal, shall preside over such tribunal. In the even that the Parties are unable to agree upon the third arbitrator within ninety (90) days after receipt of a proposal, either Party may request the Secretary-General of the Permanent Court of Arbitration at the Hague to appoint such arbitrator who shall not be a national of either country.

3. The procedures of the arbitration shall be determined by the arbitration tribunal and the decision of a majority of the arbitrators shall be the decision of the tribunal. The proceedings of the tribunal shall be conducted in English and the decision of such a tribunal shall be in writing. Both the Parties shall accept the decision as final, definitive and binding.

4. Provision for the venue of arbitration, the administrative support of the arbitration tribunal and the remuneration and expenses of its arbitrators shall be as agreed in an exchange of notes between the Parties. Both the Parties may also agree by such exchange of notes on alternative procedures for settling differences arising under this Treaty.

Article 12

1. Following the conclusion of this Treaty, the earlier understandings reached between the Parties concerning the utilization of the waters of the Mahakali River from the Sarada Barrage and the Tanakpur Barrage, which has been incorporated herein, shall be deemed to have been replaced by this Treaty.

2. This Treaty shall be subject to ratification and shall enter into force on the date of exchange of instruments of ratification. It shall remain valid for a period of seventy-five (75) years from the date of its entry into force.

3. This Treaty shall be reviewed by both the Parties at ten (10) years interval or earlier as required by either Party and make amendments thereto, if necessary.

4. Agreements, as required, shall be entered into by the Parties to give effect to the provisions of this Treaty.

IN WITNESS WHEREOF the undersigned being duly authorized thereto by their respective governments have hereto signed this Treaty and affixed thereto their seals in two originals each in Hindi, Nepali and English languages, all the texts being equally authentic. In case of doubt, the English text shall prevail.

Done at New Delhi, India, on the twelfth day of February of the year one thousand nine hundred ninety six.

(SHER BAHADUR DEUBA)
PRIME MINISTER
HIS MAJESTY'S GOVERNMENT OF NEPAL

(P.V.NARASIMHA RAO)
PRIME MINISTER OF INDIA

Letter Exchanged with the Treaty

KATHMANDU
NEPAL

The Prime Minister

February 12, 1996

Excellency,

I have the honour to refer to the Treaty concluded between us concerning the Integrated Development of the Mahakali River including Sarada Barrage, the Tanakpur Barrage and Pancheswar Project (Treaty). At this juncture, may I also recall for Your Excellency the decisions taken in the Joint Commission dated 4-5 December, 1991 and the Joint Communique issued during your visit to Nepal on 21st October, 1992.

In order to give effect to the desires expressed by our respective Governments, I have the honour to make the following proposals on the basis of the provisions of the said understandings and the said Treaty.

1. The all-weather link road connecting the Tanakpur Barrage to the East-West Highway at Mahendranagar in Nepal shall be completed by India within one (1) year from the date of the entry into force of the Treaty.

2. The supply of 20 millions kilowatt-hour of energy annually, free of cost, to Nepal from the Tanakpur Power Station as indicated in the said Joint Communique from the date of commissioning of the Tanakpur Power Station in July 7, 1992 till the start of the supply of 70 millions kilowatt-hour (unit) of energy annually, free of cost, to Nepal as provided for in the Treaty, shall be reconciled with the energy procured or to be procured by Nepal from India under the existing power exchange arrangement.

3. Regarding Pancheshwar Multipurpose Project (Project), the following principles shall be adopted and arrangements made for finalization of the Detailed Project Report (DPR) completion of negotiation and implementation of the Project:

   (a) The DPR shall be finalized by both the countries within six (6) months from the date of the entry into force of the Treaty. For this purpose, necessary data and reports shall be exchanged expeditiously. While assessing the benefits from the Project during the preparation of the DPR, net power benefit shall be assessed on the basis of, *inter alia*, saving in costs to the beneficiaries as compared with the relevant alternatives available. Irrigation benefit shall be assessed on the basis of incremental and additional benefits due to augmentation of river flow and flood control benefit shall be assessed on the basis of the value of works saved and damages avoided.

(b) It is understood that Paragraph 3 of Article 3 of the Treaty precludes the claim, in any form, by either Party on the unutilized portion of the shares of the waters of the Mahakali River of that Party without affecting the provision of the withdrawal of the respective shares of the water of the Mahakali River by each Party under this Treaty.

(c) Agreement for the financing and implementation of the Project, including the proposal for the establishment of the Pancheshwar Development Authority shall be negotiated and finalized by both the countries within one (1) year from the finalization of the DPR.

(d) In order to expedite the implementation of the Project, field investigation and detailed design including tender document preparation shall start immediately after the finalization of the DPR and run parallel to the negotiation on agreement for implementation of the Project. For this purpose, a separate financing arrangement for such activities shall be agreed upon by both the countries.

(e) The Project shall be aimed to be completed within eight (8) years from the date of the agreement for its implementation, subject to the provision of the DPR.

I shall be grateful if Your Excellency will kindly confirm that the above correctly sets out the understanding reached between our two Governments. This letter and Your Excellency's reply confirming the understanding will constitute an agreement between our two Governments which also shall come into force on the date of exchange of instruments of ratification between the Parties as set forth in Paragraph 2 of Article 12 of the Treaty.

Please accept, Your Excellency, the assurances of my highest considerations.

(Sher Bahadur Deuba)

H.E. Mr. P.V. Narasimha Rao
Prime Minister of India
New Delhi

Appendix IV

Partial Accord between India and Bangladesh on Farakka. Dacca, April 18, 1975

The delegation from India led by Shri Jagjivan Ram, Minister of Agriculture and Irrigation, met the delegation from Bangladesh led by Mr. Abdur Rab Serneabat, Minister of Flood Control, Water Resources and Power, in Dacca from April 16 to 18, 1975. The talks were held in a cordial atmosphere and were characterised by mutual understanding that exists between two friendly countries.

The Indian side pointed out while discussions regarding allocation of fair weather flows of the Ganga during lean months in terms of the Prime Minister's declaration of May, 1974 are continuing, it is essential to run the feeder canal of the Farakka Barrage during the current lean period. It is agreed that this operation may be carried out with varying discharges in ten-day periods during the months of April and May, 1975 as shown below ensuring the continuance of the remaining flows for Bangladesh:

Month	Ten-day Period	Withdrawal
April, 1975	21st to 30th	11,000 ft^3/s
May, 1975	1st to 10th	12,000 ft^3/s
	11th to 20th	15,000 ft^3/s
	21st to 31st	16,000 ft^3/s

Joint teams consisting of experts of two Governments shall observe at the appropriate places in both the countries the effects of the agreed withdrawals at Farakka, in Bangladesh and on the Hooghly River for the benefit of Calcutta Port. A joint team will also be stationed at Farakka to record the discharges into the feeder canal and the remaining flows for Bangladesh. The teams will submit their reports to both the Governments for consideration.

Appendix V

Treaty between the Government of the Republic of India and the Government of the People's Republic of Bangladesh on Sharing of the Ganga/Ganges Waters at Farakka. New Delhi, 12 December 1996

Determined to promote and strengthen their relations of friendship and good neighbourliness,

...

Being desirous of sharing by mutual agreement the waters of the international rivers flowing through the territories of the two countries and of making the optimum utilisation of the water resources of their region in the fields of flood management, irrigation, river basin development and generation of hydro-power for the mutual benefit of the peoples of the two countries,

...

Being desirous of finding a fair and just solution without affecting the rights and entitlements of either country other than those covered by this Treaty, or establishing any general principles of law or precedent,

Have agreed as follows:

Article 1

The quantum of waters agreed to be released by India to Bangladesh will be at Farakka.

Article 2

(i) The sharing between India and Bangladesh of the Ganga/Ganges waters at Farakka by ten day periods from the 1st January to the 31st May every year will be with reference to the formula at Annexure I and an indicative schedule giving the implications of the sharing arrangement under Annexure I is at Annexure II.

(ii) The indicative schedule at Annexure II, as referred to in sub para (i) above, is based on 40 years (1949-1988) 10-day period average availability of water at Farakka. Every effort would be made by the upper riparian to protect flows of water at Farakka as in the 40-years average availability as mentioned above.

(iii) In the event flow at Farakka falls below 50,000 ft3/s in any l0-day period, the two governments will enter into immediate consultations to make adjustments on an emergency basis, in accordance with the principles of equity, fair play and no harm to either party.

Article 3

The waters released to Bangladesh at Farakka under Article 1 shall not be reduced below Farakka except for reasonable uses of waters, not exceeding 200 ft3/s, by India between Farakka and the point on the Ganga/Ganges where both its banks are in Bangladesh.

Article 4

SELECTED DOCUMENTS

A Committee consisting of representatives nominated by the two Governments in equal numbers (hereinafter called the Joint Committee) shall be constituted following the signing of this Treaty. The Joint Committee shall set up suitable teams at Farakka and Hardinge Bridge to observe and record at Farakka the daily flows below Farakka Barrage, in the Feeder Canal, and at the Navigation Lock, as well as at the Hardinge Bridge.

Article 5

The Joint Committee shall decide its own procedure and method of functioning.

Article 6

The Joint Committee shall submit to the two Governments all data collected by it and shall also submit a yearly report to both the Governments. Following submission of the reports the two Governments will meet at appropriate levels to decide upon such further actions as may be needed.

Article 7

The Joint Committee shall be responsible for implementing the arrangements contained in this Treaty and examining any difficulty arising out of the implementation of the above arrangements and of the operation of Farakka Barrage. Any difference or dispute arising in this regard, if not resolved by the Joint Committee, shall be referred to the Indo-Bangladesh Joint Rivers Commission. If the difference or dispute still remains unresolved, it shall be referred to the two Governments, which shall meet urgently at the appropriate level to resolve it by mutual discussion.

Article 8

The two Governments recognise the need to cooperate with each other in finding a solution to the long-term problem of augmenting the flows of the Ganga/Ganges during the dry season.

Article 9

Guided by the principles of equity, fairness and no harm to either party, both the Governments agree to conclude water-sharing Treaties/Agreements with regard to other common rivers.

Article 10

The sharing arrangement under this Treaty shall be reviewed by the two Governments at five years' interval or earlier, as required by either party and needed adjustments, based on principles of equity, fairness, and no harm to either party made thereto, if necessary. It would be open to either party to seek the first review after two years to assess the impact and working of the sharing arrangements as contained in this Treaty.

Article 11

For the period of this Treaty, in the absence of mutual agreement on adjustments following reviews as mentioned in Article X, India shall release downstream of Farakka Barrage, water at a rate not less than 90% (ninety per cent) of Bangladesh's share according to the formula referred to in Article II, until such time as mutually agreed flows are decided upon.

Article 12

This Treaty shall enter into force upon signature and shall remain in force for a period of thirty years and it shall be renewable on the basis of mutual consent.

…

DONE at New Delhi 12th December, 1996 in Hindi, Bangla and English languages. In the event of any conflict between the texts, the English text shall prevail.

ANNEXURE – I

Availability at Farakka	Share of India	Share of Bangladesh
70,000 ft^3/s or less	50%	50%
70,000 -75,000 ft^3/s	Balance of flow	35,000 ft^3/s
75,000 ft^3/s or more	40,000 ft^3/s	Balance of flow

Subject to the condition that India and Bangladesh each shall receive guaranteed 35,000 ft^3/s of water in alternate three 10-day periods during the period March 1 to May 10.

[Annexure II is not reproduced]

Appendix VI

The Helsinki Rules of the International Law Association

The Helsinki Rules on the Uses of the Waters of International Rivers – Helsinki, 1966.

Chapter 1

General

Article I

The general rules of international law as set forth in these chapters are applicable to the use of the waters of an international drainage basin except as may be provided otherwise by convention, agreement or binding custom among the basin States.

Article II

An international drainage basin is a geographical area extending over two or more States determined by the watershed limits of the system of waters, including surface and underground waters, flowing into a common terminus.

Article III

A 'basin State' is a state the territory of which includes a portion of an international drainage basin.

Chapter 2

Equitable utilization of the waters of an international drainage basin

Article IV

Each basin State is entitled, within its territory, to a reasonable and equitable share in the beneficial uses of the waters of an international drainage basin.

Article V

(1) What is a reasonable and equitable share within the meaning of Article IV is determined in the light of all the relevant factors in each particular case.

(2) Relevant factors, which are to be considered, include, but are not limited to:

(a) the geography of the basin, including in particular the extent of the drainage area in the territory of each basin State;

(b) the hydrology of the basin, including in particular the contribution of water by each basin State;

(c) the climate affecting the basin;

(d) the past utilization of the waters of the basin, including in particular existing utilization;

(e) the economic and social needs of each basin State;

(f) the population dependent on the waters of the basin in each basin State;

(g) the comparative costs of alternative means of satisfying the economic and social needs of each basin State;

(h) the availability of other resources;

(i) the avoidance of unnecessary waste in the utilization of waters of the basin;

(j) the practicability of compensation to one or more of the co-basin States as a means of adjusting conflicts among uses; and,

(k) the degree to which the needs of a basin State may be satisfied, without causing substantial injury to a co-basin State.

(3) The weight to be given to each factor is to be determined by its importance in comparison with that of other relevant factors. In determining what is a reasonable and equitable share, all relevant factors are to be considered together and a conclusion reached on the basis of the whole.

Article VI

A use or category of uses is not entitled to any inherent preference over any other use or category of uses.

Article VII

A basin State may not be denied the present reasonable use of the waters of an international drainage basin to reserve for a co-basin State future use of such waters.

Article VIII

(1) An existing reasonable use may continue in operation unless the factors justifying its continuance are outweighed by other factors leading to the conclusion that it be modified or terminated so as to accommodate a competing incompatible use.

(2) a. a use that is in fact in operation is deemed to have been an existing use from the time of the initiation of construction directly related to the use or, where such construction is not required, the undertaking of comparable acts of actual implementation.

b. such a use continues to be an existing use until such time as it is discontinued with the intention that it be abandoned.

(3) A use will not be deemed an existing use if at the time of becoming operational it is incompatible with an already existing reasonable use.

Chapter 3

Pollution

Article IX

As used in this Chapter, the term 'water pollution' refers to any detrimental change resulting from human conduct in the natural composition, content, or quality of the waters of an international drainage basin.

Article X

(1) Consistent with the principle of equitable utilization of the waters of an international drainage basin, a State:

(a) must prevent any new form of water pollution or any increase in the degree of existing water pollution in an international drainage basin which would cause substantial injury in the territory of a co-basin State, and

(b) should take all reasonable measures to abate existing water pollution in an international drainage basin to such an extent that no substantial damage is caused in the territory of a co-basin State.

(2) The rule stated in paragraph (1) of this Article applies to water pollution originating:

(a) within a territory of the State; or

(b) outside the territory of the State, if it is caused by the State's conduct.

Article XI

(1) In the case of a violation of the rule stated in paragraph (1) a. of Article X of this Chapter, the State responsible shall be required to cease the wrongful conduct and compensate the injured co-basin State for the injury that has been caused to it.

(2) In a case falling under the rule stated in paragraph (1) b. of Article X, if a State fails to take reasonable measures, it shall be required promptly to enter into negotiations with the injured State with a view toward reaching a settlement equitable under the circumstances.

Chapter 4

Navigation

Article XII

(1) This Chapter refers to those rivers and lakes portions of which are both navigable and separate or traverse the territories of two or more States.

(2) Rivers or lakes are 'navigable' if in their natural or canalized state they are currently used for commercial navigation or are capable by reason of their natural condition of being so used.

(3) In this Chapter the term 'riparian State' refers to a State through or along which the navigable portion of a river flows or a lake lies.

Article XIII

Subject to any limitations or qualifications referred to in these Chapters, each riparian State is entitled to enjoy rights of free navigation on the entire course of a river or lake.

Article XIV

'Free navigation', as the term is used in this Chapter, includes the following freedom for vessels of a riparian State on a basis of equality:

(a) freedom of movement on the entire navigable course of the river or lake;

(b) freedom to enter ports and to make use of plants and docks; and,

(c) freedom to transport goods and passengers, either directly or through transhipment, between the territory of one riparian State and the territory of another riparian State and between the territory of a riparian State and the open sea.

Article XV

A riparian State may exercise rights of police, including but not limited to the protection of public safety and health, over that portion of the river or lake subject to its jurisdiction, provided the exercise of such rights does not unreasonably interfere with the enjoyment of the rights of free navigation defined in Articles XIII and XIV.

Article XVI

Each riparian State may restrict or prohibit the loading by vessels of a foreign State of goods and passengers in its territory for discharge in such territory.

Article XVII

A riparian State may grant rights of navigation to non-riparian States on rivers or lakes within its territory.

Article XVIII

Each riparian State is, to the extent of the means available or made available to it, required to maintain in good order that portion of the navigable course of a river or lake within its jurisdiction.

Article XVIII bis[1]

1. A riparian State intending to undertake works to improve the navigability of that portion of a river or lake within its jurisdiction is under a duty to give notice to the co-riparian States.

---

[1] Approved by the 56th Conference of the International Law Association New Delhi, 1974. Text in: Report of the Committee on International Water Resources Law of the International Law Association, *Report of the 56th Conference*, p. 15.

2. If these works are likely to affect adversely the navigational uses of one or more co-riparian States, any such co-riparian State may, within a reasonable time, request consultation. The concerned co-riparian States are then under a duty to negotiate.

3. If a riparian State proposes that such works be undertaken in whole or in part in the territory of one or more other co-riparian States, it must obtain the consent of the other co-riparian State or States concerned. The co-riparian State or States from whom this consent is required are under a duty to negotiate.

Article XIX

The rules stated in this Chapter are not applicable to the navigation of vessels of war or of vessels performing police or administrative functions, or, in general, exercising any other form of public authority.

Article XX

In time of war, other armed conflict, or public emergency constituting a threat to the life of the State, a riparian State may take measures derogating from its obligations under this Chapter to the extent strictly required by the exigencies of the situation, provided that such measures are not inconsistent with its other obligations under international law. The riparian State shall in any case facilitate navigation for humanitarian purposes.

Chapter 5

Timber floating

Article XXI

The floating of timber on a watercourse which flows through or between the territories of two or more States is governed by the following Articles except in cases in which floating is governed by rules of navigation according to applicable law or custom binding upon the riparians.

Article XXII

The States riparian to an international watercourse utilized for navigation may determine by common consent whether and under what conditions timber floating may be permitted upon the watercourse.

Article XXIII

(1) It is recommended that each State riparian to an international watercourse not used for navigation should, with due regard to other uses of the watercourse,

authorize the co-riparian States to use the watercourse and its banks within the territory of each riparian State for the floating of timber.

(2) This authorization should extend to all necessary work along the banks by the floating crew and to the installation of such facilities as may be required for the timber floating.

Article XXIV

If a riparian State requires permanent installation for floating inside a territory of a co-riparian State or if it is necessary to regulate the flow of the watercourse, all questions connected with these installations and measures should be determined by agreement between the States concerned.

Article XXV

Co-riparian States of a watercourse which is, or is to be used for floating timber should negotiate in order to come to an agreement governing the administrative regime of floating, and if necessary to establish a joint agency or commission in order to facilitate the regulation of floating in all aspects.

Chapter 6

Procedures for the prevention and settlement of disputes

Article XXVI

This Chapter relates to procedures for the prevention and settlement of international disputes as to the legal rights or other interests of basin States and of other States in the waters of an international drainage basin.

Article XXVII

(1) Consistently with the Charter of the United Nations, States are under an obligation to settle international disputes as to their legal rights or other interests by peaceful means in such a manner that international peace and security, and justice are not endangered.

(2) It is recommended that States resort progressively to the means of prevention and settlement of disputes stipulated in Articles XXIX to XXXIV of this Chapter.

Article XXVIII

(1) States are under a primary obligation to resort to means of prevention and settlement of disputes stipulated in the applicable treaties binding upon them.

(2) States are limited to the means of prevention and settlement of disputes stipulated in treaties binding upon them only to the extent provided by the applicable treaties.

Article XXIX

(1) With a view to preventing disputes from arising between basin States as to their legal rights or other interest, it is recommended that each basin State furnish relevant and reasonably available information to the other basin States concerning the waters of a drainage basin within its territory and its use of, and activities with respect to each waters.

(2) A State, regardless of its location in a drainage basin, should in particular furnish to any other basin State, the interests of which may be substantially affected, notice of any proposed construction or installation which would alter the regime of the basin in a way which might give rise to a dispute as defined in Article XXVI. The notice should include such essential facts as will permit the recipient to make an assessment of the probable effect of the proposed alteration.

(3) A State providing the notice referred to in paragraph (2) of this Article should afford to the recipient a reasonable period of time to make an assessment of the probable effect of the proposed construction or installation and submit its views thereon to the State furnishing the notice.

(4) If a State has failed to give the notice referred to in paragraph (2) of this Article, the alteration by the State in the regime of the drainage basin shall not be given the weight normally accorded to temporal priority in use in the event of a determination of what is a reasonable and equitable share of the waters of the basin.

Article XXX

In case of a dispute between States as to their legal rights or other interests, as defined in Article XXVI, they should seek a solution by negotiation.

Article XXXI

(1) If a question or dispute arises which relates to the present or future utilization of the waters of an international drainage basin, it is recommended that the basin States refer the question or dispute to a joint agency and that they request the agency to survey the international drainage basin and to formulate plans or recommendations for the fullest and most efficient use thereof in the interests of all such States.

(2) It is recommended that the joint agency be instructed to submit reports on all

matters within its competence to the appropriate authorities of the member States concerned.

(3) It is recommended that the member States of the joint agency in appropriate cases invite non-basin States which by treaty enjoy a right in the use of the waters of an international drainage basin to associate themselves with the work of the joint agency or that they be permitted to appear before the agency.

Article XXXII

If a question or a dispute is one which is considered by the States concerned to be incapable of resolution in the manner set forth in Article XXXI, it is recommended that they seek the good offices, or jointly request the mediation of a third State, of a qualified international organization or of a qualified person.

Article XXXIII

(1) If the States concerned have not been able to resolve their dispute through negotiation or have been unable to agree on the measures described in Article XXXI and XXXII, it is recommended that they form a commission of inquiry or an ad hoc conciliation commission, which shall endeavour to find a solution, likely to be accepted by the States concerned, of any dispute as to their legal rights.

(2) It is recommended that the conciliation commission be constituted in the manner set forth in the Annex.

Article XXIV

It is recommended that the States concerned agree to submit their legal disputes to an ad hoc arbitral tribunal, to a permanent arbitral tribunal or to the International Court of Justice if:

(a) a commission has not been formed as provided in Article XXXIII; or
(b) the commission has not been able to find a solution to be recommended; or
(c) a solution recommended has not been accepted by the States concerned; and
(d) an agreement has not been otherwise arrived at.

Article XXXV

It is recommended that in the event of arbitration the States concerned have recourse to the Model Rules on Arbitral Procedure prepared by the International Law Commission of the United Nations at its tenth session in 1958.

Article XXXVI

Recourse to arbitration implies the undertaking by the States concerned to consider the award to be given as final and to submit in good faith to its execution.

Article XXXVII

The means of settlement referred to in the preceding Articles of this Chapter are without prejudice to the utilization of means of settlement recommended to, or required of, members of regional arrangements or agencies and of other international organizations.

Annex

Model rules for the constitution of the conciliation commission for the settlement of a dispute
(In implementation of Article XXXIII of Chap. 6)

Article I

The members of the Commission, including the President, shall be appointed by the States concerned.

Article II

If the States concerned cannot agree on these appointments, each State shall appoint two members. The members thus appointed shall choose one more member who shall be the President of the Commission, If the appointed members do not agree, the member-president shall be appointed, at the request of any State concerned, by the President of the International Court of Justice, or, if he does not make the appointment, by the Secretary-General of the United Nations.

Article III

The membership of the Commission should include persons who, by reason of their special competence, are qualified to deal with disputes concerning international drainage basins.

Article IV

If a member of the Commission abstains from performing his office or is unable to discharge his responsibilities, he shall be replaced by the procedure set out in Article I or Article II of this Annex, according to the manner in which he was originally appointed. If, in the case of:

(1) a member originally appointed under Article I, the States fail to agree as to a replacement; or

(2) a member originally appointed under Article II, the State involved fails to replace the member;

a replacement shall be chosen, at the request of any State concerned, by the President of the International Court of Justice, or, it he does not choose the replacement, by the Secretary- General of the United Nations.

Article V

In the absence of agreement to the contrary between the parties, the Conciliation Commission shall determine the place of its meetings and shall lay down its own procedure.

Appendix VII

UN Convention on the Law of the Non-Navigational Uses of International Watercourses, 21 May 1997

The Parties to the present Convention,

Conscious of the importance of international watercourses and the non-navigational uses thereof in many regions of the world,

Having in mind Article 13, paragraph 1 (a), of the Charter of the United Nations, which provides that the General Assembly shall initiate studies and make recommendations for the purpose of encouraging the progressive development of international law and its codification,

Considering that successful codification and progressive development of rules of international law regarding non-navigational uses of international watercourses would assist in promoting and implementing the purposes and principles set forth in Articles 1 and 2 of the Charter of the United Nations,

Taking into account the problems affecting many international watercourses resulting from, among other things, increasing demands and pollution,

Expressing the conviction that a framework convention will ensure the utilization, development, conservation, management and protection of international watercourses and the promotion of the optimal and sustainable utilization thereof for present and future generations,

Affirming the importance of international co-operation and good-neighbourliness in this field,

Aware of the special situation and needs of developing countries,

Recalling the principles and recommendations adopted by the United Nations Conference on Environment and Development of 1992 in the Rio Declaration and Agenda 21,

Recalling also the existing bilateral and multilateral agreements regarding the non-navigational uses of international watercourses,

Mindful of the valuable contribution of international organizations, both governmental and non-governmental, to the codification and progressive development of international law in this field,

Appreciative of the work carried out by the International Law Commission on the law of the non-navigational uses of international watercourses,

Bearing in mind United Nations General Assembly resolution 49/52 of 9 December 1994,

Have agreed as follows:

PART I

INTRODUCTION

Article 1
Scope of the present Convention

1. The present Convention applies to uses of international watercourses and of their waters for purposes other than navigation and to measures of protection, preservation and management related to the uses of those watercourses and their waters.

2. The uses of international watercourses for navigation is not within the scope of the present Convention except insofar as other uses affect navigation or are affected by navigation.

Article 2
Use of terms

For the purposes of the present Convention:

(a) 'Watercourse' means a system of surface waters and ground waters constituting by virtue of their physical relationship a unitary whole and normally flowing into a common terminus;

(b) 'International watercourse' means a watercourse, parts of which are situated in different States;

(c) 'Watercourse State' means a State Party to the present Convention in whose territory part of an international watercourse is situated, or a Party that is a regional economic integration organization, in the territory of one or more of whose Member States part of an international watercourse is situated;

(d) 'Regional economic integration organization' means an organization constituted by sovereign States of a given region, to which its member States have transferred competence in respect of matters governed by this Convention and which has been duly authorized in accordance with its internal procedures, to sign, ratify, accept, approve or accede to it.

Article 3
Watercourse agreements

1. In the absence of an agreement to the contrary, nothing in the present Convention shall affect the rights or obligations of a watercourse State arising from agreements in force for it on the date on which it became a party to the present Convention.

2. Notwithstanding the provisions of paragraph 1, parties to agreements referred to in paragraph 1 may, where necessary, consider harmonizing such agreements with the basic principles of the present Convention.

3. Watercourse States may enter into one or more agreements, hereinafter referred to as 'watercourse agreements', which apply and adjust the provisions of the present Convention to the characteristics and uses of a particular international watercourse or part thereof.

4. Where a watercourse agreement is concluded between two or more watercourse States, it shall define the waters to which it applies. Such an agreement may be entered into with respect to an entire international watercourse or any part thereof or a particular project, programme or use except insofar as the agreement adversely affects, to a significant extent, the use by one or more other watercourse States of the waters of the watercourse, without their express consent.

5. Where a watercourse State considers that adjustment and application of the provisions of the present Convention is required because of the characteristics and uses of a particular international watercourse, watercourse States shall consult with a view to negotiating in good faith for the purpose of concluding a watercourse agreement or agreements.

6. Where some but not all watercourse States to a particular international watercourse are parties to an agreement, nothing in such agreement shall affect the rights or obligations under the present Convention of watercourse States that are not parties to such an agreement.

Article 4
Parties to watercourse agreements

1. Every watercourse State is entitled to participate in the negotiation of and to become a party to any watercourse agreement that applies to the entire international watercourse, as well as to participate in any relevant consultations.

2. A watercourse State whose use of an international watercourse may be affected to a significant extent by the implementation of a proposed watercourse agreement that applies only to a part of the watercourse or to a particular project, programme or use is entitled to participate in consultations on such an agreement and, where appropriate, in the negotiation thereof in good faith with a view to becoming a party thereto, to the extent that its use is thereby affected.

PART II

GENERAL PRINCIPLES

Article 5
Equitable and reasonable utilization and participation

1. Watercourse States shall in their respective territories utilize an international watercourse in an equitable and reasonable manner. In particular, an international watercourse shall be used and developed by watercourse States with a view to attaining optimal and sustainable utilization thereof and benefits therefrom, taking into account the interests of the watercourse States concerned, consistent with adequate protection of the watercourse.

2. Watercourse States shall participate in the use, development and protection of an international watercourse in an equitable and reasonable manner. Such participation includes both the right to utilize the watercourse and the duty to cooperate in the protection and development thereof, as provided in the present Convention.

Article 6
Factors relevant to equitable and reasonable utilization

1. Utilization of an international watercourse in an equitable and reasonable manner within the meaning of article 5 requires taking into account all relevant factors and circumstances, including:

(a) Geographic, hydrographic, hydrological, climatic, ecological and other factors of a natural character;
(b) The social and economic needs of the watercourse States concerned;
(c) The population dependent on the watercourse in each watercourse State;
(d) The effects of the use or uses of the watercourses in one watercourse State on other watercourse States;
(e) Existing and potential uses of the watercourse;
(f) Conservation, protection, development and economy of use of the water resources of the watercourse and the costs of measures taken to that effect;
(g) The availability of alternatives, of comparable value, to a particular planned or existing use.

2. In the application of article 5 or paragraph 1 of this article, watercourse States concerned shall, when the need arises, enter into consultations in a spirit of cooperation.

3. The weight to be given to each factor is to be determined by its importance in comparison with that of other relevant factors. In determining what is a reasonable and equitable use, all relevant factors are to be considered together and a conclusion reached on the basis of the whole.

Article 7
Obligation not to cause significant harm

1. Watercourse States shall, in utilizing an international watercourse in their territories, take all appropriate measures to prevent the causing of significant harm to other watercourse States.

2. Where significant harm nevertheless is caused to another watercourse State, the States whose use causes such harm shall, in the absence of agreement to such use, take all appropriate measures, having due regard for the provisions of articles 5 and 6, in consultation with the affected State, to eliminate or mitigate such harm and, where appropriate, to discuss the question of compensation.

Article 8
General obligation to cooperate

1. Watercourse States shall cooperate on the basis of sovereign equality, territorial integrity, mutual benefit and good faith in order to attain optimal utilization and adequate protection of an international watercourse.

2. In determining the manner of such cooperation, watercourse States may consider the establishment of joint mechanisms or commissions, as deemed necessary by them, to facilitate cooperation on relevant measures and procedures in the light of experience gained through cooperation in existing joint mechanisms and commissions in various regions.

Article 9
Regular exchange of data and information

1. Pursuant to article 8, watercourse States shall on a regular basis exchange readily available data and information on the condition of the watercourse, in particular that of a hydrological, meteorological, hydrogeological and ecological nature and related to the water quality as well as related forecasts.

2. If a watercourse State is requested by another watercourse State to provide data or information that is not readily available, it shall employ its best efforts to comply with the request but may condition its compliance upon payment by the

requesting State of the reasonable costs of collecting and, where appropriate, processing such data or information.

3. Watercourse States shall employ their best efforts to collect and, where appropriate, to process data and information in a manner, which facilitates its utilization by the other watercourse States to which it is communicated.

Article 10
Relationship between different kinds of uses

1. In the absence of agreement or custom to the contrary, no use of an international watercourse enjoys inherent priority over other uses.

2. In the event of a conflict between uses of an international watercourse, it shall be resolved with reference to articles 5 to 7, with special regard being given to the requirements of vital human needs.

PART III

PLANNED MEASURES

Article 11
Information concerning planned measures

Watercourse States shall exchange information and consult each other and, if necessary, negotiate on the possible effects of planned measures on the condition of an international watercourse.

Article 12
Notification concerning planned measures with possible adverse effects

Before a watercourse State implements or permits the implementation of planned measures, which may have a significant adverse effect upon other watercourse States, it shall provide those States with timely notification thereof. Such notification shall be accompanied by available technical data and information, including the results of any environmental impact assessment, in order to enable the notified States to evaluate the possible effects of the planned measures.

Article 13
Period for reply to notification

Unless otherwise agreed:

(a) A watercourse State providing a notification under article 12 shall allow the notified States a period of six months within which to study and evaluate the possible effects of the planned measures and to communicate the findings to it;

(b) This period shall, at the request of a notified State for which the evaluation of the planned measures poses special difficulty, be extended for a period of six months.

Article 14
Obligations of the notifying State during the period for reply

During the period referred to in article 13, the notifying State:

(a) Shall cooperate with the notified States by providing them, on request, with any additional data and information that is available and necessary for an accurate evaluation; and

(b) Shall not implement or permit the implementation of the planned measures without the consent of the notified States.

Article 15
Reply to notification

The notified States shall communicate their findings to the notifying State as early as possible within the period applicable pursuant to article 13. If a notified State finds that implementation of the planned measures would be inconsistent with the provisions of articles 5 or 7, it shall attach to its finding a documented explanation setting forth the reasons for the finding.

Article 16
Absence of reply to notification

1. If, within the period applicable pursuant to article 13, the notifying State receives no communication under article 15, it may, subject to its obligations under articles 5 and 7, proceed with the implementation of the planned measures, in accordance with the notification and any other data and information provided to the notified States.

2. Any claim to compensation by a notified State, which has failed to reply within the period applicable pursuant to article 13, may be offset by the costs incurred by the notifying State for action undertaken after the expiration of the time for a reply, which would not have been undertaken if the notified State had objected within that period.

Article 17
Consultations and negotiations concerning planned measures

1. If a communication is made under article 15 that implementation of the planned measures would be inconsistent with the provisions of articles 5 or 7, the notifying State and the State making the communication shall enter into consultations and, if necessary, negotiations with a view to arriving at an equitable resolution of the situation.

2. The consultations and negotiations shall be conducted on the basis that each State must in good faith pay reasonable regard to the rights and legitimate interests of the other State.

3. During the course of the consultations and negotiations, the notifying State shall, if so requested by the notified State at the time it makes the communication, refrain from implementing or permitting the implementation of the planned measures for a period of six months unless otherwise agreed.

Article 18
Procedures in the absence of notification

1. If a watercourse State has reasonable grounds to believe that another watercourse State is planning measures that may have a significant adverse effect upon it, the former State may request the latter to apply the provisions of article 12. The request shall be accompanied by a documented explanation setting forth its grounds.

2. In the event that the State planning the measures nevertheless finds that it is not under an obligation to provide a notification under article 12, it shall so inform the other State, providing a documented explanation setting forth the reasons for such finding. If this finding does not satisfy the other State, the two States shall, at the request of that other State, promptly enter into consultations and negotiations in the manner indicated in paragraphs 1 and 2 of article 17.

3. During the course of the consultations and negotiations, the State planning the measures shall, if so requested by the other State at the time it requests the initiation of consultations and negotiations, refrain from implementing or permitting the implementation of those measures for a period of six months unless otherwise agreed.

Article 19
Urgent implementation of planned measures

1. In the event that the implementation of planned measures is of the utmost urgency in order to protect public health, public safety or other equally important interests, the State planning the measures may, subject to articles 5 and 7, immediately proceed to implementation, notwithstanding the provisions of article 14 and paragraph 3 of article 17.

2. In such case, a formal declaration of the urgency of the measures shall be communicated without delay to the other watercourse States referred to in article 12 together with the relevant data and information.

3. The State planning the measures shall, at the request of any of the States referred to in paragraph 2, promptly enter into consultations and negotiations with it in the

manner indicated in paragraphs 1 and 2 of article 17.

PART IV

PROTECTION, PRESERVATION AND MANAGEMENT

Article 20
Protection and preservation of ecosystems

Watercourse States shall, individually and, where appropriate, jointly, protect and preserve the ecosystems of international watercourses.

Article 21
Prevention, reduction and control of pollution

1. For the purpose of this article, 'pollution of an international watercourse' means any detrimental alteration in the composition or quality of the waters of an international watercourse, which results directly or indirectly from human conduct.

2. Watercourse States shall, individually and, where appropriate, jointly, prevent, reduce and control the pollution of an international watercourse that may cause significant harm to other watercourse States or to their environment, including harm to human health or safety, to the use of the waters for any beneficial purpose or to the living resources of the watercourse. Watercourse States shall take steps to harmonize their policies in this connection.

3. Watercourse States shall, at the request of any of them, consult with a view to arriving at mutually agreeable measures and methods to prevent, reduce and control pollution of an international watercourse, such as:

(a) Setting joint water quality objectives and criteria;

(b) Establishing techniques and practices to address pollution from point and non-point sources;

(c) Establishing lists of substances the introduction of which into the waters of an international watercourse is to be prohibited, limited, investigated or monitored.

Article 22
Introduction of alien or new species

Watercourse States shall take all measures necessary to prevent the introduction of species, alien or new, into an international watercourse, which may have effects detrimental to the ecosystem of the watercourse resulting in significant harm to other watercourse States.

Article 23
Protection and preservation of the marine environment

Watercourse States shall, individually and, where appropriate, in cooperation with other States, take all measures with respect to an international watercourse that are necessary to protect and preserve the marine environment, including estuaries, taking into account generally accepted international rules and standards.

Article 24
Management

1. Watercourse States shall, at the request of any of them, enter into consultations concerning the management of an international watercourse, which may include the establishment of a joint management mechanism.

2. For the purposes of this article, 'management' refers, in particular, to:
   (a) Planning the sustainable development of an international watercourse and providing for the implementation of any plans adopted; and
   (b) Otherwise promoting the rational and optimal utilization, protection and control of the watercourse.

Article 25
Regulation

1. Watercourse States shall cooperate, where appropriate, to respond to needs or opportunities for regulation of the flow of the waters of an international watercourse.

2. Unless otherwise agreed, watercourse States shall participate on an equitable basis in the construction and maintenance or defrayal of the costs of such regulation works as they may have agreed to undertake.

3. For the purposes of this article, 'regulation' means the use of hydraulic works or any other continuing measure to alter, vary or otherwise control the flow of the waters of an international watercourse.

Article 26
Installations

1. Watercourse States shall, within their respective territories, employ their best efforts to maintain and protect installations, facilities and other works related to an international watercourse.

2. Watercourse States shall, at the request of any of them which has reasonable grounds to believe that it may suffer significant adverse effects, enter into consultations with regard to:

(a) The safe operation and maintenance of installations, facilities or other works related to an international watercourse; and
(b) The protection of installations, facilities or other works from wilful or negligent acts or the forces of nature.

PART V

HARMFUL CONDITIONS AND EMERGENCY SITUATIONS

Article 27
Prevention and mitigation of harmful conditions

Watercourse States shall, individually and, where appropriate, jointly, take all appropriate measures to prevent or mitigate conditions related to an international watercourse that may be harmful to other watercourse States, whether resulting from natural causes or human conduct, such as flood or ice conditions, water-borne diseases, siltation, erosion, salt-water intrusion, drought or desertification.

Article 28
Emergency situations

1. For the purposes of this article, 'emergency' means a situation that causes, or poses an imminent threat of causing, serious harm to watercourse States or other States and that results suddenly from natural causes, such as floods, the breaking up of ice, landslides or earthquakes, or from human conduct, such as industrial accidents.

2. A watercourse State shall, without delay and by the most expeditious means available, notify other potentially affected States and competent international organizations of any emergency originating within its territory.

3. A watercourse State within whose territory an emergency originates shall, in cooperation with potentially affected States and, where appropriate, competent international organizations, immediately take all practicable measures necessitated by the circumstances to prevent, mitigate and eliminate harmful effects of the emergency.

4. When necessary, watercourse States shall jointly develop contingency plans for responding to emergencies, in cooperation, where appropriate, with other potentially affected States and competent international organizations.

PART VI

MISCELLANEOUS PROVISIONS

Article 29
International watercourses and installations in time of armed conflict

International watercourses and related installations, facilities and other works shall enjoy the protection accorded by the principles and rules of international law applicable in international and non-international armed conflict and shall not be used in violation of those principles and rules.

Article 30
Indirect procedures

In cases where there are serious obstacles to direct contacts between watercourse States, the States concerned shall fulfil their obligations of cooperation provided for in the present Convention, including exchange of data and information, notification, communication, consultations and negotiations, through any indirect procedure accepted by them.

Article 31
Data and information vital to national defence or security

Nothing in the present Convention obliges a watercourse State to provide data or information vital to its national defence or security. Nevertheless, that State shall cooperate in good faith with the other watercourse States with a view to providing as much information as possible under the circumstances.

Article 32
Non-discrimination

Unless the watercourse States concerned have agreed otherwise for the protection of the interests of persons, natural or juridical, who have suffered or are under a serious threat of suffering significant transboundary harm as a result of activities related to an international watercourse, a watercourse State shall not discriminate on the basis of nationality or residence or place where the injury occurred, in granting to such persons, in accordance with its legal system, access to judicial or other procedures, or a right to claim compensation or other relief in respect of significant harm caused by such activities carried on in its territory.

Article 33
Settlement of disputes

1. In the event of a dispute between two or more Parties concerning the interpretation or application of the present Convention, the Parties concerned shall,

in the absence of an applicable agreement between them, seek a settlement of the dispute by peaceful means in accordance with the following provisions.

2. If the Parties concerned cannot reach agreement by negotiation requested by one of them, they may jointly seek the good offices of, or request mediation or conciliation by, a third party, or make use, as appropriate, of any joint watercourse institutions that may have been established by them or agree to submit the dispute to arbitration or to the International Court of Justice.

3. Subject to the operation of paragraph 10, if after six months from the time of the request for negotiations referred to in paragraph 2, the Parties concerned have not been able to settle their dispute through negotiation or any other means referred to in paragraph 2, the dispute shall be submitted, at the request of any of the parties to the dispute, to impartial fact-finding in accordance with paragraphs 4 to 9, unless the Parties otherwise agree.

4. A Fact-finding Commission shall be established, composed of one member nominated by each Party concerned and in addition a member not having the nationality of any of the Parties concerned chosen by the nominated members who shall serve as Chairman.

5. If the members nominated by the Parties are unable to agree on a Chairman within three months of the request for the establishment of the Commission, any Party concerned may request the Secretary-General of the United Nations to appoint the Chairman who shall not have the nationality of any of the parties to the dispute or of any riparian State of the watercourse concerned. If one of the Parties fails to nominate a member within three months of the initial request pursuant to paragraph 3, any other Party concerned may request the Secretary-General of the United Nations to appoint a person who shall not have the nationality of any of the parties to the dispute or of any riparian State of the watercourse concerned. The person so appointed shall constitute a single-member Commission.

6. The Commission shall determine its own procedure.

7. The Parties concerned have the obligation to provide the Commission with such information as it may require and, on request, to permit the Commission to have access to their respective territory and to inspect any facilities, plant, equipment, construction or natural feature relevant for the purpose of its inquiry.

8. The Commission shall adopt its report by a majority vote, unless it is a single-member Commission, and shall submit that report to the Parties concerned setting forth its findings and the reasons therefor and such recommendations as it deems appropriate for an equitable solution of the dispute, which the Parties concerned shall consider in good faith.

9. The expenses of the Commission shall be borne equally by the Parties

concerned.

10. When ratifying, accepting, approving or acceding to the present Convention, or at any time thereafter, a Party which is not a regional economic integration organization may declare in a written instrument submitted to the Depositary that, in respect of any dispute not resolved in accordance with paragraph 2, it recognizes as compulsory ipso facto and without special agreement in relation to any Party accepting the same obligation:

(a) Submission of the dispute to the International Court of Justice; and/or

(b) Arbitration by an arbitral tribunal established and operating, unless the parties to the dispute otherwise agreed, in accordance with the procedure laid down in the annex to the present Convention.

A Party, which is a regional economic integration organization, may make a declaration with like effect in relation to arbitration in accordance with subparagraph (b).

PART VII

FINAL CLAUSES

Article 34
Signature

The present Convention shall be open for signature by all States and by regional economic integration organizations from 21 May 1997 until 20 May 2000 at United Nations Headquarters in New York.

Article 35
Ratification, acceptance, approval or accession

1. The present Convention is subject to ratification, acceptance, approval or accession by States and by regional economic integration organizations. The instruments of ratification, acceptance, approval or accession shall be deposited with the Secretary-General of the United Nations.

2. Any regional economic integration organization, which becomes a Party to this Convention without any of its member States being a Party shall be bound by all the obligations under the Convention. In the case of such organizations, one or more of whose member States is a Party to this Convention, the organization and its member States shall decide on their respective responsibilities for the performance of their obligations under the Convention. In such cases, the organization and the member States shall not be entitled to exercise rights under the Convention concurrently.

3. In their instruments of ratification, acceptance, approval or accession, the regional economic integration organizations shall declare the extent of their competence with respect to the matters governed by the Convention. These organizations shall also inform the Secretary-General of the United Nations of any substantial modification in the extent of their competence.

Article 36
Entry into force

1. The present Convention shall enter into force on the ninetieth day following the date of deposit of the thirty-fifth instrument of ratification, acceptance, approval or accession with the Secretary-General of the United Nations.

2. For each State or regional economic integration organization that ratifies, accepts or approves the Convention or accedes thereto after the deposit of the thirty-fifth instrument of ratification, acceptance, approval or accession, the Convention shall enter into force on the ninetieth day after the deposit by such State or regional economic integration organization of its instrument of ratification, acceptance, approval or accession.

3. For the purposes of paragraphs 1 and 2, any instrument deposited by a regional economic integration organization shall not be counted as additional to those deposited by States.

Article 37
Authentic texts

The original of the present Convention, of which the Arabic, Chinese, English, French, Russian and Spanish texts are equally authentic, shall be deposited with the Secretary-General of the United Nations.

IN WITNESS WHEREOF the undersigned plenipotentiaries, being duly authorized thereto, have signed this Convention.

DONE at New York, this ____ day of one thousand nine hundred and ninety-seven.

ANNEX

ARBITRATION

Article 1

Unless the parties to the dispute otherwise agree, the arbitration pursuant to article 33 of the Convention shall take place in accordance with articles 2 to 14 of the present Annex.

Article 2

The claimant party shall notify the respondent party that it is referring a dispute to arbitration pursuant to article 33 of the Convention. The notification shall state the subject matter of arbitration and include, in particular, the articles of the Convention, the interpretation or application of which are at issue. If the parties do not agree on the subject matter of the dispute, the arbitral tribunal shall determine the subject matter.

Article 3

1. In disputes between two parties, the arbitral tribunal shall consist of three members. Each of the parties to the dispute shall appoint an arbitrator and the two arbitrators so appointed shall designate by common agreement the third arbitrator, who shall be the Chairman of the tribunal. The latter shall not be a national of one of the parties to the dispute or of any riparian State of the watercourse concerned, nor have his or her usual place of residence in the territory of one of these parties or such riparian State, nor have dealt with the case in any other capacity.

2. In disputes between more than two parties, parties in the same interest shall appoint one arbitrator jointly by agreement.

3. Any vacancy shall be filled in the manner prescribed for the initial appointment.

Article 4

1. If the Chairman of the arbitral tribunal has not been designated within two months of the appointment of the second arbitrator, the President of the International Court of Justice shall, at the request of a party, designate the Chairman within a further two-month period.

2. If one of the parties to the dispute does not appoint an arbitrator within two months of receipt of the request, the other party may inform the President of the International Court of Justice, who shall make the designation within a further two-month period.

Article 5

The arbitral tribunal shall render its decisions in accordance with the provisions of this Convention and international law.

Article 6

Unless the parties to the dispute otherwise agree, the arbitral tribunal shall determine its own rules of procedure.

Article 7

The arbitral tribunal may, at the request of one of the Parties, recommend essential interim measures of protection.

Article 8

1. The parties to the dispute shall facilitate the work of the arbitral tribunal and, in particular, using all means at their disposal, shall:

(a) Provide it with all relevant documents, information and facilities; and

(b) Enable it, when necessary, to call witnesses or experts and receive their evidence.

2. The parties and the arbitrators are under an obligation to protect the confidentiality of any information they receive in confidence during the proceedings of the arbitral tribunal.

Article 9

Unless the arbitral tribunal determines otherwise because of the particular circumstances of the case, the costs of the tribunal shall be borne by the parties to the dispute in equal shares. The tribunal shall keep a record of all its costs, and shall furnish a final statement thereof to the parties.

Article 10

Any Party that has an interest of a legal nature in the subject matter of the dispute which may be affected by the decision in the case, may intervene in the proceedings with the consent of the tribunal.

Article 11

The tribunal may hear and determine counterclaims arising directly out of the subject matter of the dispute.

Article 12

Decisions both on procedure and substance of the arbitral tribunal shall be taken by a majority vote of its members.

Article 13

If one of the parties to the dispute does not appear before the arbitral tribunal or fails to defend its case, the other party may request the tribunal to continue the proceedings and to make its award. Absence of a party or a failure of a party to defend its case shall not constitute a bar to the proceedings. Before rendering its final decision, the arbitral tribunal must satisfy itself that the claim is well founded in fact and law.

Article 14

1. The tribunal shall render its final decision within five months of the date on which it is fully constituted unless it finds it necessary to extend the time limit for a period which should not exceed five more months.

2. The final decision of the arbitral tribunal shall be confined to the subject matter of the dispute and shall state the reasons on which it is based. It shall contain the names of the members who have participated and the date of the final decision. Any member of the tribunal may attach a separate or dissenting opinion to the final decision.

3. The award shall be binding on the parties to the dispute. It shall be without appeal unless the parties to the dispute have agreed in advance to an appellate procedure.

4. Any controversy, which may arise between the parties to the dispute as regards the interpretation or manner of implementation of the final decision, may be submitted by either party for decision to the arbitral tribunal, which rendered it.

Appendix VIII

The International Law Association Rules on Water Resources

TABLE OF CONTENTS

CHAPTER I
SCOPE

Article 1
Scope

1. These Rules express international law applicable to the management of the waters of international drainage basins and applicable to all waters, as appropriate.

2. Nothing in these Rules affects rights or obligations created by treaty or special custom.

Article 2
Implementation of These Rules

1. States shall, where appropriate, enact laws and regulations to accomplish the

purposes set forth in these Rules and shall adopt efficient and adequate administrative measures, including management plans, and judicial procedures for the enforcement of these laws and regulations.

2. States shall undertake educational and research programmes as necessary to assure the technical capacity necessary for State and communal authorities to fulfil the obligations specified in this Chapter and in other Rules.

Article 3
Definitions

For the purposes of these Articles, these terms have the following meanings:

1. 'Aquatic environment' means all surface waters and groundwater, the lands and subsurface geological formations connected to those waters, and the atmosphere related to those waters and lands.

2. 'Aquifer' means a subsurface layer or layers of geological strata of sufficient porosity and permeability to allow either a flow of or the withdrawal of usable quantities of groundwater.

3. A 'basin State' is a State the territory of which includes any portion of an international drainage basin.

4. 'Damage' includes:
   (a) loss of life or personal injury;
   (b) loss of or injury to property or other economic losses;
   (c) environmental harm; and
   (d) the costs of reasonable measures to prevent or minimize such loss, injury, or harm.
5. 'Drainage basin' means an area determined by the geographic limits of a system of interconnected waters, the surface waters of which normally share a common terminus.

6. 'Ecological integrity' means the natural condition of waters and other resources sufficient to assure the biological, chemical, and physical integrity of the aquatic environment.

7. 'Environment' includes the waters, land, air, flora, and fauna that exist in a particular region at a particular time.

8. 'Environmental harm' includes:
   (a) injury to the environment and any other loss or damage caused by such harm; and
   (b) the costs of reasonable measures to restore the environment actually undertaken or to be undertaken.

9. 'Flood' means a rising of water to levels that have detrimental effects on or in one or more basin States.

10. 'Flood control' means measures to protect land areas from floods or to minimize damage there from.

11. 'Groundwater' means water beneath the surface of the ground located in a saturated zone and in direct contact with the ground or soil.

12. 'Hazardous substances' means substances that are bio-accumulative, carcinogenic, mutagenic, teratogenic, or toxic.

13. An 'international drainage basin' is a drainage basin extending over two or more States.

14. 'Management of waters' and 'to manage waters' includes the development, use, protection, allocation, regulation, and control of waters.

15. 'Person' means any natural or juridical person.

16. 'Pollution' means any detrimental change in the composition or quality of waters that results directly or indirectly from human conduct.

17. 'Regional economic integration organization' means an organization constituted by sovereign States of a given region, to which its member States have transferred competence in respect of matters governed by these Rules.

18. 'State' means a sovereign State or a regional economic integration organization.

19. 'Sustainable use' means the integrated management of resources to assure efficient use of and equitable access to waters for the benefit of current and future generations while preserving renewable resources and maintaining non-renewable resources to the maximum extent reasonably possible.

20. 'Vital human needs' means waters used for immediate human survival, including drinking, cooking, and sanitary needs, as well as water needed for the immediate sustenance of a household.

21. 'Waters' means all surface water and groundwater other than marine waters.

CHAPTER II
PRINCIPLES OF INTERNATIONAL LAW GOVERNING THE MANAGEMENT OF ALL WATERS

Article 4
Participation by Persons

States shall take steps to assure that persons likely to be affected are able to participate in the processes whereby decisions are made concerning the management of waters.

Article 5
Conjunctive Management

States shall use their best efforts to manage surface waters, groundwater, and other pertinent waters in a unified and comprehensive manner.

Article 6
Integrated Management

States shall use their best efforts to integrate appropriately the management of waters with the management of other resources.

Article 7
Sustainability

States shall take all appropriate measures to manage waters sustainably.

Article 8
Minimization of Environmental Harm

States shall take all appropriate measures to prevent or minimize environmental harm.

Article 9
Interpretation of These Rules

1. All of these Rules are to be interpreted consistently with the principles of this Chapter.

2. References to States in these Rules encompass States acting individually or jointly and States acting with or through international organizations, as appropriate.

CHAPTER III
INTERNATIONALLY SHARED WATERS

Article 10
Participation by Basin States

1. Basin States have the right to participate in the management of waters of an international drainage basin in an equitable, reasonable, and sustainable manner.

2. Basin States shall define the waters to which an international agreement regarding the management of waters of an international drainage basin applies; such an international agreement may apply to all or part of the waters of an international drainage basin or to a particular project or use, except that a use by one or more basin States shall not cause a significant adverse effect on the rights of or uses in another basin State without the latter State's express consent.

Article 11
Cooperation

Basin States shall cooperate in good faith in the management of waters of an international drainage basin for the mutual benefit of the participating States.

Article 12
Equitable Utilization

1. Basin States shall in their respective territories manage the waters of an international drainage basin in an equitable and reasonable manner having due regard for the obligation not to cause significant harm to other basin States.

2. In particular, basin States shall develop and use the waters of the basin in order to attain the optimal and sustainable use thereof and benefits therefrom, taking into account the interests of other basin States, consistent with adequate protection of the waters.

Article 13
Determining an Equitable and Reasonable Use

1. Equitable and reasonable use within the meaning of Article 12 is to be determined through consideration of all relevant factors in each particular case.

2. Relevant factors to be considered include, but are not limited to:
   a. Geographic, hydrographic, hydrological, hydrogeological, climatic, ecological, and other natural features;
   b. The social and economic needs of the basin States concerned;
   c. The population dependent on the waters of the international drainage basin in each basin State;
   d. The effects of the use or uses of the waters of the international drainage basin in one basin State upon other basin States;
   e. Existing and potential uses of the waters of the international drainage basin;
   f. Conservation, protection, development, and economy of use of the water resources of the international drainage basin and the costs of measures taken to achieve these purposes;

g. The availability of alternatives, of comparable value, to the particular planned or existing use;
h. The sustainability of proposed or existing uses; and
i. The minimization of environmental harm.

3. The weight of each factor is to be determined by its importance in comparison with other relevant factors. In determining what is a reasonable and equitable use, all relevant factors are to be considered together and a conclusion reached on the basis of the whole.

Article 14
Preferences among Uses

1. In determining an equitable and reasonable use, States shall first allocate waters to satisfy vital human needs.

2. No other use or category of uses shall have an inherent preference over any other use or category of uses.

Article 15
Using Allocated Water in Other Basin States

1. Allocation by agreement or otherwise to one basin State does not prevent use by another basin State to the extent that the basin State to which the water is allocated does not in fact make use of the water.

2. Use of a water for purposes of this Article includes water necessary to assure ecological flows or otherwise to maintain ecological integrity or to minimize environmental harm.

3. Use of water by a basin State other than the one to which the water is allocated does not preclude the basin State to which the water is allocated from using the water when it chooses to do so.

Article 16
Avoidance of Trans-boundary Harm

Basin States, in managing the waters of an international drainage basin, shall refrain from and prevent acts or omissions within their territory that cause significant harm to another basin State having due regard for the right of each basin State to make equitable and reasonable use of the waters.

CHAPTER IV
RIGHTS OF PERSONS

Article 17
The Right of Access to Water

1. Every individual has a right of access to sufficient, safe, acceptable, physically accessible, and affordable water to meet that individual's vital human needs.

2. States shall ensure the implementation of the right of access to water on a non-discriminatory basis.

3. States shall progressively realize the right of access to water by:
   a. Refraining from interfering directly or indirectly with the enjoyment of the right;
   b. Preventing third parties from interfering with the enjoyment of the right;
   c. Taking measures to facilitate individuals' access to water, such as defining and enforcing appropriate legal rights of access to and use of water; and
   d. Providing water or the means for obtaining water when individuals are unable, through reasons beyond their control, to access water through their own efforts.

4. States shall monitor and review periodically, through a participatory and transparent process, the realization of the right of access to water.

Article 18
Public Participation and Access to Information

1. In the management of waters, States shall assure that persons subject to the State's jurisdiction and likely to be affected by water management decisions are able to participate, directly or indirectly, in processes by which those decisions are made and have a reasonable opportunity to express their views on programmes, plans, projects, or activities relating to waters.

2. In order enable such participation; States shall provide access to information relevant to the management of waters without unreasonable difficulty or unreasonable charges.

3. The information subject to access under this Article includes, without being limited to, impact assessments relating to the management of waters.

4. In providing information consistently with this Article, States need not provide access to information that would compromise:
   a. Intellectual property rights, including commercial or industrial secrets;
   b. Rights of individual privacy;

c. Criminal investigations or trials;
d. National security; and
e. Information that could endanger ecosystems, historic sites, and other naturally or culturally important objects or locations.

Article 19
Education

States shall undertake education at all levels to promote and encourage understanding of the issues that arise under these Rules.

Article 20
Protection of Particular Communities

States shall take all appropriate steps to protect the rights, interests, and special needs of communities and of indigenous peoples or other particularly vulnerable groups likely to be affected by the management of waters, even while developing the waters for the benefit of the entire State or group of States.

Article 21
Duty to Compensate Persons or Communities Displaced by Water Projects or Programmes

States shall compensate persons or communities displaced by a water programme, plan, project, or activity and shall assure that adequate provisions are made for the preservation of the livelihoods and culture of displaced persons or communities.

CHAPTER V
PROTECTION OF AQUATIC ENVIRONMENTS

Article 22
Ecological Integrity

States shall take all appropriate measures to protect the ecological integrity necessary to sustain ecosystems dependent on particular waters.

Article 23
The Precautionary Approach

1. In implementing obligations under this Chapter, States shall apply the precautionary approach.

2. States shall take all appropriate measures to prevent, eliminate, reduce, or control harm to the aquatic environment when there is a serious risk of significant adverse effect on or to the sustainable use of waters even without

conclusive proof of a causal relation between an act or omission and its expected effects.

Article 24
Ecological Flows

States shall take all appropriate measures to ensure flows adequate to protect the ecological integrity of the waters of a drainage basin, including estuarine waters.

Article 25
Alien Species

States shall take all appropriate measures to prevent the introduction, whether intentionally or otherwise, of alien species into the aquatic environment if the alien species might have a significant adverse effect on an ecosystem dependent on the particular waters.

Article 26
Hazardous Substances

States shall take all appropriate measures to prevent the introduction of hazardous substances into the waters subject to its jurisdiction or control.

Article 27
Pollution

1. States shall prevent, eliminate, reduce, or control pollution in order to minimize environmental harm.

2. When there is a relevant water quality standard established pursuant to Article 28, States shall take all appropriate measures to assure compliance with that standard.

3. States shall ensure that wastes, pollutants, and hazardous substances are handled, treated, and disposed of using the best available techniques or the best environmental practices, as appropriate to protect the aquatic environment.

Article 28
Establishing Water Quality Standards

1. States shall establish water quality standards sufficient to protect public health and the aquatic environment and to provide water to satisfy needs, in particular for:

a. Providing drinking water of sufficiently good quality for human health;
b. Preserving ecosystems;
c. Providing water for agriculture, including irrigation and animal husbandry; and
d. Providing for recreational needs with due regard for sanitary and aesthetic requirements.

2. Standards established under this Article shall include, among others:
   a. Specific quality objectives for all waters within a State's jurisdiction or control, taking into account the uses of the particular waters;
   b. Specific quality objectives applicable to a particular basin or part of a basin.

CHAPTER VI
IMPACT ASSESSMENTS

Article 29
The Obligation to Assess Environmental Impacts

1. States shall undertake prior and continuing assessment of the impact of programmes, projects, or activities that may have a significant effect on the aquatic environment or the sustainable development of waters.

2. Impacts to be assessed include, among others:
   a. Effects on human health and safety;
   b. Effects on the environment;
   c. Effects on existing or prospective economic activity;
   d. Effects on cultural or socio-economic conditions; and
   e. Effects on the sustainability of the use of waters.

Article 30
Participation in Impact Assessments in Another State

A person who suffers or is under a serious threat of suffering damage from programmes, projects, or activities relating to the waters in another State shall be entitled in the other State to the same extent and on the same conditions as a person in that State to participate in an environmental impact assessment procedure.

Article 31
The Impact Assessment Process

Assessment of the impacts of any programme, project, or activity shall include, among others:
   a. Assessment of the waters and the environments likely to be affected;
   b. Description of the proposed activity and its likely effects, with particular emphasis on any trans-boundary effects;

c. Identification of ecosystems likely to be affected, including an assessment of the living and non-living resources of the relevant water basin or basins;
d. Description of mitigation measures appropriate to minimize environmental harm;
e. Appraisal of the institutional arrangements and facilities in the relevant drainage basin or basins;
f. Assessment of the sources and levels of pollutants in the relevant drainage basin or basins, and of their effects on human health, ecological integrity, and amenities;
g. Identification of human activities that are likely to be affected;
h. Explanation of predictive methods and underlying assumptions as well as the relevant data used, including identification of gaps in knowledge and uncertainties encountered in compiling the required information, including assessment of the risk of major accidents;
i. Where appropriate, an outline for monitoring and management programmes and plans for post-project analysis;
j. A statement of the reasonable alternatives, including a no-action alternative; and
k. An adequate non-technical summary.

CHAPTER VII
EXTREME SITUATIONS

Article 32
Responses to Extreme Conditions

1. States shall take all appropriate measures to prevent, reduce, eliminate, or control all conditions of waters, whether resulting from human conduct or otherwise, that pose a significant risk:
   a. To human life or health;
   b. Of harm to property; or
   c. Of environmental harm.

2. States, promptly and using the most expeditious means available, shall notify other potentially affected States and competent international organizations of any harmful condition of waters under this Article that originates within its jurisdiction or control.

3. States shall develop notification systems and contingency plans for responding to harmful conditions under this Article.

Article 33
Polluting Accidents

1. States shall take all appropriate measures as quickly as possible to reduce,

eliminate, or control pollution resulting from accidental events.

2. States shall use the most expeditious method available to notify other affected States and competent international organizations of accidents that pose a significant risk of serious pollution to waters within another State's jurisdiction or control, in particular when pollution involves hazardous substances.

3. States shall develop notification systems and contingency plans for responding to accidents under this Article.

Article 34
Floods

1. States shall cooperate in developing and implementing measures for flood control, having due regard to the interests of other States likely to be affected by the flooding.

2. States likely to be affected by flooding shall use the most expeditious method available to communicate among themselves and with international organizations as soon as possible regarding any events likely to create floods or dangerous rises of water levels in their territory, establishing:
   a. An effective system of transmission in order to fulfil this obligation;
   b. Measures to ensure priority to the communication of flood warnings in emergency cases; and
   c. A special system of translation, if necessary, between the basin States.

3. States shall jointly develop contingency plans for responding to foreseeable flood conditions.

4. In addition to contingency plans, cooperation with respect to flood control shall, by agreement between affected States and when appropriate international organizations, include among other matters:
   a. The collection and exchange of relevant data;
   b. The preparation of surveys, investigations, studies, and flood plain maps, and their mutual exchange;
   c. The planning and designing of relevant measures, including flood plain management and flood control works;
   d. The execution, operation, and maintenance of flood control measures;
   e. Flood forecasting and communication of flood warnings;
   f. Developing or strengthening necessary legislation and appropriate institutions for achieving these goals; and
   g. The setting up of a regular information service charged to transmit the height of water levels and the discharge quantities.

5. States shall maintain all flood control measures in good order, and shall ensure the prompt execution of repairs or other emergency measures taken to assure the minimization of damage from flooding.

6. The use of the channel of rivers and lakes for the discharge of excess waters shall be free and not subject to any limitation provided such discharge is not incompatible with the object of flood control and does not adversely affect the rights or interests of other states.

Article 35
Droughts

1. States shall cooperate in the management of waters to prevent, control, or mitigate droughts, having due regard to the interests of other basin States.

2. Cooperation with respect to drought shall, by agreement between affected States and when appropriate with international organizations, include among other matters:
   a. An integrated strategy for addressing the physical, biological, and socio-economic aspects of the drought;
   b. The definition of criteria that activate the provisions of this Article;
   c. An integrated strategy for mitigating the effects of drought and moving towards the sustainable use of waters;
   d. The development or strengthening necessary legislation and appropriate institutions for achieving these goals; and
   e. The allocation of adequate resources to achieve these goals in accordance with their circumstances and capabilities.

3. States likely to be affected by drought shall promptly communicate among themselves and with competent international organizations whenever the criteria specified pursuant to paragraph 2(b) are met.

4. Nothing in this Article limits the rights of States to protect themselves unilaterally from the effects of droughts so long as the measures taken do not violate obligations under these Rules or otherwise violate the rights of other States.

CHAPTER VIII
GROUNDWATER

Article 36
Application of These Rules to Aquifers

1. The Rules of this Chapter apply to all aquifers, including aquifers that do not contribute water to, or receive water from, surface waters or receive no significant contemporary recharge from any source.

2. States, in managing aquifers, are subject to all Rules expressed in these Articles, taking into account the special characteristics of groundwater.

Article 37
Managing Aquifers Generally

States shall manage groundwater conjunctively with the surface waters of any basin of which it is a part, taking into account any interconnections between aquifers or between an aquifer and a body of surface water, as well as any impact on aquifers caused by activities within the State's jurisdiction or control.

Article 38
Precautionary Management of Aquifers

States, in accordance with the precautionary approach, shall take early action and develop long-term plans to ensure the sustainable use of groundwater and of the aquifers in which the groundwater is contained.

Article 39
Duty to Acquire Information

In order to comply with this Chapter, States shall take all appropriate steps to acquire the information necessary to manage groundwater and aquifers efficiently and effectively, including:

a. Monitoring groundwater levels, pressures, and quality;
b. Developing aquifer vulnerability maps;
c. Assessing the impacts on groundwater and aquifers of industrial, agricultural, and other activities; and
d. Any other measures appropriate to the circumstances of the aquifer.

Article 40
Sustainability Applied to Groundwater

1. States shall give effect to the principle of sustainability in managing aquifers, taking into account natural and artificial recharge.

2. The rule in paragraph 1 does not preclude the withdrawal of groundwater from an aquifer that is receiving no significant contemporary recharge.

Article 41
Protecting Aquifers

1. States shall take all appropriate measures to prevent, insofar as possible, any pollution of, and the degradation of the hydraulic integrity of, aquifers.

2. States in fulfilling their obligation to prevent pollution of an aquifer shall take special care to prevent, eliminate, reduce, or control:
   a. The direct or indirect discharge of pollutants, whether from point or non-point sources;
   b. The injection of water that is polluted or would otherwise degrade an aquifer;
   c. Saline water intrusion; or
   d. Any other source of pollution.

3. States shall take all appropriate measures to abate the effects of the pollution of aquifers.

4. States shall integrate aquifers into their programmes of general environmental protection, including but not limited to:
   a. The management of other waters;
   b. Land use planning and management; and
   c. Other programmes of general environmental protection.

5. States shall specially protect sites where groundwater is withdrawn from or recharged to an aquifer.

Article 42
Trans-boundary Aquifers

1. The Rules applicable to internationally shared waters apply to an aquifer if:
   a. It is connected to surface waters that are part of an international drainage basin; or
   b. It is intersected by the boundaries between two or more States even without a connection to surface waters that form an international drainage basin.

2. Whenever possible and appropriate, basin States sharing an aquifer referred to in paragraph 1 shall manage an aquifer in its entirety.

3. In managing the waters of an aquifer referred to in paragraph 1, basin States shall consult and exchange information and data at the request of any one of them and shall cooperate in the collection and analysing additional needed information pertinent to the obligations under these Rules.

4. Basin States shall cooperate according to the procedures in Chapter XI to set drawdown rates in order to assure the equitable utilization of the waters of an aquifer referred to in paragraph 1, having due regard for the obligation not to cause significant harm to other basin States and to the obligation to protect the aquifer.

5. Basin States sharing an aquifer referred to in paragraph 1 shall cooperate in

managing the recharge of the aquifer.

6. Basin States sharing an aquifer referred to in paragraph 1 shall refrain from and prevent acts or omissions within their territory that cause significant harm to another basin State, having due regard to the right of each basin State to make equitable and reasonable use of the waters.

CHAPTER IX
NAVIGATION

Article 43
Freedom of Navigation

1. Subject to the limitations or qualifications in this Chapter, each riparian State is entitled to freedom of navigation on the entire watercourse to which they are riparian on a basis of equality and non-discrimination.

2. A 'riparian State' for purposes of this Chapter is a State traversed by or separated from another State by the navigable portion of a watercourse.

3. A 'watercourse' for purposes of this Chapter is a river, lake, or other surface body of water on which navigation is possible from one riparian State to another or from a riparian State to the high seas.

4. A watercourse is 'navigable' for purposes of this Chapter if, in its natural or canalized condition, the watercourse is currently used for commercial navigation or is capable of being so used in its natural condition.

5. 'Freedom of navigation' for the purposes of this Chapter includes:
   a. Freedom of movement on the entire navigable course of the watercourse;
   b. Freedom to enter ports and to make use of plants and docks; and
   c. Freedom to transport goods and passengers, directly or through trans-shipment, between the territory of one riparian State and the territory of another riparian State and between the territory of a riparian State and the open sea.

Article 44
Limitations on Freedom of Navigation

1. Absent special arrangements, only vessels of a riparian State are entitled to exercise freedom of navigation.

2. Movement by vessels exercising freedom of navigation shall be continuous and expeditious, and not prejudicial to the peace, good order, or security of the riparian State.

3. Stopping or anchoring is allowed when incidental to ordinary navigation or if necessary because of *force majeure*, distress, or for the rendering of assistance to persons, ships, or aircraft in danger or distress.

4. Riparian States may restrict or prohibit the loading by vessels of a foreign State of goods and passengers in its territory for discharge in such territory.

5. Non-discriminatory fees may be charged by a riparian State to recover the costs of services provided to vessels exercising freedom of navigation.

Article 45
Regulating Navigation

In order to achieve good order in the navigable portion of a watercourse within its jurisdiction, a riparian State may regulate, limit, or suspend navigation, as appropriate for the purposes of protection of public safety, health, or the environment, over that portion of the watercourse within its jurisdiction, provided the State does not discriminate against the shipping of another riparian State and does not unreasonably interfere with the enjoyment of the rights of freedom of navigation defined in Articles 43 and 44.

Article 46
Maintaining Navigation

Each riparian State is, to the extent of the means available, required to maintain in good order that portion of a navigable watercourse within its jurisdiction.

Article 47
Granting the Right to Navigate to Non-riparian States

Riparian States, individually or jointly, may grant rights of navigation to non-riparian States on watercourses or other waters within its or their territory.

Article 48
Exclusion of Public Vessels

Freedom of navigation does not apply to the navigation of warships or of a government vessel used for non-commercial purposes except by agreement of the States concerned.

Article 49
Effect of War or Similar Emergencies on Navigation

1. In time of war, other armed conflict, or public emergency constituting a threat to the security of a riparian State, it may take measures derogating from its

obligations under this Chapter to the extent strictly required by the exigencies of the situation.

2. No measures taken under this Article are to violate a State's other obligations under international law.

3. Riparian States shall in any case facilitate navigation for humanitarian purposes.

CHAPTER X
PROTECTION OF WATERS AND WATER INSTALLATIONS DURING WAR OR ARMED CONFLICT

Article 50
Rendering Water Unfit for Use

Combatants shall not poison or render otherwise unfit for human consumption water indispensable for the health and survival of the civilian population.

Article 51
Targeting Waters or Water Installations

1. Combatants shall not, for military purposes or as reprisals, destroy or divert waters, or destroy water installations, if such actions would cause disproportionate suffering to civilians.

2. In no event shall combatants attack, destroy, remove, or render useless waters and water installations indispensable for the health and survival of the civilian population if such actions may be expected to leave the civilian population with such inadequate water as to cause its death from lack of water or force its movement.

3. In recognition of the vital requirements of any party to a conflict in the defence of its national territory against invasion, a party to the conflict may derogate from the prohibitions contained in paragraphs 1 and 2 within such territories under its own control where required by imperative military necessity.

4. In any event, waters and water installations shall enjoy the protection accorded by the principles and rules of international law applicable in war or armed conflict and shall not be used in violation of those principles and rules.

Article 52
Ecological Targets

Combatants shall not, for military purposes or as reprisals, destroy or divert waters, or destroy water installations, when such acts would cause widespread, long-term, and severe ecological damage prejudicial to the health or survival of the population or if such acts would fundamentally impair the ecological integrity of waters.

Article 53
Dams and Dikes

1. In addition to the other protections provided by these Rules, combatants shall not make dams and dikes the objects of attack, even where these are military objectives, if such an attack may cause the release of dangerous forces and consequent severe losses among the civilian population.

2. This protection ceases if the dam or dike is used for other than its normal function and in regular, significant, and direct support of military operations and such attack is the only feasible way to terminate such use.

Article 54
Occupied Territories

1. An occupying State shall administer water resources in an occupied territory in a way that ensures the sustainable use of the water resources and that minimizes environmental harm.

2. An occupying State shall protect water installations and ensure an adequate water supply to the population of an occupied territory.

Article 55
Effect of War or Armed Conflict on Water Treaties

1. Treaties creating legal regimes for an international watercourse or part thereof are not terminated by war or armed conflict between the parties to the treaty.

2. Such Treaties or parts thereof shall be suspended only where military necessity requires suspension and where suspension does not violate any provision of this Chapter.

CHAPTER XI
INTERNATIONAL COOPERATION AND ADMINISTRATION

Article 56
Exchange of Information

1. Basin States shall regularly provide to other basin States all relevant and available information on the quantity and quality of the waters of a basin or aquifer and on the state of the aquatic environment and the causes for any changes in waters, in an aquifer, or in the aquatic environment, including, but

not limited to, a list of all known water withdrawals and sources of pollution.

2. Basin States shall employ their best efforts to collect and, where appropriate, to process data and information in a manner that facilitates its use by other basin States to which it is to be communicated.

3. The exchange of information under this Article shall include all relevant technical information for a programme, plan, project, or activity, including the results of any relevant impact assessment.

4. Basin States shall cooperate with other basin States to provide as much information as possible under the circumstances having due regard for the provisions of paragraph 5.

5. States need not provide information that would compromise:
   a. Intellectual property rights, including commercial or industrial secrets;
   b. Rights of individual privacy;
   c. Criminal investigations or trials;
   d. National security; and
   e. Information that could endanger ecosystems, historic sites, and other naturally or culturally important objects or locations.

Article 57
Notification of Programmes, Plans, Projects, or Activities

1. Basin States shall promptly notify other States or competent international organizations that may be affected significantly by a programme, plan, project, or activity.

2. Basin States shall also promptly inform other States or competent international organizations whenever necessary to accomplish obligations set forth in these Rules.

3. A basin State that has reasonable grounds to conclude that a programme, project, or activity to be undertaken or already undertaken within another State may involve a significant effect on waters or the aquatic environment within the first State shall so inform the other State, providing documentary support for the conclusion, and request the other State to exchange information under Article 56 and to consult under Article 58.

Article 58
Consultations

1. Basin States shall consult one another and with competent international organizations on actual or potential issues relating to their shared waters or to the

aquatic environment in order to reach, by methods of their own choice, a solution consistent with their rights and duties under international law.

2. Basin States that conclude that a programme, plan, project, or activity would significantly adversely affect them shall promptly notify the State responsible for the programme, plan, project, or activity of those conclusions along with corroborating documentation. Upon receipt of such a claim, the interested States shall promptly consult each other

3. In conducting consultations and negotiations under paragraphs 1 and 2, basin States shall proceed in good faith to give reasonable regard to the rights and legitimate interests of the other basin States involved, and if necessary, to coordinate approaches to the programme, plan, project, or activity in order to arrive at an equitable and sustainable resolution of the situation.

4. During consultations, a basin State planning a programme, project, or activity shall, if requested by another interested State, refrain from implementing or allowing the implementation of the programme, plan, project, or activity for a reasonable period.

5. Consultation shall not be used to delay unreasonably the implementation of programs, plans, projects, or activities that are the subject of the consultation.

Article 59
Failure to Consult

1. If a State subject to a duty to consult pursuant to Article 58 does not enter into consultations or negotiations within a reasonable time, the other interested States may implement a proposed programme, plan, project, or activity so long as it is consistent with the State's obligations under international law.

2. A State's obligation to pay compensation for violations of customary international law to another interested State may be offset by expenses incurred by the obligated State as result of the other State's failure to respond.

Article 60
Requests for Impact Assessments or Other Information

1. A basin State, at the request of another basin State likely to be affected by a programme, plan, project, or activity envisaged to occur or occurring within the requested State, shall undertake an impact assessment of the programme, plan, project, or activity on an ongoing basis.

2. A basin State, at the request of another basin State likely to be affected by a programme, plan, project, or activity envisaged to occur within the requested State, shall provide all relevant information in the requested State's possession

or which the requested State can acquire through reasonable efforts, limited as in Article 56(2).

3. A basin State requested by another basin State to provide information or to conduct an impact assessment pursuant to this Article shall employ its best efforts to comply with the request but may condition its compliance upon reciprocal exchanges by the requesting State or upon reimbursement for the reasonable costs of collecting and processing the information.

Article 61
Urgent Implementation of Programmes, Plans, Projects, or Activities

1. When implementation of a programme, plan, project, or activity is of the utmost importance to the public health, public safety, or similar interests, the basin State considering the programme, project, or activity may proceed immediately to implement the programme, project, or activity without awaiting the completion of the consultation process, but without violating the other obligations expressed in these Articles.

2. A basin State that undertakes to implement a programme, plan, project, or activity pursuant to this Article shall immediately notify other basin States and shall disclose all relevant data and information.

3. Notwithstanding a basin State's decision to implement a programme, plan, project, or activity pursuant to this Article, the implementing basin State shall, at the request of another interested basin State, consult and negotiate as provided in Article 58.

Article 62
Harmonization of National Laws and Policies

In enacting national laws pursuant to this Article, basin States shall consult other interested States with a view to harmonizing the laws and policies regarding the equitable use and sustainable development of waters and of the aquatic environment.

Article 63
Protection of Works

1. Basin States shall, within their territories, use their best efforts to maintain and protect installations, facilities, and other works related to the management of waters of an international drainage basin.

2. Basin States shall, at the request of another basin State that has reasonable grounds to conclude that its interests may be significantly adversely affected by an installation, facility, or other work related to waters or the management

of waters, enter into consultations regarding:

a. The safe operation and maintenance of the installation, facility, or other work; and
b. The protection of the installation, facility, or other work from intentional or negligent acts or the forces of nature.

Article 64
Establishment of Basin Wide or Other Joint Management Arrangements

1. When necessary to ensure the equitable and sustainable use of waters and the prevention of harm, basin States shall establish a basin wide or a joint agency or a commission with authority to undertake the integrated management of waters of an international drainage basin.

2. When appropriate, basin States shall establish other joint mechanisms for the management of waters.

3. The establishment of basin wide management mechanism is without prejudice to the creation, existence, or designation of any joint management agency, conciliation commission, or tribunal by the basin States for the resolution of any question or dispute relating to the present or future management of transboundary waters.

Article 65
Minimal Requirements for Basin Wide Management Arrangements

1. A basin wide management mechanism under Article 64 shall have authority over:
   a. The coordination and pooling of their scientific and technical research programmes;
   b. Establishment of harmonized, coordinated, or unified networks for permanent observation and control; and
   c. Establishment of joint or harmonized water quality objectives and standards for the whole of or each significant part of a basin.

2. An agreement creating a mechanism under Article 64 shall provide expressly for the mechanism's:
   a. Objective and purpose;
   b. Nature and composition;
   c. Form and duration;
   d. Legal status;
   e. Area of operation;
   f. Functions and powers; and
   g. Financial arrangements.

Article 66
Compliance Review

Basin States shall undertake recurring review at regular intervals of the implementation of their commitments under agreements relating to waters, including, when applicable, their implementation of joint management mechanisms, in either event including in the review:

a. Assessment, on the basis of all information available, of the overall affects of measures relating to the management of waters or of the aquatic environment;
b. Examination of the obligations of the States involved in a joint management mechanism in light of the objectives for which the mechanism was established and of the evolution of scientific and technological knowledge;
c. Promotion of appropriate responses by States involved to climate change;
d. Facilitation of the refinement of methodologies for the effective implementation of the joint management mechanism or other agreements;
e. Establishment of subsidiary bodies as necessary or proper for the implementation of the joint management mechanism or other agreements;
f. Mobilization of additional financial resources as necessary and as available for the joint management mechanism or for other agreements;
g. Arrangement, where appropriate, for the services or cooperation of international organizations, of intergovernmental bodies, and of non-governmental bodies; and
h. Recommendations regarding any matter necessary or proper for the implementation of the joint management mechanism or other agreements.

Article 67
Sharing Expenses

1. Expenses for the collection and exchange of relevant information and other joint activities, including the establishment and operation of a basin wide management mechanism, shall be allocated among the basin States based upon:
   a. Receipt of economic benefits;
   b. Receipt of environmental benefits; and
   c. Ability to pay.
   d.
2. Expenses for special works undertaken by agreement in the territory of one State at the request of another State shall be borne by the requesting State, unless otherwise agreed.

CHAPTER XII
STATE RESPONSIBILITY

Article 68
State Responsibility

States are responsible for breaches of international law relating to the management of waters or to the aquatic environment in accordance with the international law of State responsibility.

CHAPTER XIII
LEGAL REMEDIES

Article 69
Access to Courts or Administrative Authorities

1. A person who suffers or is under a serious threat of suffering damage from the management of water or the aquatic environment in a State shall be entitled to institute proceedings before a competent court or administrative authority of that State in order to obtain an appropriate remedy as specified in Article 70.

2. Public bodies and non-governmental organizations with a proven interest regarding waters or the aquatic environment in a State shall be entitled, under appropriate terms and conditions, to institute proceedings or to participate in proceedings instituted by others.

Article 70
Remedies for Damage to Persons

1. States shall take all appropriate steps to ensure the availability of effective administrative and judicial remedies for persons whose legal rights have been violated and who suffer or are under a serious threat of suffering damage arising from programmes, plans, projects, or activities relating to waters or to the aquatic environment subject to the State's jurisdiction or control.

2. Remedies under this Article shall, as appropriate, provide for:
   (a) Determination whether the damaging programme, plan, project, or activity should be permitted;
   (b) Preventive remedies;
   (c) Compensation for damage; and
   (d) Any other proper remedy.

Article 71
Remedies for Persons in Other States

1. In providing access to courts and remedies to persons who suffer or are under a serious threat of suffering damage, States shall not discriminate on the basis of the nationality or residence of the person claiming damage or the place where the damage occurred or may occur.

2. States shall take all appropriate measures to ensure cooperation between their courts and authorities to ensure that persons who suffer or are under a serious threat of suffering damage resulting from actions in another State relating to the waters of an international drainage basin shall have access to such information as is necessary to enable them to exercise their right to a remedy in a prompt and timely manner.

3. Public bodies and non-governmental organizations with a proven interest regarding waters or the aquatic environment in States other than the States in which they are established shall be entitled to institute proceedings or participate in procedures in that other State to the same extent and on the same conditions as public bodies and non-governmental associations established in the other State.

4. States shall provide, by agreement or otherwise, relative to proceedings involving persons or events in more than one State for:
   a. The jurisdiction of courts or administrative bodies;
   b. The determination of the applicable law; and
   c. The enforcement of judgments.

CHAPTER XIV
SETTLEMENT OF INTERNATIONAL WATER DISPUTES

Article 72
Peaceful Settlement of International Water Management Disputes

1. States shall resolve disputes concerning issues within the scope of these Rules through peaceful means.

2. States involved in the dispute shall consult one another and, when appropriate, competent international organizations, in order to reach, by methods of their own choice, a solution consistent with their rights and duties under international law.

3. Where the facts are in dispute, the States involved in the dispute shall appoint a body to investigate and to determine the disputed facts, the decision of the fact-finding body binding the States only if they have consented to such binding effect.

4. In any procedure to resolve the dispute, the States involved shall invite other States likely to be affected by resolution of the dispute to present their views at an appropriate early stage in the dispute.

5. The means of settlement referred to in this Article are without prejudice to recourse to means of settlement recommended to, or required of, members of regional arrangements or agencies or other international organizations.

Article 73
Arbitration and Litigation

1. If the procedures set forth in Article 72 of these Rules have not succeeded in resolving the dispute, the States or international organizations involved shall agree to submit their dispute to an *ad hoc* or permanent arbitral tribunal, or to a competent international court.

2. Recourse to arbitration or litigation implies an undertaking by the States involved in the dispute to accept any resulting award or judgment as final and binding.

Bibliography

1. BOOKS AND BOOK CHAPTERS

Arthur, D.J. (1964) *Conflict in Laos: the Politics of Neutralization*. London: Pall Mall Press.

Baxter, R.K. 'The Indus Basin' in Garretson A.H., R.D. Hayton and C.J. Olmstead (1967) *The Law of International Drainage Basins*. New York: Oceana Publication.

Berber, F.J. (1959) *Rivers in International Law*. London: Stevens & Sons.

Birnie, P.W. and A.E. Boyle (1992) *International Law and the Environment*. Oxford: Clarendon Press.

Biswas, A.K. 'Management of International Rivers: Opportunities and Constraints' in Biswas, A.K. and J.I. Uitto, (Eds.) (2001) *Sustainable Development of the Ganges-Brahmaputra-Meghna Basins*. Tokyo: United Nations University Press.

Boer, B., R. Ramsay and D. Rothwell (1998) *International Environmental Law in The Asia Pacific*. London: Kluwer Law International Ltd.

Boyle, A. and D. Freestone (Ed.) (1999) *International Law and Sustainable Development*. Oxford: Oxford University Press.

Brans, E.H.P., et al. (Eds.) (1981) *The Scarcity of Water: Emerging Legal and Policy Response*. The Hague: Martinus Nijhoff.

Brownlie, I. (1998) *Principles of Public International Law*. (5th ed,) Oxford: Oxford University Press.

Bull, D. (1983) *The Poverty of Diplomacy: Kampuchea and the Outside World*. Oxford: Oxfam.

Caflisch, L. 'Regulation of the Uses of International Watercourses' in Salman, S.A. and L.B. de Chazournes (Eds.) (1998) *International Watercourses- Enhancing Co-operation and Managing Conflict*. Washington D.C: The World Bank.

Caflisch, L. 'The Use of International Waterways: The Contribution of the United Nations' in Glassner, M.I. (Ed.) (1998) *United Nations at Work*. London: Praeger.

Caflisch, L. 'The Law of International Waterways and its Sources' in Macdonald, R.St.J. (Ed.) (1994) *Essays in Honor of Wang Tieya*. Dordrecht: Martinus Nijhoff.

Caponera, D. 'Shared Waters In International' in Blake, B., et al. (Eds.) (1995) *Peaceful Management of Transboundary Resources*. Graham Trotman: Martinus Nijhoff.

Chandler, D.P. and E. Kiernan (Eds.) (1988) *Pol Pot, Plans the Future: Confidential Leaderships Documents from Democratic Kampuchea, 1976-1977*. New Haven: Yale Center for International and Area Studies.

Chapman, G.P., A.K. Dutt and R.W. Bradnock (Eds.) (1999) *Urban growth and Development in Asia: Vol. 1: Making the Cities*. Aldershot UK: Ashgate Publishing.

Chapman, G.P, and M. Thompson (Eds.) (1995) *Water and the Quest for Sustainable Development in the Ganges Valley*. London: Mansell Publishing.

Chauhan, B.R. (1992) *Settlement of International and Inter State Water Dispute in India*. Bombay: N.M Tripathi Pvt.

Chonchai, P. 'Management of Trans boundary Water resources: A case Study of the Mekong' in Glassner, M.I. (Ed.) (1998) *The United Nation at Work*. USA: Praeger.

Chowdhury, S.R. 'International Equity: Substratum of the Right to Development' in Chowdhury, S.R., E.M.G. Denters and P.J.M. de Waart (Eds.) (1992) *The Right To Development in International Law*. The Hague: Martinus Nijhoff Publishers.

Clarke, R. (1991) *Water: the International Crisis*. London: Earthscan Publication.

Coupland, R. (1943) *Report on the Constitutional Problem in India, Pt III: The Future of India*. Oxford: Oxford University Press.

Crow, B., A. Lindquist and D. Wilson (Crow et al.) (1997) *Sharing the GANGES. The politics and technology of river* development. Dhaka: The University Press Ltd.

Crow, B., A. Lindquist and D. Wilson (Crow et al.) (1995) *Sharing the GANGES. The politics and technology of river Development*. New Delhi: Saga Publication.

Davidson, P.B. (1991) *Vietnam at War: the History 1946-1975*. Oxford: Oxford University Press.

Dubey, M. 'Some Reflection on Indo-Nepal Relations' in Lok Raj Baral (Ed.) (1996) *Looking to the Future: Indo-Nepal Relations in Perspective*. (5th ed,) New Delhi: Anmol Publication Pvt.

Duncanson, D.J. (1968) *Government and Revolution in Vietnam*. Oxford: Oxford University Press.

Edward, H.P., Brans, et al. (Ed.) (1997) *The Scarcity of Water: Emerging Legal and Policy Responses*. The Hague: Kluwer Law International.

Elkins, T.H. 'The Rhines Basin: A Geographical Introduction' in Chatham House Study Group (1975) *Regional Management of the Rhines. Papers of the Chatham House Study Group*. London: Chatham House.

Ferry Dobbs (1967) *The Law of International Drainage Basin*. New York: Oceana Publications.

Garreston et al., (Ed.) (1967) *The Law of International Drainage Basins*. New York: Dobbs Ferry Oceana (Published for the Institute of International Law).

Gleick, P.H. (1993) *Water in Crisis: A Guide to the World's Fresh Water Resources (Pacific Institute for Studies in Development, Environment and Security, Stockholm Environmental Institute)*. Oxford: Oxford University Press.

Goldberg, D. 'World Bank Policy on International Waterways in the Context of Emerging International Law and the Work of International Law Commission' in Blake, G.H., J. Ridley and C.H. Schofield (Eds.) (1995) *The Peaceful Management of Transboundary Resources*. London: Graham & Trotman.

Govardhan, V. (1993) *Environmental Impact Assessment of the Tehri Dam*. New Delhi: Ashish Publishing.

Gulhati, N.D. (1982) *Development of Inter-State Rivers: Law and Practices in India*. New Delhi: Allied Publisher.

Gunn, G.C. (1988) *Politics Struggle in Laos, 1930-2954: Vietnamese Communist Power and The Lao Struggle for National Independence*. Bangkok: Duang Kamol.

Gywali, D. 'Himalayan Waters: Between Euphoric Dreams and Ground Realities' in Bahadur, K. and M.P. Lama (ed.) (1995) *Nepal Perspectives on Indo-Nepal Relations*. New Delhi: Har-Anand Publication.

Iftekharuzzaman, 'The Ganges Water sharing issue: Diplomacy and Domestic Politics in Bangladesh' in Ghoshal, B.D. (Ed.) (1996) *Diplomacy and Domestic Politics in South Asia*. New Delhi: Konarak.

Johnson, R.W. 'The Columbia Basin' in Hayton, G.R. and C. Olmstead (1967) *The Law of International Drainage Basins*. New York: Oceana Publications.

Kaushik, P.D. 'Indo-Nepal Relations and Gujral Doctrine-Bouquets and Brickbats' in Dharmdasani, M.D. (Ed.) (2001) *India and Nepal: Big Power-Small Power Relations in South Asia*. New Delhi: South Asian Publishers.

Kharat, R.S. (1999) *Bhutan in SAARC: Role of a Smaller State in a Regional Alliance*. New Delhi: South Asian Publication.

Krishna, R. 'The Evolution and Context of the Bank Policy for Projects on International Waterways' in Baker, G.H., J. Ridley and C.H. Schofield (Eds.) (1995) *The Peaceful Management of Transboundary Resources*. London: Graham Trotman.

Lammers, J. (1984) *Pollution of International Watercourses: A Search for substantive Rules and Principles of Law*. The Hague: Martinus Nijhoff.

Lipper, J. 'Equitable Utilisation' in Garretson, Hayton, and Olmstead (Eds.) (1967) *The Law of International Drainage Basins*. New York: Oceana Publications, Dobbs Ferry, Inc.

Michel, A.A. (1967) *The Indus Rivers: A Study in the Effects of Partition*. New Haven and London: Yale University Press.

Muchlinski, P. (1997) *Multinational Enterprises and the Law*. (2nd ed.) United Kingdom: Blackwell Publisher.

Muni, S.D. (1973) *Foreign Policy of Nepal*. New Delhi: National Publishing House.

Natt, T. and R.C. Matson (Eds.) (1989) *Water in the Middle East: Conflict or Cooperation?* Boulder: Westview Replica Edition.

Nollkaemper, A. (1993) *The Legal Regime for Transboundary Water Pollution: Between Discretion and Constraint*. Dordrecht: Kluwer Law International.

Osborne, M. (1973) *Politics and Power in Cambodia, the Sihanouk years*. Camberwell: Longman.

Parker, D.J. (Ed.) (2000) *Floods, Vols. I and II*. London: Routledge.

Pearce, F. (1992) *The Damned. Rivers, dams and the coming of the world water crises*. London: The Bodley Head.

Porras, I. (1994) 'The Rio Declaration: A new Basis for International Co-operation' in Philippe Sands (Ed.) (1994) *Greening International Law*. New York: The New Press.

Rangachari, R., K.B.S. Rasheed and B.G. Verghese (Adhikari et al.) (Eds.) (2000) *Cooperation on Eastern Himalayan Rivers. Opportunities and Challenges*. New Delhi: Konarak Publishers Pvt. Ltd.

Reisner, M. (1993) *Cadillac Desert. The American West and Its Disappearing Water*. New York: Viking Penguin.

Robinson, N.A. (Ed.) (1993) *Agenda 21 & The UNCED Proceedings (Vol. IV)*. New York/London/Rome: Oceana Publications.

Saeijs, H.L.F. and M.J. van Berkel ((ed.) E.H.P. Brans, E.J. de Haan, A. Nollkaemper and J. Rinzema) (1997) *The Global Water Crisis: The Major Issue of the Twenty- first Century, A Growing and Explosive Problem, in The Scarcity of Water, Emerging Legal and Policy Response*. The Hague: Kluwer Law International.

Salman, S.M.A. 'Sharing the Ganges Waters between India and Bangladesh: An Analysis of the 1996 Treaty' in Salman, S.M.A. and L.B de Chazournes, (Eds.) (1998) *International Watercourses: Enhancing Cooperation and Managing Conflict*. Washington D.C: The World Bank.

Sands, P. (1995) *Principles of International Environmental Law, Vol. I: Frameworks, Standards and Implementation*. Manchester: Manchester University Press.

Schrijver, N. (1997) *Sovereignty over Natural Resources, Balancing Rights and Duties*. Cambridge University Press.

Shaw, M.N. (1997) *International Law*. Cambridge: Cambridge University Press.

Shrestha, G.D. 'Perspectives on Regional Cooperation' in Thapa, B.B. and B.B. Pradhan (Eds.) (1995) *Water Resources Development: Nepalese Perspectives*. Delhi: Konarak Publishers.

Shrestha, H.M. and L.M. Singh 'The Ganges-Brahmaputra System: A Nepalese Perspective in the Context of Regional Cooperation' in Biswas, A.K. and T. Hashimoto (Eds.) (1996) *Asian International Waters From Ganges-Brahmaputra to Mekong*. New Delhi: Oxford University Press.

Singh, L. (1966) *The Politics of Economic Co-operation in Asia*. Columbia: University of Missouri Press.

Smith, H.A. (1931) *The Economy Use of International River*. London: P.S. King & Son.

Smith, R.B. (1983) *An International History of the Vietnam War*. London: Macmillan.

Stuart-Fox, M. (1997) *A History of Laos*. Cambridge: Cambridge University Press.

Subba, B. (2001) *Himalayan Waters*. Katmandu: Panos South Asian.

Subedi, S.P. (2002) *Contemporary Issues in International Law: A Collection of the Josephine Onoh Memorial Lectures* (edited with D. Freestone, S. Davidson and S. Subedi). The Hague/London: Kluwer Law International.

Subedi, S.P. (2005) *Dynamics of Foreign Policy and Law: A Study of Indo-Nepal Relations*. New Delhi: Oxford University Press.

Subedi, S.P. 'The United Nations and the Trade and Transit Problems of Land-locked States' in Glassner, M. (Ed.) (1998) *The United Nations at Work*. London: Praeger Publishers.

Subedi, S.P. 'Indo-Nepal Relations: the Causes of Conflict and their Resolution' in Mitra, S.K and D. Rothermund (Eds.) (1997) *Legitimacy and Conflict in South-Asia*. New Delhi: Manohar Publishing.

Subedi, S.P. 'Indo-Nepal Relations: The Causes of Conflict and their Resolution' in Mitra, S.K. and D. Rothermund (Eds.) (1997) *Legitimacy and Conflict in South-Asia*. New Delhi Branch of Heidelberg University & Manohar.

Subedi, S. P. (1996) *Land and Maritime Zones of Peace in International Law*. Clarendon: Oxford University Press.

Subedi, S.P. (1989) *Land-Locked Nepal and International Law*. Kathmandu: K. Gautam Publishers.

Syed, A.S. (1998) *Introduction to Environmental Laws of Bangladesh*. Dhaka: Ace Data Products.

Teclaff, L. 'Harmonizing Water Use and Development with Environmental Protection' in Utton, A. and L. Teclaff (Eds.) (1978) *Water in Developing World: The Management of a Critical Resource*. Colorado: Westview Press.

Thapa, B.B. and B.B. Pradhan (Eds.) (1995) *Water Resources Development: Nepalese* Perspectives. Delhi: Konark Publishers.

Toye, H. (1968) *Laos: Buffer State or Battleground*. Oxford: Oxford University Press.

Trelease, F.J. 'Arizona versus California: Allocation of Water Resources to People, State and nations' in Kurland, P.B. (Ed.) (1963) *Supreme Court Review*. USA: The University of Chicago Press.

Upreti, B.C. (1993) *Politics of Himalayan River Waters*. New Delhi: Nirala Publications.

Upreti, B.C. (2001) *Uneasy Friends: Reading on Indo-Nepal Relations*. Delhi: Kalinga Publication.

Verghese, B.G. (1990) *Water of Hope*. New Delhi: Oxford & IBH Publishing Co.

Verghese, B.G. and R.R. Iyer (Eds.) (1994) *Harnessing the Eastern Himalayan Rivers: Regional Cooperation in South Asia*. New Delhi: Konark Publishers.

Verghese, B.G., R.R. Iyer, Q.K. Ahmad, B.B. Pradhan and S.K. Malla (Eds.) (1994) *Converting Water Into Wealth Regional Co-operation in Harnessing the Eastern Himalayan Rivers*. New Delhi: Konark Publishers.

Wallensteen, P. and A. Swain (1997) *Comprehensive Assessment of the Freshwater Resources of the World*. Stockholm: Stockholm Environment Institute.

Waterbury, J. 'Transboundary Water and the Challenge of International Cooperation in the East' in Rogers, P. and P. Lydon (Eds.) (1994) *Water in the Arab World: Perspectives and Prognosis*. Harvard University: Division of Applied Sciences.

Wightman, D. (1963) *Towards Economic Co-operation in Asia*. New Haven: Yale University Press.

World Commission on Dams (WCD) (2000) *Dams and Development: A New Framework for Decision Making; WCD Report, November 2000*. London: Earthscan Publication.

Young, M.B. (1991) *The Vietnam Wars 1945-1990*. New York: HarperCollins.

Zacklin, R. and L. Caflisch (Eds.) (1981) *The Legal Regime of International Rivers and Lakes*. The Hague: Martinus Nijhoff.

Zasloff, J.J. and L. Unger (1991) *Laos: Beyond the Revolution*. Basingstoke: Macmillan.

2. ARTICLES

Arora, V.K. and G.J. Boer 'The effects of simulated climate change on the hydrology of major river basins' (online). Available from: <http://www.ccma.bc.ec.ca/~varora/papers/impact_report_for_wgne.pdf>.

Benvenisti, E. (1996) 'Collective Action in the Utilization of Shared Freshwater: The Challenges of International Water Resources Law.' *American Journal of International Law*, Vol. 90, pp. 384-415.

Biswas, A.K. (1992) 'Indus Water Treaty: The Negotiation Process.' *Water International*, Vol. 17, p. 209.

Bourne, C.B. (1997) 'The Case Concerning the Gabcikovo-Nagymaros Project: An Important Milestone in International Water Law.' *Yearbook of International Environmental Law*, Vol. 8.

Bourne, C.B. (Spring 1996) 'The International Law Association's Contribution to International Water Resources Law.' *Natural Resources Journal*, Vol. 36, No. 2, pp. 155-216.

Boyle, A.E. (1997) 'The Gabcikovo-Nagymaros Case: New Law in Old Bottles.' *Yearbook of International Environmental Law*, Vol. 8.

Brunnee, J. and S.J. Toope (1997) 'Environmental Security and Freshwater Resources: Ecosystem Regime Building', *American Journal of International Law,* Vol. 91, pp. 26-59.

Canelas de Castro, P. (1997) 'The Judgement in the Case Concerning the Gabcikovo-Nagymaros Project: Positive Signs for the Evolution of International Water Law.' *Yearbook of International Environmental Law*, Vol. 8.

Caponera, D.A. (1993) 'Legal Aspects of Transboundary River Basin in the Middle East: The Al Asi (Orontes), The Jordan and the Nile.' *NRJ*, Vol. 33, p. 654.

Chakravarty, S. (1997) 'Indo-Bangladesh Treaty on Sharing of Ganga Waters.' *Mainstream*, January 11, p. 32.

Crook, J.R. and S.C. McCaffrey (1997) 'The United Nations Start Work on a Watercourse Convention.' *American Journal of International Law*, Vol. 91, pp. 374-377.

Crow, B. (1998) 'New Actors and New Space for Environmental Agreement.' *Water Nepal*, Vol. 6, No.1, pp. 25-41.

Datta-Ray, S.K. 'Living with Nepal: Must busybodies Queer the Pitch' *Statesman Weekly*, 17 February, p. 11.

Desai, B. (1998) 'Sharing of International Water Resources: The Ganges and Mahakali River Treaties.' *Asia Pacific Journal of Environmental Law*, Vol. 3 Issue 2, pp. 172-177.

Dickstein, H.L. (1973) 'International Lake and River Pollution: Question and Method.' *Columbia Journal of Transnational Law*, Vol. 12, p. 492.

Dhungel, H. (1999) 'Risks and Reward of Mega Projects: The Political Economy of Paraguayan Hydropower.' *Water Nepal*, Vol. 7, P. 25-26.

Eddy, H.R., R. Lammens and E. Marteijn (1992) 'Ecological Rehabilitation of Floodplains, The State of the Art.' *Contributions To the European Workshop*

Ecological Rehabilitation of Floodplains (International Commission for the Hydrology of the Rhines-Basin, Report II-6) p. 183.

Faisal, I.M., A. Nishat and S. Tanzeema (1999) 'Managing Common Waters between India and Bangladesh.' Paper read at the *International Conference in South Asia: Resolution of Inter-State Conflicts* held at Jawaharlal Nehru University New Delhi, 29-30 March, p. 8.

Farooque, M. and S.R. Hassan (1996) 'Laws Regulating Environment in Bangladesh', *Bangladesh Environmental Lawyers Association,* Dhaka, pp. 310-333.

Fitzmaurice, M. (1997) 'Convention on the Law of Non-navigational Uses of International Watercourses', *Leiden Journal of International Law*, Vol. 10, pp. 501-508.

Fitzmaurice, M. (1995) 'The Law of Non-Navigational Uses of International Watercourses- he International Law Commission completes its Draft', *Leiden Journal of International Law*, Vol. 8, pp. 361-375.

Fuentes, X. (1996) 'The Criteria for the Equitable Utilization of International Rivers.' *British Yearbook of International Law* Vol. 67, pp. 337-412.

Gerritsen, G.J. (1992) 'Ecological Rehabilitation of the River Ijssel', *Contributions To the European Workshop Ecological Rehabilitation of Floodplains* (International Commission for the Hydrology of the Rhines-Basin, Report II-6) p. 79.

Gyawali, D. and A. Dixit (1998) 'Mahakali Impasse and Indo-Nepal Water Conflict.' *Economic and Political Weekly*, February 27, pp. 553-564.

Gyawali, D. (1999) 'Water beyond the State: Resolving Conflicts with Institutional Pluralism.' Paper read at the *International Conference in South Asia: Resolution of Inter-State Conflicts* held at Jawaharlal Nehru University, New Delhi. 29-30 March, p. 3.

Gyawali, D. (1998) 'Patna, Delhi and Environmental Activism: Institutional Forces Behind Water Conflict in Bihar.' *Water Nepal,* Vol. 6 No. 1, pp. 67-115.

Havinga, H. (1992) 'Floodplain Restoration: A challenge for River Engineering.' *Contributions To the European Workshop Ecological Rehabilitation of Floodplains* (International Commission for the Hydrology of the Rhines-Basin, Report II-6) p. 95.

Hey, E. (1998) 'The Watercourses Convention: To What Extent Does it provide a Basis for Regulating Uses of International Watercourses?' *Review of European Community & International Environmental Law* (RECIEL) Vol. 7 No. 3, pp. 291-300.

Hussain, S.M. 'International Law and the Ganga Water Problem.' *Law and International Affairs,* Vol. 9, No.2, pp. 8-102.

ILA Helsinki Rules (1967) 'Uses of the Waters of International Rivers (Helsinki, 20th August, 1966).' *The International Law Association, Report of the Fifty-Second Conference*, Helsinki, 14-20 August, 1966.

ILI Report of the Rapporteur of the ILI concerning the question of 'determining the rules of international law relating to international rivers from the point of view of the utilization of their energy' in *Annuaire de l'Institut de Droit*

International, Vol. 24, Madrid Session, April 1911, Paris, 1911, which was also published in the *Revue Generale de Droit International Public*, 1910.

ILI Resolution on International Regulations regarding the Use of International Water Courses in *Annuaire de l'Institut de Droit International*, Vol. 24, Madrid Session, April 1911, Paris, 1911, which has been reproduced in the United Nations General Assembly, 'Legal Problems Relating to the Utilization and Use of International of International Rivers', UN Doc.A/5409 of 15th April, 1963.

ILI Resolution on The Use of International Non-Marine Waters, Salzbourg, 11th September 1961, in *Annuaire de l'Institut de Droit International*, Vol. 49-II, Salzbourg Session, September 1961, Basle, 1961.

Iyer, R.R. (2000) 'Water; Charting a Course for the Future.' *Economic and Political Weekly*, March 31-April 6, pp. 1115-1123.

Iyer, R.R. (1999) 'Conflict Resolution: Three Rivers Treaties'. *Economic and Political Weekly,* June 12, pp. 1509-1511.

Jacobs, L.M. (1993) 'Sharing the Gifts of the Nile: Establishment of a legal regime for Nile Waters Management.' *Temple International and Comparative Law Quarterly,* Vol. 7, p. 101.

Josse, M.R. (1994) 'The Case for New Thinking.' *Water Nepal*, Vol., 4, Nepal, p. 260.

Karim, A.T. (1998) 'The Bangladesh-India Treaty on Sharing of the Ganges Waters: Genesis and Significance.' *Bangladesh Institute of International and Strategic Studies* (BIISS) Vol. 20, pp. 216-235.

Koudstall, R. (2001) 'The Water resources system in Bangladesh and the Netherlands.' *The Daily Star*, Dhaka, 30th April, p. 18.

Lammers, J. (1998) 'The Gabcikovo-Nagymaros Case Seen in Particular From the Perspective Of the Law of International Watercourses and the Protection of the Environment.' *Leiden Journal of International Law*, Vol. 11, pp. 287-321.

Litjens, G.J.J.M. (1992) 'World Wildlife Fund Reanimates Delta of Rhine.' *Contributions To the European Workshop Ecological Rehabilitation of Floodplains* (International Commission for the Hydrology of the Rhines-Basin, Report II-6) p. 105.

McCaffrey, S.C. (1995) 'The International Law Commission adopts Draft Articles on International Watercourses.' *American Journal of International Law*, Vol. 89.

McCaffrey, S.C. (1989) 'The Law of International Watercourses: Some Recent Developments and Unanswered Questions.' *Denver Journal of International Law 7 & Policy* Vol. 17, pp. 505-526.

McCaffrey, S. C. and M. Sinjela (1998) 'The 1997 United Nations Convention on International Watercourses.' *American Journal of International Law,* Vol. 92, pp. 97-107.

McCaffrey, S.C. and M. Sinjela (1986) 'Second Report on the Law of Non-navigational Uses of International Watercourse.' *Yearbook of the International Law Commission,* Vol. II, Part I, p. 130.

McCaffrey, S.C. and M. Sinjela (1998) 'The UN Convention on the Law of Non-navigational Uses of International Watercourses: Prospects and Pitfalls.' *World Bank Technical Paper* No. 414.

McCaffrey, S.C. and M. Sinjela (1996) 'An Assessment of the Work of the International Law Commission' *Natural Resources Journal.* Vol. 36 (spring), pp. 276-318.

Nazem, N.I. and M.H. Kabir (1986) 'Indo-Bangladesh Common Rivers and Water Diplomacy.' *Bangladesh Institute of International and Strategic Studies Papers*, Dhaka, No. 5 (December), pp. 7-9, 42-46.

Nollkaemper, A. (1996) 'The Contribution of the International Law Commission to International Water Law: Does it reverse the Flight from Substance?' *Netherlands Yearbook of International Law* Vol. 27, pp. 39-73.

Nussbaum, T. (1996) 'Report of the Working Group to Elaborate a Convention on International Watercourses.' *Review of European Community & International Environmental Law* Vol. 6, pp. 47-54.

Paukert, M. (2002) 'The Indus Umbilical.' *Himal* (July), pp. 1-4.

Postel, S. (1997) 'Changing the course of transboundary water management.' *Natural Resources Forum,* Vol. 21, No.2, pp. 85-90.

Prasad, T. (1997) *'Comprehensive Water Resources Development in Indo-Nepal Region: Perspective and Prospects.*' Presented at a conference on the Large Scale Water Management held in Kathmandu, October, p.18.

Pun, S.B. 'The Evolving Role of the Public and Private Institutions in the Nepalese Power Sector.' *Annual Report of Water and Energy Commission Secretariat*, Adm./060799/1/1, Seq. 041, pp. 38-49.

Salman, S.A. (1998) 'Co-Management of Resources: The Case of the Ganges River.' (October. 1998). (online). Available from:<http//gurukul.ucc.american.edu/maksoud/water98/present/.htm>

Salman, S.M.A. and K. Uprety (1999) 'Hydro-Politics in South Asia: A Comparative Analysis of the Mahakali and the Ganges Treaties.' *Natural Resources Journal*, Vol. 39, pp. 295-343.

Sarup, A. (1972) 'Transit Trade of Land Locked Nepal', *International Comparative Law Quarterly*, Vol. 2, pp. 277-306.

Shah, R. (1994) 'Politics of Water Power in Nepal,' *Water Nepal*, Vol. 4, No. 1, p. 286-287.

Sharma, K. (1997) 'The Farakka fallout', *The Hindu,* April 29, p. 12.

Shrestha, G.D. (1994) 'Himalayan Waters: Need for Positive Indo-Nepal Co-operation.' *Water Nepal*, Vol. 4, No. 1, p. 272.

Singh, K.N. (1990) 'Agenda for Talks with K.P Bhattarai.' *The Times of India*, 7th June 1990.

Sinha, C.P. 'Sediment Management; A Co-operative Indo-Nepal Ventures.' *Water Nepal*, Vol. 4, No. 1, pp. 158-163.

Subba, B. (1994) 'Tapping Himalayan Water Resources: Problems, Opportunities and Prospects From a Bhutanese Perspective.' *Water Nepal*, Vol. 4, No. 1, p 210.

Subedi, S.P. (2003) 'Resolution of International Water Disputes: Challenges for the 21st Century.' International Bureau of the Permanent Court of Arbitration,

Resolution of International Water Disputes, Vol. 6 in the PCA Peace Palace Papers series. The Hague: Kluwer Law International, pp. 33-47.

Subedi, S.P. (2003) 'The Legal Regime Concerning the Utilization of the Water Resources of the River Ganges Basin.' *German Yearbook of International Law,* Vol. 46, pp. 452-493.

Subedi, S.P. (2003) 'The Concept in Hinduism of 'Just War'.' *Journal of Conflict and Security Law,* Vol. 8, No. 2, pp. 339-361. Oxford University Press.

Subedi, S.P. (2003) 'The Himalayan Frontier Policy of British-India and the Significance of the 1923 Treaty of Friendship between Great Britain-Nepal.' *Journal of the Britain-Nepal Society,* Vol. 27 (December 2003), pp. 35-39. London

Subedi, S.P. (2002) 'Regulation of Shared Water Resources in International Law: The Challenge of Balancing Competing Demands.' *Nepal Law Review* Vol. 15 (1 & 2), July 2002, pp. 1-14. Faculty of Law, Tribhuvan University.

Subedi, S.P. (2002) 'Incorporation of the Principle of Sustainable Development into the Development Policies of the Asian Countries.' *Environmental Policy and Law,* Vol. 32, No. 2, (April 2002), pp. 85-90. International Council of Environmental Law, Bonn.

Subedi, S.P. (1999) 'Constitutional Accommodation of Ethnicity and National Identity in Nepal.' *International Journal on Minority and Group Rights,* Vol. 6, No. 1/2, pp.121-147. Kluwer Law International, The Hague.

Subedi, S.P. (1999) 'Hydro-Diplomacy in South Asia: The Conclusion of the Mahakali and Ganges River Treaties.' *American Journal of International Law,* Vol. 93, No. 4, p. 957.

Subedi, S. P. (1998) 'Environmental Inputs into the Planning Process and Access to Justice.' *Environmental Policy and Law,* Vol. 28, No. 2, May 1998, pp. 96-103. International Council of Environmental Law, Bonn.

Subedi, S.P. (1997) 'Transit Arrangements between Nepal and India: A Study in International Law.' *Geopolitics and International Boundaries,* Vol. 2, No.1, pp. 175-196. London: Frank Cass.

Subedi, S.P. (1996) 'When is a Treaty a Treaty in Law? An Analysis of the Views of the Supreme Court of Nepal on a Bilateral Water Agreement between Nepal and India.' *Asian Yearbook of International Law,* Vol. 5, pp. 201-210.

Subedi, S.P. (1994) 'India-Nepal Security Relations and the 1950 Peace and Friendship Treaty: Time for New Perspectives.' *Asian Survey,* Vol. 34, No. 3, pp. 273-284. University of California Press.

Subedi, S.P. (1989) 'Obligations and Responsibilities of Transit and Land-Locked States in the Absence of a Transit Treaty.' *The Rising Nepal,* 20 May 1989, p. 2.

Subedi, S.P. (1987) 'The Marine Fishery Rights of Land-locked States with Particular Reference to the EEZ.' *International Journal of Marine and Coastal Law* Vol. 2, No. 4, pp. 227-239 (London).

Swain, A. (1998) 'Reconciling Disputes and Treaties: Water Development and Management in Ganga Basin', *Water Nepal*, Vol. 6, No. 1, pp. 43-65.

Tanzi, A. (1997) 'Codifying the Minimum Standards of the Law of International Watercourses: Remarks on part one and half.' *Natural Resources Forum,* Vol. 21, No. 2, pp. 109-117.

Thapa, P.J. (1997) 'Water-Led Development in Nepal: Myths, Limitations and Rational Calculations,' *Water Nepal* Vol. 5, No.1 Jan-July 1997 pp. 35-57.

Thapa, A.B. (2002) 'Kosi Floods.' *Spotlight*, Nepal, 22-29 September 2002.

Thapa, A.B. (1997) 'Urgent Need for Controlling Kosi Floods.' *Water and Energy Commission Secretariat*, Vol. 8, pp. 7-10.

Thapa, A.B. (2002) 'Landlocked Austria's Lesson for Nepal', *Spotlight*, Vol. 22, Sept 27-Oct. 3, 2002.

Thapa, A.B. 'Kosi Navigational Canal,' *Water and Energy Commission Secretariat Bulletin*, Vol. 8, No. 2 Kathmandu, p. 5-7.

The 1996 Mekong River Commission Annual Report, 3.

The 1991 Interim Mekong Committee Annual Report, 11.

The 1973 Mekong River Committee Annual Report, 28.

The United States Bureau of Reclamation, *Reconnaissance Report-Lower Mekong River Basin* (1995).

The 1956-57 Annual Report of the Economic Commission for Asia and the Far Eas,t 15th February 1956 - 25th March 1957, E/CN. 11/454.

United Nations, *Reports of International Arbitral Awards*, Vol. X.

United Nations, *Reports of International Arbitral Awards*, Vol. III.

United Nations, (1963) 'Legal Problems relating to the Utilization and Use of International Rivers.' *United Nations General Assembly Doc. A/5409 of 15th April 1963, Part IV and Annexure I.*

Upreti, T. (2000) 'A perspective on Downstream Benefits.' *Kathmandu Post,* June 25, p. 10.

Verma, U.K. (1994) 'Socio-economic Renaissance Through Dynamic Indo-Nepal Co-operation in Water resources Development.' *Water Nepal*, Vol. 4, No. 1, p. 140-142.

Weiss, E.B. (1995) 'Intergenerational Fairness for Fresh Water Resources.' 25 (4/5) *Environmental Policy and Law.*

Wouters, P.K. (1996) 'An Assessment of Recent Development in International Watercourse Law through the Prism of the Substantive Rules Governing Use Allocation.' *Natural Resources Journal*, Vol. 36 (spring), pp. 417-439.

Yearbook of the International Law Commission II 1974, part two, 357.

Yearbook of the International Law Commission II 1980, part one, 194.

3. CASES

The Case concerning the River Meuse (*Belgium v the Netherlands*), PCIJ, Series A/B, No. 70, 1937.

The Arbitral Awards of 19th August 1872 and 10th April 1905 in the *Helmand River Delta Case* between Afghanistan and Persia.

Report of the Helmand River Delta Commission, Afghanistan and Iran, February 1951.

Award of 22nd March 1888 by Grover Cleveland, the President of the United States of America, as arbitrator in the *San Juan River Case* between Costa Rica and Nicaragua.

Award in the *Faber Case* by a German-Venezuelan Mixed Claims Commission, constituted under the Protocol of 13th January 1903.

Awards of 16th April 1938 and 11th March 1941 by an Arbitral Tribunal in the *Trail Smelter Case.*

Arbitral Award of 16th November 1957 by an Arbitral Tribunal in the *Lake Lanoux Case* between Spain and France, *Revue Generale de Droit International Public*, Vol. LXII, 1958.

Case concerning the Gabcikovo-Nagymaros Project (*Hungary v Slovakia*, 37 ILM 162 (1998)).

Index